D1412218

Praise for other books in the Poor Richard's Series . . .

Poor Richard's Web Site

"Makes it possible for ordinary people to set up effective business websites without going broke or spending forever online. It's a great read for anyone who wants to build a business site, and it becomes a part of our recommended library."

—CMPnet's Techweb

"A good source with easy step-by-step directions." —*Publishers Weekly*

"Offers clear advice to help you defend against jargon-happy sales people and computer magazines." —Fortune.com

"If you really want to build a functional Web site [this] might just be the book for you." —CNN Interactive

Poor Richard's E-mail Publishing

"The single most authoritative and helpful guide an entrepreneur can turn to when it's time to move beyond a Web site." —*The Newsletter on Newsletters*

"Unites commonsense advice with clear explanations of e-mail technology . . .The book is packed with marketing know-how and tells you how to make money with your newsletter . . .Don't click Send without [this book]." —*PC World*

"Transforms what could be boring technical jargon into an easy-to-understand tutorial on the ins and outs of Email publishing." —*Website Success Monthly* newsletter

Poor Richard's Building Online Communities

"An extensive course on creating a vital Web community." —Entrepreneur.com

"Create a web community for a business or family using the power of the Internet and this *Poor Richard's* guide, which focuses on inexpensive methods of achieving such a goal. From locating and participating in mailing lists to joining web-based communities for business and pleasure, this imparts the basics of understanding how such groups function." —Review's Bookwatch

"Another great book from the *Poor Richard's* Series. This book will help the novice or expert build a online community that will make the most out of the different components that turn a Web site into a community."

—Nathan Allan, Community Development Manager, Sausage Software

POOR RICHARD'S HOME AND SMALL OFFICE NETWORKING

Room to Room or Around the World

by
John Paul Mueller

This book is dedicated to Aunt Barb and Aunt Mary—
I can't imagine life without their pleasant company.

Poor Richard's Home and Small Office Networking:
Room to Room or Around the World

SAN#: 299-4550
Top Floor Publishing
8790 W. Colfax #107
Lakewood, CO 80215

Feedback to the author: feedback@topfloor.com
Sales information: sales@topfloor.com
The Top Floor Publishing Web Site: http://TopFloor.com/
The Poor Richard Web Site: http://PoorRichard.com/
Cover design/illustration by Marty Petersen, http://www.artymarty.com

Library of Congress Catalog Card Number: 2001086046

ISBN: 1-930082-03-7

03   02   01   6 5 4 3 2 1

ACKNOWLEDGEMENTS

Thanks to my wife, Rebecca, for working with me to complete this book. I really don't know what I would have done without her help in proofreading my rough draft. She also helped research, compile, and edit some of the information in this book.

This book contains numerous real world examples, many of which other people contributed. Space doesn't allow me to mention them all by name, but I appreciate them all.

Matt Wagner, my agent, deserves credit for helping me get the contract for this book in the first place and taking care of all the details that most authors don't really think about. I always appreciate his help.

Finally, I would like to thank Missy Ramey, Jerry Olsen, Fred Kloepper, Sydney Jones, Joann Woy, and Liz Cunningham for their assistance in bringing this book to print. I especially appreciate their willingness to work with me on a demanding schedule.

ABOUT THE AUTHOR

John Mueller is a freelance author and technical editor. He has writing in his blood, having produced 48 books and almost 200 articles to date. The topics range from networking to artificial intelligence and from database management to heads down programming. Some of his current books include a COM+ programmer's guide and a Windows 2000 performance, tuning, and optimization book. His technical editing skills have helped over 24 authors refine the content of their manuscripts, some of which are certification related. In addition to book projects, John has provided technical editing services to both *Data Based Advisor* and *Coast Compute* magazines. A recognized authority on computer industry certifications, he has also contributed articles to magazines including *SQL Server Professional, Visual C++ Developer*, and *Visual Basic Developer*.

When John isn't working at the computer, you can find him in his workshop. He's an avid woodworker and candle maker. On any given afternoon, you can find him working at a lathe or putting the finishing touches on a bookcase. One of his newest craft projects is glycerin soap making. You can reach John via email at JMueller@mwt.net. John is also setting up a new Web site at: http://www.mwt.net/~jmueller/. Feedback is always welcome. One of his current projects is creating book FAQ sheets that should help you find the book information you need much faster.

TABLE OF CONTENTS

INTRODUCTION

In the beginning, networking was about saving money. Vendors wanted to provide a way to share equipment in order to reduce costs. The network started as a means to make an already good idea better. The beginnings of networks are rooted in the efforts of many experimenters who thought there had to be a better way, and companies like Novell who saw an opportunity to make money while saving money for someone else. People still use networks for that essential reason today. Even in the world of commodity computing, the need to save money by sharing equipment remains real.

Of course, networks also allow people to share data. Early networks concentrated on secure data access without frills. At one time, it was enough to know that the document you needed to edit was in a central data store somewhere on the server. Today, data sharing takes on a whole new meaning in addition to the old. People want to collaborate on documents and hold conferences in an effort to make working together less expensive.

The scale of networking has changed, too. An early network might connect a few people in a departmental workgroup together—that's why these networks are called local area networks (LANs). As companies began to see the cost benefits and performance enhancements of the LAN, wide area networks (WANs) were born. This led to further expansion in the form of the metropolitan area network (MAN). Finally, the Internet seems to connect the whole mess together, creating one super network. All of us can extend our reach anywhere in the world today with the proper equipment.

A home office or small business can no longer afford to ignore the cost savings, collaboration, and outreach benefits of networking. If you're not connected, you aren't working at maximum efficiency. Since it's almost certain your competitor will make use of networking technology, it becomes more of a must-have business tool than a nice expansion to consider sometime in the future. While you may not need a network to make your next big sale, it will help you in many other ways. Communication takes many forms, and networks often help in areas where businesses need help most.

So, why read this book? There are perhaps as many networking books on the market as there are networks. What this book offers that the others don't is the home office and small business perspective. Many other books, articles, papers, and Web sites provide clearly written prose about the corporate network—few people even consider the small network. A small network isn't simply a down-sized version of the networks used by large businesses; it's an entirely different entity. Small networks can serve businesses in ways that the large corporate networks never could because the scale of such networks makes this impossible.

In this book, we'll look at issues that are important to the home business and small office alike. Networks can become a bottomless pit, grabbing all of your free cash and then some, if you let them. Large corporations spend thousands of dollars to build a single workstation and thousands more each year to maintain it. When viewed from this perspective, networks sound like the toy of the rich, not the tool of the poor. However, good design and careful maintenance of a network can reduce these costs immensely. A home office or small business network can often become a profit center rather than a cost to list at the bottom of a financial report.

Your network can become an extension of you. It allows you the freedom to communicate with others over vast distances without traveling. A well-designed network can reduce the effort required to accomplish tasks and allow those tasks to serve more than the single purpose for which you originally designed it. In fact, you can perform some tasks with a network that you can't perform otherwise.

Of all of the things that a network can do for a home office or a small business, communication is key. Members of a small organization wear many hats, and the loss of even one member due to a business trip or illness can have far reaching effects. Unlike large corporations, where an employee is simply a cog in a wheel, easily replaced at the whim of management, workers in a small organization are members of a family—cherished for all of the things they do to make the organization run. Even if you never use a network for any other purpose, using it to expand the communication capabilities of your organization will net results that you may not be able to imagine.

The goal of this book is to help the home office or small business entrepreneur get the most from networking. We'll look at issues that you need to consider for your organization—issues that big business may not consider. This book also looks at the benefits of being a small business with a network. In many respects, a small business has far more opportunities to exploit a network than a large corporation does. Finally, we'll look at ways you can avoid the problems that the big guys experience. You won't have to spend thousands to keep your network running.

CHAPTER ONE

Do You Need a Network?

Networks have been a hot topic for quite some time now and will continue to be a hot topic because of constant advancements in networking technology. Since networks are a hot topic, you'll find more than a little incorrect, incomplete, or incomprehensible information about them in magazines and some sources on the Internet. Some people will tell you that a network can do things like make your business more productive or help you work faster simply because you install one. Like anything else, true gains in productivity with a network represent hours of hard work.

Besides the hype, there are problems with terminology. Many people are completely confused about networking terms and what they really need to build one. Let's look at the term *networking* first. We have many ways to look at the term *network* as it relates to computers, but here's a simple definition:

A method of connecting two computers together for the purpose of sharing data, resources, or services.

Using this definition, you can include everything from two machines hooked together with a serial cable for exchanging files to a local area network (LAN) to the Internet as examples of a network. Networks typically include some type of physical connection through cables or the airwaves (as in the case of a wireless network) and some type of software to control the transaction. Networks also rely on protocols (standardized rules for communication) to control the flow of data between workstations. A network provides services to the client, but those services might be limited to printer and file sharing. The first PC networks provided just these two services and still managed to help businesses become more productive. Today's network also includes some type of security, but the security measures might be exceptionally limited in scope. A Windows 95 network provides the barest hint of security, while a Windows 2000 network provides robust security that will protect even the most sensitive data.

It seems today that anyone with two machines thinks they need to be connected, whether such a connection makes sense or not. Networks can be very beneficial by allowing you to work faster, collaborate with other people, or share resources like printers. However, knowing what a network can do for anyone in general and what it can do for you in specific are two entirely different questions. In fact, in some circumstances, there's every reason to believe you won't need a network at all to achieve your data exchange goals. As I see it, you have three issues to resolve before you begin installing a network in your home or small business.

The first issue you have to resolve is whether you need a network. You might be able to resolve any data sharing needs you have using alternative methods and avoid the cost of installing a network. The simple act of using a floppy disk as a transfer medium might be all you need to avoid the cost of installing a network. (Using the floppy disk approach is also known as a sneaker network—a topic that we talk about in the "What a Network Can Do That Sneakers Can't" section later in the chapter.) In fact, the floppy was once one of the more popular methods of getting data from one machine to another. Microsoft Windows still supports this concept through the use of the Briefcase—an electronic version of the real thing that you can use to move data from one machine to another using a floppy.

Using Someone Else's Network—*Some people view the question of whether to install a network as a matter of determining whether removable media will work, but the real answer is somewhat more complex. In the past, small companies often installed networks because removable media wouldn't work and there were no other viable solutions. While floppies and other removable media might be too limited in their storage capacity, too slow, or simply too cumbersome, you have other solutions today—many of which cost little to implement. With the Internet, you have the world's largest network at your disposal for an extremely low cost and few hassles. The Internet and other alternative solutions make it possible for some small companies to get by without a network today, even if they would have needed a network in the past.*

A second issue is determining what a network would provide that alternate solutions wouldn't provide and then finding solutions to those problems. You'll find, for example, that you can't run a database application without a network. (While you can run a database manager like Access on a single machine, the purpose of using a database application in most cases is to provide a shared data resource, which is why you require a network.) If a centralized database is something that your company has to have, you'll have to install a network or find some viable alternative. The same holds true for home networks. You may find that some applications require a dedicated network connection when working from home. For example, you may want to play the latest game over a network and find that using alternatives like the Internet produce less than stellar results. If your goal is to share data between your home and office computer, however, solutions like **Symantec's** pcAnywhere (http://www.symantec.com/pca/) work just fine.

The third issue is how much network you need when you decide to install one. Networks come in a variety of shapes and sizes. A network that won't work for a small company may work just fine for a home installation. Finding the right-size network will save you money, time, and frustration. Using the right type of network will also enhance your ability to get work done quickly.

We aren't going to cover every potential topic presented by these three issues in this chapter, but we will look at the most basic issue that you need to resolve, the need for a network. There isn't any reason to install a network if you can find a networking alternative that will cost less and work just as well. You may still need to implement some networking strategies (like adding data security) even if you decide to use a networking alternative. But in the long run you'll save both time and money by using the alternative whenever possible. The following sections describe some of the issues you should know about when determining your need for a network.

Networks Cost Money

When considering a network for your home or business, you need to determine how you're going to use the network. You won't need specifics immediately, but you should have some idea of what you're going to do. If you're going to use the network for database management, you'll need to consider how the database manager will affect your business. Ask yourself how much the database manager will produce in income over the course of a year. It's important to answer two questions. First, you need to know how much the network will cost. Second, you need to know how the network will pay you back for the initial investment. The following sections discuss these two topics in more detail. (It may seem like I'm almost arguing against any use of networks in these sections. My main point is people overlook many alternatives to networks because they are fixated on the network solution—networks do serve an important purpose and they have a definite purpose that we'll discuss as the book progresses.)

Discovering the Sources of Network Costs

You have a lot of ways to create a network, but all standard networks (those that are used by corporations and small companies alike) require an initial outlay of money, and then a smaller sum for maintenance. In other words, no matter how large or small your network is, it will cost you some money. Even if you get the hardware or software for free, you'll still end up paying a price for the convenience a network provides. So, it's important to have some idea of just where your money will go when you initially build the network and continue to use it. Here's a list of the most common expenses for any network.

Hardware—Depending on what type of network you install, you'll need to buy several pieces of hardware that could include cabling, network interface cards (NICs), a server, hubs (places to plug in all of the cables), and network-compatible devices like printers with an NIC installed. We'll talk about many of these issues in Chapter 3, *Designing a Standard Network*, and Chapter 5, *Cabling and Other Masses of Wire*.

Software—Your network will require software to make it operate. Many modern operating systems come with network software that allows you to create a peer-to-peer network (more on this term in Chapter 3). If you want to create other kinds of networks, however, you'll need to purchase a network operating system (NOS) like Novell NetWare. In addition to an operating system, you may need to buy one or more network-compatible applications to perform network-specific tasks.

Training—Any network is going to offer enough differences from a standard desktop configuration to change the way users perform tasks. A good design will get rid of some of these problems, but you'll still find that you need to perform some level of training to get users up to speed on the new network configuration.

Support—Networks are more complex than one, stand-alone machine. In most cases you're going to need some type of infrastructure for the network and the users it supports. This represents two levels of support that you'll need to consider as part of a network design.

Consulting fees—No matter how experienced your staff is, setting up a network can become difficult without the proper skills. In some cases it's less expensive to pay a consulting firm to perform the initial setup and then use in-house staff to maintain the network once it's running.

Maintenance—Networks contain hardware and software, both of which require periodic maintenance. Hardware requires replacement as it ages and you'll find that software, no matter how perfect out of the box, will require a patch or two to make it work acceptably. (Software without bugs is one of the rarest commodities in the computer arena.)

Keeping Consulting Costs Under Control—*Every consultant I've ever met is hungry; he or she wants the big job. In many cases, getting the big job means convincing clients that their company needs more hardware or software than required to do the job. I'm not saying that the consultant is dishonest, simply ambitious. Most small businesses have no need for a large network—all they really need is some Windows 95 or Windows 98 machines connected together to share a centralized database (at the most). To keep consulting costs under control, decide what type of network you want before you call the consulting firm. Better yet, see if the vendor you buy the hardware from also provides installation. Using the store's installation team will make it possible to avoid using a consultant at all.*

Dealing with Hidden Costs

The hidden costs of a standard network make it feasible to pursue other paths first; then install a network if nothing else will do the job. You don't have to install and test these alternatives, but you should learn about them and determine their strengths and weaknesses in relation to the tasks you need to perform. For example, some radio frequency (RF) network alternatives transmit data at 1 Mbps, which is fine for word processing, but won't work well with a complex database management system. Here's an easy way to summarize the idea of network cost:

A network should always provide enough services to pay for its initial cost within a year or two of installation.

Networks can become expensive gadgets rather than useful tools if you don't count the cost of owning one at the outset. Make sure you include hidden costs like training and consulting fees because these costs can quickly mount. Determine how much value a network will add to your business and compare this benefit to the money that you're going to invest.

Determining how much a particular piece of your network will cost is difficult, to say the least. For example, there's always a difference between the vendor's list price and the product's street price (the amount you actually pay at the store). Vendors also make a point to use different methods to tell you about their product—making any direct comparison between two vendors impossible without buying one of each product and examining them yourself. It helps to have some gauge to use when determining the value of a product versus the amount you'll pay. Here are a few Web sites you can use for pricing and product review information when you're performing a preliminary analysis of your networking needs:

Price Watch
http://www.pricewatch.com/

Product ReviewNet
http://www.productreviewnet.com/splash.html

ZDNet Reviews
http://www.zdnet.com/reviews/

ZDNet Shopping
http://www.zdnet.com/shopping/

Tom's Hardware Guide
http://www.tomshardware.com/

CDW.com
http://www.cdw.com/

PC Connection
http://www.pcconnection.com/

CNET.com
http://www.cnet.com/

Computer Shopper
http://www.compshopper.co.uk/

All of these sites have one thing in common: they make it easier for you to see the hidden costs of buying a network. Knowing the hidden costs helps you make a better decision when looking at alternatives to installing a network. You'll know, for example, that you'll pay four times as much for a network that can keep your data secure and transfer it quickly than you would for a simple serial cable that will transfer the data at an incredibly slow pace and in a nonsecure manner. After spending some time looking at network prices, you'll come to the conclusion that networks are a lot more expensive than you originally thought and that those alternatives are starting to look better than ever.

The Employee Cost of Networks—*Most businesses assume that all employees will be happy to have a computer on their desk because the computer will save them time and make their jobs easier to perform. In reality, you can expect some employees to fight working with computers because they fear the computer will eventually replace them. In addition, some employees don't feel capable of learning how to use the computer or are simply unwilling to learn. Part of the hidden cost of installing a new network might be the loss of valuable employees. Unlike large corporations where the loss of one employee isn't going to stop anything, small businesses are much more reliant on having good employees in key areas. You need to consider this cost as part of your decision to install a network.*

Inexpensive Networking Alternatives

Everyone likes to save money when starting on a new venture. We talked about a lot of hidden costs for installing a network in the previous section of the chapter. These hidden costs are a necessary evil when you really need the services that a network can provide, but they can also turn into an unnecessary expenditure if you have other solutions to the problem.

Networking alternatives will often cost less, yet provide the same features that you hope to get from a standard network. For example, you may need to share data between two computers like a desktop machine and a laptop. When you go on a trip, you need to place data for the trip on your laptop; when you return home, the updated data will need to move from the laptop to your desktop machine. You have a number of alternatives to this common scenario that fall short of networking:

- Use a serial or parallel cable to connect the two computers.
- Transfer the data using a floppy or other removable media.
- Replace the two-computer setup with a single-computer solution consisting of a laptop and a docking station.
- Rely on infrared (IR) data transfer.
- Use e-mail to transfer the data from one machine to the other (making the Internet your network).
- Create a connection using a product like pcAnywhere.
- Use the pre-Internet solution of setting up a bulletin board system (BBS) on your computer so that you can dial in using a direct number.

No matter which technique you choose, you will have trade-offs that you need to consider as part of the alternative solution. For example, IR data transfers rely on line of sight, so the two computers have to be in the same room. E-mail data transfers are slow and could encounter a variety of problems like data corruption and the inability to get through firewalls.

The issue that you must deal with when working with network alternatives is that none of them will provide the full capabilities of a network. Limitations in the design will prevent you from transferring data at full speed, reduce your ability to perform required network tasks, or hamper security measures required to protect sensitive data. You may find that these alternatives provide limited printer support or that some types of services like transaction processing are missing. In fact, you can boil the whole issue of using a network down to this simple statement:

Network alternatives provide low-cost solutions to one or two standard network problems, but don't provide the full set of services that a standard network provides.

Two Machines and a Cable

One of the simplest network incarnations is two machines connected by a cable. A lot of networks start out and stay at this simple level. It could be that all you really need to do is have a master–slave relationship between the two machines to provide some level of control over network resources. The master machine would control what the slave is able to do.

The following sections are going to look at two simple network scenarios and some of the trade-offs you have to consider. We'll look at several important questions as part of the discussion. For example, if you use a networking alternative, will you actually spend more money waiting for the system to perform a task? Human time always costs more than network hardware, so you'll find times where a little added money spent up front will net productivity in the long run.

The Home Network

The vast majority of home gaming machine networks use this simple network setup. Few gamers need more than two machines—one for personal use and a second for a friend. With a little clever wiring, these setups can often get by without the additional expense of a hub, making it necessary to purchase only the cable and two NICs.

Of course, you also need an operating system like Windows 95, 98, or Millennium installed on both machines to make the required software connections. Considering that Windows has come with basic networking since Windows for Workgroups, you'll find that the vast majority of Windows systems on the market will allow you to set up a network. In fact, few, if any, PC workstation operating systems produced today lack basic network capabilities.

You Get What You Pay For—*The network services provided by Windows 95, 98, and Millennium are simple at best. All you get is the ability to transfer data between machines and share some basic resources like printers and disk drives. Newer versions of Windows also come with the ability to share an Internet connection using Internet Connection Sharing (ICS). Apple's Macintosh provides services similar to what Windows provides, although the exact features vary by operating system version, just as they do for Windows users. What you give up by using these products are good security (minimal security is provided), standard network administration utilities, and the ability to control the network through services like bandwidth throttling. In other words, even though these operating systems can help you achieve your goals at an exceptionally low cost, you get what you pay for.*

Despite the low cost of a gaming network and the ease of setting it up, game enthusiasts could be better served by other alternatives that cost even less. Consider for a moment that such a network provides a relatively limited number of services to the user, even though it's capable of doing much more. The only data gamers need to exchange is the type generated by games—these enthusiasts often are completely unconcerned by any other criteria. You also need to consider that this setup is more expensive than some of the other alternatives we've talked about so far. So, why would a gaming enthusiast need an expensive solution like a network when you could potentially play games across the Internet?

The main factor in this case is speed. Games exchange a lot of data and the 56 Kbps connection provided by a dial-up Internet connection just won't provide the required data processing capability. So, sometimes the two-machine mini-network is necessary, because you need more speed than alternatives can provide. However, you might be able to use a low-speed, low-cost solution like the ones presented in Chapter 2, *Cheap Alternative Networks*, instead of creating a full-fledged network. Many of these low-cost networks provide a 1 Mbps or higher transfer rate, which is more than enough for many games.

The Small-Business Network

Small businesses, especially home offices, often require the services of a small, two-machine network. However, the criterion in this situation isn't speed. A home office seldom exchanges data between machines at a high enough rate to use all of the available bandwidth provided by even a 10 Mbps Ethernet network. Home office networks are often put together for security and convenience reasons. In some situations, the primary machine is used by Mom or Dad for office work, while a second machine is used by children for homework. In other cases (many more than you might suspect), the main machine is used by the owner of the business, while an assistant uses the second machine for business-related tasks.

A two-machine home office network represents another situation where care in creating the connection can result in large cost savings. Even though you can get the required networking software for free when setting up a simple network, you still have hardware and other networking costs. These costs might reduce the ability of a small business to buy appropriate peripherals for a small, two-machine network. You can get a better network by using one of the less expensive network alternatives in Chapter 2 than by creating a standard 10 Mbps or higher-speed network using NICs, hubs, and cabling. For example, a network that relies on your house wiring in place of network cabling is a flexible alternative in a home where network cabling wasn't installed as part of the original construction. Using house wiring as a data conduit allows you to plug a computer into any room of the house and get acceptable performance.

Whatever your reason for creating the simple two-machines-and-a-cable network, you'll find that you normally use it for data exchange, not for the services or resources that a network can provide. As a result, it's almost always possible to get great performance at a fraction of the cost using other alternatives.

This leads me to the "exception to the rule" scenario. Few people begin their first networking experience by connecting a hundred or so machines. Almost everyone starts by building a two-machine network—even if that network is going to be a complex configuration somewhere along the way. Even though we'll cover less expensive solutions for two-machine networks in Chapter 2, always begin building a network with more machines in mind unless you know that you'll never expand beyond that two-machine limit. We'll talk about designing a network in more detail in Chapter 3, *Designing a Standard Network*.

Making Infrared Work

One of my favorite nonnetworks is the infrared (IR) connection. The reason this type of connection is so great is that all you need to do is point your laptop at the machine you want to communicate with and the operating system normally allows the two machines to start talking. This point-and-transfer method has the advantage of requiring no cables, being fast to connect and disconnect, and being far less expensive than just about any alternative. Since the laptop vendor often provides IR support in the form of drivers, all you need to worry about is a compatible operating system, rather than an operating system with specific features.

Every laptop machine I've ever owned has an IR port installed on it that the machine sees as a serial connection. Several desktop machine motherboard makers like Asus also include IR ports as part of their systems (often as an option, rather than a standard component). Even my LaserJet printer includes an IR port (again, as an option rather than a standard component), so when I want to print with my laptop I just point it at the printer and voila, a document appears at the output. In fact, you'll find that many network-compatible devices also include an option for using IR.

Anything that's free, or nearly so, will have limitations. Some limitations, like the need to install IR ports on devices that only offer them as options, are obvious. (You can get an IR port add-on for far less than an NIC in most cases—my motherboard vendor charged under $10 for the one in my desktop.) Here's a list of the most glaring problems with the IR alternative to networking.

Line-of-sight connection—An IR connection only works when the two machines are directly lined up with each other. This means that you couldn't use an IR connection between rooms.

Low-speed connection—IR ports emulate a serial port for the operating system. In many cases this means you'll be limited to 115 Kbps connections, rather than the 1 Mbps transfer rate of a low-cost network or the 10 Mbps (or above) transfer rate of a standard network.

Higher-Speed IR Connections—*A new Infrared Data Association (IrDA) standard allows data transfers of 4 Mbps, but this new data exchange rate isn't a common feature on PCs yet. The two standard transfer rates as of this writing are 115 Kbps asynchronous and 1.152 Mbps synchronous. Any IR port will support the 115 Kbps asynchronous transfer rate—the other two transfer rates require newer equipment. You can find out more about IrDA standards at* http://www.irda.org/.

Connection reliability—The line-of-sight nature of IR means that you have to point the client machine toward the server. A relatively small margin for error exists in many cases, which means that making the connection can be error-prone and maintaining it can be problematic. While this transfer technology works fine for one-time transfers of files, you wouldn't want to use it for applications like database management that rely on good connections.

Multiple standards—Currently two common standards exist for IR. Generally you won't have any problem getting one machine to talk with another, but because of the two standards, you'll find a few situations where you might have problems. It's important to realize that you may not always get a connection with every IR device; testing is an essential part of using IR in place of a network.

One-to-one connectivity—IR relies on the same protocol as a serial port to transfer data; it doesn't use packets like Ethernet or other network protocols do. As a result, a one-to-one relationship exists between the client and server. Without any way to filter data from two machines, this technology is limited to one data stream at a time.

There may be other problems with your IR setup as well. This list represents a few of the more common problems. For example, one laptop that I owned insisted that I use COM3 for the IR port. Nowhere in the documentation did it state that this was a requirement, nor did the technical support staff provide me a reason for the odd behavior of my machine. In fact, I found the one port that the machine would work with through trial and error. Since IR ports are a marriage of several pieces of equipment on your machine and require vendor-specific drivers to operate, you may find, as I did, that you run into some strange problems.

Figure 1.1: The presence of an Infrared applet in your Control Panel indicates the IR port is installed and ready for use.

One problem I ran into that's easily corrected (at least in Windows) is that the IR port on some machines is disabled by default. The port is installed, the driver is set up, and you can see the port in Device Manager, but it still won't work for some reason. If you see an Infrared applet in the Control Panel like the one shown in Figure 1.1, the port is most likely ready for use, it just isn't turned on. Unfortunately, unless the vendor who sold you your laptop placed the IR status icon in the taskbar tray, you won't know whether the IR port is turned on.

Open the Infrared applet and you'll see the Infrared Monitor dialog box. The Status tab will tell you whether the IR port is enabled. If it's not enabled, you can enable it using the Enable infrared communication option on the Options tab shown in Figure 1.2. Notice that this tab also allows you to change other essential settings like the polling interval for the IR port.

There's a lot of good information available on IrDA. For example, some people consider it a viable alternative to radio frequency (RF) technologies like Bluetooth in some cases. Here's a list of URLs where you can find additional information about IR technologies:

IrDA Infrared Communications:
An Overview
http://www.countersys.com/tech/
overview.html

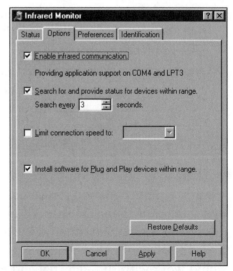

Figure 1.2: The Options tab of the Infrared Monitor dialog box allows you to enable the IR port.

ACTiSYS Corporation
http://www.actisys.com/

IrDA Versus Bluetooth: A Complementary Comparison
http://www.countersys.com/tech/bluetooth.html

Parallax Research
http://www.parallax-research.com/

IrDA Serial Infrared Interface
http://cesdis.gsfc.nasa.gov/linux/misc/irda.html

More Information on IrDA
http://www.jdresearch.com/irdrive/irda.html

What is Bluetooth?—*Bluetooth is a new technology standard that defines how computers can connect without wires. A radio frequency (RF) connection similar to the one used with walky-talkies is used to connect two computers together. RF technology is in its infancy, so a strong standard is needed to ensure that everyone develops compatible devices. You can find out more about Bluetooth at* http://www.intel.com/mobile/bluetooth/.

What a Network Can Do that Sneakers Can't

We've talked about a lot of network alternatives in the chapter so far and discussed a number of reasons why you should avoid using networks unless you absolutely have to. Of course, a lot of people use networks and for good reason—you can't replace the network in many situations. Running around with a floppy in hand (the infamous sneaker net) is a ridiculous solution to a data-sharing problem when more than a few people need to share information. A network allows you to share resources in a secure environment and provide users with services that make many tasks a lot easier (or doable in the first place). The following sections are going to explore the issues behind what a network can do that sneakers can't.

Understanding Why Networks are Important

For many people, the issue of network usage becomes a matter of what you can do. A car with a larger engine can go faster and haul more cargo than a car with a small engine. Likewise, a network can be viewed as the high-powered solution to the problem of managing data. All networking tasks end up manipulating data in some way. A business' data is the most important asset the company owns and the safe manipulation of that data is essential. A task can be viewed as one or more data manipulation exercises. Here are a few tasks that you can perform only with a network:

- Work with any type of centralized database.
- Share many types of devices with more than one person at a time.
- Ensure data remains secure.
- Maintain usage records or accounting data for users.
- Manage resources from a central location.
- Build any type of data server like a Web server.
- Establish a reliable data environment.

As you can see, networks provide a lot of features that some small businesses will require, but others won't. For example, the ability to manage resources from a central location isn't much of an issue when you have three workstations and a printer. Even 20 workstations and several printers don't provide much of a management challenge. It's when you become a network administrator with hundreds of machines to manage and several floors of printers to maintain, plus other peripheral devices, that the ability to manage resources from a central location becomes important.

In fact, of all of the things you can't do with a sneaker network, the only two that apply to networks for small business or home users are working with centralized databases and keeping your data secure. The reason this book is important is that small businesses do need to keep data secure and work with databases. A network is an important part of a home setup or a small business because it can help people perform specialized tasks faster than they could ordinarily. In fact, you can summarize the reasons for deciding between a standard network and a network alternative as follows:

Network alternatives work fine for printing reports or sharing data between two machines, but they aren't useful for activities that require any type of collaborative effort (simultaneous sharing of data).

The Effect of Reliability on Your Decision

There's one issue to consider when deciding whether to use a network that applies to everyone equally: reliability. You'll find that a reliable system is incredibly important to anyone who uses a computer. I've seen gamers tear their hair out (literally, in fact) when they lost the data on their system due to a computer crash. Some businesses will take out insurance on their data, because the loss of that data could ruin their company. Reliability is a central theme for every computer system. Reviewers often include reliability as one of the key issues for any new product. In fact, reliability issues often appear as the central topic in computer news articles.

I won't go so far as to say that a direct correlation exists between how much you spend and the reliability of your data environment; however, you'll find definite reliability problems inherent in low-cost solutions. Your data gets assaulted from a variety of sources, even if you keep your data on a single machine and never share it with anyone. A failed hard drive, lost password, or something as innocuous as pressing the wrong key can damage your data. Here is a list of the common sources of reliability problems:

- Human error
- Software glitches
- Hardware failures
- Acts of nature
- Crackers
- Lost communications
- Unexplained phenomena

A Windows 2000 client/server network offers you a lot more reliability than a Windows 95 peer-to-peer network. Likewise, any network will offer more in reliability than a network alternative. The reliability of a system boils down to the number of failure points and the quality of the components used. Increase the number of failure points and the reliability of the system suffers. Likewise, raise the quality of the components you use and reliability gets better.

When you install a network, you add some hidden reliability boosters that you really need to consider as part of your overall strategy. For example, most networks include the ability to back up both server and client data. A single tape drive can keep all of the data on your network safe and secure. When a failure occurs, you can restore the data from the tape, rather than attempt to overcome the loss.

Networks provide you with both options and flexibility. If the single printer connected to your workstation fails, you have to get the printer fixed before you can output any more documents. A network, however, might have two or three printers that are shared by the people who use it. The business saves money, because the company needs fewer shared printers for individual users. The user gains printer availability. A single printer failure won't be enough to keep users from creating output from their machines.

Some networked PCs also offer the advantage of failover support. When one machine fails, another can take its place. This means that a user could potentially lose access to a workstation and use another workstation until the first one is fixed. Failover support is an important issue, because it reduces the number of failure points and therefore the vulnerability of the network to disaster. Of course, this service isn't available on every network; it's one of the new features of Windows 2000 and appears as a standard part of other operating systems as well.

Do Networks Really Cost More?

After all of the things you've read in this chapter, you may come to the conclusion that networks are expensive and error-prone solutions to the common problem of resource sharing between employees. Networks do have a lot to offer—I wouldn't want you to feel that a network is the option of last choice and that every other choice is better.

If your company is growing and you use a lot of custom applications, then trying the alternatives listed in this chapter is probably a waste of time. You really do need a network to fulfill your company's needs. Using the floppy shuffle to exchange small amounts of data between two employees is one thing; attempting to do the same thing between five employees borders on madness.

A low-cost alternative turns into a costly solution when you really do need a network to get the job done. You'll eventually get the network anyway and in the mean time you'll waste both time and money on a solution that won't work. So, what's the easy way to determine whether you need a network? Here's the simple way that I look at things:

Use a network when more than two people need to share data, when the data resides within a database, or any time complex sharing requirements exist.

Whether a network is worth the cost is based solely on what you need to do and how fast you need to do it. It's important to separate fact from fiction when it comes to networking. A network won't automatically make your business more productive or save you money unless you need the features that a network can provide. As the book progresses, I'll help you find the answers you need to make a network into a solution that really will make your business more productive and save you money.

CHAPTER TWO

Cheap Alternative Networks

Most small businesses I've worked with don't have the money required to build a huge expensive network. Even if they had the money, I'd probably recommend they forgo installing a high-speed network if they really don't need one. If your home office or small business has two or three computers connected together and all you work on is word-processed files, a full-scale network is a waste of money. An inexpensive alternative network will work just as well, be easier to maintain, and cost a lot less to build.

Home networks are especially easy to serve with alternative networks, because the builder often uses them to meet family and business needs. The main computer is the one that Mom or Dad uses to communicate with work or perform household tasks, like pay the bills. A network allows the children's computers to access resources on the large machine used by Mom and Dad. The family might use the network for gaming and other recreational needs as well. In short, home networks often serve both light-business and family needs. An alternative network solution provides everything required in such cases.

Even if a home network is used for serious business needs all of the time, you need to consider how many people will use the network and what type of work they'll perform. For example, if you're running a home sales business, the main computer will probably have all the accounting and database information stored on it. An administrative assistant will use a secondary computer for word processing and occasional database lookup. Again, a network scenario like this doesn't require all of the features that a full-fledged network can provide.

Of course, at this point, you're probably asking what constitutes an inexpensive alternative network. The first section of the chapter answers that question. You may be surprised at the variety of ways that a business can move data from one machine to another. As home-office networks become more prevalent, I'm sure that we'll see even more solutions on the market. The only requirement for many networks is the ability to move data from one machine to another—speed really isn't much of a factor in many cases.

But don't get the impression that these networking alternatives are just as good as the big expensive models. There are tradeoffs in any cost-based solution to a problem. The second section of the chapter helps you understand what you gain with an alternative-network solution and what you lose. In most cases, you'll gain more than some extra cash in your pocket and you'll lose more than just a little data-transfer speed. It's important to understand the hidden costs of an alternative-network purchase before you actually make it.

The last three sections look at the most prevalent networking alternatives in detail. In some cases, you may find that a solution that looks attractive at first has drawbacks that your business can't live with. For example, a house-wiring system may look attractive because of the extremely low cost, but may turn out to be the wrong choice because of the poor security it provides. The purpose of these last three sections is to show you the good, the bad, and the ugly of alternative networks. You may find that a solution that didn't look realistic at first really can do the job for your business and save you a lot of cash as a result.

Two Tin Cans and a String

If you're like me, you spent at least a little time marveling over the wonder of two tin cans and a string as a child. I remember that my brother and I had a lot of fun times as children having secret conversations using our special telephones. The principle behind the tin-can-and-string telephone is easy to understand and even easier to implement. Sound gets concentrated in the first can, travels down the string as a vibration, and ends up in the second can as a sound. It works, but it doesn't work well. I'd often ask my brother to repeat something, because the tin can and string didn't do a good job of transferring the information.

Alternative networks are much like the tin-can-and-string telephone. They use a well-known principle to move data from one point to another. Most of them are like the tin-can-and-string telephone in that they're cheap, work reasonably well over short distances, and are easy to implement and configure. They also have the same failings at the tin-can-and-string telephone; namely, they aren't an industrial-strength solution to anyone's problems. For example, anyone within earshot knew what my brother and I were discussing in our supposedly secret conversation. An alternative network can have security gaps as well that have nothing to do with the network, but result from the way the technology transfers the data from one location to another. An alternative network allows a small number of machines to transfer small amounts of data extremely well. However, you have to watch for technological failings while congratulating yourself on saving your business money.

Most alternative network vendors try to provide you with a quality product— at least within the limitations of the technology. For example, you'll find that some vendors provide data encryption to overcome security problems inherent with some types of alternative-network technology. Other vendors overcome power problems by carefully tuning their systems to provide enough, but not too much signal amplification. Obviously, you want to get your data transmitted to all of the computers in your home; but you don't want your competitor who lives ten miles away to know your business' innermost secrets.

The following sections provide a quick look at some of the more popular alternative networking technologies. We'll talk about these technologies in general, so that you can decide whether to read about them in detail later in the chapter. All of these options offer low cost and ease of installation. In addition, all offer enough bandwidth for simple gaming, word processing, low-end databases, and other simple networking needs. Not many of these solutions handle video-data transfer or other network intensive tasks; you need a full-fledged network for these needs.

What is SOHO?—*You may see the term SOHO on some vendor sites and no explanation of what the term means. In fact, a few vendors use the term SOHO in their name or as part of product names. SOHO stands for small office, home office. When you see SOHO, you know that the vendor is talking about your networking needs—at least from the vendor's point of view. You need to examine what a vendor means by this term. In some cases, the vendor is making an honest attempt to make networking easy and less costly. In other cases, vendors market last year's product that didn't sell in the corporate world as this year's great product for small businesses. Don't get caught with an inferior system. Always check product reviews and the business' reputation before you buy a product—especially online.*

House-Wiring Systems

One of the problems with building a home network is finding a way to run cabling without ripping out walls or causing other major damage. Unlike offices, where false ceilings, cubicle stanchions, and hollow walls offer places to put cables, a home often has permanent ceilings and voids (areas between walls or floors where cables are run) with plenty of obstacles. Running a cable of any kind can prove frustrating. In some cases, the only way to run a cable is to tear out part of the wall, something a landlord will look upon with disfavor or may mean expensive repairs for homeowners.

Fortunately, your home already contains all of the cable you need to transfer data from one machine to another. Every electrical outlet is part of a web of cabling that encompasses the entire house. A house-wiring network makes use of this feature to get around the problem of running cables in a home. Data moves from receptacle to receptacle, just as it would with standard network cable.

Of course, just having cabling in place won't allow the network to run. All of these systems require a special plug-in box that isolates the computer from the voltage the house wiring is designed to carry, but allows the computer to transfer signals. One end of the box has a standard two-or three-pronged receptacle plug. The other end has a cable with an adapter on the end that plugs into the computer. The appeal of the house-wiring system is that it's easy to set up and configure. If anything goes wrong with the plug-in device, you simply pull out the old one and plug in a new one; it's akin to changing a light bulb. The only difficulty you might encounter is installing the software. While the vendor normally automates this process, you might run into configuration problems in some rare cases.

Control More Than Your Computer—*Some house-wiring network vendors provide more than just networking solutions. A few also provide solutions for the appliances in your home. For example, Intelogis sells the Powerline (http://www.intelogis.com/power/) kit that allows you to control appliances with your computer, as well as connect computers together using your house wiring. As a home-office user, this is a good feature to consider, because you can automatically set up lighting or applications to turn on right before you get home. Theoretically, you could also connect a remote-network setup, so that you could control appliances while away from home. We'll talk about remote-network connections in Chapter 10, Remote Communications.*

Home Phoneline Systems

In the previous section, I noted that homes come with lots of cable used for electrical outlets. Homes also come with telephone cables, and modern homes commonly have at least one telephone outlet in each room. Each of these telephone outlets can support three telephone lines using three sets of wires (6 wires total). The home's main number uses up one set of wires. That leaves two sets of wires free.

Some vendors have begun using the second or third set of wires as another method to move data from one point to another. You can access the second set of wires without changing anything in the telephone outlet box. Other vendors have begun piggybacking the network signal on top of the normal telephone signals. A well-designed system won't interfere with your telephone conversations as you work at the computer. The result is the same using either strategy; your data goes from one computer to another using a standard telephone connection.

This network-connection scheme works much like the home-wiring system. You connect a cable between the computer and the telephone line (instead of a power receptacle). The telephone wiring does the rest. The only major difference is that some home phoneline systems require that you install a network interface card (NIC). Low cost versions of these cards are about $20, which increases overall network cost a little, but not much. You normally get higher data-transfer rates using a home phoneline system in exchange for the slightly higher installation cost.

***Get a Standardized Home Phoneline System**—Unlike many of the alternatives we'll talk about in this chapter, there are standards for the home phoneline system. These standards specify the speed at which system communicates and how it transfers data from one point to another. Using a standardized system means that you don't need to worry quite as much about getting updates and additions from the same vendor you used for the original installation. You can find out more about the home phoneline standards at Home Phoneline Networking Alliance at* http://www.homepna.org/.

USB Systems

USB systems are really a new implementation of existing technology. When working with most of these systems, you create a connection by plugging one end of a double-ended adapter into each of the two machines you want to connect together. If you want to connect three machines, the machine in the center will have two connections: one to machine 1, and one to machine 3. This is *daisy chaining*, a technique used by other networking technologies.

Some USB systems rely on an Ethernet-like block. You plug one end of the USB cable into the computer; the other end goes into the block. These systems tend to have fewer reliability problems and transfer data slightly faster than the daisy-chained models. However, they're also more cumbersome to set up and tend to cost a little more than the daisy-chained models do.

The feature that makes this solution easier than creating a full-fledged Ethernet network is that you don't need to open the machine to set up the network. The USB port and external adapter take care of all of the required network connections. A simple automated software setup completes the installation process. In most cases, the only question the installation program will need to ask is what you want to call your machine. (Every machine on the network has to have a unique name.) Here are some of the more popular vendors of this technology:

ActionTec USB Networking Kit
http://www.actiontec.com/products/usb-homenet/actionlinkusb_ovrview.html

Anchor Chips EZ-Link USB
http://www.ezlinkusb.com/

Entrega 3Plus Port
http://www.entrega.com/

When it comes to speed, USB systems fall short of new home phoneline systems, but far exceed the capabilities of home-wiring systems. You'll find that you can get about 2 to 5 Mbps transfer rate from a USB system. The one area where USB systems shine is in a low latency time of 1 ms to 20 ms. *Latency* is the time required for one system to respond to a request made by another system. The latency levels for USB compare favorably with the higher rates generally experienced by both home phoneline and home-wiring system users. See "Using the Power Lines" and "Using the Telephone Lines" sections later in this chapter for performance data on these other networking systems.

Radio-Frequency Systems

Unlike every other alternative networking systems we've talked about so far, radio-frequency systems require no cables at all. Most depend on low-power radio-frequency transmissions in ranges that the Federal Communications Commission (FCC) doesn't regulate. The vendor selects frequencies that avoid potential problem areas with your PC's normal function.

Most radio-frequency systems use 2.4 GHz as their transmission frequency. This frequency has the least chance of interfering with other devices in your office, although some interference will occur. For example, some people have complained that their wireless network produced a low-level hiss on their computer speakers, while other people complained about problems with other wireless computing devices. You'll want to avoid the systems that use a 900 MHz transmission frequency, because many home devices, like cordless telephones, use this frequency range. Imagine having your telephone calls interrupted while working at the computer.

When using a radio-frequency system, you'll need to install an expansion card in most cases. Desktop machines need an industry standard architecture (ISA) or peripheral component interconnect (PCI) card, while laptops can use a Personal Computer Memory Card International Association (PCMCIA) card (also known as a PC Card). Some vendors also provide hubs that you can plug into standard network cards. However, using a hub with wireless capability wouldn't make sense for a small business—you may as well use a standard network setup.

Radio-frequency systems vary greatly in features. However, any good radio-frequency system adheres to the Institute of Electrical and Electronics Engineers (IEEE) 802.11 and IEEE 802.1Q standards. The first standard tells how a radio-frequency system should work. The second standard describes how a virtual local area network (LAN) should operate. A radio-frequency network needs to perform both tasks. You can find out more about **The IEEE** at http://www.ieee.org/.

The biggest reason to use a radio-frequency network is that you don't have to rely on existing house wiring or run any new cable to create a connection. If your landlord will make a fuss about all of those new holes in the wall, a wireless network is a good way to avoid trouble. Radio-frequency networks are also extremely portable. You can attach a radio-frequency connection to a notebook or palmtop and walk around while you compute without losing your network connection.

Get a Standardized Radio-Frequency System—Like users of a home phoneline system, radio-frequency system users have a place to go to find out about new standards in radio-frequency networks, HomeRF Web Site at http://www.homerf.org/. The standards proposed by this group aren't the same as those for Bluetooth (see the "Making Infrared Work" section of Chapter 1, Do You Need a Network?). Bluetooth answers the needs of short-haul communication between PDAs, laptops, cell phones, and printers in the range of 30 feet. This group is concentrating on long-range network communication and higher speed data transfers. (The FCC just approved 10 Mbps data transfers.)

Getting Additional Help

The rapid pace of technology makes it possible that there are newer and more exciting technologies available even as you read this. That's why it's important to know where to get additional help for your networking needs. The Internet has a lot to offer for the home-office or small-business network builder. Here are some sites to consider:

Absolutely Straight Talk on Computer Networks for the Small Office/Home Office
http://www.rubyan.com/

Computer Networking
http://compnetworking.about.com/

Cyber Office Solutions
http://www.cyberofficesolutions.com/

Home Networking News
http://www.home-networking.org/

The Home PC Network Site
http://www.homepcnetwork.com/

Wireless LAN.com Answer Page
http://www.wirelesslan.com/

ZDNet Family PC Home
http://familypc.zdnet.com/

Cheap Network Pros and Cons

The two best reasons to get an alternative network are price and speed of installation. Most of these solutions require no special wiring and little or no effort to install on the PC. The lack of wiring alone saves you considerable time when getting an alternative network operational. Of course, the fact that vendors design these networks for simple setups of two or three machines helps, too. The cost of an alternative network is extremely low, because there isn't any complex hardware, wiring, or even software to worry about. Most of these kits contain a small adapter and a simple driver.

The following sections look at the pros and cons of using an alternative network. For a home-office or small-business user with simple needs, you'll find that the pros far outweigh the cons. If you are an ambitious small-business owner with thoughts of corporate power in your head, an alternative network presents some major hurdles. Many of these hurdles are insurmountable, and you'll quickly find yourself looking at a full-fledged network at the outset.

Potential Problem Areas

The biggest problem with alternative networks is speed. For the most part, they rely on unshielded household wiring to transport the data. There isn't any way to determine how long the cabling run is, because walls hide cable and associated connections. In some cases, there isn't even any way to determine which path the electrical signal will take from one machine to another. Consequently, alternative-network designers need to consider a worst-case wiring scenario and design their systems accordingly. About the only alternative-network systems that provide the same speed as a low-end business network are the new home phoneline systems that provide a 10 Mbps transfer rate. Even so, latency and other factors keep this system from performing at full speed.

Most of the cons I just mentioned won't surprise you, because even the alternative network vendors talk about them. However, there are hidden cons to consider. For example, you normally get what you pay for when it comes to computer equipment. An alternative-network system vendor has less reason to provide top-notch support because of the low cost of the equipment and the relative simplicity of the setup. You'll find there are few problems with these systems, but if you do run into one and can't solve it on your own, the vendor may not be there to help. In other words, make sure you check the vendor's support plan before you buy, just in case you run into problems.

Another hidden problem is scalability. Alternative-network vendors may claim that you can run a whole office on one of their systems. A practical limit is three computers and up to three peripheral devices if you don't intend to load the network down with high-end applications. So, when your business grows and you need to add the fourth computer to the network, you may find you need to add an entirely new network as well. An alternative system is designed for small networking needs—most of them even contain *home* or *home office* right in the product name or description.

***Speed Tips for the Windows Gamer**—There's nothing better than playing games against a real opponent rather than the computer, unless you're suffering from a slow network connection. In many cases, the network has more than sufficient bandwidth; the setup's to blame for the speed problems. There are two quick fixes to speed up game playing on the network. First, open the Network Properties dialog box by right-clicking Network Neighborhood and selecting Properties from the shortcut menu. Highlight the TCP/IP entry for the NIC on each machine, click Properties, and then click IP Addresses. Select Specify an IP address and hard code the IP addresses for each machine on the network using 192.168.0.XXX (where XXX is a unique number between 1 and 254) and a subnet mask of 255.255.255.0. This allows the network to resolve addresses faster. Click OK. Second, highlight the IPX entry for the NIC, click Properties, and then click Bindings. Clear the File and printer sharing for Microsoft networks option; then click OK. This change reduces the time that Windows spends processing file and print requests. Click OK again to close the Network Properties dialog box. Windows will ask you to reboot the machine. You should notice a speed increase when you play games over the network.*

One problem that most people don't consider is security. If you're running a house-wiring network, there's a good chance that your neighbor will be able to see everything transmitted on your network. The signal runs out of your house to the power pole and back down to the neighbor's house. The same problem occurs (albeit less frequently) with home phoneline systems and radio-frequency systems. All of these alternative networks transmit information in an uncontrolled environment, making interception of data quite easy. Of course, your neighbor would need the right equipment to read your network signals and a reason to do so. Still, it's important to remember this security concern when purchasing your equipment. Some vendors include encryption as part of the package. While encryption costs a little in network bandwidth, it also protects your data so no one else can see it.

I'm not saying that alternative networks are poorly designed or that they won't live up to vendor promises; but you need to be realistic about the capabilities of these systems. Alternative-network vendors design these systems for home offices or small businesses that will never grow beyond a certain size. For example, I installed one of these systems in a doctor's office. He's never called me back, because he's never needed any help with the system. It does everything he needs it to do and his office will never grow, because he has all of the patients he can handle. This is a perfect example of when the limitations of an alternative network are a non-issue. The fact that the vendor has probably gone out of business and that there isn't any way to add new nodes to the network doesn't matter.

Planning for Failure—Alternative networks are exceptionally simple and easy to run. However, just like any other device (even a simple one), you can damage the components of an alternative network. Since standardization isn't common with alternative networks, you're normally stuck getting devices from a single vendor once you decide on a solution. This means that if a device fails, you'll have to get a new one from that vendor. What if the vendor is out of business or doesn't make that part anymore? It may mean that you're out of luck and will need to buy a whole new network. It pays to get one extra of each device for the network. That way, if the inevitable failure does occur, you'll be prepared for it. Of course, by the time a second failure occurs, you're normally ready for a new network with the enhanced capabilities vendors have added since your original installation.

Perks of Using an Alternative Network

One of the most important pros of using an alternative network is simplicity. As an alternative-network user, you don't need to learn about complex networking terms, weird setup routines, or difficult maintenance tasks. Once you set the alternative network up, it either works or it doesn't. Except for occasional diagnostic tests (if there are any), an alternative network shouldn't require any maintenance. You'll find that most of the boxes, cables, and other hardware pieces for an alternative network are completely sealed. When one fails, unplug it and replace it with a new one.

The total cost of ownership (TCO) for an alternative network is quite low. You may have read that TCO is something that large companies worry about all of the time. Some articles that I've read include some scary figures about the cost of maintaining an individual PC, which directly affects the cost of maintaining a network as a whole. What these articles don't mention is all of the contributing factors for TCO. Large companies usually have a large support staff of network engineers and help-desk personnel. That's because the complex systems they use can't be easily learned or fixed by the people using them. The simplicity of an alternative network makes problems like a steep learning curve a non-issue for most users. It doesn't take long to learn how to use them and maintenance is a snap. Your TCO will be relatively low, because you don't need to hire a support staff of any kind for your network.

A full-fledged network requires special cabling and peripheral devices like hubs to run. An alternative network requires a simple plug-in device attached to the back of the computer. In many cases, this means that you can move computers around if you like and still not have to do much with the network. For example, if you're using a house-wiring network alternative, all you need is another wall plug to get the network reconnected. Since you'll need a wall outlet for your computer anyway, reconnecting the network doesn't represent a major undertaking. Again, the simplicity of alternative networks makes it easy to reconfigure your system in any way you require.

Chapter 3, *Designing a Standard Network*, looks at what people who need to build a full-fledged network go through to prepare for the network installation. An alternative-network user may have to perform some level of planning, but nothing quite as extensive as the planning as we'll talk about in Chapter 3. Given that you only need to think about the number of machines and peripheral devices that you want to run on the alternative network, all you really need to do is know how to count. Total the number of network nodes you need, and buy enough alternative-network packages to handle that number of nodes.

Using the Power Lines

Using house-wiring is one of the more popular alternative networking technologies, because it requires so little work on the part of the installer. Some systems don't even require a three-prong outlet—any two-prong outlet will do. This feature makes some systems acceptable for any house, no matter how old, as long as it has power wiring of some kind. You will find that setting up this alternative network takes about 10 minutes. You begin by plugging the two plug-in boxes into outlets. Connect the other end of each box to the computer and complete the process by sticking a CD-ROM with the required software into each machine. Once both machines have the required software in place, they should be able to communicate. The only installation decision that you might need to make is which plug to use on the back of the computer.

There are four methods used to make the connection to the computer. Which method you choose depends on how much you want to spend and your networking needs. The fastest data-transfer method is to connect the plug-in box to a standard NIC. Of course, this is also the most expensive method, because you have to buy a NIC in addition to the plug-in box. The theoretical speed of this connection is 10 Mbps, but you'll rarely get it, because of the poor performance characteristics of house wiring. The second fastest method at 1 to 2 Mbps is to make the connection to the USB port in the back of the computer. Unfortunately, the plug-in box requires special intelligence for the USB port, which raises the cost of the system, so it's not as popular as other methods. The most common method is to use the parallel port. The advantage of using this technique is that the plug-in box requires no special intelligence, and you can still get around 360 Kbps transfer rate. Finally, some plug-in boxes rely on a serial-port connection, which is the slowest method at a maximum 115 Kbps transfer rate. All of these methods provide better performance than the maximum dial-up speed of 56 Kbps, so even gamers should be happy with the results.

The Advantages of a Passthrough Connector—We've been talking about the requirement for a serial or parallel port when using these technologies. What happens if you don't have a port to spare? Some, but not all, of these products include what's known as a passthrough connector. A passthrough connector allows you to use the serial or parallel port for its normal purpose in addition to using it for network connections. Passthrough connectors allow you to double the usage of a serial or parallel port on your machine. The disadvantage is that the passthrough connector can become confused, making it impossible to use the port for any purpose until you reboot. Although the confusion problem is rare, you do need to take it into account when complete network reliability is a factor.

Transfer rate isn't the only concern when connecting two machines together. You also need to consider latency. House wiring has extremely poor data-transfer characteristics, and there's a chance that the receiving machine will have to ask for the same data several times before it actually receives a good copy. This means that the time to transfer a single piece of information (called a packet) increases dramatically as the quality of the electrical cable decreases. A standard 10 Mbps Ethernet network has a latency of about 1 ms for a short cable. A house-wiring network has a typical latency of 40 ms; but this can be has high as 400 ms if the wiring in your home has a lot of flaws, like kinks, in it. Unfortunately, there isn't any way to determine what the latency of the network connection will be until you connect everything. In some cases, you can fix a latency problem in a home-wiring network by moving the plug-in to another receptacle.

A potential concern for this networking technology is the voltage on the other side of the plug-in. If the plug-in should fail in such a way as to connect the house current directly to the parallel or serial port of a computer, the excess voltage will most likely destroy the port and damage the computer. I've never heard of this particular problem happening. It would seem that the vendor selling the kit would ensure that the plug-in includes safety measures to guard against this problem; but it pays to check the vendor documentation to be certain.

Another concern is that lightning will strike and damage the system. You should plug your computer into a surge suppressor to guard against this problem. However, there isn't any guarantee that the plug-ins will be able to communicate through a standard surge suppressor, because of the way that some vendors design them. Look for a house-wiring kit that includes a surge suppressor that you can use with the kit. This special surge suppressor allows a higher data-transfer rate and still protects your system from harm. If the house-wiring network kit you choose doesn't include a surge suppressor, check with the company to ensure your standard surge suppressor will work.

Now that you know what to look for in a house-wiring kit, let's talk about specific vendors. Here's a list of vendors to check:

Intelogis Passport
http://www.intelogis.com/products/

X-10 ActiveHome
http://www.x10.com/products/

Using the Telephone Lines

Home phoneline systems are becoming more popular as more homes get telephone lines in every room. This is a solution for modern home offices, where the quality of the telephone wiring is relatively high. There are currently two common speeds for home phoneline systems: 1 Mbps and 10 Mbps, although other speeds are available. Whether you actually get the throughput that vendors promise depends on the quality of the adapters you use, how the contractor ran the telephone cable in your house, the amount of ambient noise, and the quality of the telephone wiring. However, it doesn't take much to see that using a home phoneline system results in higher throughput than the home-wiring system discussed in the previous section.

Using telephone wires in place of standard house wiring reduces latency as well. Telephone cabling is better suited to transmitting data than electrical wire. You can expect latency in the 20 to 50 ms range in most cases. If the cable run between two computers is short (like between two adjoining rooms), you may see latency as low as 1 ms, which would be equal to standard Ethernet cabling.

Some home phoneline systems aren't quite a simple as the house-wiring systems discussed in the previous section. A higher percentage of these systems require that you open your machine and install a NIC. While installing a NIC isn't hard, it does add to the cost of the system. If you're using one of the network alternatives, you want to keep costs to a minimum. Including a NIC also raises the complexity level, something else most people want to avoid when working with a network. In short, you still gain flexibility and don't need to run cables to get your network setup; but some home phoneline systems do create more problems than they should.

Home phoneline systems are available from a number of vendors. Because there's a standard these vendors can use when designing their systems, you'll find that many of these systems are interchangeable. However, you should try to get all of your parts from the same vendor to ensure there aren't any compatibility problems. Here's a list of some home phoneline system vendors:

3Com Residential—HomeConnect
http://www.3com.com/solutions/personal/

ActionTec ActionLink
http://www.actiontec.com/products/homenet/

Best Data Home PC Link
http://www.bestdata.com/products.htm

D-Link DHN910 Phoneline and DHN-920 USB Phoneline
http://www.dlink.com/products/kits/

Diamond HomeFree Phoneline
http://www.thedigitaldreamhome.com/

Intel AnyPoint Phoneline
http://www.intel.com/anypoint/

Linksys HomeLink Phoneline
http://www.linksys.com/products/

Tut Systems HomeRun
http://www.tutsys.com/products/expressomdu/

Working with Wireless Technologies

Most wireless technologies rely on either infrared or radio-frequency transmissions to perform their work. When using an infrared transmission, the computers all have to be in the same room, which tends to limit the usefulness of infrared as a networking technology. On the plus side, it's extremely unlikely that an infrared network will interfere with anything else in your home or office. We talked about techniques you can use to make infrared work better for networking in the "Making Infrared Work" section of Chapter 1, *Do You Need a Network*.

Radio-wave setups don't rely on specific computer locations. The two computers have to be in range of the radio signal; but that's the only requirement. Unfortunately, no matter what radio frequency you choose, there's bound to be some type of interference with something else, even if it's only your radio. The radio-frequency spectrum has filled up quickly as cell phones and cordless devices proliferate, so it pays to be careful about which radio-frequency technology you choose.

Even radio waves experience problems getting through certain obstacles, so you need to exercise care when setting up your office. For example, if you place a large metal filing cabinet between two of the computers that you want to connect, the transmission rate will decrease due to interference. Radio-frequency systems designed for home office use, like Diamond's HomeFree, normally have a throughput of 1 Mbps, which is sufficient for word processing and other low-bandwidth tasks. BreezeCOM and other companies provide higher speed wireless networks that provide a throughput of 11 Mbps, which is actually a little better than a low-end Ethernet system. Latency for all radio-wave networks is between 1 ms and 10 ms. That's a little higher than Ethernet, but better than some of the other technologies we've talked about so far.

Distance is another concern with radio-frequency networks. Low-energy systems, like HomeFree, tend to top out at a 150-foot range. That's because they use a lower power signal that won't interfere with other electronic devices. Higher power systems, like BreezeNET, allow for a much larger range. They can transmit data at 11 Mbps up to 175 feet and 1 Mbps up to 500 feet range. There are transmission increments of 1 Mbps, 2 Mbps, 5.5 Mbps, and 11 Mbps for most high power radio-wave systems, so the transmission will degrade in increments. Other radio-frequency networking systems, like SOHOware CableFREE, promise a midrange of distance with penetration through difficult surfaces like concrete.

Of course, these ranges are all inside ranges in an office environment. Some companies specify an open environment inside range (such as in a warehouse) of as much as 1,000 feet for a network that would normally travel 175 feet in an office environment. Companies often use radio-frequency networks to create connections outside a building. For example, some companies use them to connect two buildings. A small business that requires workers to spend time outdoors could use radio-frequency networks to stay in touch. Ranges outside a building are often in miles, because there are fewer obstructions and surfaces to absorb the energy. For example, BreezeNET is rated at 15 miles when using high-gain antennas.

One of the more interesting choices in radio-frequency networks is WebGear Aviator. This choice is one of the few radio-frequency networks designed to connect to the parallel port instead of requiring a NIC in the PC. Not only does this make Aviator a lot easier to install, but less expensive as well. Unfortunately, the ease of using a parallel port comes at the price of speed. The Aviator transfers data at approximately 360 Kbps instead of the 1 Mbps or more allowed by other radio-frequency networks. An upcoming USB Aviator release should allow much higher throughput in the 1.2 to 2 Mbps range.

Now that you have a better idea of how wireless technologies work, let's talk about where you can get a network based on this technology. The following list contains some of the vendors you'll want to check out:

BreezeCOM BreezeNET and BreezeACCESS
http://www.breezecom.com/

Diamond HomeFree Wireless
http://www.thedigitaldreamhome.com/

InnoMedia InfoAccess
http://www.innomedia.com/

Intel AnyPoint Wireless
http://www.intel.com/anypoint/

Proxim Symphony and RangeLAN2
http://www.proxim.com/products/selector/

SOHOware CableFREE
http://www.sohoware.com/Products/Products.htm

WebGear Aviator
http://www.webgear.com/

As you can see, there are a number of wireless network suppliers today. This number will only increase as wireless technologies grow in popularity.

CHAPTER THREE

Designing a Standard Network

Designing even a small network may be one of the most important parts of getting your network up and running. I've received more than a few calls from people who want a network because they really feel they need one. Precisely what this network will do or why the people need the network are questions that they've never stopped to consider. All they know is that the network will save them money somewhere along the way, having read a success story in a trade journal or a general magazine. It's important to know why you need a network and what you expect it to do for you before you begin to put it together.

Another type of call that I get is one where the user or company has a specific purpose in mind for the network. They become so fixated on that particular use for the network that other uses seem out of the question, even if the alternative use has more potential to save the company money than the original idea and wouldn't cost any more to implement. Networks are extremely versatile and flexible. You can always get more functionality from a network as long as the required capacity is provided as part of the installation.

Both of these situations point out the need to design the network. Creating a network without designing it first usually results in something that doesn't do what you originally anticipated, at least not well. A good network design will help an individual or company in the following ways:

- Obtain some specific level of functionality today.
- Provide for more features in the future.
- Reduce installation costs.
- Reduce complexity by installing the hardware and software in an orderly fashion.
- Enhance user productivity by ensuring all users have what they need.
- Reduce the time required to get the network operational.
- Decrease the cost of owning the network.
- Allow you to see new uses for the network.
- Ensure the network will perform the tasks you want it to do.

This chapter will help you design your own network with a minimum of fuss and for less cash than those high-priced consultants will tell you a network requires. Of course, the first problem for many people who want to build a network is that they don't see a need to perform any design at all. That's what the first section of the chapter is all about. It tells you why even a small network will benefit from some type of design phase, even if that phase consists of a half an hour's work scrawling some notes on a napkin.

The computer industry uses a lot of terms to describe networks. Even a small network can be described in several different ways. If you don't know what these terms mean, trying to design a network can become a very frustrating exercise. The two terms you must understand are *peer-to-peer* and *client/server*, both of which describe types of networks by the way they share resources. The second section of the chapter will help you understand some of these terms and what they mean to you. More importantly, it will help you understand why one type of network will work better in some cases than in others.

Once you've gotten some basics down, it's time to begin designing your network. The final sections in this chapter won't discuss every potential element for every kind of network you'll ever see; I've concentrated on the requirements for a small business or home network. As a result, you'll find discussions on topics like deciding what resources to share and getting the right workstation or server. We won't discuss large network needs like creating clusters (even though I'll tell you what this term means so that you can impress your friends with your new networking knowledge).

Networks with a Frankenstein Complex

Most people know what a network is, or at least they think they do. In many cases, someone building a network views it as a collection of stand-alone machines that just happen to have wires connecting them together. Networks that are built using a piece of this and a part of that often end up having a Frankenstein complex and turn on their creator in the long run. A poor network design will always have problems and will create more work for their owners, even if you use the best equipment. What types of problems do networks with a Frankenstein complex have?

- Poor reliability
- High operating and training costs
- Slow response time
- Potential data loss

A network is a cohesive unit and should work as a single entity when it comes to network-specific tasks. A user who needs to use the shared network printer shouldn't have to worry about the location of the printer, how it's connected to the network, or whether the correct software is installed. All the user should need to do is click Print and allow the network do the rest of the work of getting the data from the workstation to the printer.

***Checking for a Frankenstein Complex**—You may not know if your network has a Frankenstein complex. If you're unsure about how well your network is constructed, try printing a document locally and then again across the network. If you have to work any harder to print the document across the network than you do locally, then there's a problem with your network setup. This may seem like a simplistic way to make a decision, but printing is one of the most common activities on a network. If a network doesn't handle printing well, it likely has other problems as well. Networks with a Frankenstein complex are a common occurrence.*

Networks with a Frankenstein complex also have organizational problems. One company that hired me complained about reduced productivity after the network was installed, rather than the productivity increase they had anticipated. A look at the network design showed that the network had been put together using mismatched pieces of hardware and software, and that the network itself wasn't designed around the workflow of the company. A simple example of the workflow problem was the printer, which was located in a back room to keep things quiet in the work area, but made access to printed documents nearly impossible. (The room was a closet that could hold at most one person at a time.) Since the business was a law firm, you can imagine that printer access is a requirement, not an optional network feature. Moving the printer to the middle of the office and placing it in a soundproof enclosure reduced access problems, increased productivity, and still kept the office reasonably quiet.

The location of data presented another problem. Since no one's hard drive had sufficient space for everything they need, the network administrator (actually an administrative assistant) ended up shuffling data all over the network. The result was that no one ever knew where to find data from one day to the next. The addition of a large hard drive on one machine cleared up this problem and made the network administrator's job easier. In addition, using a single large hard drive made it easier for everyone to search for information.

There were other problems at this company, but you get the picture. A network with a Frankenstein complex ended up turning against its owners and reduced productivity by a noticeable amount. Even though this example represents a small network for eight people, the problems imposed by a poor design are real. Here's a good way to look at the cure for the Frankenstein complex:

Every network requires some amount of design, even if it's a gaming platform for home use.

Of course, some networks require more design than others. We'll talk about how much design time your network needs as the chapter progresses. You may find that just a few minutes planning your home network on a scrap sheet of paper will save hours later when you put the network together. Business networks almost always require more planning than home networks used for entertainment or family purposes, but you can still control the time and money required to design the network by eliminating unnecessary work.

Peer-to-Peer versus Client/Server

There are many ways to categorize networks. The two most common network designations are peer-to-peer and client/server. You may have heard these terms before, but because they're used inconsistently within the computer industry, the meanings of these terms might be difficult to figure out just by listening to the experts speak. There is, in fact, some confusion over just how these designations apply to some network operating systems (NOSs), because the vendors keep changing the designation of their operating system (OS) to meet current industry demand for a specific product.

There are two visible differences between peer-to-peer and client/server networks: resource sharing and console availability. In a peer-to-peer network, all of the computers can share resources in common. (Whether you actually want to share all of the resources the network contains is another question, which we'll answer in the "Deciding What to Share" section later in this chapter.) Every workstation can act as both a client and a server, which means that every piece of hardware is also available for shared use. In all cases, you can use the server (the computer that provides resources to other computers) as a workstation in a peer-to-peer network. Here are some examples of peer-to-peer networks:

- All recent versions of **Microsoft Windows** (http://www.microsoft.com/windows/)
- Apple **AppleShare** and **AppleShare IP** (http://www.apple.com/appleshareip/)
- **SpartaCom** LANtastic (http://www.spartacom.com/products/lantastic.htm)

A client/server network is one where all of the workstations connect to one or more centralized computers and use resources only on those computers. Even if a workstation can host a resource such as a printer, requests for that resource must go through the central server. In almost every case, the machine you use as a server can't be used as a workstation in a client/server network. The server console is normally used to manage the network instead of working with user data. Here are some examples of client/server networks:

- **Novell NetWare** (http://www.novell.com/products/)
- All minicomputer and mainframe OSs
- **IBM OS/2 Warp** (http://www-4.ibm.com/software/os/warp/)
- **Linux** (http://www.linux.com/)

One of the more important decisions you can make about your network is what type of network you really need. In many cases, a peer-to-peer network will work just fine and at a much lower cost than a client/server setup. In other cases, you'll need the additional flexibility that a client/server setup can provide. Since the type of network you choose will affect everything from the kind of NOS you install to the type of hardware you buy, it's the first design decision you have to make.

Now that you have some idea of where operating systems fall in the networking arena, let's look at them in detail. The four sections that follow will introduce you to four networking models: peer-to-peer, client/server, NOSs that fall somewhere in between these two extremes, and hybrid networks that contain both peer-to-peer and client/server elements. Learning about these four models will help you make a better operating system purchase.

Peer-to-Peer Advantages and Disadvantages

You can categorize networks in many ways. The two most common network designations are peer-to-peer and client/server. In fact, it's unlikely that you'll see a client/server setup used in the home. There are a lot of reasons to use peer-to-peer networks. Here are a few of the most common reasons:

Less expensive—The best reason to use a peer-to-peer network is cost. Not only do you save on the price of a server, but you can also more efficiently use all of the resources available to the company as a whole.

More cost-efficient—From an equipment usage perspective, a peer-to-peer network can be the most efficient way to reuse equipment. If you have an older PC that no longer has enough oomph to serve as a workstation, you can connect it to the network and still continue to use the hard drive and other resources.

Easier to set up—A peer-to-peer network is commonly created using workstations. So, there's no server to set up and there may not be any major setup on the workstations either. In some cases, such as Windows, the client software is automatically installed during setup if the OS detects network hardware.

Easier to learn—A server normally requires that the user learn special commands and use server-specific software. This increases the amount of time required to get a network operating and reduces the probability that anyone but the network administrator will be able to fix even simple problems. The learning curve for some client/server networks is so steep that the vendor creates special schools to train network administrators (as in the case of Novell NetWare).

Don't get the idea that peer-to-peer networks are the perfect solution for every network. They do have certain limitations that make them less than perfect for many needs. Here are a few of the problems to look out for when working with peer-to-peer networks:

Size limits—Peer-to-peer networks are limited in the number of workstations that the network can handle. In most cases, you can connect ten machines to a peer-to-peer network. Adding more than ten machines normally results in very poor performance and can increase the chance that the network will freeze or lose data.

Speed—Client/server networks provide all kinds of speed enhancements that peer-to-peer networks don't enjoy. For example, it's very common for servers to include additional memory that will buffer (temporarily store) requests for data. This allows the client to resume whatever task it's performing more quickly and use server resources more efficiently. In addition, most servers include some type of software to speed disk access and even predict what data the client will request next so that the data is retrieved before the client even asks for it.

Security—All of the machines for a peer-to-peer network are accessible by anyone with access to the network. In addition, OSs commonly used for peer-to-peer networks like Windows 95 or 98 don't include many of the same security features as a server would. As a result, it's much easier for a cracker to break into your network and damage it in some way (or worse yet, steal your data).

Maintainability—Peer-to-peer networks are harder to maintain than a client/server network in one important way. Because a peer-to-peer network is decentralized, you'll have to update files on each machine individually every time you want to add some new level of server or client functionality.

All of these items are important, but there's an even simpler way to look at peer-to-peer networks:

Peer-to-peer networks are best used for networks of ten or less machines where security isn't an issue.

Client/Server Advantages and Disadvantages

Client/server networks are normally found in medium to large business offices, with some exceptions. A small business may need features like the added security a client/server network can provide. We discussed several disadvantages of using peer-to-peer networks in the previous section; in most cases, client/server networks don't have these problems. The client/server model was first used with mainframes, so the technology has been around for a while. Here are some of the advantages of client/server networks:

Easier management—Client/server networks normally come with tools that make management tasks easier. For example, it's fairly common to include tools that can assess the state of client machines through the use of an agent. This same agent may allow the server to perform tasks like backing up the remote machine.

More reliable—In most cases, a client/server network will be more reliable, because it's designed with large network features like remote backup, higher bandwidth processing, better security, and transaction processing. In addition, most client/server technologies have been thoroughly tested over a number of years, which means you should see fewer bugs and few situations where the server becomes nonoperational.

Security—While the completely secure network is a myth (see Chapter 8, *Network Security Essentials*, for details), client/server networks do provide better security than peer-to-peer networks can provide. The server itself is normally locked in a separate room or equipment closet, making it difficult for anyone to access the server. Data is better protected because the underlying security is better and the network administrator has more options when assigning security to a particular item. The hard drive itself is often encrypted, making it hard for others to get at your data even if they do manage to log onto the network.

Flexibility—Many vendors sell add-on products for the client/server networks, something that peer-to-peer networks don't offer. An add-on product may do something as simple as allow you to create backups faster or continuously. Add-on products also make management tasks easier or extend a specific server capability. You'll also find add-ons in the form of server-based applications like database management systems (DBMSs).

Centralized data source—Once a company reaches a specific size, it begins to build an infrastructure in the form of custom applications. All of these custom applications require a centralized data source if the company is to get any benefit from the application as a resource. While you could create a centralized data source with a peer-to-peer network, it's not always the best choice because of performance and security issues.

Scalability—This fancy term refers to the ability of a client/server network to continue handling user requests, even when the number of users increases or the complexity of each request increases. Client/server networks include special technologies like clustering (a group of servers connected together in order to better handle a processing load) that allow it to continue processing even when the load is inconsistent.

One reason that peer-to-peer networks became popular is that client/server technology can't do everything. We've already talked about some of the advantages of using a peer-to-peer network in the previous section. All of these advantages are areas where client/server technology fails to help the small business. Here are a few other disadvantages you should consider:

Cost—The number one reason to avoid using a client/server network is cost. A minor cost is the server; there are other costs in the form of maintenance and training that make a client/server network a lot more expensive than a peer-to-peer network of similar capability. Ongoing maintenance costs are also a factor, because you continue paying for them as long as the network is operating.

Complexity—A client/server network is more complex than a peer-to-peer network, which means you need to spend at least a little additional time creating a design for it. You have to consider things like the placement of the server and running additional cable for the server and its peripherals.

No automatic failover—When an error occurs with one of the machines on a peer-to-peer network, you lose one machine. If a server fails, on the other hand, you've lost the entire network. This is such a severe problem with client/server networks that vendors have created all kinds of strange technologies to handle the problem. None of these technologies is completely successful, but many of them come very close.

Your could spend a lot of time trying to figure out client/server networks. However, for most people the whole issue comes down to this:

Client/server networks are best used for small-office networks when security or performance is an issue and a higher installation and maintenance cost isn't a problem.

Network Operating Systems that Fall Somewhere Between

Some people will try to convince you that simply because Windows NT Server and Windows 2000 Server will allow access by hundreds of people given enough hardware, they're a true client/server NOS. The truth is that the underlying technology for these NOSs is still based on the peer-to-peer model. Every installation of these NOSs that I've ever performed has created a fully functional workstation as well as provided server software. In addition, a Windows NT Server or Windows 2000 Server setup can use resources like a hard drive on a client machine (as long as the proper sharing is in place)—something that a client/server NOS normally won't allow.

Windows NT Server and Windows 2000 Server do share some features of the client/server model. For example, they're normally set up to provide centralized services. The server is commonly locked up in an equipment closet and not used as a workstation. The security provided by Windows NT Server and Windows 2000 Server is better than the security commonly offered by peer-to-peer networks, but I still wouldn't place it on an equal footing with products like NetWare and definitely not on the same level as a mainframe OS. Windows 2000 Server also provides better administrator utilities than previous versions of this OS, and it includes support for features that are normally associated with client/server NOSs like clustering and the ability to use extended disk storage methodologies like storage area networks (SANs). (A SAN is a special hard drive that resides outside the server and allows access by more than one server. SANs are used to increase network reliability; a single downed server won't prevent users from accessing their data.)

Does this mean that Windows NT Server or Windows 2000 Server is a less capable OS that you should avoid? Both NOSs are capable in their own right, but they do tend to have many of the same problems that any peer-to-peer network has. You can avoid some of these problems by locking the server away in a closet and removing both keyboard and monitor. The fact remains, however, that every version of Windows still relies on the peer-to-peer network model.

Linux is another NOS that could actually fit in either category. Though Linux is used almost exclusively for servers today, there's a potential to use it for workstation purposes as well. The method in which Linux makes connections to other systems is much like UNIX, which means that it follows the client/server path.

One of the interesting things about working with a Linux server in a Windows environment is that Linux makes itself look like a Windows NT server through the use of a piece of GNU software called Samba. The Samba Web Administration Tool (SWAT) allows you to administer the Linux server from the comfort of your Windows workstation. Linux will also work with Apple computers through the use of Netatalk (Net AppleTalk), which is built into the kernel.

Hybrid Networks

Many networks today are hybrid networks—networks that rely on a combination of peer-to-peer and client/server technology. Even a small company can benefit from a hybrid solution by using it to reduce overall system cost, while enhancing system performance and reliability.

Figure 3.1 shows a typical hybrid network setup. Notice that the central database application used for all of the company's internal data relies on a client/server configuration. All other data sharing occurs between peers. In addition, since this is a small network, all peripherals are shared using the peer-to-peer network setup. For example, two workstations provide access to a printer connection (one laser and one color), while another shares a relatively expensive DVD.

A hybrid configuration like this means that you get maximum utilization of every workstation and the server can be a lot smaller (read: less expensive) than a typical client/server network setup. Though you're working with what amounts to two networks, this network still relies on a single set of connections (Ethernet in this case). A hybrid network relies on two different protocols (sets of rules) to keep the two networks separate. If the workstation OS is designed

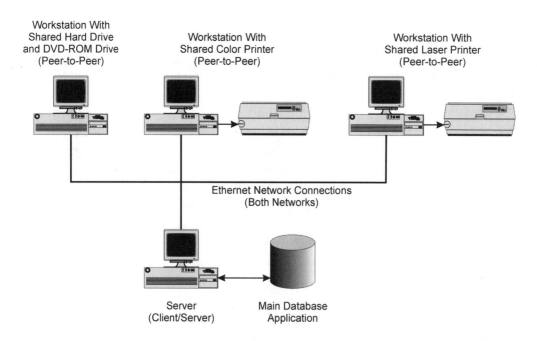

Figure 3.1: A typical hybrid network setup.

correctly, it will work with both protocols to make both networks appear as a cohesive whole to the user.

Hybrid networks share the advantages and disadvantages of their component parts, the client/server and peer-to-peer network. The reason that this kind of network is so attractive is that you can eliminate some of the disadvantages of using the other network types, yet make use of the advantages they provide. For example, you can reduce the reliability and security problems of a peer-to-peer network by placing sensitive data on the client/server portion of the network.

There's one issue you can't avoid when working with a hybrid network. What you're doing in essence is creating two networks. This adds complexity to the network design. You'll spend more time designing such a network and the complexity may add to the administrator's burden. As with anything else in life, there's no free lunch. Building a hybrid network means getting the best of both worlds when you create a good design, but getting the worst of both worlds when the design is less than perfect.

Deciding What to Share

Some networks are hard to use because every potential resource is shared with everyone on the network. For example, if you have a peer-to-peer network, it's possible to share every hard drive on every machine. In most cases, this is a bad idea because no one will know where to find specific pieces of information and you'll have problems maintaining a secure environment. Figure 3.2 shows an example of a machine where the drives are at least identified by type, but you still don't know what information the drive holds. In addition, sharing all of these resources will reduce network efficiency and performance. In short, you need to consider what to share as part of the design process.

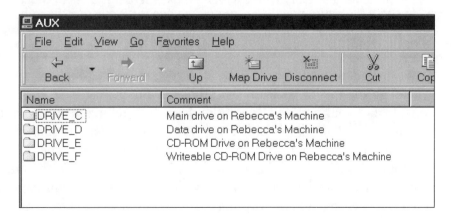

Figure 3.2: A peer-to-peer network machine where all resources are shared.

You really need to consider three problems when determining what you want to share. First, you need to determine if anyone needs the resource in question. The network administrator's hard drive is probably one resource that no one will need to use. This drive should be kept private so that all of the network administrator's tools and data remain secure.

The second consideration is security. Sharing a resource that someone needs is a good idea, but you need to consider how much access they require. For example, a data folder may allow users to read data, but not write it. An in-box may allow users to write data, but not read it (you can send in a report, but not read reports made by other people). A database directory may allow someone to both read and write data, but not to create or delete files (you wouldn't want any employees to erase your client database because they got angry). Users' personal directories on the server will probably allow all rights for files, but not allow the users to create new or delete existing directories, to ensure they don't create hidden data areas on the server.

The third consideration is who should access the resource. It may seem that everyone on the network should have access to every printer, but that may not be the best choice. You may want one group of people to use one printer, and another group of people to use a second printer. In some cases, you want to restrict access to a resource to ensure everyone gets a fair chance to use it, rather than for security reasons. Printers are the most abused piece of office equipment, so it makes sense to share this resource based on user zones, departments, or some other criterion that assures fair access.

***Sometimes Less Sharing Is More Efficient**—There will be times when you want to share a resource, but may not need to share the entire resource. For example, an administrative assistant may need a shared in-box on his or her machine. So, sharing that particular directory with everyone makes sense. It doesn't make sense, however, to share the entire drive. All that anyone needs is access to the in-box. The other resources on the administrative assistant's drive should remain private to ensure that other data they're working on remains secure.*

As a network administrator, you have access to everything, everywhere, making it tough for you to envision the problems a user may have with access restrictions. Part of your network design should include telling people what they can access and why. This allows individual users to request additional access if they really need it to perform their jobs. In some cases the network administrator or developer designing a network isn't aware of all of the nuances of every individual's job; it's very easy to overlook data access requirements if you're not actually engaged in performing that job. Besides asking for user input, you should perform test cases to ensure the users get the access required to perform their jobs. These test cases are important because some users may not know that a lack of network access is causing a problem and will avoid reporting it to the network administrator.

Hard Drives

Hard drive space was rare and expensive at one time. Even a small hard drive could double the price of a workstation. Of course, hard drives of the mainframe era were huge—most required substantial floor space. In addition, workstations of the mainframe era didn't have any intelligence, making hard drive integration difficult, to say the least. As a result, hard drives were one of the first "precious" resources shared on a network. A single large hard drive could serve many users more efficiently than placing hard drives in individual machines.

Today, hard drives are one of the least expensive parts of workstations when you consider how much they do for you and at what cost. Most workstations have a minimum of a 10 GB hard drive, and some come with even larger main storage. So, why do you need to continue sharing a hard drive if this has become a commodity resource? There are two good reasons to share hard drives even now, and you may find others as you design your network:

Security—Workstations are inherently nonsecure because they're accessible by the public at large and users are notorious for not following company security policies. A workstation is suitable for storing application code and a user's personal data, but sensitive company data should be stored on a secure server's hard drive.

Collaboration—Most corporate applications require some level of collaboration between employees. Because a server is online all the time, the data required for the collaborative effort is available as well. Workstations are shut down at the whim of the user assigned to them, making collaborative efforts difficult if the user isn't available when needed.

These reasons form the basis of your decision to create a centralized storage area when designing your network. Personal data and applications should appear on the user's machine; company-sensitive data must get stored on a server if you want to keep it safe. Of course, the most common company data storage requirement is the database application, which is naturally stored on the server to ensure everyone can access the information when needed.

Storage for data that could fall into either realm can be a judgment call. For example, word processing files may not require collaboration between employees and could therefore be viewed as personal user data that gets stored on the user's machine. However, since a word processing file could contain sensitive company information, you might want to store it on the server anyway for safe keeping. On the other hand, e-mail files are rarely stored on the server in a peer-to-peer setting, because they require no collaboration between employees that isn't handled by message traffic and because the amount of sensitive data is minimal when employees follow published company guidelines.

Network Printers

Network printers have come down in price, but they still aren't the commodity products that hard drives are and probably never will be. Like hard drives, the main reason to share printers during the era of the mainframe was cost. Today, however, there are other reasons to share printers like the ones shown here:

Efficiency—It's extremely unlikely that a single user could print enough documents to keep a printer busy all of the time. As a result, it's inefficient to give each user a separate printer to use. A single printer can service several users and still allow the individual users to retrieve documents quickly.

Functionality—Look at Figure 3.1 earlier in this chapter. This hybrid network contains two printers because users are likely to require the services of both. There are situations (like creating a simple report) when the high-resolution black and white output of a laser printer works better than color. In other situations (like creating a chart), color is preferred because it provides a better presentation. Some users will require both kinds of output to perform their tasks efficiently.

Maintainability—Printers tend to be complex and they require periodic maintenance by a qualified technician. Paper dust and other environmental pollutants can become a problem for any printer. In addition, while a user can easily add paper to any printer, changing ink or toner cartridges might require the services of someone who has worked with the printer before. Sharing a printer reduces maintenance requirements and therefore the number of network personnel your company requires.

Unlike many other areas of shared computing, a printer user doesn't have to use a printer in a particular way. While a network administrator can say who will use the shared printer and who can administer it, the output from the device is still under the user's control. Figure 3.3 shows a typical printer configuration dialog box for Windows 98. Notice that the user has control over basics like the number of copies, whether the printer outputs a banner (a page between print jobs), and whether the server notifies the user after a print job is complete. In short, the user

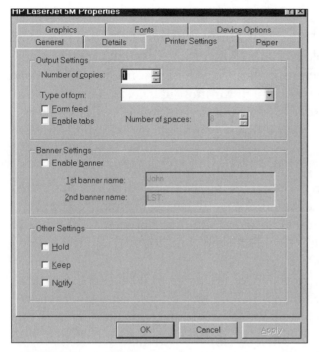

Figure 3.3: Printers can feel like personal devices even when they're shared.

will feel as if the network printer is connected locally if it's shared properly.

Unlike other devices, printers are normally shared. (We do talk about one exception in the "Hardware You Can't Normally Share" section later in this chapter.) The problem is figuring out whom to share them with. If a network is small and you have just one printer for everyone, the answer is pretty easy to figure out.

Complications arise when there's more than one printer to share. Looking again at Figure 3.1, there are two printers connected to this relatively small network. In this case, the printers have differing capabilities, so you may choose to share them by perceived need. The per-page cost of using a laser printer is lower than using a color printer, so encouraging use of the laser printer will save the company money.

When you design your network, you need to consider the cost of using devices that have consumable resources, like a printer. The ink for a color printer will allow a user to create a more dramatic presentation, but will also cost the company at least twice as much per page to print. In the example network in Figure 3.1, you'll probably want to give everyone access to the laser printer, but restrict access to the color printer. Only those users who need the features of a color printer should use it.

Performance is also an issue when sharing certain types of network resources like a printer. A printer will place a burden on the workstation that it's attached to, because the file will get downloaded from the client machine, spooled (stored) onto the local hard drive, and then sent to the printer at a pace the printer can accept. All of these activities drain performance from the workstation; performance that could be used for user-specific tasks.

Other Peripherals

Many peripherals fall into the "other" category of sharing. Windows will allow you to share something as simple as a floppy drive. Since data files are fairly large today and very few people distribute applications on floppy, most machines have just a single floppy drive and that's enough for most uses. Normally, you won't want to share this drive, because it's not a mainstream storage device. However, there are times when sharing a floppy drive might make sense. Since this is a small, removable storage device found on just about any machine, it's a good medium when you can't be sure of the capabilities of someone else's machine. You can create multiple floppies at once by using the shared drives on more than one machine. A shared drive also comes in handy when you want to copy data from one floppy to another without constantly shuffling floppies. A shared drive will also allow you to make multiple copies of the same floppy without swapping the master floppy in and out of the drive.

Just about every machine on your network requires a CD-ROM drive today, because a lot of software is distributed on CD. However, there are other types of optical drive support you should consider. You'll want to include at least one rewritable (CD-RW) drive in the collection for backup purposes. In many cases, a CD-RW drive can be more flexible than a tape backup and less expensive as well. A CD-RW drive will allow you to burn (create) data CDs, read standard CDs, or use rewritable media for backup and restore (or even as a removable hard drive). Unlike tape drives, CD-RW drives tend to use standard drivers and are no harder to install than a standard CD-ROM drive. They're also easier to use and maintain than tape drives.

There are other types of drives that you won't want to purchase for every machine. A DVD-ROM drive is one of them. These drives are quite a bit more expensive than CD-ROM drives. As application data requirements expand well beyond the limits of a single CD, you'll likely see more DVDs introduced on the market. For example, Microsoft provides their Microsoft Developer Network (MSDN) subscription on a single DVD, making it possible to perform a minimal install on any one machine, use the DVD as an archive for most data searches, and save a lot of hard drive space as a result. Because of the high cost of DVD-ROM drives and the rash of updates by vendors, you'll want to share this one high-capacity drive with all of the machines on the network for now.

A fairly new player on the market is the DVD-RAM drive. This drive allows you to read CDs or DVDs. You can also use it as a DVD read/write device using special media. You can't use it to burn your own CDs or DVDs. The read/write media used by a DVD-RAM drive isn't the same as the permanent media used by vendors for movies. A DVD-RAM drive does allow you to create much larger backups than a CD-RW drive, so you may want to consider it as an alternative when a CD-RW won't meet your needs and you don't want to install a tape drive on any of your workstations or servers.

Other devices fall into the realm of the arcane. For example, you can attach a 3D modeler to your network to create a 3D version of a drawing you create using a CAD application. Since such devices are not only rare and expensive, but often require specialized operation as well, you'll want to share it to reduce network costs. A user can create a drawing on a local workstation, rather than the network. Once the drawing is complete, the user can create a 3D rendition of it for presentation, manufacturing, or verification purposes. In short, one person won't use some specialized devices enough to be cost-effective.

DVDs—*Two Drives in One—DVD-ROM and DVD-RAM drives are actually two drives in one box. A DVD drive will read CDs and DVDs with equal ease, even though the technologies for the two storage media are different. To perform this feat of magic, a DVD drive normally contains two read heads: one for CDs and another for DVDs. It's possible (and I've had this happen) for one of the lasers used for reading media on a DVD drive to burn out long before the other laser. As a result, you could end up with a DVD drive that can only read CDs or DVDs, but not both. I normally mark which laser failed and put the drive back as a spare. When I need a temporary DVD or CD reader, I'll take my spare out of storage and put it in the machine until the new drive arrives in the mail.*

Hardware You Can't Normally Share

You normally can't share some pieces of hardware. For example, unless you have special software installed, you can't share your personal modem with someone else. Whether the software is available depends on how many people need to share modems and the vendor's ability to create the required product. Newer versions of Windows include a feature called Internet Connection Sharing (ICS) that allows you to share your Internet connection with someone else. If this connection happens to go through your modem, you get what effectively amounts to modem sharing.

Even if you were to have the proper software to share a device, some devices would defy sharing because of their design. For example, it's pretty hard to share someone's scanner, because you have to be at the machine where the scanner is connected. The same holds true for devices like digital cameras. There just isn't any way to use this device without accessing the machine that it's connected to, so there isn't any point in trying to share the device.

There are other situations where you could share a device, but it doesn't make sense to do so because of limitations in the device itself. For example, you may have a slower dot matrix printer on the network for printing multiple-part invoices. Many consultants would tell you to replace such a device with a laser printer, but if the old dot matrix can keep up with the work, there isn't any reason to replace it. Of course, you don't want to overload the printer either (which is another reason to design the network to account for such requirements). Unless everyone on the network prints invoices, you'll want to keep sharing limited to the single machine used to enter the invoices or share the printer between the two or three machines responsible for this task.

Another category of device that you don't want to share is a scientific instrument. For example, you might have a data logger (a device that measures something and keeps the readings in a log) attached to your network. Such a device is normally self-contained and no one needs to operate it. A data logger keeps reporting whatever it needs to report to the machine that it's attached to. What you need to share in this case is the logs the data logger creates, rather than the device itself.

There are a lot of reasons that some devices fall into the "can't share" category. However, you can use this simple rule to determine when a device isn't a good candidate for sharing:

Never share a device if the user will spend more time using the device from a remote location than using it locally.

Developing a Peripheral Sharing Plan

It's important to use all of the clues you've gathered to develop a peripheral sharing plan. Map out which devices will get shared and who will use them. This plan will allow you to further develop a map for the network. Let's look at how you might assign workstations given the structure of the network in Figure 3.1 earlier in this chapter. (I'll use the term network administrator in the following paragraphs to indicate the person responsible for keeping the network running—this isn't necessarily a full-time network administrator.)

The first workstation could be given to one of the more technical employees in the company. It has the largest hard drive and the higher-end peripheral devices. Since the technical (or power) user will require these resources more often than other people in the company, making them local resources will reduce the load on the network and provide additional bandwidth for other tasks. A technical user will also be one of the better choices to watch the local machine for errors and notify the network administrator quickly when something happens. If security is an issue, then you may want to assign this workstation to the network administrator.

The second workstation will normally service the network administrator. The color printer load on this machine will be relatively light because fewer people will use it. Keeping the color printer at the network administrator's desk will also allow the network administrator to better track printer usage and keep costs down. Printers also cause a number of problems—keeping one of them within easy reach of the network administrator will reduce the amount of time the network administrator spends running around.

The third workstation, the one with the laser printer, is a good workstation for an administrative assistant for several reasons. The most important reason is that the administrative assistant will place the smallest load on a workstation. Word processing and small database management tasks hardly use any of the workstation resources, leaving plenty of those resources for use with the laser printer. Other network users will get timely printouts without hindering the efforts of the person using the workstation.

Setting a Limit on Expenses

So far in this chapter, I've talked a lot about network design principles like deciding which resources to share and how to assign peripherals to individual machines. A lot of home and small-office users will consider these issues but will fail to address the most important issue of all, cost. You probably have some idea of what you want to spend, but you might find that a trip to the computer store results in catastrophe for your budget unless you also plan ahead for any unforeseen expenses. A fully deployed network consists of these elements:

- Hardware required to create the network, including peripheral devices
- Consumables required to keep the hardware operating, including paper for printers and cleaning supplies to maintain the various machines
- OS support used to make a workstation or server operational
- Commercial software used to address common needs like e-mail and word processing
- Custom software used to address company-specific needs like an order entry system or other database application
- Training designed to make users productive quickly
- User support to answer questions quickly and fix problems as they arise

Failure to include any of these elements in your network design will result in cost overruns or a network that fails to perform to your expectations. It's important to consider all of the costs for your network as part of the design process. That way, you can make changes to the design as needed before you've spent any money to build the network. It's easier to make compromises when your bank account is full, rather than wait until you've spent everything set aside for the network. The following sections will help you compute the following expenses:

- Hardware
- Consumables
- Operating system
- Application software
- User training
- User support
- Miscellaneous network expenses

Hardware and Consumables

The first task you need to perform when setting a limit on network expenses is to create a functional picture of your network. The picture doesn't have to be as pretty as the one in Figure 3.1, but it should be functional. Assign workstations to particular rooms or cubicles. Make sure you understand where every piece of equipment will go, who will use it, why they need it, and what tasks they'll perform with it.

Once you have a picture of your network, use it to develop cost estimates. For example, list every machine and every peripheral device on the network. Call local computer stores and check the Internet for equipment prices. You'll also want to check with used-equipment dealers. In some cases you can purchase a perfectly functional piece of used equipment for pennies that will work fine for low-end uses. Refurbished monitors are an especially good buy, because a monitor is the one piece of equipment that doesn't change in functionality very often. I've purchased several computers for my network in the last two years because of changes in technology, but the monitors haven't changed in years.

Choosing Between Local and Internet Purchases—*Many people will look at price alone when shopping for network equipment, but price isn't the only consideration for a home or small-office network. Support plays an important part of an equipment purchase for someone who can't afford the assistance of a full-time support staff. Local companies tend to provide higher-quality service because they have to satisfy the needs of the community to stay in business. Internet companies can usually offer better price breaks because they don't have the infrastructure of a local store. In many cases, buying a monitor or printer from an Internet source is a low-risk proposition because the local store wouldn't service these items anyway. On the other hand, the computer itself is filled with parts that a local store can service. In many cases, you'll find that the trade-off in price is more than paid back in superior service.*

OS and Commercial Software

You'll find that the OS and commercial software costs are almost constant. It's the one area that you can't really save any money on, unless you're a very smart shopper. Develop a list of tasks for every workstation, choose an appropriate OS, determine which commercial software will work best for the task at hand, and then price all of the software. A large company will try to get a deal from each of the software vendors that produce the required software—home offices and small companies don't have the same option. You can, however, look at the bargain bins at your local computer store. In many cases you can buy last year's software for greatly reduced prices.

It may seem at first that buying last year's commercial software will only lead to trouble, because you won't have the latest and greatest product on your system. The truth is that few people use all of the capabilities in any software built today—most of those capabilities will go to waste. If last year's software will do the job, then there isn't any reason to get this year's software at a higher price. You'll save in two other important ways. First, today's software will be filled with bugs—the software that a company put out last year will already have patches available on their Web site, so you'll end up with a more stable product. Second, companies that provide training services usually lag behind the software vendor. You'll find that you can get training services for last year's software with relative ease and that the training will cost less in most cases.

Custom Software

Custom software has caused more problems for companies than any other piece of the network; and yet no other piece is of such great importance. Without the custom software required to run your company, you'll find that the reason for creating a network in the first place is greatly reduced or even eliminated. While a precise formulation on how to get custom software for the lowest cost is outside the scope of this book, it's important to get a solid estimate from the consultant writing the software as part of the design process. Make sure the consultant provides you with a detailed development plan. The consultant should also include a software specification that details every part of the custom application.

Training

People constantly complain about the price of training, yet they won't shop around for a better alternative to the classroom experience. I recently priced a class for a word processing application for a small company. At $800, the class was going to be well out of their price range. I then stumbled upon a tape with lessons on a floppy disk at a local Sears store, of all places. The tape cost $19.95 and demonstrated how to perform all of the common tasks that the user needed to perform with the word processing application. This was one instance when using last year's application really paid off, because the tape wasn't available for this year's application.

Of course, price isn't the only consideration for training. Classroom instruction has an advantage that you can't replace with a tape—a classroom has an instructor. Instructors can answer questions, provide a personal perspective, and tailor the class to meet the needs of the students. Tapes are created for a generic student and there isn't any way to ask the "teacher" questions.

However, tapes also have advantages you need to consider. For one thing, you can play the tape when it's convenient for you to learn, rather than when it's convenient for the training company. A tape can be played more than once, which means that you also have the option of viewing the same material over and over until you feel that you know it well enough to perform a given task.

The cost for training can vary quite a bit, so make sure you ask more than one company and look for training alternatives like tapes. Combining two training methods can often help users over a steep learning curve with specific types of complex software like graphics applications or even high-end desktop publishing systems. You'll also need to factor in hidden training costs like lost user productivity, travel expenses, and textbooks.

I don't want to sound like a commercial for my particular trade, but books are also a real steal when it comes to training. Books usually provide more information than either classes or tapes, and you can review them as needed. In some cases a book author will also provide an e-mail address, so you can get answers to questions you may have. While this isn't quite as good as having an instructor at your beck and call, an author can usually provide detailed answers to questions about a book's contents and help you over time.

User Support

User support of some kind is a requirement for every network, but discovering just what type of user support you need and can afford can be an adventure. Hiring someone to fulfill the role of user support person is out of the question for most small companies and home office scenarios, so you'll need to come up with something else.

When working with commercial software, you can usually rely on the vendor to provide some level of support. Unfortunately, that support may come in exchange for a payment. You may have to sign up for an extended level of product support with the vendor. Check the terms of any agreements carefully, because paid support may not equate to unlimited support. In some cases, the terms of the support agreement will state that the vendor will provide assistance a specific number of times within a given period.

There are also hidden costs when dealing with the support staff for a commercial vendor. I often find myself waiting on hold for what seems like hours when calling a vendor for support. The hold time is annoying, but the resulting telephone bill can really cause problems. If you have several users who all need help at the same time, you may find yourself paying a substantial amount of money to the local telephone company instead of getting increased productivity from your staff. It's absolutely essential that you don't pay twice for support. Make sure that any paid support you get includes an 800 number so that you don't end up paying both the software vendor and the telephone company.

Custom software presents the greatest user support challenge. There are several problems that you need to be aware of when it comes to custom software support:

Not a professional trainer—Most consultants are either great software engineers or great trainers; they seldom fulfill both roles well. Unless the company you choose to develop your custom software has professional support, plan on spending a lot of time trying to get adequate training and user support.

Poor documentation—Even companies that provide great software, training, and customer support can produce manuals that can't be read without the help of a cryptographer. Some manuals appear to be written in some other language; most likely geek speak.

Company stability problems—I've gotten called a number of times to "fix" software left behind by a consultant who's no longer in business. Even the most conscientious developer can take a plunge, so you have no way of knowing whether your custom software will have support tomorrow. Because custom software has a small installed user base, you can't rely on peer support either.

The best way to ensure you'll get proper user support for your custom software is to take a proactive approach when working with a consultant. Make sure the company has professional trainers on staff. Ask to read manuals that the company has produced for other clients. Ensure the company you're dealing with is large enough that they'll be around for a few years so that you can ask questions as users become proficient with the piece of custom software.

The Bottom Line

Once you've obtained prices or at least estimates for all of the elements of your network, you may find that you need to spend more time planning the network before you buy anything. It's not uncommon for companies to have cost overruns, even if they plan carefully. There are too many variables in the equation to plan precisely, so you need to get the network for a little under the price you had in mind, rather than spend everything you have up front. Still, you'll find that the more time you spend on planning, the better your final results will be. Here's the list of items you can trim in order of highest probability for savings:

1. Reduce the amount of custom software. One of the most expensive pieces of your network will be the custom software that you use to answer company-specific needs. The price you get from a consultant can vary quite a bit and depends on quite a few factors (including how many other consultants are bidding on the same project). You can often trim the price of this element by asking for fewer features or finding commercial software that can answer all or part of a specific custom software requirement. For example, commercial printing packages are usually highly flexible and cost much less than a custom alternative.

2. Use training alternatives whenever possible. You probably won't find any deals by calling around to different training centers for a quote on a piece of commercial software; the variation between training centers is minimal at best. However, it's easy to reduce training costs by using alternatives to classrooms. For example, training tapes can do a good job of teaching the fundamentals. There are also software alternatives known as computer-based training (CBT) that take a hands-on approach to teaching users how to use commercial software.

3. Get the hardware you need, rather than what you want. You don't need every new device out there. The price difference between a fully loaded workstation and one that's usable, but not state-of-the-art, can be as much as $4,000. Servers that have usable versus state-of-the-art hardware can save you even more. A good network design can help you reduce the server requirements and therefore the equipment you need to build the server.

4. Consider alternatives for user support. The cost for user support can vary a lot depending on what type of user support you choose. In some cases, it might cost less to buy paid support than have users wait for hours on the phone. Another alternative is to send one user to a school on your software, then allow that user to become the local expert.

5. Buy commercial software with an eye toward savings, rather than state-of-the-art. The only way to save money on commercial software is to hit the bargain bin as often as possible. Smart shopping at online stores can also help, as can looking for low-cost alternatives to expensive commercial software, like shareware.

6. Think ahead when buying consumables. You can save a little on consumables by purchasing them in bulk or waiting for sales. However, consumables are the smallest cost for your network and it's not necessarily a good idea to spend hours looking for the one place that will save you a cent or two on paper. Your time is precious, too; wasting it to save a modicum on a consumable resource will only end up costing you money in the long run.

Developing a Deployment Plan

At this point, you've created some type of development plan for your network. All of the elements for building the network are in place except one, a deployment plan. You have to determine when to install various network elements. For example, you'll want to have all of the hardware operational before getting the commercial software. In most cases, you'll want to install the custom software last to ensure there are no compatibility problems with the commercial software and to allow users time to adjust to the network before you burden them with a new application.

It's also important to coordinate network installation with user requirements like training. In some cases users can go to school while the installation of hardware and software proceeds at their desks. In this way, the users are productive, and they won't be in the way of the installer. When the users come back from training, they'll have the new network to test their new knowledge on.

A deployment plan should spell out specific milestones for network installation. While it's important to include approximate dates for milestone delivery, you should also include some slack time to ensure that unforeseen events don't compromise the eventual goal of getting your network running by a certain date. The date that's easiest to meet is the installation of hardware, since the process for installing and testing it is relatively well known. User training schedules should be easy to meet as well, but you never know when an unexpected event will keep an employee at home or on a trip. Commercial software installation shouldn't be a problem either—in most cases the installation process is well documented and perhaps even automated.

One of the harder elements to gauge in your deployment plan is user support. You need to have user support in place by the time the network is fully operational. If you use vendor-specific support, then you'll find that most user support requirements can be met in a timely manner. However, there are still going to be problem areas. You'll need to assign personnel to perform even mundane tasks like caring for the printers and maintaining the equipment.

The biggest deployment plan killer is the consultant for the custom software. It's true that creativity doesn't work on a schedule and you'll find that custom software is a true test of this principle. I normally check a company's delivery schedule when planning custom software delivery dates. In many cases I'll double or even triple the company's estimated delivery time, especially if a project is complex or the company isn't going to use a lot of off-the-shelf programmer's resources for the project.

Chapter Four

Connections Require Software

I get a lot of e-mail and telephone calls about networks. The one topic that always comes up is hardware. For some people, networking is all about hardware—the creation of physical connections between machines using NICs, cables, and hubs. I get the feeling that most people assume that the software is a moot point—they'll be able to create any required connections using Windows or the Macintosh OS since both provide built-in networking capability.

After a few minutes of discussion, however, I usually persuade the caller that there are other concerns to discuss before the hardware. The physical connection between your computer and the network is just one part of the networking picture. You actually have four levels of networking to consider, which are shown in order here:

1. User and company
2. Applications
3. Operating system (OS)
4. Hardware

In Chapter 3, *Designing a Standard Network*, we looked at the user and company portion of the network as part of the design process. A good network design answers both the user's and the company's needs. After all, there's little point in creating a network that doesn't serve the users by allowing them to work faster, more efficiently, and with less effort. A company requires the output of the network users to provide services to customers or a product that it can sell to others. The design phase, in other words, considers the needs of the company, all of the users as a whole, and when necessary, the needs of individual users.

As you can see from this list, two levels of networking deal in some way with software—applications and operating system. In fact, it's the requirements of the software that drive hardware selection, not the other way around. The applications you select will determine the OS selection because the OS needs to support the user and the applications the user needs to complete given tasks. So, network connections require you to decide which applications will satisfy user needs specified during the design phase, find an OS that will run those applications, and finally base your hardware decisions on the software's requirements.

We're going to explore the software portion of the network in this chapter. Software comes in many shapes and sizes, so it's important to plan for the kinds of software that you'll need to accomplish specific tasks. This chapter examines five important topics as part of the software-selection process as described here:

> **User applications**—The main reason for installing a network is to allow users to share resources, work faster and more efficiently, and accomplish tasks that they find difficult to complete otherwise. User applications provide the interface the user will use to interact with the network and accomplish given tasks. As a result, you need to select the user applications that will provide the best set of features for the users first and then base other decisions on this software's requirements.

> **Diagnostic and utility software**—Depending on the requirements for your network and the applications you want to use with it, you'll need several kinds of diagnostic and utility software. You'll choose some of this software immediately after application software and other diagnostics and utilities after choosing an OS. For example, database utilities like form-generation tools are normally purchased with the database to ensure the two pieces of software will work together. On the other hand, a virus scanner is OS specific and you wouldn't purchase it until you knew which OS you would use. We'll talk more about diagnostic and utility software in Chapters 6, *Configuring Windows for Network Use,* and 7, *Working With NetWare.*

> **Operating system**—It's important to choose an OS that best supports the user applications for your network. In some cases, you may need to mix two or more OSs on the same network to get the best performance and flexibility. For example, it's common to buy two OSs for a client/server network. The first is for any workstations on the network, while the second supports the needs of the server.

What Is Shareware and Freeware?—Many aspiring programmers have great ideas and even better programming talents, but little or no money for marketing. In addition, some companies often try alternative methods of gaining market penetration for their products. These groups often resort to distributing their software as shareware or freeware. You can download both products from the Internet and begin using them right away. Neither product is in the public domain—the authors still retain a copyright to their software. However, in the case of shareware the author is hoping that you will try the software and like it so much that you'll buy it. In the case of freeware, the author isn't looking for any monetary return, but may want public recognition for a great application or want to use the software as a jumping off point for other business ventures.

Installation requirements—Once you've decided on a set of applications, diagnostics, utilities, and an OS, you need to define an installation strategy. Software vendors have done a lot to make software easier to install than ever before. In fact, the installation of some software is almost automatic. It's not the 95 percent of the installations that go well that you need to worry about; it's the 5 percent that cause problems (and a lot of hair pulling).

Buying smart—Once you have made all of the purchasing decisions, it's time to get the software. You can use various techniques to get more for your money. For example, you might choose to use a shareware or freeware version of the software you need rather than pay a higher price for commercial software. This last section of the chapter will help you get the best possible software for the lowest price.

Deciding Which Applications to Run

One of the problems with designing a network is that many companies start out small and then expand as they discover their network can perform tasks that they didn't envision it could at the outset. In addition, your company will hopefully grow, which means that you'll be adding more users to the network at some point. What many people end up with is a confusing array of applications that aren't optimized and a network that performs slowly. Part of the cure for this problem is to decide which applications you need to perform specific tasks and then stick with that list.

To prevent your network from becoming a haven for unused applications, use the divide-and-conquer approach to the tasks the network needs to perform. By knowing what tasks each type of software can perform, you can reduce the number of applications you purchase and install. You can divide applications into six categories. Each category performs a different task, as outlined here:

Word processing—This is the most common of all software. Every company requires some type of word-processing capability to write letters, create reports, and perform tasks like creating labels. Some word processing software, like Microsoft Word, has so many bells and whistles that it's hard for any single person to use all of the capability it provides. You can use this flexibility to your advantage by allowing the word processor to replace some of the software you might otherwise need to buy.

Spreadsheet and accounting—Many companies have more than their fair share of spreadsheet applications. At one time, I had no less that four spreadsheet applications on my machine: general spreadsheet (Excel), accounting program, complex math calculations (Mathematical), and a little calculator application I kept around for quick number crunching. Today, I've cut that to two spreadsheet applications and saved a whopping $700.00 on every one of my workstations. We'll look at how you can perform this magic as well.

Database—Depending on your personal and company needs, a database program may dominate your desktop. This type of application is used for everything from client lists to inventory-control systems. Database applications also come in two basic forms: off-the-shelf and custom. Most companies have at least one custom database application for maintaining their customer list and orders list.

***Combined E-mail Systems**—Some companies use a single e-mail application for all of their communication needs. For example, the version of Outlook that comes with Microsoft Office provides all of the internal and external e-mail communication that many companies need. Be sure to shop wisely if you choose an all-in-one solution, however. You'll want an application that can handle every requirement and maintain the security of internal communication.*

Communication—Because of the Internet, it's unlikely that you'll find any company that has less than two communication programs: One program for internal communication could be as simple as e-mail. (Most internal communication systems, however, are more complex than simple correspondence.) The second program is used for communication outside the company and includes a browser, like Internet Explorer, and an e-mail application, like Outlook Express. Other communication applications your company may need include remote collaboration programs. NetMeeting allows two people to collaborate over the Internet, which saves both time and money by reducing travel time and expenses.

Graphics—This is one category of application that you won't find on every desktop, and fewer people than you might think actually require one. Graphics applications can include everything from a program designed to capture screenshots to high-end computer-aided design (CAD) applications designed to create complex drawings. This application category also includes charting and graphing applications that turn mundane data into graphical representations of things like your company's profits and losses. Graphics applications tend to be expensive, resource hungry, and difficult to master. They also represent one category of application where you can save a lot of money if you plan wisely.

Other application types—Other types of applications don't easily fit within the broad categories that we've already discussed. For example, a virus-checking utility is one type of application that fits into the other category. Some of these utilities are extremely useful; others are widgets that consume resources but return little of value. We'll talk about how you can keep this other category of applications to a manageable size and save both time and resources as a result.

Word Processing

Word processors represent one of the most common applications in use today. In fact, most OSs produced today include one or two word processors as part of the package. For example, Windows 9x and Windows 2000 both come with both NotePad (a plain text editor) and WordPad (a formatted document editor). So, one of the first things you need to consider is whether these OS offerings provide enough functionality to meet your needs. In at least some cases, they will, so you won't need to purchase another word processing application.

I obviously spend a lot of time writing, so my word processor is an extremely important part of my daily computing experience. This might lead you to believe that I need a feature-packed word processor that does everything except brush my teeth in the morning. Actually, content is my main concern; so while a good word processor is important, all of the widgets designed to make formatting easier aren't. Seldom do I need to output presentation-quality data. It's not surprising, therefore, that I didn't install most of the optional features that Microsoft Word has to offer, because I simply don't need them. The point I'm trying to make is that while Word is a great word processor, it actually has too many features—so many, in fact, that I don't know of anyone who uses every feature that Word has to offer.

Not every word processor is as complex as Word. Some allow you to type text and not much more. For the most part, however, commercial word-processing products today are bloated pieces of code that will almost certainly give you more than you bargained for. Even so, you need to make a decision about buying a word processor. Once you've decided to buy a word processor, it's important to get the right one. The following sections tell you how to save money when you buy your word processor and how to choose the right one the first time.

Three Ways to Save Money with Word Processors

The fact that Word is such a robust word processor has allowed me to save some cash along the way. First, I don't upgrade Word every time Microsoft introduces a new version. I'm already using exceptionally few of the features, so unless

Microsoft develops a new file format that my publishers say I just have to have, I doubt I'll upgrade anytime in the near future. Companies that upgrade an application like Word too often are probably suffering a case of gadgetitus—a disease that appears to affect computer junkies far too often. Not only do upgrades take money away from other projects that you do need to get done, but they also cost the company money in additional support and training costs. Finally, as applications like Word get more bloated, an upgrade can force an accompanying hardware upgrade as well.

The second way I save money is by carefully using some of the features that Word does provide. For example, I don't have to create charts often, but at times they come in handy for one of my books. Rather than purchase a separate charting application, I use the charting features provided with Word as a separate option. Given the cost of most graphics applications, I probably saved $200.00 per workstation by going this route. Which leads me to this simple truth about applications like word processors:

> *Use all of the application features that you can, but don't install any features that you'll never use.*

A third method for saving money is to get all of the service packs or patch files that the vendor provides. These updates are usually free for the price of a download. Some vendors, most notably Microsoft, include additional features as part of the service pack or patch. In short, you get a free application update along with the bug fixes that the service pack or patch file is supposed to provide.

There's one word of warning when it comes to service packs, however: make sure that the service pack's feature set is something you really want on your computer. Vendors usually provide a README file that outlines all of the changes of the service pack or patch file and details some of the things they won't fix. It always pays to read this file before you download the patch file or service pack so that you know what to expect. In some cases, vendors use service packs as a means to force their agenda on consumers by including features that the customers may not want. In other cases, the fix is worse than the original problem (such as some of the recent security patches put out by vendors that turn much-needed features off, rather than fix the security hole).

Finding the Right Word Processor

So, how do you find a word processor that provides an optimum array of features, yet keep costs to a minimum? It really depends on your business. Consider, for a moment, the construction company that I helped set up with computer equipment. The person running this company needed a good accounting program for making bids and keeping track of customer accounts. However, given that this was a small company and that the owner got most of his business through word of mouth, he had little need for presentation-quality word processing. He certainly wasn't going to write *War and Peace* anytime soon. After looking at the available alternatives, I set him up with a shareware word processing application that cost a mere $50 to register (license)—a bargain for both the shareware vendor and the construction company.

Many bargains are available to the home office or small company network user. Of course, there aren't any perfect solutions either—just solutions that work better in a given set of circumstances. Here's a list of things that you should look out for if you decide to go the shareware route with your word processor:

- Talk with other users of the shareware product to ensure the word processor works as advertised and the vendor has a good, customer-support record.
- Make sure the software has all the features you'll need, since shareware vendors are less likely to produce updates that address esoteric needs.
- Since shareware is sold on a try-before-you-buy basis, make sure you actually try the product for the full evaluation time. Even a 30-day trial is a short time to try a product for your business.
- Look at several shareware packages before you decide on a single product. You may find that after looking through several choices, none of them really meets your needs and you'll need a commercial package.
- Always check the documentation and help files for completeness.
- Find out what level of support the shareware vendor is willing to offer. Don't expect the same level of support that you get from a commercial vendor (some shareware vendors actually provide better support), but you should expect to get free updates and some type of notification about product changes.
- Ask the shareware vendor about testing current beta products. In many cases, a beta will give you a better idea of what the shareware vendor plans for the product and testing allows you to provide input on product features.

Shareware Isn't Freeware—*Just like everyone else, a shareware vendor has to make a living to stay in business. Make sure you support shareware vendors by paying for the products you use after you know they'll fulfill your needs. Check out the Association of Shareware Professionals (ASP) Web site at* http://www.asp-shareware.org/ *for further information about shareware and what you can do to support it. If you're interested in viewing the best of the shareware available today, check out the Shareware Industry Awards Foundation Web site at* http://www.sic.org/.

Shareware isn't always the best product choice; sometimes a commercial product provides a superior level of support that you can't ignore. However, I was surprised to find that a little over half of the applications on my workstations are of the shareware variety. Here are a few URLs for the better shareware choices that you should try (all shareware word processors are for the Windows platform, except as noted):

Breeze for Windows
http://www.ozemail.com.au/~kevsol/sware.html

Easy Word (DOS)
http://ourworld.compuserve.com/homepages/Easysoftware/

Medialingo BuddyPad
http://www.medialingo.com/

Microvision Development Inc. WordExpress
http://www.mvd.com/wordexpress/

Nisus Writer (Macintosh)
http://www.nisus.com/

SourceGear Corporation AbiWord (Windows and UNIX)
http://www.abisource.com/

Sun Microsystems StarOffice Personal Edition (Windows, Solaris SPARC, Solaris Intel, and Linux x86)
http://www.sun.com/dot-com/staroffice.html

Tykewriter – Word Processor for Kids (Macintosh)
http://users.erols.com/lazarus2/tykewriter.html

Word Place Yeah Write
http://www.wordplace.com/

Sun Microsystems StarOffice (originally created by the German company StarDivision) is one of the more interesting pieces of freeware in this list. This product is actually a suite of applications that includes word processor, spreadsheet, presentation manager, and drawing applications; a calendar and to-do list; an e-mail and Internet news reader; a database, and a complex formula processor. Not only is this product freeware, you get source code with it so you can customize your application. If you decide that you don't want to download StarOffice, Sun will send you a CD-ROM and documentation for a modest fee. There are more than a few politically charged reasons for Sun's benevolent actions, in this case, but you're the winner. StarOffice is one of the few freeware products that can provide a robust application environment for any home or small-office. The ability to get this product in Danish, Dutch, English, French, German, Italian, Portuguese, Polish, Russian, Spanish, and Swedish is a real perk.

You'll still run into times when commercial software is the only option, because the type of word processing that you perform will exceed the capabilities of shareware. Here are a few guidelines that you can use to make the choice quickly:

- Most shareware products won't allow you to perform desktop publishing.
- Many shareware products provide limited support for embedded objects like graphics.
- If you need to interface your word processor to your e-mail application, it's probably best to go with a commercial product that supports the e-mail application directly.
- In many cases, you'll need a commercial word processor if you intend to use automation (scripts) to any extent.
- While most shareware word processes are network friendly, some are intended for local use only.
- Collaboration normally requires the use of a commercial package, because shareware products lack features like version control and revision marks that show who made a change.

Additional Places to Find Shareware and Freeware—*You may not find the shareware you want within the confines of this book, because there are a lot of shareware authors out there. Trying to find what you need with a standard Internet search engine probably won't work either. Two of the better places to search for shareware of all types are the SoftSeek Web site at* http://www.softseek.com/ *and CNET Shareware.com at* http://shareware.cnet.com/. *If you want to look for freeware only, look at the Freeware Home Web site at* http://www.freewarehome.com/. *Macintosh users will want to check out the ZDNet Mac Download Library Web site at* http://www.zdnet.com/downloads/mac/download.html.

Spreadsheet

At one time, the sole purpose for having a computer was to perform calculations quickly. In fact, that's where the name computer comes from. Computers are still the kings of calculations today. The spreadsheet application exposes the math capability of the computer so that you can use it to perform calculations of various types. Most of us are familiar with the grid-based application like Excel that allow the creation of freeform calculations and common calculation formats like matrices. However, most accounting programs are just glorified spreadsheets, some of which include a database at the back end to manage the data you create.

The problem with the spreadsheet application is that people get addicted to them rather quickly. I mentioned earlier in this chapter that I had four spreadsheet applications on my workstation at the same time and reduced costs by getting rid of two of them. A single, general purpose spreadsheet is generally all a small business needs—especially if that application provides advanced capabilities like the ones found in products like Excel. In most cases, this single application can take the place of your calculator, accounting program, and complex math program. So the first thing you need to consider when you begin a list of applications for your network is whether a single, general-purpose spreadsheet like Excel will do the job for you. In many cases, you'll find that it will and can save you money by buying one general application rather than several custom applications.

Excel can be overkill if all you want to do is add up a list of numbers. People who have system memory constraints or who keep a lot of applications open like I do will probably want a small application to use for quick number crunching. Since Windows comes with a good calculator as part of the product, I simply set it up on my machine during installation. As a result, I have two spreadsheet- or calculation-type applications on my machine: Excel and Windows Calculator.

Most companies have to perform some type of accounting, if for no other reason than to address government regulations or other tax purposes. Depending on your business, you may not have a lot of accounting to perform. For example, one wood worker I know concentrates on building large artistic projects. He can work on the same project for six or seven months at a time, so the number of customer-related entries is small.

In most cases, small businesses with few accounting needs can get by with something less expensive than a commercial product. Here are some shareware offerings that you may want to consider for your network that won't cost you nearly as much as commercial accounting packages or spreadsheet applications (all spreadsheets are for the desktop Windows platform, except as noted):

Bye Design Spread32 and SpreadCE (Windows and Windows CE)
http://www.byedesign.freeserve.co.uk/

JPS-Development.com GS-Calc
http://www.jps-development.com/

Lucid 3D (DOS and Windows)
http://www.lucid.com/

Trius, Inc. As-Easy-As
http://www.triusinc.com/

This list of spreadsheet programs is modest; you'll find a plentiful supply on the Internet. Of the spreadsheets in this list, GS-Calc comes closest to matching the capabilities found in commercial products like Excel. It includes a full set of 2D and 3D graphs, and over 180 functions of various types. Worksheets can contain up to 2,097,152 rows × 512 columns and you can have as many worksheets as memory will permit. At under $20 (at the time of this writing), GS-Calc is another one of those products that fall into the real steal category.

Another interesting product in the list is Spread32 and SpreadCE. They're both the same spreadsheet, but one is designed for your desktop; while the other will work on palmtops equipped with Windows CE. If you use a palmtop on the road or in a work area and transfer any data you collect to your desktop machine, using this duo will ensure your data is compatible with both machines. In addition, you'll have the benefit of using a similar interface on both machines.

Database

The database application is another type of program that has been around for a while. In physical terms, a database is simply an electronic filing cabinet. Of course, some databases are extremely complex filing cabinets that hold a lot more data than the average company would want to keep around in physical form. The fact that databases can replace the filing cabinet and offer features that a filing cabinet can't, like instance searches, makes them highly popular. Most companies have several database applications, and many have new databases in development all the time.

Some people are uncertain about what a database application is all about. Part of the reason is that database applications tend to be complex and they don't reside on just one machine. An attempt to get the big picture might be met with reams of documentation, most of which aren't understandable by the average human. So, here are the four basic parts of a database application that you'll need to think about when you put the list of software together for your network:

Database manager—The engine (or intelligence) that interprets database commands and allows users to request information. It also adds, deletes, indexes, and modifies database records. One database manager is usually sufficient to run any number of database applications.

Database application—A set of instructions that the database manager interprets and acts upon. You have a lot of ways to create database applications. The complexity of the application and the kind of language used to develop it will partially determine the cost of the database application as a whole.

Data store—This is the filing cabinet. In most cases, it's one or more files that are used to hold the actual data. The database application requests changes to the data store by querying the database manager.

Business logic—One or more sets of rules that reside outside the database applications. These rules determine exceptions to the way in which the database application interact with the data store. For example, you might need to check a customer's credit in some cases, but not in others. The database application receives instructions from the business logic about when to make such checks. In other words, the business logic is the changeable intelligence that controls the database application in the background.

Unlike any of the other application types we've talked about so far, the database application often defies precise pricing. The cost of the database manager is predictable, as are the costs for any supplementary products required to make the database application work. It's the cost of the database application itself that's variable. In most cases, database applications are written by consultants, which means that you won't necessarily have enough information about the database application when you put your network together to add its price to the estimated cost of the network.

Generally, you'll want to search for off-the-shelf solutions for your specific database needs before you contact a consultant. Trade magazines for your industry normally have ads for these products included near the back. Make sure you ask these vendors for a demonstration copy of their product. Check their return policy in case you're not satisfied with the product and ask to speak to some of their satisfied customers. Specialty applications can be difficult to find, but if you can get them off the shelf, you'll pay a lot less, get a better product in many cases, and be able to get your network running faster. Best of all, any off-the-shelf solutions that you find will have a precise cost that you can add to the cost of your network as you complete the design.

If you do have to contract someone to write a custom database application, make sure you spend plenty of time looking at credentials. Always get a complete specification for any custom software and a price estimate. Ask for a guaranteed price or at least a price range as part of the original contract so you won't overspend because of custom software price overruns. It also pays to ask for previous customer contacts and spend some time talking with those customers.

Shareware isn't quite as good a deal for database managers as it is for other application categories. For one thing, the potential for loss is much greater. If you lose a single word-processed document, it might take one person a few hours to put it back together again. On the other hand, losing your database might mean hiring a staff of workers for weeks to input the missing data again—

if the data can be recovered at all. However, shareware databases do work well enough, in most cases, for small or personal database applications. For example, you might want to create a personal address book or perhaps maintain a to-do list. Here's a list of database managers that you might want to consider for small projects (all database managers are for the Windows platform, except as noted):

JPS-Development.com GS-Base
http://www.jps-development.com/

JR-Info cmVodbx32
http://www.rayonline.com/jrinfo/

Stevenson Technical Services Incorporated Infodex Pro
http://www.stsi.com/

Unvisible Universe Software EZGather (Macintosh and Windows)
http://www.unvisibleuniverse.com/

FileMaker Pro—*One of the excellent nonshareware products not mentioned in the list in this section is FileMaker's FileMaker Pro. You can download a demonstration copy of the product at* http://www.filemaker.com/. *A lot of third-party support is available for this database manager and you'll find that it works with both Windows and the Macintosh. FileMaker Pro also provides integration with Microsoft Office. Unlike most of the shareware offerings in this section, FileMaker Pro is designed to provide Web site support. You'll find that even though this product is modestly priced, it has features that look and act like the more expensive commercial products.*

You can also obtain off-the-shelf, shareware database applications. In many cases, these applications are written in a language the database application author converted to a standard application. You get an executable file for a database application that's good for one purpose like archiving documents scanned into your computer, managing contacts, or keeping track of employee hours. Here are some shareware database applications you may want to consider for your network (all database applications are for the Windows platform, except as noted):

Abritus International Abritus Business 2000
http://www.abritus-int.com/b2000/

Archive Power Systems, Inc. Archive Power SB (Small Business)
http://www.archivepower.com/

CISglobal IMAD2000 (Java-based so it runs on any platform with a Java interpreter including Macintosh, UNIX, Linux, OS/2, and Windows)
http://www.imad2000.com/

Cory R. Rauch DataQuip
http://www.crrweb.com/dataquip/

Davidson Software Davidson Maintenance System
http://www.davisonsoftware.com/

GovindaWare Contact Manager Deluxe
http://www.govindaware.com/

NextWord Accordia
http://www.nextword.com/

Software Techniques, Inc. E-2000 Employee Records
http://www.softwaretech.com/

One of the more interesting marketing angles for shareware database applications is that the database application author offers to customize the application for your company's specific requirements. For example, DataQuip is a sales and inventory management application that comes with a fairly substantial set of general-purpose features. You may like how this application works, but may want to add customizations like your company name and special reports. Since the database-application author offers this service, you can try the application for a while and then customize it once you know what you'd like to change. In the meantime, you have a fully functional product to work with.

Many people build their own simple database applications because many database managers come with wizards and other aids that make creating the database application simple. If you decide to try creating a database application yourself, it's important to read all of the developer-related information that comes with the database product first. A wizard or other aid will help you get the database application started, but normally won't fill in all of the blanks for you—these aids rely on a consultant to put the details in place.

Writing a simple database application isn't hard, but it can be time consuming. You need to decide whether saving money on your network is more important than the time you'll spend creating the required database application. Always use a consultant when you need complex or mission-critical database applications—network administrators who write complex database applications are like patients who perform their own operations to save money.

Don't forget to look for shareware database tools and utilities. For example, instead of building your own search engine, you might be able to use an off-the-self alternative. There are tools that will automatically generate SQL scripts for you and others that will create reports based on your database structure. One of the more common uses for tools is the creation of data-entry forms—something that can take a lot of time if you aren't familiar with design techniques commonly used by developers. Using these automated tools can help even a complete novice create professional looking database applications, but again, they're limited and you'll have to do some programming eventually. That's why you want to reserve these tools for building simple databases if you don't have programming experience. Still, there isn't any reason to pay a consultant if your needs are simple and you have the tools to do a good job.

Communication

Communication programs take many different forms, but the two most common communication programs in use today are the Internet browser and the e-mail application. In some cases, you'll still need an application to call bulletin board systems (BBSs) of some companies, but this is quickly dying out because Internet sites are easier to maintain and less costly in terms of company resources. The good news is that you get all three of these applications for free as part of Windows (Internet Explorer, Outlook Express, and HyperTerminal) and may get them free with other OSs as well. Good communications are so important today that no self-respecting OS vendor is going to send out a product without some type of communication program included.

The question you need to ask is whether these free applications will do the job. If all you want to do is get online to do some research or work with newsgroups and e-mail, the answer is yes. The free programs are more than capable of allowing you to work with several different e-mail accounts and they all perform tasks like tracking your Web site history so that you can find that really great site you visited yesterday.

Of course, in some situations you need something more than just e-mail communications. This is where some smart shopping can be helpful. You'll find communication programs bundled with other software in a lot of cases. For example, if you buy Microsoft Office, you get Microsoft Outlook with it. Outlook is the full-fledged version of Outlook Express that ships with Windows. You can use this product for e-mail and newsgroup communication, just as you would with Outlook Express, but it will also help you schedule company events and perform other communication tasks.

Needless to say, there's a healthy, but diminished, shareware market for communication programs. For example, you'll find that Easy Mail Plus by **Home Plan Software** (http://www.homeplansoftware.com/) is a full-function communication program that also allows you to perform tasks like print labels and maintain a complete contact list for your company. In addition to communication, this product includes a fully functional document editor that you could potentially use as your word processing program. In short, while shareware products are available, they just aren't as available as other kinds of shareware applications.

If you decide that you can't get by without a commercial product like Lotus Notes or Novell GroupWise, make sure that you have the resources set aside to use them. (Notes and GroupWise are two group collaboration products that enhance communication beyond e-mail—they're designed for large corporations that normally experience communication problems because employees are physically separated.) These products require a centralized server, which means you must use them with a client/server model network, in most cases. These products are definitely designed for the enterprise and you'll find that they're severe overkill for most small business and home office networks. So, the first thing you should do is make sure these products will pay for themselves in increased business. Make sure you're actually going to generate enough e-mail to warrant such a large investment of company resources. You'll also want to make sure your network administrator knows how to work with these products, because the centralized post offices they use require maintenance from time-to-time to keep the product operating correctly.

Graphics

Graphics applications were once the domain of professional artists and crafters who wanted to add pizzazz to birthday cards using cheesy bitmapped graphics. Today, anyone can create great looking graphics with an ease unheard of as little as four years ago. Not only do you have the traditional option of drawing the art yourself, but scanners allow you to import graphics from any printed source as well. The use of modified clip art from vast libraries makes it almost too easy to create presentations that look like they were designed by graphic artists and Web site presentations that will knock the socks off anyone visiting them. In short, what was once a niche application has now become a mainstream concern for any company.

The problem, of course, is finding just the right graphics application for your needs. I have to admit that I still have a number of graphics applications on my machine and this isn't likely to change anytime soon. Each graphic application has a specific purpose that can't be addressed by the others. Of course, it doesn't help that there's a whole list of graphics file formats that everyone needs to worry about. Needless to say, every time you want to use a really interesting graphic from a clip art library, it's likely to be in a format that none of your graphics applications support. So, the first thing you need to do when looking at this category of application is cut through some of the myriad of conflicting facts so that you can make some reasonable choices. The following sections of the chapter will help you decide what types of graphic support you need and what applications will best help you gain the required level of support for the least cost.

What Kinds of Graphics Do You Need?

The world of graphic applications is filled with confusing terms that mean little, if anything, to anyone outside of that community. It's easy to get lost when looking for a graphic application, because the application package tends to be filled with this jargon, making it impossible for you to make any kind of decision about which package you want. In many cases, you really don't need to know all of those confusing terms if you want to get a graphic application for business use. Most high-end professional packages, like CorelDraw, are designed for artists and you really don't need to consider them unless you want to become a professional computer artist. So, let's take a divide-and-conquer approach to the terms you do need to know. Here are some terms that you'll want to know before we begin:

Pixel—A single picture element—a single dot on the display. Each dot is a single color and is used to make up the picture as a whole; sort of like a mosaic, but using smaller tiles.

Resolution—A measurement of the number of pixels used to make up a picture. For example, if you have a 640 × 480 picture, there are 640 pixels across the picture (horizontal resolution) and 480 pixels up and down (vertical resolution). If you multiply the horizontal resolution by the vertical resolution, you get the number of pixels used to create the picture (307,200 pixels in the case of a 640 × 480 picture).

Color depth—The number of bits of information used to make up the color for an individual pixel. A pixel's color is determined by a red, green, and blue color value—the combination of the three-color values is the color depth. For example, if you wanted to display a 256-color image, you'd need a color depth of 8 pixels. Most monitors and graphics cards today support 32-bit color or 4,294,967,296 color combinations.

Computers support essentially three main kinds of graphic image today. The first type is called bitmap or raster graphics. A bitmap graphic uses one storage unit within the graphic file to represent each pixel of the image. The color depth of the picture determines the size of the storage unit. So, if you wanted to store a 256-color image, each storage unit would consume 8 bits or 1 byte of storage space. The second kind of image is a vector graphic. Instead of storing individual pixels, this file format stores math equation values that allow the graphics application to redraw the image every time you load it from disk. The metafile format is a combination of both a raster and a vector graphic. The raster graphic is used for displaying a thumbnail (small) version of the graphic, while the vector graphic is used for image modification and printing.

Other Types of Graphic Image—*I'm not going to cover the whole range of graphic image formats in this book, because other books on the market do a much better job than I can. For example, graphics with the Microsoft RIFF file extension are described as a multimedia format. One of the best books on the market for learning about how graphics are stored, compressed, and drawn by the computer is Encyclopedia of Graphics File Formats by James D. Murray and William vanRyper (ISBN: 1-56592-161-5).*

The first decision you need to make is whether you want to use raster or vector images. Most graphic applications specialize in one or the other, but not both. There are advantages and disadvantages to both storage methods. A raster graphic is easy to edit—you can modify each pixel individually. In addition, raster graphics have a broader base of support, which means that more people can read them without special software. Unfortunately, raster graphics tend to take up a lot of hard drive space unless you compress them. Some file formats support compression, others don't.

Vector graphics have the advantage of small size and infinite resolution. Since a vector graphic is drawn (or rendered) at the time it is displayed, the graphic application can size the image to match the resolution of your display. The result is that you don't get the jagged appearance that you would with a raster graphic. Because of the resolution independence of a vector image, you can usually print it at any size desired and get great results every time. One of the biggest disadvantages of the vector graphic is that you normally require a higher priced graphic application to work with them (although viewers are relatively inexpensive). Programs like CorelDraw and AutoCAD use vector graphics to ensure you get the best presentation of your drawings at all times.

Common Graphics File Formats

The second decision you'll need to make is the file formats that you want the graphic application to support. Some file formats are better than others are for specific uses. In addition, file formats only support one type of graphic format, raster or vector, so you need to choose the appropriate file format for the kind of image storage you want. Here are some of the more common file formats:

File Extensions (Storage Type)—Description

BMP (Raster)—Windows or OS/2 bitmap graphic format. It does offer compression, but only certain applications support this feature. BMP files aren't normally compressed. This is the standard file format for all drawing programs supplied with Windows and OS/2 OSs.

CGM (Metafile)—Computer graphics metafile format. This is one of the few standards-based graphic file formats that has been approved by the American National Standards Institute (ANSI). You can expect to find a broad range of support for this file format.

DXF (Vector)—AutoCAD data exchange format. This is the file format commonly used by computer-aided design (CAD) programs.

EPS (Metafile)—Encapsulated PostScript graphic format that originally allowed PostScript printers to output superior quality graphic images and is used extensively for desktop publishing.

GIF (Bitmap)—CompuServe graphics interchange format. This is one of the two file formats commonly used on the Internet for images. (The other format is JPEG.) The GIF format is known for high data compression. A special type of GIF can contain multiple images and allows for animated effects.

JPG/JPEG (Bitmap)—Joint Photographic Experts Group (JPEG) format. A high color image format used to display photographs and other high resolution graphics, in many cases on the Internet. This file format does allow for some level of file compression and the loss of some image detail.

PCX (Bitmap)—An image format originated by ZSoft for the PC Paintbrush drawing program. It offers relatively high file compression. The main problem with the PCX file format is that several incompatible versions used by older applications may prove impossible for newer applications to read.

PICT (Metafile)—An image format originated by Apple for the Macintosh. This file format is supported by all Macintosh drawing programs and represents one of the reasons that the Macintosh is considered a superior platform for graphics work. Apple has consistently updated the PICT file format to add new capabilities. For example, PICT2 supports 32-bit color.

TIF/TIFF (Bitmap)—Tagged image file format. This is the most widely used of all the bitmap graphic file formats. It supports several different compression methods, making it possible to create extremely small files. Windows, Macintosh, DOS, and OS/2 machines (among others) can read the same file. If the ability to move graphics between operating systems is important, this is one file format you want your graphic application to support. The only problem with this file format is that there was a lack of standards for it when it was first introduced. So, it's not unheard of for a graphics application that is supposed to read TIFF to fail to open a TIFF file it didn't create. This problem has become less prevalent as vendors work to standardize TIFF, but you could still see it.

WMF (Metafile)—Windows metafile format. The only vector format supported directly by the Windows application programming interface (API). This file format isn't supported by the operating system supplied utilities, but is used by many developers for application graphics.

Getting Your Graphic Applications for Less

Now that you have some idea of what you want your graphic application to support in the way of resolution, color depth, graphic format, and file extension, it's time to talk about the applications that are available on the market. If your graphics expertise consists of drawing stick figures and basic shapes, you can stop right here. The graphics application supplied with the OS for your machine should be all that you need. Even Windows provides some decent drawing capability for the stick figure artists among us.

At the other end of the spectrum is the graphic artist. People who spend their entire day drawing on the computer have a pretty good idea of what's available. Two of the more popular drawing programs on the market are CorelDraw for artistic needs and AutoCAD for drafting and mechanical drawing. The one thing that I want to caution you about is ensuring that you buy equipment to match the capability of the drawing program. Trying to use CorelDraw or AutoCAD on anything less than a 19-inch monitor is a waste of time. Since you'll be generating a lot of image information, you'll want a fast graphics adapter as well.

There's a third group of computer users who need to view graphic images on a regular basis and tweak them in one way or another. No, this group can't be considered artists by any long shot of the imagination, nor would they spend hours creating a mechanical drawing. People in this group could go out and spend a lot of money for one of those professional packages, but it would be waste of time because they'll never use all of the features the professional package offers. Shareware is the perfect answer, in this case, because there are many products to choose from; the quality of the programs is high, and they offer enough tools for most of us to do something worthwhile without getting totally confused. Here are some shareware offerings you may want to consider for your network that won't cost you nearly as much as commercial drawing applications (all drawing applications are for the Windows platform, except as noted):

Alchemy Mindworks, Inc. Graphic Workshop and GIF Construction Set
http://www.mindworkshop.com/

Jasc Paint Shop Pro
http://www.jasc.com/

TechSmith SnagIt
http://www.techsmith.com/

Trius, Inc. DCWin
http://www.triusinc.com/

***Finding Utilities on the Internet**—The Internet offers a lot of places to find graphic applications, perhaps a few too many to list here. I've listed several places where PC and Macintosh users can find a good supply of shareware applications of all types earlier in this chapter. However, when it comes to utilities, Macintosh users will want to check out the Flux Software Web site at* http://www.fluxsoft.com/.

Choosing an Operating System

Choosing an OS might seem straightforward, but it really isn't. In some respects, the choice of an OS becomes more like the proverbial chicken-or-egg question than a straightforward decision. Some people choose the OS first so they can find applications that will work with that OS. What they find is that they often have to make compromises in application functionality, security, reliability, or features due to the OS choice.

That's why I normally look for applications first, then the OS. Using this technique means that you address user and application requirements first, and then choose an OS to support those requirements. We've already looked at the effect of your OS decisions from a network design level in the "Peer-to-Peer Versus Client/Server" section of Chapter 3, *Designing a Standard Network*.

Now that you know why I chose to cover applications first, let's talk about the OS in more detail. There are ways to make the choice of OS much easier. The following sections will provide you with tips for choosing an OS and some generalizations about which OSs are best for specific uses. Of course, everything here is meant as a guide. It's important to keep this principle in mind as you read:

There is no such thing as a perfect OS; but some OSs work better than others for a specific purpose.

Tips for Choosing a Desktop OS

You need to find the best possible application products for your business needs and then determine whether there's a common denominator when it comes to an OS. If there isn't a common denominator, you'll need to make some additional choices and determine which OS will best meet your needs both now and in the future. This process demonstrates that setting up a computer network is often a matter of making careful choices for important software that affects your business directly and then making compromises in other areas as needed. Here are some criteria you can use to make the OS choice:

- Prioritize applications so that major business needs are considered before less important needs. For example, an accounting firm would need to consider the accounting software first and then consider what word processing software to use to write letters. Choose the OS that works with the majority of your high priority applications, and then find alternatives for low-priority applications.

- Determine which OS features users will need most often. For example, utility programs like a NotePad are nice, but aren't high on the list of features that most users consider essential. Choose the OS that handles more essential user needs.

- Choose an OS with good administration features. Network administration tools are expensive, so the fewer you need to buy for your network, the better. Network operating systems (NOSs) often publish specifics for network administration, but you may need to dig a little to determine what tools (if any) a desktop OS provides.

- Estimate the resource requirements (like memory and hard drive space) for the OS. In many cases, you can determine this based on the application vendor's recommended minimum requirements, but if you plan on using resource-hungry applications like CAD, you'll want to double or even triple the requirements listed on the application's box. If two OSs will support your high-priority applications and user-required features, the OS that performs well with the fewest resources is usually the right choice.

- Consider ease of use problems. Some OSs are feature rich and efficient, but require an advanced user to understand them. An OS that works well but increases your training costs isn't a good choice.

***Multiple Platform Applications**—In the previous sections, I tried to locate shareware applications that would work on more than one platform wherever possible. Commercial applications like Microsoft Office also work on more than one OS. Choosing an application that will work on more than one OS moves the choice of OS from application need to user need.*

OS Generalizations

Some OSs are well known for their ability to provide certain types of support. For example, most people would agree that the Macintosh OS is one of the more user-friendly OSs on the market and is a good choice for novice users who won't need anything more than word processing. The Macintosh OS is also well known for its support of graphics applications. Many artists consider the Macintosh their best friend after getting frustrated with the intricacies of other OSs.

Windows is another popular OS with well-known strengths. For example, Windows is considered one of the best choices for business applications. Windows also supports the completely open architecture of the PC, which means that you'll often find applications and supporting hardware for a lower cost. Gamers prefer Windows as an OS and the wealth of games for this platform (when compared to other OSs) is a testament to the flexibility of this OS.

For many people, OS/2 is the "other" business-oriented OS. It offers many of the same strengths as Windows, but in a different package. You'll find that the OS/2 interface provides certain easy-to-use features that you won't find in Windows. For example, OS/2 provides an easier to use interface—at least from some people's perspective. OS/2 does provide support for Windows 3.x and DOS applications, besides native OS/2 applications, so you'll find that many of the applications you can use with Windows also work just fine with OS/2. In addition, OS/2 falls in the middle of the pack when it comes to reliability, security, and performance.

Talk to just about any serious engineer and you'll hear about UNIX (or Linux, in some circles). UNIX has a long history in academic and scientific circles. One of the reasons that UNIX is so popular is that it's been around long enough for developers to get most of the bugs worked out. UNIX is considered one of the most stable and reliable OSs on the market, making it a good choice when reliability is a lot more important than ease of use. In fact, you might be interested to know that Microsoft uses UNIX for some purposes, including disk duplications (see http://support.microsoft.com/support/kb/articles/Q80/5/20.ASP for details). One of the major problems that you'll face if you choose UNIX is that there are many flavors of this product. UNIX is an OS designed by committee, so you'll need to compare the strengths of each version of UNIX to ensure you get the one best suited for your needs.

Interestingly enough, I still run into people who use DOS and are quite happy with it. DOS is known for extremely low resource usage and installation simplicity. This OS was never designed for multitasking or complex application usage. It does work great when your company tends to focus on a single all-inclusive application like a database-management system. The text-based interface does make DOS more difficult to use and the lack of multitasking reduces your ability to get work done—these are the two main reasons most people abandoned DOS for Windows.

There are a lot of OSs on the market and it would be difficult to generalize all of them. Windows, Linux, Macintosh OS, UNIX, OS/2, and DOS represent the major desktop OSs in use today. Of these six, Linux is the least used on the desktop, because it doesn't currently support any form of standardized user-friendly interface (see the accompanying note, "Gnome on the Horizon," for details). Windows is the most used OS on the desktop because many businesses see it as the best product for their needs. A lot of people have opinions about how these OSs compare. Some run tests, while others look at the features that each OS has to offer. Here are some links you may want to check for comparison information:

The Xunil Pages: Operating Systems Comparison Chart
http://www.xunil.com/oschart.html

The UNIX Versus NT Organization
http://www.unix-vs-nt.org/

The Great Linux-Windows NT Debate
http://www.jimmo.com/Linux-NT_Debate/

The Linux Resource Exchange - Operating Systems Comparison
http://www.falconweb.com/~linuxrx/WS_Linux/OS_comparison.html

Windows 2000 Product Guide
http://www.microsoft.com/windows2000/guide/platform/overview/

Windows 2000 Comparisons
http://www.microsoft.com/WINDOWS2000/guide/server/compare/

Gnome on the Horizon—*Linux has become the server OS of choice for many people, because it offers a combination of open source code (which means you can modify the OS if desired) and low price. However, Linux on the desktop has all of the appeal of a porcupine in a nudist colony. Some vendors, like Red Hat, have tried to change this perception by adding a GUI to Linux. Unfortunately, until now, the graphical front ends for Linux have varied by vendor and many aren't all that friendly to use. That may change with a new GUI named Gnome. Not only does Gnome look and feel very much like Windows, but it also promises to add consistency to vendor offerings since many vendors plan to use it with their Linux offerings. While I can't say that Linux is a good OS for the desktop today, it may have a bright future because of Gnome. You can find out more about Gnome at* http://www.gnome.org/.

Overcoming the Myth of the One OS Company

Some people assume that they should choose one desktop OS for their entire network. This assumption is based on the experience that network administrators have gathered over a long time. It's true that using a single operating system for all desktops does reduce the number of problems you'll have to solve while getting the network running and keeping it operational later. However, this age-old wisdom is also based on older technology operating systems. Trying to mix two OSs in the past was akin to mixing oil and water. Today, most OSs provide features that allow some level of mixing on the same network, because users of older OSs complained.

The reason this change in the OS picture is so important is that you no longer have to take an all or nothing approach to your OS selection. You may find that Windows 2000 best serves part of the network, while another part needs the Macintosh OS. In fact, the mixed-desktop scenario is becoming more popular because most companies have a graphics department that heavily relies on the Macintosh, while the business portion requires the flexibility provided by Windows. The point is that you shouldn't limit your OS choices in the name of convenience; it pays to use the best OS for the job based on the applications users have to run.

You still need to plan additional integration time if you mix two or more desktop OSs on the same network, because each OS has special requirements. For example, the Macintosh uses a different file-naming scheme than Windows uses. When you work with a NOS (which we'll talk about in the next section), the operating system requires you to load support for each of these file-naming schemes so the server will know how to interact with the client. Each of these support modules requires testing with the network as a whole.

One of the best ways to reduce the impact of using multiple operating systems on the same network is to categorize users by application requirement. If five users have the same application requirements, you can save time and effort by configuring all five machines the same way. This allows you to install the operating system faster and get applications configured using batch files. Once you know which applications a user will need and the operating system that supports those applications, the process of planning for network installation should be reduced to looking at two or three configuration types, plus the needs of the server.

Considering the Needs of the Server OS

If you're going to install a peer-to-peer network, there isn't any difference between the operating system you use and the server. Since one or more workstations on the network will double as servers, you don't have to choose a server OS. However, in a client/server network, there's a reason to consider a separate server OS, because you're using a separate machine—one that will only dispense resources in response to user requests. A server normally uses a NOS that is specially designed to dispense resources efficiently, while controlling user access.

The selection process for a server OS is different from the one you use for a desktop OS. This makes sense when you think about it, because the machines are used for completely different purposes. The main difference is that a server

OS has to handle requests from a number of clients, while a desktop OS handles the needs of one user. While a server runs applications, just as a client does, the applications tend to affect the entire organization, rather than just one user.

As with a desktop OS selection, you need to choose the applications that will run on a server before you choose the server OS. For example, if the server will host a database-management application, you need to choose the database-management system (DBMS) first. If you're using SQL Server, you need to use a Windows 2000 Server variant as the server OS. On the other hand, when working with a DBMS like Oracle, you have more choices—you could use Novell NetWare (which is discussed in detail in Chapter 7, *Working With NetWare*) if you wanted to.

The number of end user–oriented applications that you'll run on a server is small—one or perhaps two at the most, so choosing a server based entirely on the applications that you'll run is usually impossible. In addition to application support, you can use the following criteria to select a server OS:

Performance—A major consideration for any server OS is how well it performs. It's important to remember that the main purpose of a server is to allocate resources for use by a client. However, most server OSs are rated according to their ability to service a specific number of users. So, one of the features you should check is how much you're paying per user for the server—you'll find that prices vary widely by vendor.

Security—One of the reasons to use the client/server architecture is to ensure your data remains safe. A major feature for a server OS, then, is the number and type of security options that it supports. You'll want to check for features like government certification (and the level of that certification). It's also important to see whether the server supports all of the current security standards. The granularity of security support is important as well, because this determines how much control you have over security. For example, Novell NetWare defines more rights for each network object than Windows 2000 does; so at this level, NetWare provides better granularity.

Administration features—The speed at which an administrator can add or remove users, maintain user accounts, check for security breaches, and perform other types of server maintenance determines how much you'll pay in terms of human costs for your network. A feature-rich server OS greatly reduces the amount of work that an administrator has to perform to complete any given task. An extremely popular feature is the use of a directory, essentially a complex database, to store every piece of configuration information for the server. NetWare uses NetWare Directory Services (NDS) for this purpose, while Windows 2000 uses Active

Directory. Both directories make it easier for the network administrator to manage the network.

Connectivity—A server isn't useful if it can't make connections. The connectivity of a server is often measured by the number of protocols that it supports. For example, the most popular protocol in use right now is Transmission Control Protocol/Internet Protocol (TCP/IP), which is used by the Internet. Other types of connectivity include the ability of the server to provide remote connections through a dial-up line.

Resource management—Companies use servers to share resources in many cases. A resource can include everything from a printer to hard drive space to data that a user needs to make sales. Whatever the resource is, the server has to provide features that allow a network administrator to manage it. The server has to cooperate with these management settings by automatically maintaining a specific level of resource allocation for all clients. One of the best examples of this type of resource management is bandwidth throttling. The act of adding bandwidth throttling ensures that any one client gains access to a limited amount of the available bandwidth, ensuring that all users can access the server at a minimally acceptable transmission speed.

Utilities—Servers are responsible for a lot of background tasks. For example, you'll normally call upon the server to back up all the data on your system, including any user machines that may contain critical data. If your server comes with a good backup application, you won't need to invest in a third-party product. On the other hand, if the backup application that comes with the server is unreliable or difficult to use, a third-party product can end up costing a lot of money. In short, the more full-featured utilities the server provides, the fewer third-party management products you'll need to buy.

You might consider other criteria for a server OS purchase—it depends on what you expect the server to do for you. For example, if the server is going to be responsible for handling printing requests from a large number of users, you'll want to get a server OS that's good at managing printer requests like NetWare. On the other hand, if you need a server that provides Internet support, you'll want to look at a product that has this support built in like Windows 2000 or UNIX.

Installation Tips and Gotchas

At some point, you'll have an assortment of shiny new packages in your office that contain the OS and applications you selected. It's tempting to rip open the package in a reenactment of Christmas and throw the software onto the first machine you see. I know that a lot of people do this, because when I come for a visit (after they fail to get anything running) I can see the torn packages still lying in a heap in the middle of the floor. Either that, or the documentation for the software has escaped to some obscure corner of the planet, which is probably no further than the nearest dump. The fact is that most people make life a lot more difficult than it needs to be when it comes time to install their software. These failed installations add to the cost of your network, which means you should try to prevent them if possible.

There are some things you should avoid as a matter of practice when it comes to checking software installation procedures. One of the more common problems, especially with shareware, is that you need to perform some other tasks before you can install the software. For example, Microsoft (a commercial vendor) is famous for insisting that you install a certain level of OS service pack before you install a new application. If any of these prerequisites costs money to implement, you need to add them to the cost of the software package to make a fair determination of which application program package is less expensive.

Another common problem is missing an easy requirement. For example, I recently needed to add a patch to a product before I installed an add-on package. I downloaded the patch from the vendor's Web site and thought I had everything needed to install the add-on package. As soon as I tried to install the patch, however, I was asked for a password. Even though it was easy to get the password, doing so cost an entire day and caused scheduling problems. More often than not, you'll find that getting ready to put a software package together means checking details that might seem like common sense, but aren't. Here are some additional tips that will allow you to get a good installation every time:

- Always read the installation instructions, user manual, and README file. I know that Guinness has a record somewhere for the number of times a vendor changes the installation procedure at the last minute in a README file. Even if the README file doesn't contain new installation instructions, you'll find a wealth of weird conditions under which the program will fail to work. It's important to clear up any problems before you attempt to install your software.

- Back up your machine immediately after you install the operating system, and again after all of the applications have been installed. Most people don't back up their systems and end up without a method to recover their system setup when failures occur as a result. This is such a big problem that third-party vendors have come up with new products like Norton Ghost that make the whole process easier. In many cases, you can get great results by creating backups. Make sure you label the backup tapes and keep the operating system-only backup separate from the backup that contains the applications as well.

Recovery Disks that Don't Recover Anything—*Windows gives many people a false sense of security with the emergency boot disk. A recovery disk of this sort will allow you to boot the machine if part of the hard drive gets wiped out. However, it won't allow you to do anything else. The emergency boot disk is a partial measure—it won't protect your installation.*

- Check for add-on package requirements. Some software ships in modular format. It's especially common to see this approach in complex products like high-end accounting packages. For example, the main application package may ship with tax tables for the federal government. If you also require state tax tables, you'll have to buy an add-on package for the state in question. The vendor isn't trying to be dishonest; complex packages are often sold in modularized form to reduce costs by allowing customers to buy only what they need to perform a particular task.

- Spend some time on the vendor's Web site (assuming the vendor has one). Check the support area for patches. It almost always pays to patch the program as part of the initial installation before users have time to make changes to the application environment. You'll also want to check the vendor Web site for support notes that talk about issues that the vendor didn't know about when the product was originally shipped.

- Get some feedback from other network administrators if possible. I'll take a trip to an appropriate newsgroup and ask members about problems with a product that I want to install on my machine. Make sure you know about any real-world problems that the vendor is trying to hide.

So, what does all this have to do with choosing applications and an OS for your network? It pays to plan the installation of the software before you actually buy the hardware. You never know when a particular piece of software will require additional memory, peripheral devices, or other resources. Planning the installation, knowing where all of the hidden problems are, is one way to ensure you get the right hardware put together the first time. In short, this section is all about insurance—making sure you have all the little things on paper before you attempt to get hardware that won't work with the software you need to use.

Getting More for Less (Purchasing Tips)

Selecting software for your network often boils down to a simple matter of getting the most product for the amount of money spent. Once you decide that one or more products will meet your needs, it's time to decide which of these products offer the best deal. Sometimes it isn't the least expensive product that offers the most; in many cases, you'll have to weigh the cost of training and support as part of the cost of the software transaction. With these issues in mind, here are some ways you can get more products for less money:

- Make bulk product purchases, because many vendors will give you a discount for buying larger quantities of their product.
- Get on-site training for all of your staff at the same time—some vendors will provide a training discount when you do so and you'll save in travel expenses as well.
- Shop online whenever possible—doing so allows you to comparison-shop faster and with greater accuracy.
- Compare product prices accurately. If the first vendor provides product support as part of the package and the second doesn't, you'll need to add the cost of product support to the second vendor's price to get a true comparison.

There are also alternatives to buying software on the horizon. The most popular alternative is the application service provider (ASP). You download the application from the vendor as you need it. Because you don't own the application, you pay rental charges for using it, so this alternative isn't the best solution for mainstream applications like word processors. Once ASPs become common, the price you pay for using an application online will be a lot less than purchasing it outright in many cases. The ASP alternative to software purchases is so popular that large companies like Microsoft are getting into the picture.

Renting an application may seem ludicrous given today's computing environment. Some changes definitely need to take place on the Internet before ASPs will become viable alternatives. One of the most pressing changes is that more people will need to have broadband (high-speed connectivity like digital subscriber line) access to the Internet before application renting will make sense. However, once these issues are taken care of, renting an application rather than buying it will have the following advantages:

Lower equipment costs—You'll be able to use machines with less intelligence to do your work.

Lower software costs—You only need to pay for the amount of application you actually use.

Reduced cost of ownership—The ASP will handle all product updates for you.

Smaller company support staff—The ASP will likely provide support as part of the application rental.

Fewer network problems—Most of the applications on your network will be custom applications designed specifically for your needs.

CHAPTER FIVE

Cabling and Other Masses of Wire

It's finally time to begin looking at the hardware for your network. By the time you reach this point in the book, you should have a network design down on paper (see Chapter 3, *Designing a Standard Network*). You should also know which operating system (OS) and applications you want to run (see Chapter 4, *Connections Require Software*). Getting the hardware ready and connecting the computers together is a relatively easy part of the network-installation process in some respects, because you've already made many of the required decisions as part of the design and software selection process.

Of course, you have hardware elements to consider. Even though the two-step design and software selection process determines that you'll have a particular number of machines that are connected in a certain way, these phases still don't tell you precisely what hardware to get. You also need to consider how fast the network has to run to maintain an appropriate level of application performance. Some applications use more network bandwidth (a term I'll talk about in the "How Fast is Fast Enough?" section of this chapter) than others do. These decisions are made easier because you've already considered the details of what you expect your network to do and what needs it must address.

Another difficult issue you face is how to run cabling, if you decided to go that route. I know from experience that running cable in a house can be difficult—running it in someone else's building that you rent for your office can be pretty close to impossible. In addition to figuring out how to run the cable, you need to consider what type of cable to run. There are several types of network cable and each one is designed for a different type of network. The media for the cable might be copper or fiber optic, both of which require different handling and skills when it comes to performing tasks like splicing. In fact, you may decide that cabling won't work at all and that you'll need to use wireless technology to get a good installation that won't damage the walls of your landlord's building.

Another consideration is network-specific hardware. Every machine connected to the network requires a network interface card (NIC). However, there are different types of NICs, and you need to know which type is best for your implementation. In addition to a NIC, some network designs will require a hub—a central place into which you plug all the cabling. Fortunately, there are ways that you can get around buying this piece of hardware for some networks.

Finally, most people don't consider some nuances of network installation until it's too late. We've all heard of lightning hitting a computer and wiping out all the data it contains, so most of us use surge suppressors. However, what happens to your server during a brown out? You can still lose data, but most people don't consider the protection required for this situation.

This chapter will help you overcome many of the problems I've just mentioned. We'll look at the hardware choices you'll need to make and discuss the relative merits of each hardware selection. You'll learn the best techniques for running your cable and the ins and outs of wireless when using a cable is out of the question. We'll also talk about the various types of protection you should consider, especially where your server is concerned.

Understanding Network Hardware

A network creates both physical and software connections between machines, which means you'll need to invest in some hardware to get your network up and running. The pieces of hardware required to create a network are surprisingly small. Here's the rundown for a typical network:

Network interface card (NIC)—Every computer on the network will require a NIC. The NIC plugs into one of the motherboard expansion slots and has one or more plugs on the back. The plugs determine the type of cable you can connect to the NIC. I'll discuss cabling more in the section, "Getting the Right Cable," later in this chapter.

Cable—The physical connection between computers is normally created using a cable. However, as you saw in Chapter 2, *Cheap Alternative Networks*, this isn't always the case. You can also create the connection using radio waves, house wiring, or infrared. As long as you can get the signal from one point to another, the media isn't all that important.

Hub or T-connectors—Some types of cabling schemes require a hub. (Some texts use the term concentrator in place of hub.) You run the cable from each machine to a central location that includes the hub. Each cable plugs into the back of the hub and the hub makes the required connections. If the cabling scheme you choose doesn't require a hub, you still need to connect the computers and the most common method is to use a T-connector. Essentially, a T-connector acts as a splice between cable segments. When working with this type of cabling scheme, you also need terminators on each end of the cable.

So, if network hardware is this simple, why all of the confusion about it? Even though the concept of the network is simple, the hardware can vary a great deal between implementations. For example, an Ethernet setup can use three completely different kinds of cable and there are variations within those cable categories.

Because the cables use different connection schemes and even vary by the type of signal they're designed to carry, the NIC has to provide the correct connector for the cable and create a different signal for each type. Depending on the configuration of the network, you may need a hub or use T-connectors to connect the cables between computers together. The cabling is arranged in specific ways, which means that even the cable runs will differ depending on the hardware you choose to use.

The internal configuration of your PC also determines the kind of hardware you need. A motherboard must provide expansion slots to support a NIC (unless the NIC is built in—a topic I'll talk about in the section, "Pros and Cons of Motherboard NICs," later in this chapter). You might need a NIC that can work with industry standard architecture (ISA) or a peripheral component interconnect (PCI) slot. Figure 5.1 shows how the expansion slots are commonly arranged on a motherboard. The figure shows typical locations for many motherboard elements. The motherboard in your machine will probably vary from the one shown here; but the expansion slots are always the same. The point is that you need a NIC that's designed to work with the expansion slots in your machine, so you'll have to consult the vendor manual for your motherboard or computer as a whole before you make any NIC decision.

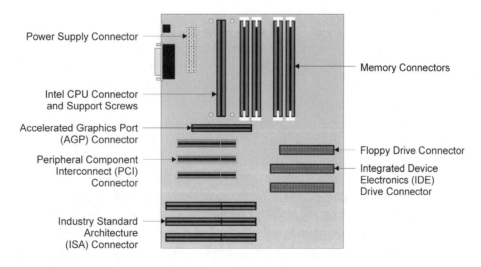

Figure 5.1: Expansion slot layout of a typical motherboard.

Hubs vary a great deal as well. For example, you need to get a hub that will handle the speed of your network. You'll also want to get a hub that can support the number of machines on your network (plus one or two connections for future expansion). If a single hub can't support all of the machines on your network, you'll need to get two hubs that are designed to work together to create what amounts to a single large hub electronically. Finally, hubs vary in features. Some of the better hubs include a full set of diagnostic and usage reporting capabilities that the network administrator can tap when looking for problem machines. In short, even though the number of hardware types is small, the variances between pieces of hardware are fairly significant.

How Fast Is Fast Enough?

One of the first questions you need to answer about your network is how fast you need to transfer data from one point to another. If you believe what you read in some trade magazines, it sounds like everyone is using gigabit networks and running fiber optic cabling. For most small businesses, such an arrangement is out of the question for one small reason, it would cost way too much. The fact is that a small business can usually get by with a lot lower network speeds and home offices can get by with even less. You don't need high speed to move a word processing file from a workstation to the server every 30 minutes or so when a user saves a document.

It's important to consider the bandwidth the network can provide when talking about network speed. However, the term bandwidth gets bandied about for all kinds of reasons, so it's important to describe how bandwidth is used in this book. Sometimes, it's easier to visualize something abstract like a network by using a concrete alternative. Think of the network cable as a pipe and the information it transfers as water. The size of the pipe is the network's bandwidth. The water consists of application data, routing information, and some other information. The water is organized into units called packets (think of a letter and associated envelope).

So, how does bandwidth work? Consider the pipe example again. A larger pipe allows more water to flow as long as there's enough water to fill the pipe. If you're not filling the pipe, making the pipe bigger won't make the water flow any faster because the pipe already provides sufficient capacity. The larger the pipe that's required to move data, the more expensive the network becomes. So, the idea is to get the smallest possible pipe to move the amount of data your company can generate at any given time without actually filling the pipe to capacity. You need enough bandwidth to address your network's needs today, plus a little more to address any needs tomorrow.

Bandwidth, or the size of the pipe, is a major concern for any network. No matter how large or small your network is, it won't provide good results if you don't have enough bandwidth to support the applications you want to use. Figuring out how big to make that pipe is the question answered in this section of the chapter. In most cases, you'll find that you can get by with less network bandwidth than you might think if you set your applications up correctly, train users to use network resources efficiently, and maintain your networking equipment. The following sections will look at how vendor claims match up to real-world expectations and what you need to consider as part of your network equipment purchase.

Real-World Speed Versus Vendor Claims

When you look at the specifications for network hardware, you need to remember that the numbers on the package are theoretical performance indicators. A vendor may say that you'll get a certain level of performance, but what you actually get depends on a lot of environmental factors that the vendor won't mention. The difference between your network and the one used by the vendor for testing purposes is that your network isn't in a lab running under ideal conditions.

Let's talk about a real-world example. When you read on the NIC package that the device is capable of transferring data at a rate of 10 Mbps, that's the theoretical delivery speed. In the real world, collisions (two computers trying to send data at once), line noise (electronic interruptions from motors, switches, radios, and a variety of other sources), and other performance inhibitors lower the amount of data that actually gets transferred. In fact, you may be surprised to learn that in a normal network setup, the 10 Mbps that you're supposed to get from a NIC actually translates into 6 Mbps real-world rates. So, if you're counting on 10 Mbps of bandwidth for your applications, you'll be disappointed with the performance of this piece of hardware.

Every Network Is Different*—The example in this section is just that—an example. Any network is going to be affected by enough outside influences that a precise calculation of network bandwidth will require on-site measurements. In addition, any change to the network will affect the performance characteristics of that network. For example, if you add a node to a network, it will change the performance characteristics of the network by increasing collisions and causing other kinds of losses.*

Of course, the first question is why the vendor doesn't tell you that the NIC is only capable of 6 Mbps, not 10 Mbps as advertised. The truth is that the vendor can't predict the losses on your network and those losses aren't even consistent. The same NIC could provide a bandwidth of 8 Mbps during one part of the day when network conditions are good and 6 Mbps later in the day when the network gets overloaded. The best the vendor can do is publish the best-case scenario statistics and allow you to modify those statistics for your particular network. The NIC is designed to provide 10 Mbps of bandwidth, so that's what the vendor puts on the package.

The point of this example is that there are certain realities in the world of networks; one of which is that there are factors outside of the realm of the OS that affect perceived network, and therefore both OS and application performance. Here's a simple way to look at what you'll need to do in order to predict the amount of network bandwidth you'll need:

When predicting network bandwidth requirements, add the amount of bandwidth that you'll need for applications to the amount of performance that will be lost due to environmental and design factors.

Measuring the Effects of Cable Length and Environment

Of course, network bandwidth is just one source of theoretical versus real-world performance problems. Networks have many limits that you need to observe. For example, every network has cable length limitations that you must observe. If you make the cable too long, the network will suffer timing problems because the signal generated by a computer on one end of the cable won't make it to a computer on the other end of the cable before a specific time elapses. Timing is important because it allows a network to move packets more efficiently, so you should get rid of the timer problem by setting the time-out value higher. In addition, the resistance of the cable will tend to reduce the size of the packet signal, which means that the packet will accumulate errors because the network won't be able to differentiate the packet signal from line noise.

The rules that define the physical and electrical characteristics of a network are known as the *network topology*. The theoretical versus real-world problem comes into play again because many network administrators will take the rules at face value and extend their network within the limitations of the topology-specified length criteria. However, these specifications assume a network operating in perfect environmental conditions. Unfortunately, there are few perfect environments. For example, as the noise around the network increases, the length that you can make the network cabling decreases in proportion to the noise level. Obviously, many network administrators don't account for this problem and pay with decreased network bandwidth as the network attempts to compensate for the noise. If you have to make the network a certain length, then ensure you consider environmental factors like electronic noise when figuring out the required bandwidth for your network.

It's important to remember that the specifications for a network topology are really a guideline. These specifications always assume that your network is operating under perfect conditions, because the engineers who create the specification can't anticipate every network problem. They assume that the on-site network administrator will take noise and other environmental hazards into consideration during the network design process and act accordingly. In short, if you need 10 Mbps worth of bandwidth, don't count on getting it with a 10 Mbps network—you'll really need the next size up.

Understanding the Effects of Network Load

Real world performance is also based on the load that the unique combinations of your company's applications provide. Theoretical performance values are usually created using test suites of applications that your company may not use. Someone writing a specification will very likely try to achieve a generic application load—one that could reflect the load that a majority of companies will place on the network. Unfortunately, there isn't any such thing as a generic company or a generic load. As a result, the performance you actually see when you design a network will vary from the theoretical norm.

Let's consider the problem of application load for a moment on the theoretical versus real-world network throughput. If your company uses applications that place large, continuous loads on the network like a graphics application, you can expect that the network will provide maximum throughput, but that the applications could appear to run slowly because of their ravenous appetites for network bandwidth. On the other hand, a database application creates small, record-sized packets that may require padding. The use of padding characters wastes network bandwidth, so the efficiency of the network will decrease. However, because of the kind of load that the database places on the network, you might see very little in the way of performance drop on a fully loaded network. There are other applications that place other kinds of load on the network—depending on how they create a load, you may see a loss of either performance or efficiency; or, in some cases, both.

There's one final real-world consideration to make. When the theoretical limits of a network topology are created, the engineers use lab type equipment in a lab setting. This equipment is specially designed to help the engineers make the required measurements. In short, even if everything else is equal, the hardware that you'll use to create a network isn't equal to the hardware used for testing.

There just isn't any way that you'll achieve the highest performance that's possible with a network because no one will purchase lab equipment for general office use.

Deciding How Much Bandwidth to Get

At this point, you may have decided that you'll never get the right network setup because there isn't any easy way to figure out how much bandwidth to get. The truth is that designers of enterprise network systems use a lot of extremely complex equations to figure out how much bandwidth they need and often get the wrong numbers, because they didn't take something into account. Knowing all of the things that will drain your network of bandwidth is an important first step to figuring out how much bandwidth you need—that's why I described the various problems in detail in preceding sections of this chapter. Once you do that, you can use the following simple chart to calculate how much bandwidth you'll actually use per network node. I'll talk about how to use the chart in a moment.

Word processing	0.05 Mbps
Spreadsheet	0.05 Mbps
Drawing	0.10 Mbps
Database	0.15 Mbps to 0.30 Mbps (per running application)
Graphics (streaming video or audio)	0.25 Mbps to 2 Mbps (per stream)

Let's use the chart in a simple example. If you have a three-node, peer-to-peer network and need to work with a word processor and one database application, each machine would likely use 0.20 to 0.35 Mbps of bandwidth. Multiply that by three nodes and you get 0.60 to 1.05 Mbps application bandwidth requirement for the network. This means that using one of the low-cost solutions in Chapter 2 might work, but you'd probably get better results with a 10 Mbps Ethernet network since we haven't factored in anything for noise, cable length, or other problems.

Notice that my chart doesn't include some application types that you might need to consider if you have the right network setup. For example, a lot of businesses will use a shared Internet connection. Everyone connects to the Internet through one machine, which means that Internet data flows from that machine, through the network, to the requesting machine. If you're using a 56 K modem to make the connection to the Internet, you have to add the modem bandwidth requirement (0.055 Mbps) to the overall network bandwidth requirement.

Okay, so this takes care of one end of the problem—the amount of bandwidth that the applications and other network resources will require. How do you resolve the problem of real network bandwidth versus what the vendor tells you it can provide? A 10 Mbps Ethernet network would have to be 100 percent efficient in order to provide the full 10 Mbps. I've never actually seen such a network, even though I know that it's theoretically possible. However, I'm talking real world in this section. I usually base my estimate on the two factors that will affect network bandwidth reductions the most: the length of the cable and the number of machines. The following simple chart shows what I use for my calculations:

First machine	0.15 Mbps
Additional machines	0.07 Mbps
Short cable run (up to 25% of total specification length)	0.5 Mbps
Medium cable run (up to 50% of total specification length)	1.0 Mbps
Long cable run (up to 95% of total specification length)	2.0 Mbps

So, for our example three-node network, we'd need to deduct 0.29 Mbps from the theoretical bandwidth to get the true bandwidth of the network. Of course, we also need to account for the cable run, which I'm assuming is short, in this case, so you'd need to deduct another 0.5 Mbps from the total available bandwidth. So the network has 9.21 Mbps to offer and at the most we'll use 1.05 Mbps of it for our applications—a 10 Mbps Ethernet network will work fine in this situation.

Getting the Right Cable

Getting a signal from one point on your network to another requires a cable, unless you're planning to use an alternative like wireless radio frequency (RF) connections. There are a number of cable types for networks, so choosing the right kind of cable for your particular network is important. Cables vary in three important ways:

- Media (the type of conductor)
- Shielding
- Conductor arrangement

The two most common media types are copper and glass (used for fiber optic). In most cases, a home or small-office network will use copper because it's relatively inexpensive and the tools required to work with it are readily available. Fiber optic media provides greater bandwidth potential, but at a high price.

Cables use shielding to prevent signal interference. An unshielded cable radiates RF signals that may interfere with the signals in other cables. In addition, such a cable is open to interference from other signals—increasing the probability of lost packets. Unshielded cables characteristically cost less than shielded cables, weigh less, and are more flexible. Some people will use unshielded cables in areas of low noise where cable weight in areas like false ceilings might be a problem. In most cases, you'll want to use a shielded cable because it weighs only a little more and provides protection from outside noise.

There are two popular methods for arranging the conductors within a cable: coaxial or twisted pair. Figure 5.2 shows both methods. The braided shield on the coaxial cable is used as the return path for the signal. This type of cable has few noise problems because the data conductor is completely surrounded by shielding. The main disadvantage to this arrangement is that the braided shield tends to make coaxial cable a little stiff. When a shield is included for twisted pair, it's maintained as a separate entity from the neutral conductor. This means that both the data conductor and the return path are shielded from noise. A twisted-pair cable normally uses thin copper shielding in place of braided shield. The twisting of the two conductors in a twisted-pair setup tends to reduce interference with other cables in the area because the two signals cancel each other out. The main advantages of twisted pair are cost and flexibility (it's not as stiff).

Ethernet relies on four basic types of cable, three of which are in common use today. Fiber optic cable is the high-speed solution and looks similar to the coaxial cable in Figure 5.2. The main difference is that there's no need for shielding for the glass media. The only reason to run fiber optic cable for a small business is to run your network at 1 Gbps (1,000 Mbps) and most small business don't require this much speed. Since fiber optic cable is relatively expensive and difficult to work with, you'll want to make this your option of last resort.

Coaxial (type RG58 A/U) is still in common use, but is limited to 10 Mbps networks. I find that coaxial is more resistant to damage than twisted pair and is easier to "fish" through existing walls. You'll use coaxial cable for bus config-uration network setups, which can prove easier for a small business to set up than a star configuration. The main disadvantage of this type of cable is that you need a special tool to work with it. (I'll discuss network setups in detail in

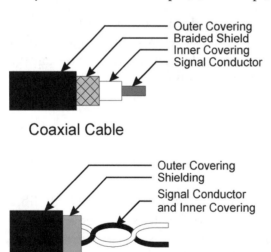

Figure 5.2: Coaxial and twisted pair are the two most popular techniques for arranging conductors within a cable.

the "Do You Need a Hub?" section later in this chapter.) However, this is the same special tool used by cable television installers (if you look at the two cables, they're similar), so finding the tool at a local **RadioShack.com** (http://www.radioshack.com/) will be easy. Coaxial cables rely on a bayonet nut connector (BNC) to create a connection to the NIC.

If you'll eventually need to run your network at 100 Mbps, Category 5 twisted-pair cable is the best option. This cable is extremely flexible, and you don't require any specialized tools to work with it. Anyone who has ever worked with telephone cables can work with Category 5 twisted pair. In fact, the connector at the end of the cable is a registered jack connector, RJ-45, which is similar to the RJ-11 connector used for the telephone. Of all the cables mentioned so far, this one is the most flexible both for installation purposes and uses. You can use Category 5 twisted-pair cable for asynchronous transfer mode (ATM), token ring, 100Base-T (100 Mbps Ethernet), and 10Base-T networking. With a special hookup, you can potentially use Category 5 twisted pair for 1000Base-T networks as well.

A fourth type of cable exists for Ethernet called ThickNet cable. It contains five heavily shielded twisted-pair cables. The cabling is difficult to work with, very stiff, and difficult to obtain. In addition, it requires a special NIC connector, which is difficult to obtain in many cases today. There are two advantages to using this cable. First, the heavy shielding makes it nearly impervious to noise, which means you can use it any environment. Second, the design of the cable allows you to create runs 500 meters (1,640 feet) long instead of the 185 meters (607 feet) for coaxial (ThinNet) cable.

Knowing Your Connector—*Every computer on the market relies on connectors to create the physical connection between devices. Unfortunately, most of these connectors have odd sounding names that don't tell you anything about how the connector looks. The Connectivity Knowledge Platform at http://www.mouse.demon.nl/ckp/ contains a wealth of information about connectors including a pictorial guide to all of the connectors that you're likely to run into on any computer.*

Tips for Running Cable Faster

Most small businesses don't have the luxury of erecting a new building, which means that they need to wire an existing building for networking needs. The problem with existing buildings is that they have finished walls, floors, and ceilings. Most people aren't too thrilled to see a lot of cables streaming across the floor (not to mention the hazards of such an arrangement), so you need to do something with the cables.

The most common solution to this problem for a room that's set up as an office space is to run the cables over the false ceiling. Generally, an installer will run the cable into one of the corners of the ceiling tile to maintain the appearances and to make it easier to remove the cable when repairs are required. You'll still want to hide the cables running up the wall if possible. The cables can be run through hollow walls, through the center of hollow cubicle supports, or along solid surfaces using self-stick cable clips. You can make cables less noticeable when you have to run them outside the wall by placing them next to door jams or other objects that normally stick out from the wall anyway. In many cases, tan colored cable will be less noticeable than black.

What happens, however, if you're like a lot of small businesses that are in a building without a false ceiling? If there's an unfinished basement below the work area, you can usually drill holes through the floor right next to the wall (to keep the hole from being noticeable) and run the cables under the floor. Make sure you support the cables with cable clips.

Finding Hidden Obstacles—*The empty spaces between the joists and studs of floors and walls usually contain electrical wiring, pipes, supports, and other hidden obstacles. You'll want to ensure you won't drill through a pipe or other object before you drill through the floor or wall when running cables for your network. Using a stud finder will help you locate some types of objects; but a stud finder isn't always accurate and it won't find thin or small objects nestled in walls. Always sight verify any location you want to drill if possible. In some cases, this will mean making a small inspection hole where you want to run a cable or place a junction box.*

If you don't have a false ceiling or an unfinished basement at your disposal, it's time to get creative. Sometimes a closet makes the perfect place to hide cables if the closet happens to be in the right space. Make sure you run the cable so that the closet can still be used if you try this approach. This is the approach that I often use in home installations. The two machines you want to network will be on opposite sides of a closet. Drill two holes directly through both walls and you have a direct connection that no one will see (at least if you're careful about how you drill).

Another method is to hide the cable within molding. This approach only works if the molding is large enough to hide the cable and has a hollow in the back. (Larger molding often does.) You'll want to be careful when using this approach because the hidden cables could be damaged if someone hits the molding. Considering that most molding is fairly solid wood, however, the risk is minimal.

There are a few cable-running practices that you should avoid. The following list is my cabling don'ts:

- Never run cables under carpeting; they'll become damaged fairly quickly and the bump in the carpet could cause accidents.
- Never stress the cable as you run it. Making the cable lie flat is good; stretching the cable isn't.
- Avoid crimping the cable or forcing it to make sharp turns. If you have to run a cable around an inside corner, allow it to stick out from the wall a little.
- Refrain from running cables through traffic areas; run them through walls, over ceilings, or under floors instead.

While most of these items are common sense, I've run into all of them. You always want to protect your network cabling and reduce any stress it might encounter. Cabling problems are difficult to find and can be expensive to fix. However, cabling that's correctly installed can last many years without failure.

Working With Network Interface Cards (NICs)

The NIC should be the easiest part of the networking equation. Just about everyone uses Ethernet today, so you normally won't need to worry about what type of network topology you're using. In addition, NICs are normally self-configuring and easily recognized by most OSs. All you really need to do is install the NIC in your machine, attach a cable, and turn it on.

There are, however, two considerations. The first is the kind of motherboard expansion slot you want to use. I talked about expansion slots in the "Understanding Network Hardware" section earlier in the chapter, so I won't talk about them again here (see Figure 5.1 for examples of expansion slots).

The second consideration is the type of network connector you want to use. Not every NIC supports every type of cable or network configuration. The NICs that do provide broad support for more than one networking solution are normally restricted to 10 Mbps operation. Figure 5.3 shows an example of a fairly common combo card— a NIC that supports more than one type of cable connection. A 100 Mbps NIC will only have the activity indicator and the RJ-45 connector on the back.

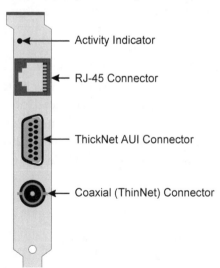

Activity Indicator

RJ-45 Connector

ThickNet AUI Connector

Coaxial (ThinNet) Connector

Figure 5.3: This combo card supports three different types of cable.

Pros and Cons of Motherboard NICs

Some motherboard vendors have recently started adding NICs to their motherboards. There are several reasons for the change in tactics. The first is the most important. Ethernet has become a de facto standard for networking. If there weren't such a standard, a motherboard vendor could never take the chance of adding a NIC to the motherboard, because such an addition could make the motherboard difficult to sell to people who wanted to use some other type of NIC.

Another reason that this has become popular is marketing. Motherboards are becoming commodity items for the most part. Vendors usually have to make their product look different by adding a necessary feature and making it look like the buyer is getting it for free.

The third reason is that miniaturization has made it possible to place more components on a motherboard than ever before. It wasn't long ago that computers were packed with expansion cards that allowed them to perform simple tasks like access a hard drive. Today, you can't buy a motherboard that doesn't already contain the required hard drive interface card built right in. It probably won't be long before you see motherboards that provide everything an average user will want—expansion cards will be relegated to specialty items.

However, for today, is getting a motherboard with the NIC already in place a good idea? In many cases, it is. If you can get the motherboard for the same price with the NIC as you can without, the NIC costs you nothing. Most motherboard NICs will support network speeds of either 10 Mbps or 100 Mbps. This makes them extremely flexible and ensures that a home or small-office user won't need to buy something else (another good reason to avoid the gigabit network as long as possible).

You need to consider some tradeoffs. If the NIC on the motherboard ever goes bad, you'll end up buying an expansion-slot NIC anyway. Of course, the problem is that you'll then have two NICs in the same machine and may experience problems getting the OS to recognize the right one. Even if you disable the motherboard NIC through the system BIOS, some OSs will insist on recognizing it. If this happens, not only will you have a bad NIC to deal with, but you'll be wasting resources, too.

Do You Need a Hub?

There are two main methods of connecting the computers in a network. You can use a bus connection where one computer is daisy chained to the next, or you can use a star connection where all of the computers are connected to a central hub. Figure 5.4 shows an example of each type of connection.

The speed of your network, the type of NIC installed in the systems, and the type of cabling used will determine the need for a hub. Almost every new

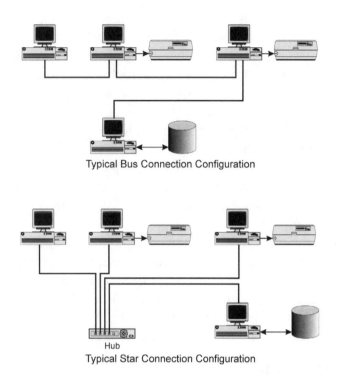

Typical Bus Connection Configuration

Hub
Typical Star Connection Configuration

Figure 5.4: The main difference between a bus configuration and a star configuration is the hub.

network setup uses a hub because there are definite advantages to using twisted-pair cable in a star configuration. The two biggest advantages are cost and troubleshooting.

Using twisted-pair cable costs a lot less than coaxial. If you just compare cabling costs, you'll come out ahead using twisted pair. A large company does just that because cabling costs become a major factor as the number of nodes in a network increase. However, what if you have a small company with only three or four nodes? The difference in cabling cost will be minimal because it takes more twisted-pair cable to do the same thing that coaxial cable will do. (Look at Figure 5.4 and you'll see the bus configuration that coaxial cable supports is more efficient at using cable.) In addition, you need to add the cost of the hub to the network. A small company is likely to lose money when working with a star configuration and twisted pair, while a large company will save money due to the vast difference in cabling costs.

The one undeniable benefit for anyone using twisted pair and a star connection is the ability to diagnose network failures fast. Look again at Figure 5.4. Since every cable in a star configuration ends up at the hub, the hub can test each machine's connection separately. If a machine fails to respond when queried, the connection is removed from the star and the hub will light an indicator showing the node failed. In short, you can simply look at the hub and know instantly which machine has failed, which allows to you fix the network faster. Again, the more machines in your network, the more beneficial this feature becomes.

Of course, it could be argued that the value of a hub's diagnostic ability is small when dealing with three or four machines. Even if you resort to trial and error, finding an error on a small network isn't going to take long. However, it's still going to be problematic and unlike the star configuration, when a bus-configured network loses a single connection, the entire network is likely to become non-operational.

The bottom line, then, for small office and home networks is: are you willing to pay the extra money for a hub to gain some specific benefits in the way of diagnostic capability. If you're not trying to save every last cent that you can on the network, using a star configuration with a hub will definitely pay you back in saved diagnostic time sometime in the future. A coaxial-bus configuration is still the best way for a small company or home network to save money.

Plugging Things In

After you have all of the cables run, machines installed, peripherals located in central areas, and hubs hidden in closets, the temptation is to plug everything in and see if it works. Unfortunately, this isn't the best way to do things because networks can experience a myriad of startup problems. I use the following steps when setting up a network.

1. Connect two computers. If you're working with a client/server network, be sure one of the computers is the server. Make sure you install any required software to test the network, but none of the application software.
2. Try to log in and fully test the connectivity of these two computers.
3. Add a new computer to the network. When working in a mixed network, test all of the computers that use a single OS first; then move on to the next OS in your list. This will allow you to check for OS-specific problems in a logical progression.
4. Repeat steps 2 and 3 until you've added all of the computers to the network.
5. Add any peripherals to the network. Test each peripheral in turn.
6. Install the remaining network software, testing connectivity after each setup is complete.

By following a logical progression when installing your network, you can save a lot of time when trying to diagnose failures. If you see a failure occur, try reversing your change. Problems that go away after the change is reversed usually indicate the new machine is faulty, something is wrong with the wiring, or there's some type of error with the network itself. The problem could be something as simple as a missing driver on the server. The point is that you have some idea of where to look and what's causing the problem.

Wireless Technology and the Network

I've spent a lot of time talking about cables in this chapter because the vast majority of you will use cables of some type for your network. However, in some situations cables just won't work. It could be something as simple as providing the right level of connectivity when you have a lot of users who are on the road all day, or perhaps you couldn't get the landlord's permission to install cabling. Whatever the reason, some network administrators need an alternative to the common method of connecting computers with cables.

Wireless technology is still in its infancy. Even though some people are trying it out and more than a few of them are finding success, there are still a lot of problems to overcome with this technology. One of the more pressing problems, as with any new technology, is the matter of standards. There are several standards out there right now and you need to make sure that any equipment you buy is going to rely on a single standard, rather than a mix of all of the available offerings. The technology that has the greatest chance of being accepted as a standard today is Bluetooth. I'm not going to discuss all of the details of this technology because most of the details don't matter if you simply want to connect two machines. However, you can read about this standardized technology at these Web sites:

Bluetooth Solutions from Ericsson
http://bluetooth.ericsson.se/

Wireless Local Loop World
http://www.telecomresearch.com/

The Official Bluetooth SIG Website
http://www.bluetooth.com/

Bluetooth Technology (Intel)
http://www.intel.com/mobile/bluetooth/

Bluetooth Mailing List
http://bluetooth.listbot.com/

Of all the problems that Bluetooth is having right now, the one you need to be concerned about the most is security. There are gaps in most technologies, but the one in Bluetooth has to do with the way data is translated as it moves from a conventional connection to a wireless connection and back again. Every time the data is translated, the device performing the translation has to decrypt any encrypted data. This means that your data is unencrypted and quite accessible for some amount of time, so a cracker could use that hole to access your data without your knowledge. Hopefully, by the time you read this, the security problems with wireless will be fixed. In the meantime, you'll want to examine this issue carefully before you buy.

Another potential problem for businesses is the relatively low bandwidth of 721 Kbps provided by Bluetooth. Data rates this low mean that you can't really support a network of more than two or perhaps three heavy database users at a time. This problem will likely go away as the technology develops, but it's something you need to consider today.

Using wireless technologies does make sense for many applications. Networking schemes like Bluetooth rely on radio waves to transmit data between nodes on the network. You don't need a physical connection to any other machine. As long as your machine is within radio range, you can communicate with other nodes. That's the beauty of wireless—no cables mean that you'll avoid a lot of problems that conventional networks incur and you'll be able to support the road warrior with greater ease.

The home user will benefit as well. Just think about the luxury of having a network for your craft business without having to tear up the walls to install it. In addition, you won't be tied to your office anymore. As long as you're within broadcast range, you can use your laptop to conduct business anywhere around your house. So, while you're in the hammock working on yesterday's receipts, other people will be sitting in stuffy offices waiting for another day to end.

Hardware Protection You Can't Live Without

A computer system is only as good as the protection it receives from the user. If you don't add a surge suppressor to your system, lightning will probably hit it at the worst possible moment. This type of protection wasn't well known when PCs first appeared on the scene, but it's well known now because of all the people who have had to purchase new equipment when they failed to protect their computer.

How much protection you give your computer depends on how valuable the data the computer manages is to you. The computer itself is a relatively low-cost item when compared to the data it's supposed to protect. Consider how long it would take your company to recover from a surge-induced hard drive crash on the computer that holds your order-entry database. You'd lose any pending sales, information about orders that you'd already fulfilled but the customer hasn't paid for, your entire customer list, and even mundane bits of data like your product catalog. If a company loses enough data, the results can be catastrophic.

The following sections aren't provided to scare you into buying protection that you don't want or need. What we'll do is look at some of the technologies that are available to protect your computer. Once you know the types of protection you can buy, it's up to you to decide how much insurance you need in the form of protection. A small purchase today can save your company in the future; but like insurance, you'll never know if that investment will pay off until the unthinkable happens.

Surge Suppressors versus the Uninterruptible Power Supply

You can add many kinds of peripherals to your system to protect it from damage. Ask any number of vendors and you'll get that many different answers on just what the best protection is. The fact remains that the power, telephone, and network cabling for your system offer opportunities for disaster to strike. Not only are there problems with power surges, but with power sags as well. Even if the power surge or sag isn't enough to damage your system, the electrical noise created by such an event could damage data on your system and will certainly affect performance in the short term.

The only device that can protect from electrical noise, surges, and sags is an uninterruptible power supply (UPS). A UPS contains a battery that will supply power to your system in the event of a power sag. In addition, it usually contains a circuitry that's superior to the type found in a surge suppressor to protect your computer from power spikes. If a spike is too high or too long in duration, the UPS will switch to battery to protect your machine from damage. Most UPS vendors also include filtering to remove any electrical noise from the system. Electrical noise is a silent killer because it quietly steals life from system components like the CPU.

Unlike a surge suppressor, most UPSs provide protection for the power cables, telephone, and network cables. Low-cost surge suppressors protect only the power cables. A higher quality surge suppressor may also protect the telephone line.

There are two types of UPS. The first makes a connection from the power line to your computer, just as a surge suppressor would. If the UPS detects a fault condition, it'll switch to battery and prevent any damage. The advantage to this type of UPS is cost and longevity. Since the UPS will rely on the power line most of the time, the battery isn't charging and discharging all the time. In addition, the circuitry for this type of UPS is simpler, which reduces cost. A simple device and a battery that's only used in emergencies add up to a UPS that costs less and has a long life span. This type of UPS is just fine for a workstation.

The second type of UPS always supplies power to the computer from the battery. The line power is used to keep the battery charged. In this way, the computer always received conditioned power—power that's supposedly perfect. This type of UPS offers several advantages. The most important advantage is constant power. The first type of UPS suffers from switching time; this one doesn't. If a power failure occurs quickly enough with the first type of UPS, there's a chance (albeit a small one) that your computer will still go offline. Since the power is always generated by the UPS for the computer, you'll see less line noise from it as well, which increases the longevity of your computer. This type of UPS is perfect for a server, but you may want to use it with more expensive workstations as well.

UPSs vary in a number of other ways. For example, you need to be careful about how the UPS is rated. Some vendors use watts for the power rating while others use volt-amperes (VA). When you compare two UPSs that have the same rating, the one rated in watts provides more capacity than the one rated in VA. Both rating systems are sound, but watts are closer to what you'll actually get from the UPS in the way of power. The amount of power that you need from a UPS varies according to the size of your system and how long you need to support the computer after a power failure. The calculations are somewhat complex, but fortunately, the UPS vendors have simplified the process by offering an online calculator. Figure 5.5 shows the one for **American Power Conversion, APC**, at http://www.apcc.com/sizing/.

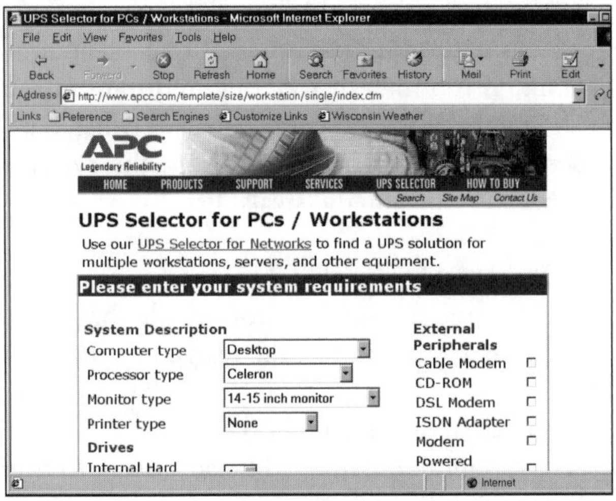

As you can see in Figure 5.5, all you need to do is fill out a simple questionnaire about your system. After you fill it out and submit the form, the vendor will display a list of solutions for your UPS needs like the one shown in Figure 5.6. The feedback information always tells you how long your system will run with the given UPS. You need to select a UPS that will at least allow you to shut down

Figure 5.5: UPS calculators help you find the right size the first time.

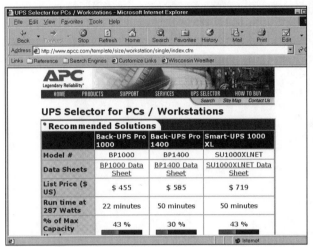

Figure 5.6: There's usually more than one UPS solution for your system.

your system normally—more time is better. Other UPS information can include the number of plugs on the back and the types of information the UPS will monitor. For example, the UPS on my server will monitor the input and output voltages, UPS temperature and humidity, battery voltage, amount of load, and the output frequency of the UPS.

Some UPS vendors will try to confuse you with a lot of rhetoric that goes beyond the simple issues. One of the more popular areas of discussion is the kind of waveform that the UPS provides as output. Whether your computer actually notices a stepped output is the least of your worries during a power outage—a true sine wave output is probably better, but your computer will run fine on either output waveform. To avoid the marketing blitz during your next UPS purchase, concentrate on these issues:

- Switching type (always battery or battery only when needed)
- Power output
- Number of receptacles
- Types of devices protected
- Computer support time
- Service and support policy

Using Built-In Monitoring

It's a warm day, but I've decided to save some cash and leave the air conditioning off in my home office. At about noon, an alarm buzzes and a dialog box like the one shown in Figure 5.7 shows on my screen. The computer is telling me that it's gotten too hot; it's time to turn the air conditioner on and cool things off. Without this warning screen, my computer would have overheated and I may have lost data. Using the built-in monitoring allows me to run the air conditioner only when needed to keep the system cool, which saves not only on the electric bill, but also ensures that I have the air conditioning on when I do need it.

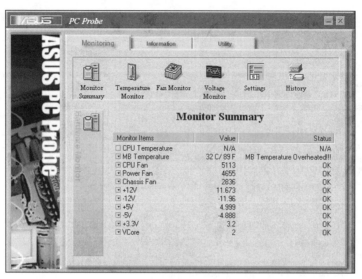

Figure 5.7: A built-in monitoring system can tell you when your computer needs attention.

Many computers, like those from ASUS (http://www.asus.com/) include some form of internal monitoring system that tells you when specific equipment has either failed, or will fail soon. In the case of my motherboard, I can monitor the CPU temperature, motherboard temperature, all the output voltages of the power supply, and the current speed of all the fans. A failure of any of these elements will display an alarm that will alert me to the problem before it becomes critical.

Even if you have a small network, using built-in monitoring can also help the network administrator. Users may not know that their computer is about to overheat, but with an alarm the network administrator can detect the problem and fix it quickly. Sometimes a computer-killing event happens because of the way that the users maintain their office. I've seen users place any number of things in front of the computer's cooling vents, which prevents hot air from escaping. No matter what the cause of failure, internal monitoring is a cheap form of insurance. It adds pennies to the cost of the motherboard, yet ensures that you'll keep your investment intact.

The Benefits of a Good Maintenance Plan

Some people play Russian Roulette with their network and can't understand why it refuses to perform to expectations. A network is a business investment, just like any other investment. If you own a company car, you don't just drive it constantly without ever changing the oil or putting in gas. You'll normally take the car to a reputable repair shop for maintenance at given intervals to protect your investment. Likewise, computers require some level of care and protection to have long and productive lives.

Of course, maintenance does need to take a back seat to the main reason you bought the computer in the first place—getting work done faster and more efficiently. You wouldn't want to perform maintenance on your car the day you need to drive to the airport to pick up a client—you'd choose a convenient time to perform the maintenance. Likewise, computer maintenance should occur on a regular basis, but at a time that's convenient for everyone. Some companies perform maintenance at night; others wait until the weekend.

Is Your Business 24/7?—*Many companies need to have their network available 7 days a week, 24 hours a day, 365 days a year to meet certain obligations. For example, your company may have a Web site that requires full-time access by potential customers. In this case, you'll want to have a spare server or use server clusters. Just because your network requires 24/7 access, doesn't mean you can get by without maintaining your machines. A single spare machine will allow you to rotate those hard working servers out and give them some tender loving care.*

Some people view any type of maintenance with the same enthusiasm as they would view a funeral. However, maintenance doesn't have to be a time-consuming and dirty task if you perform it regularly. There are four items of maintenance that are crucial for any machine:

Backup—This is one of the few bits of maintenance that many network administrators are willing to perform. Yet, it's not surprising to find that some companies still don't have a backup when they need it because the backup is performed too seldom, isn't inclusive enough, or is performed incorrectly. In one case, I visited a company that had conscientiously made a backup every night for years. The only problem is they never tested the tape drive, which turned out to be bad—their backup wasn't any good.

Cleaning—A computer has to move air to stay cool. If the vent holes are dirty, the computer will quickly overheat and parts will fail. Dust within the computer can also cause shorts and other problems. Cleaning the computer with compressed air specifically designed for the purpose will keep things running properly. Make sure you also use the special cleaners required for the optics on your machine like the CD-ROM drives.

Diagnostics—Some diagnostic programs will exercise the hardware and tell you whether everything is okay. This type of diagnostic can help you find things like bad memory locations. A bad memory location can be pretty dangerous. If the OS uses that location, you could lose data or cause the server to freeze when code in the memory location is executed. Other diagnostic programs go further and will perform predictive analysis. These diagnostic programs will help you predict when a hard drive is about to go bad, for example. Whichever type of diagnostic you use, running diagnostics on a machine is essential if you want to be sure that it won't let you down. Make sure you include tasks like defragmenting the hard drive as part of your maintenance plan to ensure the machines on the network always run at peak performance.

Minor upgrades—Computer vendors don't release a lot of computer updates, but the ones they do release are usually crucial to the operation of your system. Make sure you check the vendor Web site often and download any Flash ROM updates that you find. I recently ran into a problem with Windows 2000 that was solved by a Flash ROM update. Until I applied the update, the owner of the machine was convinced that she would need to buy a new machine. Imagine her surprise when a simple update fixed the problem. The update was free (except for the cost of my time, of course).

When you have a good maintenance plan in place, you can usually predict problems long before they become problems. You'll find that you spend a lot less time fixing emergencies and more time working on tasks that you want to perform. A good maintenance plan includes some level-of-performance monitoring to ensure that the system runs as efficiently as possible. In most cases, it's a lot easier to keep your system in a high state of readiness than to get it that way after a system failure occurs.

CHAPTER SIX

Configuring Windows for Network Use

If you've been following the book from the beginning, you have all of those shiny new boxes of software sitting at your side and at least two machines connected together. All of the decisions have been made; it's time to get your network up and running for the first time. This is the chapter where all of the preliminary work you've done will pay off, because you'll find that putting the network together with all of this information at your disposal is relatively easy. Of course, you still can't rush over to the boxes, rip them open, and act like it's Christmas—it helps to include a little sanity in the setup process.

Before you can begin installing an OS on your workstation for the first time, you need to know a little about the OS. In this chapter, we're going to be looking at Windows. It's not the only OS out there; but it's one of the most popular OSs available, which is why I decided to talk about it in this book. (Chapter 7, *Working With NetWare*, talks about another popular OS, Novell NetWare.) There are a lot of other OSs available to the home and small-office user like the Macintosh OS, UNIX, and Linux. I talked about these alternatives in Chapters 3, *Designing a Standard Network*, and 4, *Connections Require Software*, and will discuss them in future chapters as well. I'm not trying to convince you that you need to use Windows as the OS for your workstations—it's just one of many possibilities.

Linux Installation Made Easy—*Linux users have provided some pretty impressive online documentation for this operating system. You can find complete documentation, including installation instructions, for Linux at* http://www.linux.org/. *Another good place to look for Linux installation-specific information is* http://www.ibiblio.org/mdw/LDP/gs/. *Finally, if you have Red Hat Linux, you'll want to check out* http://www.thelinuxproject.com/.

Windows is an OS with a lot of potential; but all too often that potential is obscured by features you don't need, strange errors in the middle of saving your document, and scary articles in the media about the impending death of your computer by a cracker. There are a lot of things you can do to get rid of those excess features, and in many cases, getting rid of the unnecessary features makes your machine more stable. Unfortunately, the third problem will remain until Microsoft plugs all of the security holes in its product. You can get products that make your machine more secure and help you find out when someone has gotten around your security measures. We'll talk about these requirements for your network in Chapter 8, *Network Security Essentials*. For now, it's more important to get your network running.

This chapter also looks at what you need to do to get a good Windows installation. Sure, you can sit back and let the installation program do all of the work; but in many cases, the installation you get will reflect what Microsoft thinks you need, rather than what you really want. Remember that Microsoft thinks like a big corporation, so what you'll end up with, in many cases, isn't going to work in a small-business or home-office setting. We'll discuss a proactive approach to getting a good installation and how to fix any problems that occur. Performing a custom installation now will save you a lot of time later.

Getting your workstation set up is just part of the process. You'll also need to access the server. We'll look at some of the problems you'll experience getting Windows to talk with your server the first time. We won't look at every server out there; but you'll end up with a good idea of what types of problems you might see. Part of the server-access portion of the chapter includes installing server applications and diagnosing server application problems.

Finally, we'll talk about some hidden installation problems that could occur on any Windows workstation. For example, Microsoft will make assumptions about your network setup that may not be true. You'll need to ferret out these problems and fix them to produce a stable setup. In many cases, these problems won't scream out and tell you of their existence. They'll hide in the background waiting for the worst possible moment to break out and make your life miserable unless you take a proactive approach.

Windows Features You Can Live Without

Microsoft has a habit of thinking that everything it produces is the greatest thing since sliced bread. For some people, this might be the truth; but I'm willing to bet that most of you can get by without some of the bells and whistles that Microsoft thinks you need. For example, it's doubtful that many of you will need NetMeeting or Microsoft Chat installed on your machine. Yes, they're useful utilities; but if you don't need the features they provide, they just take up hard drive space. Since Microsoft feels that you really need these two programs, however, it'll cheerfully install them on your system.

Of course, Microsoft isn't the only one playing this game. I installed the vendor-supplied device drivers for all of my hardware and got a really neat utility installed with the driver. It didn't matter whether I needed the utility or not; the vendor simply assumed that I needed the utility on my machine. Of course, the utility started automatically for me, so every time I started Windows it would be there, just in case I decided to use it. Unfortunately, these little gadget utilities can rob your system of performance, can make it unstable, and generally create problems for you. Here's a general rule of thumb that I go by:

Applications that increase system performance or personal productivity are the only applications you should run on your system.

There are a lot of reasons to keep your system free of features you don't need. The most important reasons are performance and reliability. Every time you install a feature you don't need, the reliability of your system is affected. That's because applications make changes to the OS environment and install new functionality that may not work with other applications. (We'll look at these problems in detail as the section progresses.) If the application also includes features that start automatically when you start Windows, the performance of your system is affected. Every application running on your machine uses processing cycles and resources, such as memory, that are needed by the applications you do use on a regular basis.

In the following sections, we're going to look at several Windows feature issues. Of course, the best ways to keep your system running well is to keep features that you don't want installed from appearing on your machine in the first place. However, removing features you don't need is a good second option. It's also important to know what types of applications are installed with and without your knowledge. We'll look at some of the uses for those mystery applications that you may have been afraid to remove in the past. Finally, you need to consider some features that are software related, but don't fall into the application category. Some of the most difficult to understand are network features. Installing too many unnecessary network features can reduce system performance by as much as half when working with network applications. A quick look at the network functionality you actually need installed on your system will often net a significant increase in system performance by reducing the number of unneeded features.

Reducing or Eliminating Unneeded Applications

You may find that the process of installing an operating system, device drivers, and applications is a jarring experience the first few times. Getting the installations completed is only part of the process. Once you are done, you have a new installation that may or may not work as anticipated. You may find that the new system that you thought would speed you on your way languishes in application traffic. In short, you did all of that work and have a sluggish system to show for it.

One of the biggest problems that you'll run into when working with Windows is something I call "feature crawl." You start with a svelte setup and end up with a bloated installation that can't do anything fast and seems to crash when it does get something accomplished. Part of the solution to this problem is to make sure you keep your system lean in the first place—only install what you need. Another part of the solution is to reduce application fat whenever you can by removing elements that the vendor thought you needed, but you really didn't. Finally, there are techniques for disabling application features that you don't need without actually removing them. Disabling features allows you to test the operating system functionality without the feature and enable the feature again if you really do need it.

Using Custom Installs and Module Uninstalls

One of the ways you can reduce this problem is to perform a custom installation, rather than accept the default options of a typical installation. Using the custom install method allows you to choose the features you want at the beginning, which means you won't have to endure endless hours of figuring out how to remove an unwanted feature from your machine. Choosing a custom install doesn't mean you're limited to the features you choose at the outset, you can always add features later. You can summarize the need to use custom installs like this:

Manufacturers make adding features easy; removing them later can be difficult or impossible.

Some vendors will insist that you install everything in an effort to get you to try their product. However, they'll install product features in modules, making it relatively easy to remove a single module when you no longer need it. If the software doesn't provide a custom-installation option, all you need to do is find the desired entry in the Add/Remove Programs applet in the Windows Control Panel and remove it. Unfortunately, this option doesn't always work as intended. Even the best uninstall program for Windows usually leaves bits and pieces of the program behind. For example, you may find that the program folder stays in place. Hidden pieces of the program may include registry entries that the program leaves behind. (The registry is a Windows database that contains hardware and software settings, along with your personal preferences.)

Manually removing pieces of a program that you don't want is an error-prone process best left to the experts. I've repaired many systems where users thought they had correctly removed a piece of an application, only to find the system wouldn't boot later.

Forcing an Uninstall—*Some Windows features are installed automatically and there's little chance of getting rid of them short of major surgery. For example, many people see Internet Explorer as unnecessary and unwelcome if they want to use another browser. Unfortunately, Microsoft doesn't give you any choice about installing this feature; even if you remove the browser, there are still a lot of Internet Explorer files lurking on your hard drive and running while you work with Windows. This particular problem has annoyed so many people that there's a brisk third-party market devoted to removing Internet Explorer from your machine. While I can't recommend using these products, because they could make your system unstable, they do produce noticeable results in both improved system performance and reduced use of resources. (One product, 98lite,* http://98lite.net/98lite.html, *produces exceptional results, provides several configuration options, and appears to be well supported.) The point is that you can force an Internet Explorer uninstall without having to figure out which files and registry entries to change yourself. You can find out more about the 98lite product. The bigger picture is that other Web sites show how to remove other Windows features. Use these programs with caution, because the cure you're seeking for Windows feature bloat may be worse than the disease.*

There are two main causes of problems when removing individual pieces of an application. First, if the application makes registry entries where part of the program is supposed to start during the initial Windows setup and that piece is missing, Windows may freeze. Even if these registry entries don't affect the startup settings, they may affect some other area of Windows functionality like file associations. Second, many applications share dynamic link libraries (DLLs). Think of DLLs as a programmer's shortcut similar to using a packaged mix to bake a cake rather than starting from scratch. Removing a DLL needed by another application means that application can't start. If this DLL is used by a startup application, your system may not boot properly (or at all).

Using the System Configuration Utility

Fortunately, there are ways to disable pieces of a program that you don't want to start automatically—at least if you have Windows 98 or Millennium installed on your system. You can use the System Configuration utility to change the startup configuration. Accessing this application is easy; just select Start|Run to display the Run dialog box, type MSConfig in the Open field, and then click OK. The System Configuration utility will start and you'll see a System Configuration Utility dialog box like the one shown in Figure 6.1.

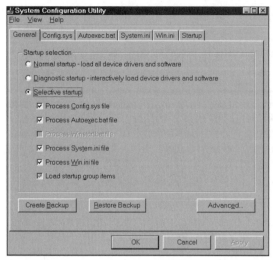

Figure 6.1: The MSConfig utility allows you to make changes to the way your system starts up.

The options on the General tab are important, because they determine which boot configuration is affected by changes you make on other tabs. System Configuration automatically chooses the current boot configuration when you start it. So, if you're currently in Safe mode, you'll see the Diagnostic startup option selected. Notice that this dialog box also allows you to create and restore backups of your current setup. Making a backup is important if you want to be sure that you can return to your original configuration if necessary. System Configuration doesn't just affect the Windows startup features, but affects those found in AUTOEXEC.BAT and CONFIG.SYS as well. AUTOEXEC.BAT and CONFIG.SYS are two files used to configure DOS and add device support that may affect Windows 9x installations. You may need to edit them to allow DOS games to run under any version of Windows 9x or to provide certain types of device support like Personal Computer Memory Card International Association (PCMCIA) with older versions of Windows 9x. For now, all you need to worry about is the Startup tab shown in Figure 6.2.

As you can see, the Startup tab contains a list of applications that run when Windows starts up. You can stop an application from running by clearing the check box next to that application's name. Clearing the name won't remove the application from the startup list; it just prevents the application from running. If you later discover that you need that application for some important work on your system, you can reopen MSConfig and check the item again. Rebooting your system will start the application for you.

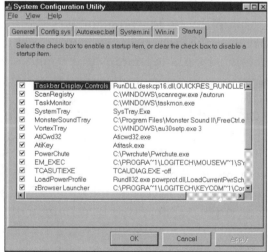

Figure 6.2: Use the Startup Tab to modify your configuration.

Since these settings won't remove the application permanently, you can experiment a little. Even if your system won't start at all, you can start it in Safe mode, choose Selective startup on the General tab, check the item you need on the Startup tab, and restart in Normal mode to fix the problem.

Another area you'll want to look for performance robbing automatic startups

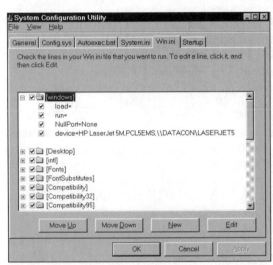

appears under the Win.ini tab shown in Figure 6.3. Open the [windows] folder and you'll see two lines; one says run= and the other says load=. In most cases, these two lines are blank as shown in Figure 6.3, because they're used by old 16-bit Windows applications. However, it doesn't hurt to check for entries. If you do see entries on this line, verify that you actually need the applications and then determine whether there are newer 32-bit versions of the product available. In many cases, a simple update will garner a noticeable improvement in system performance.

Figure 6.3: The Win.ini tab normally won't contain any entries you need to worry about, but it pays to check anyway.

Windows Applications You Can Live Without

So far we've looked at techniques for keeping your system lean and for getting it back into shape when a vendor thwarts your initial efforts. This leads me to the initial question for this section. Which Windows applications can you do without? The answer to that question depends on your networking needs. The following list contains the list of applications that I normally look at carefully. If you choose to perform a custom installation, you can select or deselect each of these items during the initial installation process and avoid the space-consuming DLLs they install.

Accessibility—Unless you have a disability or need to use the Accessibility features for productivity reasons, it's best to keep this feature off your machine. While I do find features like MouseKeys handy when creating a precise drawing, normally the features simply drain system resources and provide nothing in return. All of the accessibility features monitor the keyboard and other peripherals in an endless loop the entire time you have them activated, making this one of the more consistent performance drains on a Windows system.

Briefcase—The Briefcase allows you to move items from your desktop machine, work on them at home, and then update the items on your desktop machine the next morning. The good thing about this feature is that updates occur with a single click of your mouse, rather than one file at a time.

Decorations—This entry refers to all of the decorations that Windows will allow you to install—everything from wallpaper to themes. Any decoration you add to a workstation will use up resources. Wallpaper uses memory within the display adapter and requires additional storage space on disk. Sounds use system resources when played and hard drive storage as well. There's nothing wrong with installing decorations; but it pays to be aware of the cost of using them.

Dial-Up Server—Many small business owners want access to their work machine from home. The dial-up server provides this access through a local connection, rather than relying on the Internet. The advantage is that you don't have to worry quite as much about security breaches—most crackers are looking for easy Internet connections to break into. Of course, since this feature has to constantly monitor the phone line, it does incur a performance penalty, so you'll want to restrict installation to one or two machines.

Games—Whether games fall into the entertainment or time wasting category is a topic of much speculation—one that I won't get involved with here. The games provided with Windows are of minimal value and don't take up a lot of disk space. None of them executes automatically, so they won't use any system resources until you manually start them. However, the effect of games on the most precious resource of all, the humans running the computer, can be devastating.

Imaging—This application allows you to view images and work with a scanner. In most cases, you'll install this utility only if there's a scanner attached to your machine and you don't like the features for the capture program that comes with the scanner. In short, this is one utility that most users will want to avoid.

Internet Connection Sharing—A lot of companies need to share a single phone line for all Internet needs. Using ICS means that all the workstations (clients) will send Internet requests to the single workstation (server) that has ICS enabled. Of course, the network and server will both take a performance hit because ICS is constantly polling for requests and there's two-way communication between client and server that normally won't happen if each workstation uses a separate modem line. ICS has the advantage of saving money, because the network only needs one phone line and one modem. In addition, it's easier to secure one entry point to the network than one entry point for each workstation.

Microsoft Chat—You can use this program to talk with a buddy over an Internet connection. It doesn't offer all of the features of NetMeeting, but it's smaller in size and definitely kinder to system resources. Of course, you have to ask whether you'll actually talk with someone over the Internet. Most small business won't need anything more than an e-mail program.

NetMeeting—This is an excellent program for collaboration with other people over the Internet or even a local intranet. I've also used it as a teaching aid. The whiteboard gives me a place to write down items I want a student to remember and the ability to watch what the other person is doing without having two people crowd around the same computer is a real plus. Unfortunately, this program is better used by large corporations than small companies. It definitely requires a lot of bandwidth and system resources, so it's an option that many small companies will want to avoid.

Personal Web Server—There are only two purposes for installing PWS. The first is to allow developers to test their Web applications locally before distributing them on the network. The second is to allow a small company to create an intranet. The problem with the second use is that few small companies really need an intranet—at least if they're small enough to make PWS worthwhile to use. The server and network both experience a performance loss if you install this feature.

Virtual Private Networking—We'll talk about this feature in detail in Chapter 11, *Communicating Over the Internet*. Most small companies will want to install this feature after the main network has been running for a while and is stable. Attempting to install VPN as part of the initial installation causes problems in most cases. It's also important to realize that VPN incurs a relatively high performance hit because it has to constantly monitor the client system.

Web-Based Enterprise Management—A corporation can be spread over a large physical area, making it difficult for a network administrator to monitor the network's status. WBEM is what's known as a client-side agent that allows a network administrator to perform monitoring and administrative tasks from a remote location. The client will experience a performance loss, because WBEM remains active the entire time it's installed. There are few, if any, reasons to install this feature on a small company network.

Windows Scripting Host—One way to make your working environment more responsive and flexible is to use scripts that automate certain tasks. WSH is the primary method to accomplish this under Windows. However, WSH has also been partly responsible for some of the e-mail virus break-ins experienced by users of programs like Outlook Express. While a power user will probably benefit from this utility, you'll want to keep it off novice users' machines.

Network Features You Should Check

The networking features provided by Windows are often hidden beneath layers of terminology that many people don't understand. As a result, many users blindly accept the features that Windows installs by default and never question whether they're paying the ultimate price in performance-robbing feature overkill. Here's something you should always remember about a Windows network installation:

> *Microsoft assumes a worst-case network scenario and that users know nothing about their network, so Microsoft often installs a feature even if people will never use it.*

It's important to remember that Microsoft uses a corporate mindset when deciding what to install on your machine. This corporate mindset dictates some odd behavior for the home or small-office network user. For example, Windows promotes the use of more than one network protocol in many situations when only one protocol is needed. Those extra protocols use resources that you could

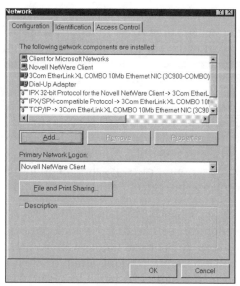

Figure 6.4: A typical Network Neighborhood setup for a small network.

Figure 6.5: The File and Print Sharing dialog box allows you to choose what level of sharing to support on an individual machine.

easily use for other purposes. To give you an example of how many features get installed, take a look at the Network dialog box shown in Figure 6.4. (You access this dialog box by right-clicking Network Neighborhood, and choosing Properties from the shortcut menu.) These are all of the things Microsoft would install for a network with a NetWare file server and a peer-to-peer configuration for other resources (a typical setup for many smaller companies).

There are a lot of ways to optimize this setup to allow your network to operate more efficiently with fewer resources. For one thing, if you tell Windows that you want to share resources with other computers, it almost always interprets that statement to mean both a printer and disk drive. Click File and Print Sharing (see Figure 6.4) and you'll see a File and Print Sharing dialog box like the one shown in Figure 6.5. Checking both boxes when you only need to share either the printer or disk drive wastes resources. Make sure these check boxes are set according to the resources that you'll actually make available to other people.

Another potential problem is the number of networking elements that you have installed on your system. Windows actually uses four different networking elements to create a complete network configuration. The following list describes each element.

Client—The part of the network installation the user sees. This element allows a user to interact with the network and provides services like printer access.

Adapter—A device driver used to access a physical device like an NIC (network interface card). If you don't have an adapter installed, Windows can't see the device.

Protocol—Essentially a set of rules for communicating on the network. A protocol describes how to package information for transmission and what limitations a client will have to obey when working with those packages. Think of a protocol as the rules two diplomats (a client and a server computer) use to negotiate a treaty (the data packet).

Service—A network-specific application. For example, sharing your hard drive with other users requires a special server application. Clients request data from the server and the server makes it available to them. NetWare Directory Service (NDS) access is also provided through a service.

Windows assumes that NetWare will always use a special protocol known as IPX for communication, even though NetWare 5 allows use of the IP protocol used by Windows and the Internet. Setting NetWare up to use IP and then installing only one protocol (IP) on your workstations, will result in a significant performance boost.

Dial-Up Network Security Concerns—*Figure 6.6 shows one of the security issues that most people don't know about. Notice that the unchecked item is the File and printer sharing for Microsoft Networks service. Since this is the dial-up adapter, you don't want this service checked. Leaving the service checked would make it possible for others to break into your network. Unfortunately, Microsoft checks this binding by default, so you have to clear it manually. As you can see, there are many reasons to check the bindings for the network elements installed on your machines.*

In some cases, the client provided with Windows is more efficient than alternatives provided by vendors. For example, the Novell NetWare Client shown in Figure 6.4 is less efficient than the standard Windows counterpart. The reason I installed the Novell NetWare Client, in this case was because the machine in question was used to administer the network. In this case, functionality overruled the need for efficiency. You may find yourself in a similar situation. There are times when you must choose the increased functionality of one client over the efficiency provided by another. We'll talk about the Novell NetWare Client more in Chapter 7, *Working With NetWare*. Installing a client isn't the end of the process in some cases. Every client can be configured for use. Microsoft assumes that you want every client to have access to every protocol installed on the machine. In addition, Windows normally installs separate clients for every adapter installed on the machine. The result is a relatively long list of clients, adapters, and protocols for even a small network setup. You can enhance performance, ensuring that the clients, protocols, and adapters are matched up. For example, the NetWare client should be matched up with either the IP or the IPX protocol and the NIC attached to the network. The NetWare client doesn't require both IP and IPX protocol access. In addition, you wouldn't want to provide a NetWare client access to the dial-up adapter. Unfortunately, Windows creates all these connections whether you need them or not.

There's a simple way to fix the problem. Figure 6.6 shows the Bindings tab of the TCP/IP protocol associated with the dial-up adapter. A binding is a connection between two networking elements. Clearing the check mark from one of the boxes in this dialog box will remove the connection between two elements. If the connection doesn't exist, Windows won't spend time trying to service it, and your machine will operate more efficiently, while providing the same level of service it always has.

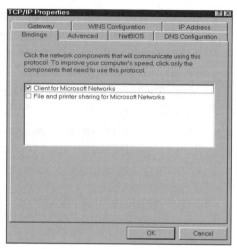

Figure 6.6: Changing the bindings for a network to match actual system requirements will improve performance.

Domains and Other Esoteric Terms

It's not surprising that computer users often get lost in the abyss of jargon they have to endure. Sometimes the terminology makes little or no sense to the user and any explanation by the network administrator sounds like so many words in a foreign tongue. Some people just don't understand geek speak and, in many cases, there isn't any reason to ask them to.

But I'll need to explain a few terms that you might not be familiar with in this chapter. You can always look in the Glossary for an explanation of a term you don't understand.

One of the terms you'll hear quite often is node. A *node* is any individual element on the network that has a network address. Workstations and servers are always nodes. Printers with a NIC installed are usually nodes as well. Think of a node as you would a stopping point along a path. Any device that can create and interpret network signals directly is a node.

The second term is *domain*. A domain is a part of a network controlled by a single computer or set of computers. Think of a domain as you would a kingdom. The king (primary domain controller) is in charge of the domain. He doesn't have charge of other domains—just this one. The king may have assistants (backup domain controllers) to help him manage the domain, but for the most part, he's the head guy.

All of the workstations in the domain are like the serfs in a kingdom. They have to ask permission to join the domain from a domain controller. It doesn't matter whether the primary or backup domain controller responds to the request—all the workstation needs is permission from someone. The domain controller monitors every workstation activity as soon as the workstation joins the domain that it controls.

A network may have more than one domain if it's large enough, just like the world has more than one kingdom. However, most small businesses will need just one domain and it's unlikely that a home-office network will ever require more than one domain (if it requires a domain at all). The important thing to remember is that you don't have to set up a domain when working with Windows; there are other options. Unfortunately, the way the Windows setup process works, you may think that a domain is required. We'll talk about this problem in detail in the "Performing the Installation" section later in this chapter.

Sometimes a network is small enough that it doesn't require a domain at all. Most home networks fall into this category. If you have fewer than ten machines, you don't need a domain unless you need to provide some special level of control for the system. In most cases, a small network is best served by a workgroup, not a domain.

Another term that you'll hear is *workgroup*, which would seem to be just another form of domain to many people. A workgroup is another way to define a group of computers on a network, but this is a group of peers. Some networks use workgroups to make up the "small towns" within the domain. So, a group of peers form the town (workgroup), but their allegiance is to the king in the castle (domain).

Installing Windows, the Short Version

There are a lot of books on the market with detailed instructions on installing Windows. You'll find everything from the low-level details of creating batch files for corporate setups to simple instructions for a standalone machine. Corporations often use batch files that contain automated answers to installation programs; in some cases, the batch file is replaced with a script that performs work like custom configuration by user job title in addition to providing simple answers. In addition to all of these other sources, Microsoft provides Windows setup instructions online that you can use:

Windows 95
http://msdn.microsoft.com/library/winresource/dnwin95/S61EA.htm

Windows 98
http://www.microsoft.com/TechNet/win98/Reskit/Part1/wrkc02.asp

Windows NT
http://www.microsoft.com/TechNet/winnt/ntwrkstn/Manuals/start/xsh05.asp

Windows 2000 Professional
http://www.microsoft.com/TechNet/win2000/win2kpro/manuals/progs/pgsch02.asp

Windows 2000 Server
http://www.microsoft.com/TechNet/win2000/win2ksrv/manuals/srvgs/sgsch04.asp

Windows 2000 Advanced Server
http://www.microsoft.com/TechNet/win2000/win2ksrv/manuals/asgs/agsch04.asp

I'm not going to repeat that vast wealth of information in this chapter. We're going to take the broad view of Windows installations instead. I'll also provide a short set of installation instructions in plain English, rather than in geek speak. The emphasis of the following sections is to get the installation done quickly, with the least amount of trouble, yet create an installation that's efficient and resource friendly.

There are two topics we'll look at in the following sections. First, We'll talk about the types of installation you can perform. In most cases, I recommend that you use the custom installation option, because it provides the greatest flexibility, a real plus since the other options are targeted at the needs of large corporations. Second, we'll look at the installation itself—not a blow-by-blow procedure, but a set of steps that tells you why each part of the installation is important and how you can optimize choices for your network.

Choosing an Installation Method

One of the installation elements that you need to think about before you get involved with the installation procedure is the type of installation you want to perform. Microsoft provides four different installation methods as shown here:

Typical Setup—This is the default setup. It installs a standard set of options for your machine. Of course, this means you'll end up with a lot of features that you don't need unless your company is one of the fortunate few that fit within Microsoft's profile.

Portable Setup—Use this setup if you're using a laptop or notebook computer. It installs a minimal set of standard utility programs—the same set included with the Compact Setup option. This installation also includes all the special utilities that Windows provides for portable computers, such as the Briefcase and Direct Cable Connection features. This is a good setup if you have a laptop and you don't mind having a few extra features installed. For the most part, Microsoft did a good job of keeping feature creep to a minimum in this installation option.

Compact Setup—This is the option to use if you're really tight on hard disk space. It installs only the bare essentials—perhaps a little too bare for many users. The nice thing about using this particular option is that you can get a minimal system started and then add other features as you need them. If you don't want to perform a custom installation on a desktop computer, this is the option to choose.

Custom Setup—The custom option provides the most flexibility of all the Setup options. It also requires the greatest amount of time to set up. This is the perfect option for those who already have a good idea of what they do and don't want out of Windows. It's the option that I always recommend to home and small-office network users because it's the only option that allows them to tailor Windows to their needs.

Performing the Installation

This section is intended as a broad overview of what you'll see during the installation procedure. Each step is a point along the installation procedure, although not necessarily in the order that you'll actually see them during installation. I've annotated each step to tell you why it's important and what kinds of problems you should look out for when completing it. The point of this section is to help you get a good installation that will work the first time you try it. These tips will also help you create an efficient setup that will allow your machine to work at its maximum capacity (or at least close to the limit).

1. Start the Setup program. You can do this in a number of ways. One way is to place the CD-ROM in the drive with your current version of Windows running and allow Setup to start automatically. Windows NT and Windows 2000 installers can place the CD-ROM in the drive and reboot their machine. The OS should be detected during system startup and you'll have the option to boot directly to the CD-ROM instead of the hard drive. Opening a command window or booting MS-DOS will allow you to start setup manually by typing the appropriate setup command at the command prompt. This method has the added advantage of allowing you to specify command-line switches that are described in the following section, "Using Command Line Switches."

2. Once you get past the initial Welcome dialog box, Setup performs some hardware checks. The number and intensity of hardware checks depends on which version of Windows you want to install and the type of hardware you own. In some cases, Setup will freeze during the hardware-checking process. Make sure you give it plenty of time to complete. If the process has

definitely stopped, however, you can reboot your machine and start Setup again using one of the command-line switches that stop hardware checks. I talk about these switches in the following section, "Using Command-Line Switches."

3. Once the hardware checks are successfully completed, Setup may display a message saying that it's installing a Setup Wizard. When Setup Wizard installation is complete, Setup displays a licensing agreement and asks you to agree to its terms. If you decide you don't like the terms, you can exit setup. At this point, you should follow the prompts and answer questions as asked. You'll eventually come to an installation type selection dialog box. This is your first real chance to customize the setup of your machine. The earlier "Choosing an Installation Method" section of this chapter described these choices and the tradeoffs you'll make by selecting them.

4. Select one of the installation types. You'll see some additional prompts. For example, Windows may ask you to enter your name and the name of your company. Answer the questions and proceed from one dialog box to the next. If you chose to perform a custom install, you'll eventually see a component selection dialog box. I talked about the various features that require special care in the "Windows Applications You Can Live Without" section early in the chapter.

5. Once you select the Windows-specific utilities and applications you want to install, Setup may copy some files to disk. It will probably perform some additional hardware inspection during this process and load some device drivers. Setup will eventually ask about your network setup. It presents a list of optional network features you can install. I discussed many of these features as part of the "Network Features You Should Check" section earlier in the chapter. Make sure you choose the options you need and not the ones that look interesting.

6. At this point, the customization process is essentially complete. You'll need to provide some additional input about your network and some of the options that you chose to install. Just follow the prompts and the installation process will eventually complete. Of course, you'll probably have to reboot your machine a few times while completing the installation process.

Using Command-Line Switches

A command-line switch is a bit of text you can add to an application name at the DOS command prompt. It's important to separate each command-line switch with a space so that DOS doesn't get confused. You access the DOS command prompt by selecting MS-DOS Prompt or Command Prompt from the Start menu, or by booting DOS directly. The command-line switch modifies the behavior of the application in some way.

Let's look at some of the Setup command-line switches. They'll help you get around any problems you might experience while installing Windows. For example, some computers might freeze when Setup tries to perform a disk scan, so you can use the /IQ or /IS switch to get around the problem. The following is a complete list of these switches for all versions of Windows; not every version supports every switch. You can determine which switches a particular version supports by typing SETUP /? or WINNT /? at the command prompt. When you see something between angle brackets in the list, it means that you have to supply a value of some kind. The description will tell you what to provide. Don't type the angle brackets when you type the switch. Likewise, square brackets tell you about optional information. You don't have to provide the information; but doing so provides more precise information to Setup. If you don't provide a value, Setup uses a default value. As with the angle brackets, you don't type the square brackets as part of the command-line switch information.

/?—Use this switch to display a list of currently documented command-line switches.

/A—The /A switch enables the Accessibility Options so that you can use the accessibility features during installation.

/B—This switch performs a floppyless installation of Windows. You use this option if you want to install Windows on a diskless workstation. You must use the /S switch with this switch to tell Windows where to find the files it needs. You'll also want to use the /B switch if you're going to install over the network.

/C—Use this switch to prevent Setup from loading the SmartDrive disk cache. Using this option slows your installation but ensures that everything gets written to disk immediately. About the only time you'd need this switch is when SmartDrive proves to be incompatible with your system.

/D—The /D switch helps you get around situations in which one or more of your Windows support files are missing or corrupted and Setup can't run properly. It tells Setup not to use the existing copy of Windows for the initial phase of the setup. As soon as the new Windows support files are copied to your drive, Setup switches back to a Windows interface.

/E—The /E switch allows you to execute a command at the end of the graphical part of the setup. For example, you might want to run a batch file that installs additional applications or performs some type of system configuration. The installation of Windows is complete when this switch takes effect.

/F—This switch tells the installation program to copy the files to the floppy disk without verifying them afterward. You can save a little time during the installation process by using this switch. Of course, the downside to using this switch is that you have no way of knowing whether the floppy disks were created successfully.

/I[:<*INF filename*>]—This switch creates a new INF file and provides its name. Normally, the installation program uses DOSNET.INF to provide a list of installation file locations. The default file assumes that you'll install Windows from a local drive. Obviously, that won't work over a network. Use a copy of DOSNET.INF as a template for your INF file.

/ID—Setup doesn't check for the required disk space when you use this switch. I can't think of any time when you'd want to use it. If your system is that short on hard disk space, you should consider clearing additional space before you try to install Windows.

/IE—If you're performing an unattended install, you probably won't want to create an emergency startup disk for the machine. This switch allows you to skip the screen that starts the emergency startup disk creation process.

/IL—This option loads a special Logitech Mouse driver for you during the setup process. Use this option if you have a Logitech Series C mouse.

/IM—There are situations when Setup might freeze while checking your system's memory. This switch allows you to disable that check.

/IN—You may not want the Setup program to set your network up immediately. If that's the case, use this switch to start the installation without the network setup module.

/IQ or /IS—Use this switch to bypass ScanDisk as the first step of the installation process when performing the installation from MS-DOS. It's not a good idea to skip this step unless your system experiences some kind of problem running ScanDisk with Setup running. Be sure to do a separate scan of your drives before beginning setup if you use this switch.

/IV—If you don't want to see the Microsoft advertisements during an installation, you can use this switch to turn them off. Essentially, this switch will turn off any billboards that Setup displays.

/L—/L creates a log file that lists any problems that Setup encounters while installing the operating system. The name of the log varies by Windows version. For example, when installing Windows NT or Windows 2000, the log file is named $WINNT.LOG.

/NR—Use this switch to skip the registry check. This option comes in handy if you suspect that there are corruption problems with your registry or you simply don't want to take the time to conduct the check.

/O—/O creates a set of boot floppy disks, but doesn't actually install Windows. This option is only used with Windows NT and Windows 2000.

/OX—This switch forces the installation program to create the boot floppy disks automatically. Unlike the /O switch, this switch does start the installation process.

/R:<*directory*> or **/RX:<*directory*>**—This switch copies an optional directory from the Windows CD-ROM. You could use this feature to copy one of the optional directories, such as Internet server, from your CD-ROM or the network to your machine's hard drive. You can also use this feature to install one of the other platforms on your server.

/S[:<*source path*>]—This switch tells Windows to use a specific source path for its installation files. That source path can include a local drive or the universal naming convention (UNC) network drive (such as //SERVER/SOURCE). The installation program assumes that you want to use the current directory if you don't specify this parameter.

/T:<Temporary Directory>—This switch enables you to tell Windows which drive to use as a temporary directory. It normally tries to use the drive you're using for installation. If the drive you chose is short on space, however, you can use this switch to redirect installation-specific items to another drive. Make absolutely certain that any temporary directory you select is empty. The Windows setup program erases the contents of any temporary directory that you select.

/U[:<*script file*>]—This switch performs an unattended installation using a script file. You must use the /S switch with this option.

/UDF:<*ID*>[, <*UDF name*>]—This switch allows you to override the basic installation question answers provided in a script file using the /U switch. You'll need to supply an ID that tells which answers in a Uniqueness Database File you want to use to override the basic script. In short, you can create a generic script file that works with all installations and specify it using the /U switch, and then provide specific answers for this particular installation using the /UDF switch.

/X—/X starts a standard installation that uses floppy disks but doesn't actually create them. You'd use this switch in cases where you had already created the boot floppy disks during a previous installation. This is a Windows NT and Windows 2000 specific switch.

<Batch>—This option enables you to use MSBATCH.INF or another batch file that contains custom installation instructions.

Fixing Installation Errors

At some point, you'll get Windows installed and the Setup program will proclaim that all has gone as expected. That's when you'll figure out that the network isn't accessible, some of your devices don't work, or a Windows feature isn't working right. While Windows is indeed installed, it may be unusable or unstable when Setup is finished.

The preparatory steps we covered in Chapters 3, *Designing a Standard Network*, and 4, *Connections Require Software*, help you avoid many installation problems, but may not help you avoid them all. Fortunately, Microsoft products have gotten more robust over the years and the number of problems you'll see should be small. The following sections provide some ideas about how you can fix the most common Windows problems. We'll talk about the three most common problems:

- Device failures
- Network accessibility
- Missing or non-working Windows features

Device Doesn't Work

One of the most common problems that you'll face when installing Windows is that one or more of the devices won't work. In some cases, the device isn't recognized, while in others one or more device features are missing. The following list outlines the common causes of these problems in the order you should check them:

1. **No device driver**—Windows requires a device driver to recognize a device. Hardware has changed dramatically over the years, so if you have an older version of Windows there's a good chance newer hardware won't be recognized. In addition, while Microsoft does solicit drivers from all major manufacturers, there are situations when a driver isn't available until long after the release of Windows, which means the driver will be unavailable during the initial installation.

2. **Incorrect device detection**—Detecting a device may prove difficult if the vendor provides too few clues or the device looks like a clone of another device. If a device is detected incorrectly, there's a good chance that it may not work at all. Even if the device does work, you'll find that it doesn't provide the same level of functionality that a correctly detected device will. For example, a display adapter that has a television tuner feature may still display data on screen, but may not allow you to watch your favorite program.

3. **Setting conflicts**—Newer hardware seldom experiences this problem, because it's designed to automatically select settings that aren't in use by other devices. Older hardware requires manual changes to the settings. If you have an older device that requires manual settings, the user manual for the device normally tells you how to set it up. This problem can also happen if you overload your machine with too many devices. The presence of an empty slot doesn't necessarily mean that your computer has the resources to support another device.

4. **Device incorrectly installed**—Expansion cards have to be firmly seated in their slots whereas hard drives require good connections through their

cables before Windows will see the device. If I think a device may not be seated correctly, I check the display that most computers present when they start. This display contains a list of the devices that the computer is installing. If the device that I'm looking for is missing from the list, I open the computer and see whether anything looks out of place. In many cases, you can simply reseat the card or cable by pulling it out and pushing it back into place. Vibration can loosen both cards and cables, so they can look like they're installed, but may not be making good contact.

5. **Device conflicts**—Some devices don't get along with each other. On one machine that I worked with, the decoder card for the DVD drive and the sound card didn't like each other. I found that if I opened the machine and installed the driver for the DVD's decoder card first and then installed the driver for the sound card, everything worked fine. In most cases, you'll need to call the vendor for information like this. Make sure you get instructions about how to fix the problem before you start pulling things out and putting them back together.

We talked about several other ways to fix problems with hardware throughout the book. For example, Chapter 5, *Cabling and Other Masses of Wire*, contains a complete overview of cabling and NICs (network interface cards). The important thing to remember is that hardware normally lends itself to logical troubleshooting. Try one change at a time, restart the computer, and see whether the change fixes the problem. In many cases, it pays to turn the power off, count to three, and then turn it back on after you make a change. (Be sure to shut Windows down properly.) Turning the power off clears the memory and resets the device. Simply restarting Windows might not be enough to ensure the changes you made will actually show up when you reboot the machine.

Network Isn't Accessible

The first thing you should look for if you're having networking problems is the Network Neighborhood icon on the desktop. If you don't have a Network Neighborhood icon on the desktop, it means that networking support wasn't installed, most likely because Windows didn't detect the NIC installed in your machine. Right-click My Computer, select Properties from the shortcut menu, and click the Device Manager tab. You'll see a list of devices, including a NIC, like the one highlighted in Figure 6.7. Notice that there are two entries in the Network adapters folder—the second is the modem installed in my machine. The moment you set up a dial-up Internet connection through a modem, Windows adds this second network adapter entry.

Figure 6.7: Windows needs to recognize your NIC before it will install network support.

You still may not have access to the network even though the Network Neighborhood icon appears on screen. Earlier in the "Network Features You Should Check" section of this chapter, I talked about the various network elements you need to make contact with the network: client, protocol, and adapter. If you can't access the network after a Windows installation, you need to check for these three elements in the Network Properties dialog box shown in Figure 6.4. It's important to have the same protocol and client installed that the other machines on the network use. So, if you're working with a peer-to-peer network, you'll most likely need the Client for Microsoft Networks, TCP/IP (or other suitable) protocol, and an adapter.

Another problem with network access is identification. Click the Identification tab in the Network Properties dialog box and you'll see three identification fields like the ones shown in Figure 6.8. The two important fields are Computer name and Workgroup. The Computer name field has to be unique. If you use the same name as someone else, there will be a conflict and you won't be able to use the network. The Workgroup field has to be the same one that everyone else uses. Otherwise, you'll belong to your own private workgroup and won't be able to access the other resources on the network.

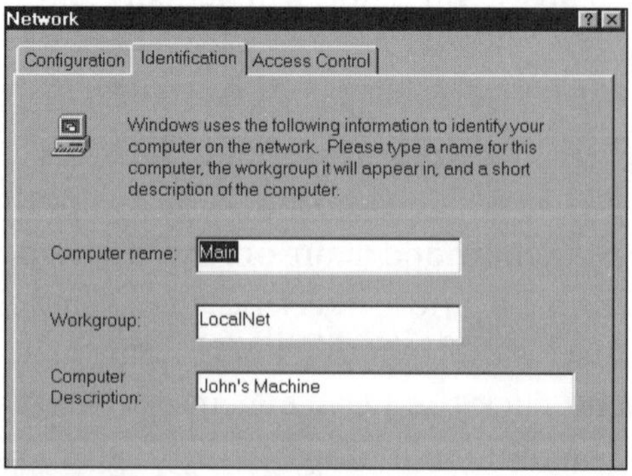

Many of the clients will have configuration options that determine where you connect on the network. For example, the Client for Microsoft Networks contains an entry like the one shown in Figure 6.9. If you belong to a Windows NT or Windows 2000 domain, it's important to provide the correct domain name in the Windows NT domain field and to check Log on to Windows NT domain. Likewise, the

Figure 6.8: The Identification tab of the Network Properties dialog box will allow you to identify yourself to other computers.

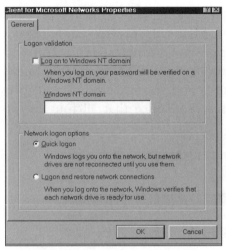

Figure 6.9: Make sure you check clients for identification information that's required when logging onto other networks.

NetWare client will ask for the name of the server, or NDS tree and context.

The final check you should make is server security. If you don't have proper access to the server, the server may not even show up in Network Neighborhood. Make sure you provide a user account and the correct access rights for everyone on the network.

Windows Feature Doesn't Work

There are a lot of reasons that a particular Windows feature might not work, but relatively few things you can do to fix these problems. Of course, the biggest problem is determining when a Windows feature stopped working. Most people don't try every Windows feature immediately after installation. Unfortunately, adding applications and devices after an installation can cause a Windows feature to stop working because of conflicts between Windows and the device or application. In this case, you'll need to do some detective work to find the problem. We'll discuss these after installation problems in Chapter 14, *First Aid for the Network*.

Finding the reason for a broken feature right after installation is somewhat easier than finding one after you've been using Windows for a while, because you haven't corrupted the environment. There are also some unique methods you can use to find the problem—methods that may not work after Windows has been running for a while. Here are three common causes of feature failure immediately after an installation:

- The feature isn't supported with your hardware setup.
- The feature didn't get installed.
- A momentary system glitch caused application or DLL corruption.

Microsoft provides README files and a wealth of other sources on the **Microsoft Windows** Web site http://www.microsoft.com/windows/ to determine whether your hardware provides the support required for a particular feature. You can also check for hardware specific information using **Microsoft.com Search** http://search.microsoft.com/us/SearchMS25.asp. For example, you can't use the CD Player if your system lacks either a CD-ROM drive or a sound card.

Even if you have the required hardware, a feature may not work if Microsoft hasn't approved it for use with Windows. Microsoft provides a hardware compatibility list that you can check at http://www.microsoft.com/hcl/. All you need to do is tell the search engine which vendor you're looking for (or choose "All Products" if you haven't selected a vendor) and select a product category. Figure 6.10 shows the results of a typical search. Notice that all four of the current Windows versions are listed.

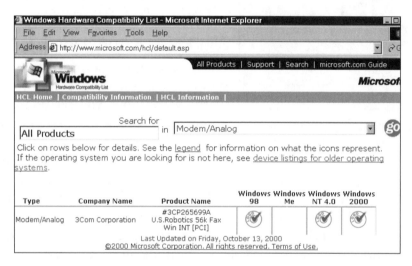

Figure 6.10: Check the Windows Hardware Compatibility List to ensure the device you want to buy is supported by the operating system.

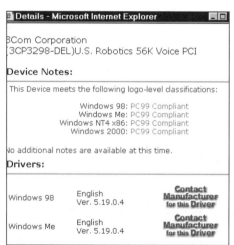

If you want details about a particular product, click it. The Windows Hardware Compatibility List Web site provides a Details window like the one shown in Figure 6.11. The Details window tells you what level of testing the device has passed and where you can get the latest drivers for it. By visiting the Windows Hardware Compatibility Web site, you can learn whether a device will work with the installed Windows feature set, how compatible the device is, and where you can get drivers to ensure the device will work as anticipated. All three of these items assure you that the Windows features you

Figure 6.11: Use the Details window to determine how compatible a device is and where you can get new drivers for it.

install will work as expected. After all, without the proper hardware, you can't expect much from the software.

Of course, you must install a feature before you can use it. You can always check the current list of installed Windows features using the Add/Remove Programs applet in the Control Panel. A special section of this applet shows which Windows features are installed. Figure 6.12 shows the dialog box for Windows 98. Windows NT uses a similar setup, while Windows 2000 uses a separate dialog box that you access through the Add/Remove Windows Components button in the Add/Remove Programs applet. In all cases, you'll see a checklist of features like the one shown in Figure 6.12. Checking the feature installs it on your computer.

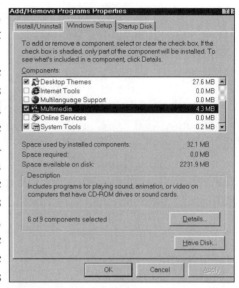

Figure 6.12: You can use this special dialog in the Add/Remove Programs applet to check whether a feature is installed.

It's possible to get a bad install during the initial Windows installation. A glitch could corrupt a DLL or a registry entry might not get made. These problems aren't frequent and usually won't repeat themselves unless your system has a problem. Still you should check for this problem and not assume you got a good install.

A feature that you installed may not work simply because it was installed incorrectly or the installation got damaged. You can reverse this situation by removing the check mark from the feature's box in the Add/Remove Programs applet (see Figure 6.12), restarting your machine, and then checking the option again to reinstall it. The reason you want to restart your machine between uninstalling and reinstalling the failed feature is to ensure any bad DLLs are removed from memory. Even though Windows won't tell you to restart the machine, this step is necessary to ensure you don't keep repeating the bad install. If reinstalling the feature doesn't work, you'll need to use the in-depth troubleshooting procedures found in Chapter 14.

Adding Devices

Windows makes adding new devices to either workstations or servers relatively painless in most cases. You'll need to turn your machine off, install the new hardware, and restart Windows. If Windows directly supports the device (see the Windows Hardware Compatibility List Web site information in the preceding section of this chapter), it automatically detects the new hardware and installs it for you. On the other hand, if the hardware is new and Windows recognizes it, you'll be asked for a vendor device driver disk. Inserting the disk and telling Windows the location of the disk are all you usually need to do to complete the device installation.

In two special cases, adding a device isn't this easy. The first is when Windows doesn't recognize the device. For example, if you plug a scanner into the serial port of your machine, Windows is unlikely to recognize this device. Normally, the vendor-supplied setup disk compensates for this lack of recognition. Make sure you read the vendor documentation before you install the device drivers on your machine. You'll find that the vast majority of the vendors provide a Setup program on a floppy or CD-ROM that you start using the Start|Run command in Windows. Once you run the Setup program, you normally have to reboot the system to gain full access to the device.

The second special case is when the default Windows driver doesn't provide all of the functionality that you want. In this case, you'll need to right-click My Computer and choose Properties from the shortcut menu. Select the Device Manager tab (see Figure 6.7); highlight the device entry in question, and then click Properties. Choose the Driver tab of the device's Properties dialog box and you'll see a display like the one in Figure 6.13. Click Update Driver and follow the prompts to update the driver.

Using the automatic search feature is a good idea when updating your driver because the Windows driver may be newer than the one on your vendor-supplied CD-ROM or floppy. Of course, you may still want to use the vendor-supplied utilities, even if the device driver is slightly older. In this case, it's a good idea to check the vendor site for a newer driver first, because that's where Microsoft most likely got the new device driver for Windows. You may have to perform a manual install by selecting Display a list of all the drivers in a specific location, so you can select the driver you want. Windows will display an Update Device Driver Wizard dialog box like the one

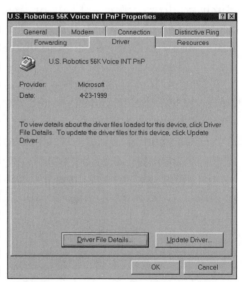

Figure 6.13: Updating a device driver will allow you to use vendor-specific files and utilities.

shown in Figure 6.14. Clicking Have Disk allows you to choose a device driver from any location on your local machine or the network. This is the option you should use to force Windows to use a specific device driver.

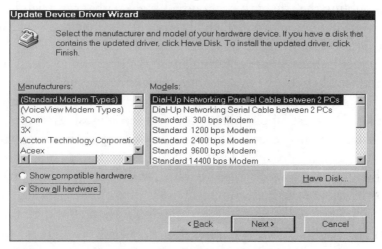

Figure 6.14: Click Have Disk if you want to force Windows to use a specific device driver setup file.

Installing Server Applications

Installing a server application is much like installing a desktop application—only larger. (It's generally more complex and affects more people.) Of course, it's the "larger" part that concerns most people. Server applications tend to require more setup steps, because they're accessed by more than one person. Whenever you have clients accessing a server, there are issues you need to resolve including the following:

- User access
- Security
- Resource usage
- Resource sharing

Most server application installations begin like desktop applications. You use Setup on the server application's floppy or CD-ROM to place files on the server. However, during the installation process, the server application may need information from you like where to store log files and what directory to use for data.

The installation decisions you make affect the performance and reliability of the server application. For example, it's common to use two separate drives on the server for database applications when two or more drives are available. The first drive contains the database's data, while the second contains log and application files. Using this two-drive approach enhances performance by increasing drive throughput. (You're using two channels to store data—effectively doubling the size of the data pipe.) It also enhances reliability because the logs and the data are stored separately. A failure of one drive will still allow you to recover the current database transactions in most cases.

As part of the installation or post installation configuration process, the server application asks which users can access the program. The users who can access the application are given certain rights apart from the rights they normally enjoy on the server. Database applications can become almost as complex as the operating system in this regard. They usually include their own security that works with the security provided by the OS. Users end up passing through two security checkpoints to access the data they need. You can make these checkpoints invisible to users through careful setup, but any crackers who gain access to the network will still see the second application checkpoint.

You may have more than one application installed on your server. So, it's important to ensure that each application has access to system resources. You need to decide which resources the application can access and how much they can use of that resource. For example, when working with Internet Information Server, you need to decide how much network bandwidth each Web server can use. This is called bandwidth throttling; but the idea is the same as any resource usage decision—limiting the amount of resources that any one application can use. Otherwise, user requests to one Web server may prevent another Web server from receiving any requests at all. We'll talk more about performance in Chapter 13, *Performance Issues*.

CHAPTER SEVEN

Working With NetWare

Sitting next to my desk is a Novell NetWare server. So far, it's been chugging away for the last three years without complaining, requiring a restart, or attracting much attention for that matter. I just keep feeding it files, cleaning out its directories from time to time, backing up its data, and checking it for problems when necessary. In short, my server has been beyond reliable, and I plan to keep it for a long time to come. I rely on my NetWare server to protect precious resources like my word processing files and to ensure I can gain access to a printer when needed. Overall, it sounds like my server has a mundane existence, but it's also something that the server has been good at for a long time.

You may wonder whether you need to install a NetWare server on your network. If you require an extremely reliable and efficient server to hold your documents and manage your printer, NetWare is probably one of the better choices out there.

Some people have wondered recently whether NetWare's days are numbered in light of all of the advances Microsoft has made with Windows 2000. The answer is quite simple when you consider how much a NetWare server can do with antiquated equipment that Windows 2000 won't even consider running on. Accessing my NetWare server is like accessing a local drive, for the most part, and it's running on a 133 MHz Pentium machine that I originally used as a workstation. Contrast this to the delayed file access I normally get from my Windows 2000 server and you'll quickly understand why NetWare is a good choice if all you need is file sharing and printer support. (The Windows 2000 server is running on a dual processor 450 MHz Pentium machine.)

Of course, Windows 2000 does have a nice GUI. It's the Hollywood version of the server; all it needs is a toothy smile to complete the picture. NetWare still relies on a character-mode interface (the GUI supplied with NetWare 5 is a bad joke someone played on Novell), so some people find it difficult to use. This is especially true of people who have spent their entire time working with Windows. NetWare is a challenge to use until you learn what the various commands can do for you. The one failing that would prevent people from using NetWare for their file server needs is the ease-of-use problem.

Installing NetWare can be tricky as well. There are quite a few places where you can easily get lost while installing this product and you can't easily correct the mistakes. Even I have had to start an installation from scratch after a failed installation attempt. Finding your mistake isn't always that easy either. However, if you figure out which features you want in advance, installing NetWare can be as easy as installing any other operating system.

We're going to look at some of the reasons that you should consider this operating system, especially if you're on a budget and don't have a lot of time to baby-sit a sick server. The following sections will tell you about the promise of NetWare and areas where it falls down on the job. I'm also going to help you get over the learning curve a bit by showing you how to perform some common tasks. For example, we'll talk about some of the options you have when installing and configuring printers. We'll also look at some of the special needs of NetWare servers when it comes to maintenance. (For general maintenance, read the "Maintenance Tasks You Can't Ignore" section of Chapter 9, *Network Administration Made Simple*.)

Why Do You Need NetWare?

One of the first serious network operating systems (NOSs) for the PC was NetWare. At the time, it was enough that NetWare provided printer and file support in a secure environment; but today people expect a lot more from a NOS than that. The file and printer support options are easy to come by now even in a peer-to-peer network setup. Security is a little more difficult to find, but small-office networks can typically get by with less security than corporate networks can. While Windows 9x isn't a good choice for networking needs, Windows 2000 Professional probably provides all that you require.

So, why use NetWare at all? For some companies, the question remains unanswered; but there are good reasons for many people to use NetWare. Novell has tried to make NetWare jump through hoops it was never designed it to jump through, mainly due to pressure from other vendors like Microsoft. In the process, they've managed to muddy the waters and dilute the features that NetWare has to offer. This section will help clear up the issue for the home-office and small-business user. It's important to understand that NetWare provides incredibly useful features at a low cost in terms of maintenance and equipment requirements. In today's computing environment, NetWare is the hidden gem that's waiting for discovery by you. There are four areas in which NetWare is considered the best of class, including the following:

- File management
- Printer management
- Directory services
- Security

I don't know of too many organizations that can get by without some type of file storage. We all produce documents and those documents require protection. The best feature of NetWare is that it does an amazingly good job of storing and retrieving files with an efficiency that continues to surprise me today. The part of the picture that many organizations fail to recognize is that you gain centralized file storage when you have a server set up for the purpose. You don't have to wait for users to start their machine in the morning to become productive, as you would when using a peer-to-peer network. Centralized storage was one of the reasons that professionals chose NetWare in the past, and it's still a good reason to select it today. However, the important issue is that you get this centralized storage at an extremely low cost compared to Windows 2000 Server.

Most professionals recognize NetWare Directory Services (NDS) as the best directory service available today. A directory service is essentially a large database that contains all of the information required to run the network, including user, server, and peripheral device data. The fact that NDS is available for many platforms, including Windows, makes it an even better choice for your network-management needs, because you can use one tool to do everything. The depth of information that NDS can store attracts many professionals. You could literally use NDS to replace your contact information database and never notice the difference.

Printers are a common item on any network, but NetWare provides more options for managing printers than most NOSs do. We'll talk about printing later in the "NetWare and Printers" section of this chapter. You'll also find that NetWare's security features offer many choices not found in other NOSs. We'll talk about these features in Chapter 8, *Network Security Essentials*. Of course, NetWare has more than just these four items to offer. You can also use it for the following purposes (many other large-corporation features aren't included in this list):

- Web server
- Database management platform
- General network services like DNS and DHCP

The Web server supplied with older versions of NetWare 5 is Netscape's Fastrack Server for NetWare. According to **Netscape's Product Support** Web page (http://www.netscape.com/products/), **iPlanet** (http://www.iplanet.com/) now provides support for the Fastrack server. Newer versions of NetWare 5 used

IBM's Websphere (http://www-4.ibm.com/software/webservers/). No matter which version of Novell's Web server you use, it doesn't provide all of the bells and whistles of Microsoft's Internet Information Server (IIS). It's an adequate Web server for an intranet or a small online Web site, but IIS still provides better Web management and the Apache server provides the most reliable support. NetWare is a good choice if you want to use a single server for all of your needs, but not the best choice if you're looking specifically for a Web server.

Unlike any other NOS on the market today, NetWare comes with a copy of **Oracle 8** (http://www.oracle.com/database/oracle8/) as part of the package. (You'll find the latest version of Oracle at the **Oracle 8i** Web site http://www.oracle.com/ip/deploy/database/8i/.) Professional developers generally acknowledge Oracle as an industrial strength database management system (DBMS) and, until recently, it held many speed records for processing data. The performance features of NetWare make Oracle 8 run faster than SQL Server on Windows 2000 in many situations when both servers have the same hardware. Of course, there's the problem of NetWare's character mode interface to consider. Some people find that using it negates some of the performance boost they would normally receive from NetWare.

Obviously, you don't have to use the DBMS that comes with NetWare; you can choose from many others. Here are a few of the DBMSs to consider if Oracle 8 doesn't meet your needs:

Advantage Database Server
http://www.advantagedatabase.com/products/adsserver/

Centura SQLBase
http://www.centurasoft.com/products/databases/sqlbase/

GP Solutions Seek Database Manager
http://www.gpsonline.com/

Inprise/Borland InterBase
http://www.borland.com/interbase/

Pervasive.SQL 2000 Server
http://www.pervasive.com/products/psql/psql_servengine/

Sybase SQL Server
http://www.sybase.com/

NetWare comes with many of the same add-on features that you'd expect from any modern NOS. You can use it as a domain name system (DNS) server and a dynamic host configuration protocol (DHCP) server. A DNS server will translate server names like www.microsoft.com into an IP address; whereas the DHCP server assigns IP addresses to clients that request one. We'll discuss many of these features in the "NetWare Features You Need to Know About" section that follows. The important consideration is that most NOSs install all of these features whether you want them or not. NetWare takes a bare-bones approach that allows you to install the features if you want, but doesn't assume that you want to do so. This bare-bones approach is one of the reasons that NetWare performs so well and is so reliable.

There are currently three versions of NetWare in use: NetWare 3.2, NetWare 4.2, and NetWare 5.1. Each version has different features, with NetWare 5.1 being the most complex. You'll find updates and patches for all three versions at the **Novell Support** Web site (http://support.novell.com/). Novell plans to discontinue the NetWare 3.2 version, but the precise date isn't known as of this writing. Interestingly enough, you can still buy all three versions of NetWare and additional licenses to upgrade existing installations at general consumer outlets like **CDW** (http://www.cdw.com/).

NetWare Versus Windows—*When it comes to NOSs, most people narrow the choice down to NetWare or Windows. (While Linux is an extremely good product, many people view it as a NOS for Web sites, not for a LAN.) There are feature differences, and if you need a feature provided by only one of these two NOSs, the choice is an easy one. Otherwise, the choice comes down to two factors. First is ease of use. Windows wins the ease-of-use battle. Novell's GUI is a complete failure, and I'd advise you to avoid it when possible. The second factor is the amount it costs to build and operate the network. NetWare wins in several ways in this arena. It's reliable to the extreme, doesn't require expensive hardware, provides easy-to-use remote management, and uses network resources extremely efficiently. The only area where you'll spend more money with NetWare is when an administrator needs to make the rare foray into the network room and use the character mode console.*

NetWare Features You Need to Know About

NetWare provides a vast number of features, yet many people know only about a few of them, and some people assume that NetWare only provides file server features. In most cases, NetWare provides all of the features required for a small network, even if you need to provide some level of Internet connectivity. You can find out more about specific versions of NetWare at these sites:

NetWare 3.x

http://www.novell.com/products/netware3/

NetWare 4.x

http://www.novell.com/products/netware4/

NetWare 5.x
http://www.novell.com/products/netware/

We've talked about many of the more important features that NetWare provides in the previous section, "Why Do You Need NetWare?" NetWare also includes many features that you may not think about right away. For example, it includes full lightweight directory access protocol (LDAP) support. LDAP is essential for allowing access to NDS information through a TCP/IP connection—the basis for communication on the Internet. In addition to LDAP, NDS Catalog Services allows an administrator to store NDS data in a local database, greatly improving data access speeds.

Like most modern NOSs, NetWare provides access to standardized security. It includes both secure socket layer (SSL) and public-key infrastructure (PKI) support. SSL allows you to send documents in an encrypted format over the Internet; PKI provides the means to issue certificates used for positive identification. The combination of SSL and PKI ensures that data sent over a public network like the Internet remains safe. Of course, all of these privacy measures aren't any good unless you can encrypt them. NetWare also provides Novell International Cryptographic Infrastructure (NICI), which is the set of modules used to encrypt the keys and documents. Novell designed NICI to provide the highest level of encryption allowed by local governments.

There are a lot of other features we haven't covered, but each of the product-specific Web sites listed in this section provides detailed information you can use to make a decision about which version of NetWare to buy. In addition to the features that we've talked about in this section, Novell also offers a lot of add-on products for NetWare. You'll find a list of add-on products at http://www.novell.com/products/. Most of these add-ons will enhance an existing NetWare feature, increase the server's reliability, or provide a new feature like the GroupWise program that allows people in large companies to remain in contact with each other.

Installing NetWare: the Short Version

Many books on the market give detailed instructions for installing NetWare. In fact, authors specifically target most of these books toward people who need to pass their Certified NetWare Engineer (CNE) exams, so they're quite detailed. Novell also makes a lot of its documentation available online in PDF format. You'll find everything from the low-level details of installing your file server to adding resources like printers. Here's where you'll find some of the documentation for specific versions of NetWare:

NetWare 3.x

http://www.novell.com/documentation/lg/nw312/docui/

NetWare 4.11

http://www.novell.com/documentation/lg/nw4/docui/

NetWare 4.2

http://www.novell.com/documentation/lg/nw42/docui/

NetWare 5

http://www.novell.com/documentation/lg/nw5/docui/

NetWare 5.1

http://www.novell.com/documentation/lg/nw51/docui/

You'll also find that Novell provides detailed documentation support of all its other products. Figure 7.1 provides you with some idea of just how detailed the documentation is.

I'm not going to repeat that vast wealth of information in this chapter. I'm going to take the broad view of NetWare installations instead. I'll also provide a short set of installation instructions in plain English, rather than in geek speak. The emphasis of this section is to get the installation done quickly, with the least amount of trouble, yet create an installation that's efficient and resource friendly.

As previously mentioned, NetWare doesn't provide as much automation as Windows does during the installation process. This means you need to do a little more planning and spend time figuring out choices as the installation proceeds. It's

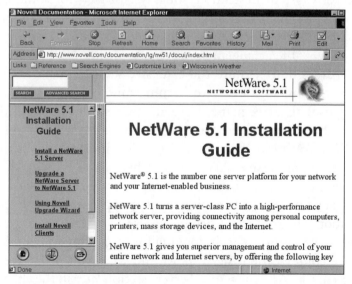

Figure 7.1: Novell provides detailed documentation for all of its products online.

unlikely that you could perform an automated NetWare installation; but then again, there's little reason to do so for a small business since you'll have one server to set up in most cases. You can divide a basic NetWare installation into four parts:

- Pre-installation planning
- NOS installation
- Adding users
- Setting security

The sections that follow look at all four of these basic requirements. In addition to these basic requirements, you may need to install additional NetWare features or set up peripheral devices as separate installation steps. For example, if you attach an uninterruptible power supply (UPS) to your server (a good idea), you'll need to install the UPS software as a separate step. NetWare won't automatically detect the device and install software for you.

Novell to Discontinue NetWare 3.x—*The following sections assume that you're using NetWare 4.x or 5.x. Since Novell is discontinuing NetWare 3.x, I decided not to cover installation for that version of the NOS. The NetWare 3.x version uses an older organizational database known as the bindery that isn't as flexible as NDS. The installation this chapter talks about relies on NDS to make your job easier.*

Pre-Installation Concerns

NetWare has a extremely robust and flexible directory service. NDS allows you to configure your system in a variety of ways. In fact, for some people, NDS almost provides too much flexibility—there's little in the way of structure for a novice to follow. So, the first step in preparing to set up a NetWare server is to plan the *NDS tree*—the arrangement of objects within NDS.

Small companies don't require the extensive setup that Novell recommends for large corporations, so it's easy to become mired in too much detail. Every NDS tree begins with a tree name. I usually use a short version of the company name followed by the word tree. So, ABC Corporation would have a tree name of ABC_TREE. You need the tree name to log into the server, so it pays to choose something unique and easy to remember.

Right below the tree name is the beginning of the tree itself—the *root*. Novell uses the unique name [Root] to define the very top of the tree. Every NDS tree has just one root. The root is the beginning of the NDS tree context. A context tells NDS where you want to begin looking for something in the tree. The better you define the context, the easier it is to find what you need. We'll talk more about contexts in the "Accessing Your Server" section later in the chapter. For right now, all you need to know is that the [Root] part of the context is always present, so you don't have to specify it unless you want to begin a search at the root.

The last required part of the NDS tree is the organization object. Some large companies have a myriad of organization names, each of which requires an *organization object*. Small companies will have a single organization object (unless you really do own more than one company). I normally use the name of the company as the organization object name. So, ABC Corporation would have an organization object name of ABC_CORP. Again, you want to make this easy to remember because you need it to log onto the server later.

Depending on the size of your company, you may want to add organizational units below the organization object in the NDS tree. However, unless you have formal departments, it's usually a good idea to skip this step. Every level you add to the NDS tree adds complexity to your network. In a large company, this added complexity is outweighed by the need to organize users and resources on the network. In a small company setup, additional levels add complexity and make things hard to manage without providing any benefit.

At this point, you'll want to make a list of resources like printers and users for your network. It pays to have all of the required configuration information on hand before you begin the installation process. NetWare automatically adds some NDS objects for you, so you don't need to record them as part of your pre-installation planning. For example, NetWare will automatically add any storage devices like hard drives that you configure for your server. The same will hold true for any device that NetWare detects automatically during installation— you'll see these devices as the installation progresses. It pays to look through the NDS tree after installation and see which NDS objects NetWare automatically adds. If you find that you need additional objects, create a list and obtain full information for the objects before you begin creating them.

One additional pre-installation concern is grouping the users into easily managed units for security purposes. NetWare makes heavy use of groups to allow you to manage entire groups of users with a single change to the group object. (Windows provides this same capability, but not to the same degree that NetWare does.) You'll want to decide in advance which users will receive what rights. Novell doesn't provide any predefined groups and only one user named "admin." We'll see how groups work in the "Adding Users" section later in this chapter.

The server also requires some pre-installation setup. If the server you choose can boot CD-ROMs, the server setup will be easy. Simply place the CD-ROM marked Operating System in the drive, boot the machine, and follow the instructions.

If your server doesn't have a bootable CD-ROM drive, you'll need a copy of DOS to boot the server. Fortunately, Novell provides almost everything you need. The License floppy contains the following:

DOS 7—This is the version of DOS marketed by Novell.

FDISK—A utility you can use to create a partition on the hard drive.

EDIT—A text editor you can use to create files.

FORMAT—A utility you can use to format the hard drive and transfer the DOS operating system to it.

NWCDEX—This application installs an extension that allows DOS to recognize your CD-ROM drive after you install the appropriate driver.

Don't modify the License disk in any way. Using it to boot your server and format the hard drive is fine; but having a separate copy of DOS is a much better idea. You'll use FDISK to create a DOS partition of at least 50 MB. FDISK will ask you to reboot after you create the partition so that DOS can see it. After you create the partition, type FORMAT C: /S and press Enter at the DOS prompt. This will make the hard drive bootable. Remove the floppy from the drive and reboot the server again—it should boot from the hard drive. Once you can boot the server to DOS, you'll need to set it up so that you can access the CD-ROM drive. This means adding a device driver statement to CONFIG.SYS, and an NWCDEX or MSCDEX statement to AUTOEXEC.BAT. Consult your CD-ROM drive owner's manual for details on how to create the required files. Boot the server a third time to install the CD-ROM device driver and activate the DOS extensions for it. Make certain that your server can access the CD-ROM drive or you won't be able to read the NetWare Operating System CD-ROM.

The last pre-installation requirement depends on the version of NetWare that you're installing—you need to follow the steps in the Network Preparation section of the user manual. If this is a new installation, there won't be much to do. You'll need to know how to add licenses to your NetWare setup, but that's about it. Make sure you quickly scan the detailed installation instructions as well. If you spot anything that looks completely unfamiliar, spend some time learning about it before you install. The quick installation procedure in plain English in the next section should help a lot in this regard. You'll also want to keep this thought in mind:

You can't prepare too much for a NetWare installation if you want success.

Performing the Installation

This section looks at some generalized steps that you can take to install NetWare. We'll be talking about areas where you can customize the installation as the procedure progresses. The procedure assumes that you've already taken care of the prerequisites discussed in the preceding "Pre-Installation Concerns" section and are ready to start the installation.

I'm assuming that you'll be installing a new server since that requires more work than an upgrade will. The upgrade choice automatically answers some of the questions for you, so you can still follow this guide—just ignore the questions Install doesn't ask. Here are the essential steps you'll take to install a NetWare 4.x or NetWare 5.x server (some steps may vary in order by version):

1. Allow the installation procedure to start automatically if you have a system that will boot from the CD-ROM drive. Otherwise, configure your machine to boot from the C: drive. Change to the CD-ROM drive. Type INSTALL and press Enter to start the installation. The NetWare installation program, Install, will perform several checks of your system. You may see a few prompts. For example, Install will ask you to choose an installation language. Eventually, you'll reach a license agreement dialog box.

2. Select Accept License Agreement and press Enter. The next dialog asks about the DOS partition on your hard drive.

Maintaining a DOS Partition—*Always retain your DOS partition. This will allow you to place a DOS-based maintenance program on your server's hard drive. You should run diagnostics on your NetWare server, just as you would any other machine on the network. The DOS partition also makes it possible for you to work with the server without starting NetWare after a reboot.*

---

3. Choose the Continue with Existing Partition option and press Enter. You'll see an installation-type selection screen. There's a choice between upgrading an existing server or installing a new one (the default). If you press F2 at the installation type selection screen, you can modify advanced settings such as the server's ID number, whether the server automatically starts after a reboot, and the server's SET parameters. (SET parameters affect settings for some types of device drivers.)

4. Press Enter to create a new server and continue the setup. Install will ask for country, code page, and keyboard information. This country-specific information will determine what language NetWare uses to display prompts and how it reacts to your keyboard.

NetWare 4.x Versus NetWare 5.x Display Modes—*NetWare 4.x doesn't require a high-resolution monitor, nor do you need a mouse. In fact, save your money and get something cheap for a monitor and display adapter. NetWare 5.x benefits from both. Even though most of the work at the console is done with the same character mode screen Novell provided in the past, NetWare 5.x does include the X Server — Graphical Console. Working with this new feature without a high-resolution display and a mouse is difficult (not as bad as Windows, but definitely not like working with the character-mode console).*

---

5. Change the country, code page, and keyboard information if necessary. Highlight Continue, and then press Enter to continue the installation. You'll see a dialog box that asks you to select a display resolution and mouse type.

6. Choose the mouse and display settings that match your machine; then select Continue and press Enter. Install will begin copying files to the server hard drive. After a while, you'll notice that Install is detecting your storage devices. You'll then see a dialog box that lists your storage adapter devices and allows you to install support for platform support modules and PCI Hot Plug support modules. NetWare always requires a storage adapter device entry—this is the driver used for the IDE or SCSI host adapter in your server. Platform support modules provide speed advantages when your server has more than one processor or some other special feature. There are three possible platform support module choices: NetWare automatically detects this entry for you, the vendor will supply one, or you don't need to worry about it. The PCI Hot Plug support module is for computers that allow removal of permanent storage devices like hard drives while the computer is running. If your server doesn't have this feature, you won't need to worry about this entry.

7. Verify that the storage adapter driver options are correct and add any required platform or Hot Plug support. Choose Continue in the Options group and press Enter. Install will perform some additional device detection and then display a list of storage device and NIC drivers.

8. Verify that the storage device and NIC driver options are correct. Press Enter to continue. At this point, Install will ask for volume SYS parameters. Normally, the default volume SYS setup works just fine.

NetWare and Volume SYS—*Volume SYS is the main hard drive on every NetWare server—you must have a volume SYS for NetWare to run. The volume SYS parameters will include the size of the partition as a whole, the amount of space you want to devote to hot fix, and the result data space. Hot fix is an automatic repair capability that detects bad spots on the hard drive and moves data in those areas to other locations.*

---

9. Press Enter to continue the installation. Install will add some more drivers to the system. After this, Install will mount volume SYS and any CD-ROM drives installed on the system. Install will begin to copy files to the SYS volume once all of the drivers are loaded. Eventually, you'll see NetWare 5's new graphical user interface (GUI) named X Server — Graphical Console (don't confuse this with ConsoleOne, which gets loaded within the X Server environment). At this point, your mouse should be active. If the mouse isn't at the port you specified or you don't want to use a mouse, the first dialog you see will tell you how to move around the display using the

keyboard. Clear the dialog box once you understand the instructions. The first task you'll need to do is give your server a name.

10. Type a name for your server. I'm going to use my company name, DataCon, for example purposes, but you could use any name you want.

11. Click Next. You'll see a Configure File System dialog box. You can add more hard drives, configure new partitions, and perform other storage-related tasks at this point.

NetWare 5.x Storage Types—*NetWare 5.x supports two different types of storage: traditional and NetWare Storage System (NSS). You'll use NSS to manage large volumes—larger than most small businesses will have. There are also problems with NSS because it doesn't support data migration, data duplexing, disk mirroring, disk striping, file compression, transaction tracking, File Transfer Protocol (FTP), VREPAIR, Network File System (NFS), or file name locks. In addition, NSS uses up more resources than a traditional NetWare volume will. Let's just say you give up a lot to use NSS— most small-business users should stick with the traditional NetWare volume.*

---

12. Click Next. You'll see a Protocols dialog box. There are four ways you can configure protocols for NetWare. You can use IPX alone, IP alone, both IP and IPX, or IP with IPX compatibility. IPX is good if you want to gain the advantages of using this protocol—Novell created IPX to overcome problems with IP. The IP choice is good if you already need to use TCP/IP on your network to access other workstations in a peer-to-peer network setup, or if you need to access the Internet through a central connection. Novell designed the IP with IPX compatibility selection for large companies that may have older workstations they need to upgrade to IP. Never choose this option because it wastes resources and slows network response time. Likewise, the IP and IPX option is designed for mixed protocol environments, something you should avoid in a small company network setup.

13. Configure the server's NIC to use IP or IPX as its protocol. Click Next. You'll see a Time Zone dialog box. Large corporations have to ensure the time settings are correct on their servers, because they may have servers spread across several times zone. Time synchronization is important to keep all of the servers communicating properly. A single server setup doesn't have such critical time constraints. It's still a good idea to get the time and time zone correct.

14. After you set the time, click Next. You'll see an NDS Install dialog box. Since we're working with a single server network, select Create a new NDS tree.

15. Click Next. You'll see the NDS dialog box. Enter the tree name, the organization (context) name, and the administrator's name, context, and password.

16. Type the appropriate values into each field; then click Next. The example server uses DATACON_TREE for the tree name, O=DataCon_Svcs for

the server object context (the organization object), and O=DataCon_Svcs for the administrator context. The next dialog box will show you an NDS summary. Make sure you copy this information down to make it easier to configure the client later.

17. Click Next. You'll see a Licenses dialog box. Insert the license floppy in the server's floppy drive.

18. Click Next. Install will load the file server and user licenses for your server. Once the license is loaded, you'll see an Additional Products and Services dialog box. In most cases, you'll want to get your server running and install additional products and services later. At this point, you'll see one or more dialog boxes asking about the services and summarizing what you selected. Click Next at each of the dialog boxes unless you want to install a service or additional product.

19. Click Finish. You'll see a variety of dialog boxes as Install analyzes your system and installation choices and then copies the appropriate files to the SYS volume. Once Install copies all of the required files, it will ask to reboot your updated server.

20. Click Yes. The server will reboot. Once the server is running, you'll be able to start configuring it.

At this point, you've probably had your fill of installing NetWare. Yes, it's a long procedure and Novell could make it easier. However, I've reformatted my hard drive and reinstalled Windows at least twice a year for the last three years on each of my five Windows machines. I installed NetWare only once in that entire time.

Adding Users

Installing NetWare is the hard part of the process. Once you complete the installation, performing tasks like adding users is much easier. You'll need to have access to your server before you can add any users. The "Accessing Your Server" section later in this chapter tells you how to install the Novell client. You must have the Novell client installed on any machine that you want to use for administration purposes. The Microsoft client that comes with Windows is designed to allow you to access the NetWare server, but doesn't provide the features required when managing one. That's one of the reasons that the Microsoft client costs you less in terms of performance and resource usage. The Microsoft client will work fine on any non-network administrator workstation. When you manage a NetWare network, all of your work will take place in the NetWare Administrator application (NWADMN32.EXE) found in the \PUBLIC\WIN32\ directory of your NetWare SYS volume.

There are several things to consider when you add a user. Here are the items we'll discuss in detail:

- Template use
- NDS tree placement
- User object creation technique

The first item to consider when adding a user is whether you want to use a template. NetWare allows you to define templates that will enter most user properties for you automatically. If you have a network with more than 20 people, it pays to define a template because it will save you time. Here are the steps you'll take to create a template (I'll assume you have NetWare Administrator running):

1. Right-click any Organization or Organizational Unit object in the NDS tree and select Create from the context menu. You'll see a New Object dialog box like the one shown in Figure 7.2. The contents of this dialog box will change according to your position in the NDS tree. For example, you can only create an Organization object at the [Root] node, so that's the only place you'll see the Organization entry in the New Object dialog box. The contents of this dialog box will also change as you add features to your NetWare server. For example, a third-party vendor may define additional objects for you to create.

Figure 7.2: The New Object dialog box contents will change to match your location in the NDS tree.

2. Highlight the Template entry in the list and click OK. You'll see a Create Template dialog box like the one shown in Figure 7.3. Notice that this dialog box allows you to use an existing template or user as the basis for the template you're about to create. The ability to nest templates allows you to create a general template that fits everyone's needs, and then refine it with other templates that meet specific needs.

3. Type a name for your template and decide whether you want to use an existing template or user as a guide for creating this one. Check Define additional pro-

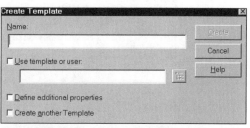

Figure 7.3: The Create Template dialog box allows you to define template properties.

perties if you want to finish defining the template now. Check Define another Template if you want to create more than one template at a time. Leaving both check boxes blank will return you to NetWare Administrator when you click Create. For a small business network you'll normally want to finish defining the template right away, so check Define additional properties.

4. Click Create. If you checked Define additional properties in the Create Template dialog box, you'll see a Template dialog box like the one shown in Figure 7.4. This dialog box allows you to define any parameters normally defined for every User object that relies on this template. So, you wouldn't add anything to the Identification or Postal Address tabs because everyone's identification and postal address is different. However, every other tab contains fields that many users will share. Of greatest concern for network administrators of small networks are the contents of the Login Restrictions, Password Restrictions, Login Time Restrictions, Login Script, and Group Membership tabs. The other tabs do contain useful entries, but Novell designed them for large network use.

5. Once you complete the Template dialog box entries, click OK. NetWare will save the new template for you.

The second User-object creation concern is where the user will be placed on the NDS tree. If your organization is small, you'll want to create the User object below the Organization object. However, if your organization has formal departments, you'll want to create Organizational Unit objects below the Organization object and place the users within their respective departments. The

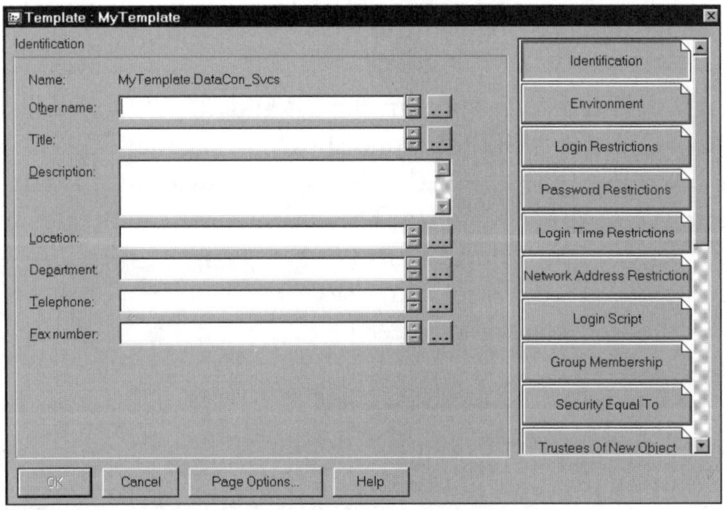

Figure 7.4: Define as many common user properties as you can using the template, but avoid properties that will change.

placement of the User object affects many facets of the user's interaction with the server, so correct placement is essential. For example, NetWare supports resource hiding by keeping users and resources for a particular department in one place. Users in other departments can't see the resources—only those in the department that owns the resource can see it. As a user's position changes in the NDS tree, logon parameters change as well. The users' logon context must match their context within the NDS tree. (We'll see how this works in the "Accessing Your Server" section later in the chapter.)

A third concern is how you create the User object. A small company may be able to rely on a template for almost every configuration concern. Larger companies will want to fill in user-specific information. This allows a network administrator to contact the user if necessary. You can also use this information as a contact database for the entire company (at least for personnel you authorize to see such information).

Let's create a User object. The following procedure is generic, just like the Template procedure earlier in this section.

1. Right-click the Organization or Organizational Unit object where you want to create the new User object and select Create. You'll see the New Object dialog box shown in Figure 7.5.

2. Highlight User and click OK. You'll see the Create User dialog box shown in Figure 7.5. Notice that this dialog box looks similar to the Template dialog box shown in Figure 7.4. However, the Create User dialog box also includes personal information like the user's name and home directory. A home directory is where the users begin their networking experience on the server. It's a place the user can store personal files.

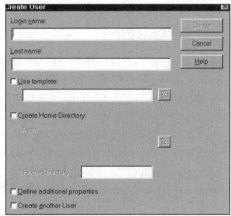

Figure 7.5: The Create User dialog box allows you to define user-specific information and perform setups based on templates.

3. Type the user's login name (normally the first name) and last name in the appropriate fields. Decide whether you want to use a template to create the new user object. In most cases, you'll check Create Home Directory and define a location on the server's hard drive for the user's personal files. Finally, you'll want to check Define additional properties unless the template contains all the required information or you want to create more than one user at a time. (You'll still need to define the user-specific properties later.)

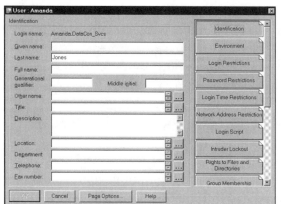

Figure 7.6: The User dialog box allows you to define all of the personal information for the user.

4. Click Create. You'll see a User dialog box like the one shown in Figure 7.6 if you checked Define additional properties in the Create user dialog box. Compare this dialog box to the template dialog box in Figure 7.4 and you'll see both differences and similarities. Look through the various tabs and you'll notice that NetWare made any template-defined property changes for you automatically. You'll still need to add any user-specific information manually.

5. Once you complete the User dialog box entries, click OK. NetWare will create the new user for you.

Setting Security

NetWare provides comprehensive security for its servers and many ways to change that security if you have the proper rights. The easiest methods of changing security is to use a data-based approach. Protect the data on your server and you won't need to worry too much about the individual user.

The traditional way to manage security on a NetWare server is to use NetWare Administrator. Right-click any object and select Details from the shortcut menu to see its Properties dialog box. If that object has security associated with it (and most do), you'll see a security tab. This tab will have different names depending on the object. For example, most data-related resource objects have a trustee tab. Click the security tab to see the security settings for that object. Figure 7.7 shows a portion of an NDS tree containing a disk drive. The disk drive uses a filing cabinet icon. Directories below the disk drive appear as green folders. Finally, files within a folder appear as white sheaves of paper.

Let's look at a directory security example in NetWare Administrator. I created a user named Amanda and

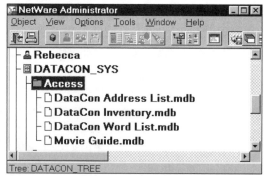

Figure 7.7: The NDS tree will contain a complete listing of each disk drive, directory, and file on your server.

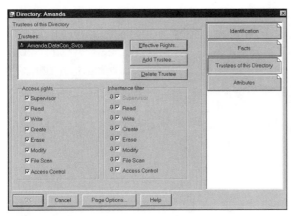

Figure 7.8: Amanda has complete rights to her home directory.

gave her a home directory of Amanda on the server's hard drive. Figure 7.8 shows the rights that NetWare assigned automatically to this directory. Notice that Amanda is the trustee of this directory and has complete rights to it as shown in the Access rights field. Amanda can do anything in her home directory.

Obviously, the network administrator also has rights to this directory as does anyone who has security equivalent to the network administrator. No one else can access the directory unless you give that person rights to do so using Add Trustee. Use Delete Trustee to remove rights to use a directory from an individual. If you don't want to remove complete access to the directory, you can always set specific rights using the Access rights field.

If you want to check the rights of other people to a directory, click Effective Rights. You'll see an Effective Rights dialog box. Click the NDS Tree button to display a list of users and groups on the server. Select a user or group and you'll see the list of effective rights change to match those of the selected individual or group.

You can always use NetWare Administrator to manage any aspect of the NDS tree. However, there may be times when you need to make a quick change and don't want to wait for NetWare Administrator to start up. If you have the Novell Client installed for Windows, you can also use Windows Explorer to set security on your server drives. Right-click the drive, directory, or file that you want to change and select Properties from the shortcut menu. Click NetWare Rights and you'll see a Properties dialog box like the one shown in Figure 7.9.

The upper pane contains a list of all of the current trustees for this object. The middle pane contains a list of the users

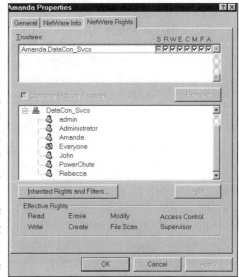

Figure 7.9: Windows Explorer provides another way to manage your NetWare drives, directories, and files if you have the right client installed.

and groups on the server. Finally, the lower pane has a list of your rights to the object. You can assign a new trustee to an object by double-clicking the user's entry in the middle pane. Adding rights to the new trustee is as simple as checking the rights listed to the right of the trustee's name in the upper pane. If you want to remove a trustee, highlight the entry and click Remove. Any changes you make to the display won't take affect until you click OK or Apply. If you click Cancel, Windows forgets all of the changes—it doesn't send them to the server.

Accessing Your Server

Windows workstation users have the luxury of two clients to access a NetWare server. As previously mentioned the Microsoft client is lean and resource friendly, while the Novell client provides complete functionality. Most users will use the Microsoft client to keep resource usage on their machines minimal. On the other hand, all network administrators will require the Novell client. Windows will automatically detect the presence of a NetWare server and install the standard software. You can also install standard support manually using the Add button in the Network Properties dialog box (see Chapter 6, *Configuring Windows for Network Use,* for details).

Installing the Novell client requires that you first download the latest client (the one on your distribution CD-ROM is almost certainly out of date). Look at the Clients section of http://www.novell.com/download/ for a list of current clients. Once you download the client, you'll need to install it on the client machine. You may have to unzip the client file before you can run the Setup program it contains—WinZip (or another ZIP utility) will lead you through the process automatically. Here is a quick view of a typical Novell client installation.

1. Double-click the Setup file. Setup will display a licensing agreement.
2. Click Yes to accept the agreement. You'll see a dialog box with two installation choices. Like Microsoft, Novell assumes that everyone is a large corporation. You'll always want to use the Custom setup option so that you can choose just the features you need. The Novell client will use quite a few system resources even without bells and whistles added, so a custom installation is a must.
3. Click Next. You'll see a Protocol Preference dialog box like the one shown in Figure 7.10. Make sure you choose the protocol that matches your server setup. In most cases, a small business setup will use the IP only or IPX selections. Remember that IPX is the extended form of IP that provides more features that standard IP will, but that IP is the standard used by the Internet.

4. Choose a protocol, and then click Next. You'll see a Login Authenticator dialog box like the one shown in Figure 7.11. Most modern NetWare setups use NDS. However, don't allow the dialog box to fool you. Some network administrators continue to use bindery emulation even with NetWare 4.x and NetWare 5.x. If your server uses a bindery (a must with

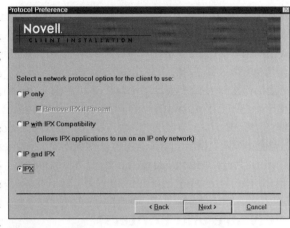

Figure 7.10: Make a protocol selection based on your server's setup.

NetWare 3.x) or bindery emulation (an option for NetWare 4.x or NetWare 5.x), choose the Bindery option.

5. Choose an authenticator, and then click Next. You'll see an optional components dialog box like the one shown in Figure 7.11. This is where you can get into real trouble with feature creep. Most small networks won't need any of these options. Many of these options require special installations at the server as well as the client, so if you performed a plain vanilla installation like we did earlier in the chapter, you won't need any of these options.

6. Click Install. At this point, everything should happen automatically. Setup will use the selections you made to install the Novell client. Once the installation is complete, Setup will ask to reboot your machine.

Care and Feeding of a NetWare File Server

A NetWare file server requires little care other than normal machine maintenance. Of course, you'll want to keep the NDS tree cleared of old entries. When someone leaves the company, make sure you remove the related user object. Otherwise, you'll have gaps in the security net that NetWare provides. It's also

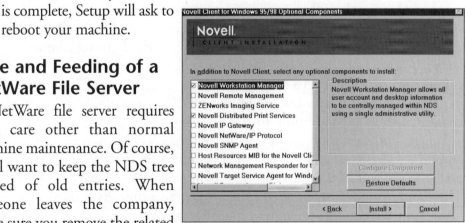

Figure 7.11: Be careful when choosing optional components—most small networks don't require any of them to operate.

important to keep the disks clear of old data and to archive information you won't use for a long time. However, you should perform these maintenance tasks with any server. We'll discuss any additional maintenance you should perform in Chapter 9, *Network Administration Made Simple*.

Novell is extremely proactive about releasing patches for problems found in the product. You should visit the **Novell Updates** Web site (http://support.novell.com/filefinder/) on a result basis to locate and download patches for your Novell products. The first question a support representative will ask when you call for support is if you've installed the latest patches for your system. This makes sense since the latest patch that Novell has released may fix the problem.

NetWare and Printers

One of the things that most professionals know NetWare for is its ability to handle printers in a way that's almost invisible to the end user. NetWare 5 provides several ways to manage printers, all of them effective in specific situations. Novell is going to try to tell you that Novell Distributed Print Services (NDPS) is the greatest thing since sliced bread. It is the greatest thing since sliced bread if you have a large network—but it's a network administrator's nightmare for small networks.

This section of the chapter is going to show you how to manage printers the traditional way. For the most part, this is the same method used from NetWare 3.x on. The only element that changed in NetWare 4.x is that the information was moved from the bindery to NDS.

Traditional NetWare printer management consists of three components: print server, printer, and print queue. The print server manages all of the print jobs submitted by clients. A printer object represents the printer physically connected to either the server or a client machine with an attached printer running a special application that allows the server to manage it. In some cases, it's much easier to connect printers directly to the server so that it can do double duty on a small network. Once your network grows beyond 20 workstations, you may want to consider setting a workstation up as a print server.

You'll add the three objects: Print Server (Non NDPS), Printer (Non NDPS), and Print Queue just as we added the User object in the "Adding Users" section earlier. Once you have these three objects in place, you'll need to connect them. The printer comes first, print queue second, and print server third.

Creating the connections is easy. Right-click a Printer object and select Details from the shortcut menu. Click Assignments and you'll see a Printer (Non NDPS) dialog box similar to the one shown in Figure 7.12 (this figure shows the print queue assignment already in place). Click Add. You'll see a Select Object

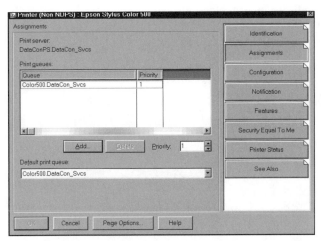

Figure 7.12: You'll choose print queue and print server assignments on the Assignments tab of a printer or print queue object.

dialog box. Select the print queue that you want to use, and then click OK. You'll see the print queue assignment add to the Queue list.

Now that we have the printer assigned to the print queue, let's assign a print server to the print queue. Right-click the Print Server (Non NDPS) object and select Details. Click Assignments. You'll need to add print queues to the Assignment tab, just as you added print queues earlier. When you add all of the print queues that you want the print server to service, click OK to close the Print Server (Non NDPS) dialog box and make the changes permanent. Reopen the Print Server (Non NDPS) dialog box and click Print Layout. Click Update so that the details of the print layout get updated. Your dialog box should show the relationship between print server, printer, and print queue. Figure 7.13 shows an example of what you'll see.

You need to perform one more task before you can start printing—load the print server. All you need to do is type LOAD PSERVER <Name of Print Server> at the NetWare server console. If you've set everything up correctly, the print server will start. You'll see the NetWare Print Server window appear on the server console screen with a status of Running near the top. The server is ready to print.

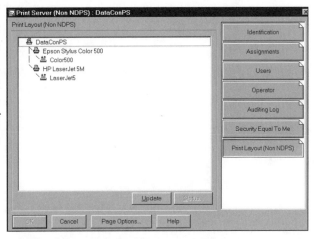

Figure 7.13: Make sure you have the printers connected correctly before you try to start the print server or send any print job to the NetWare server.

CHAPTER EIGHT

Network Security Essentials

Protecting computer systems in a hostile world is a problem that every network administrator has to deal with. Computer security of any kind is a hot topic today, because the risks continually increase seemingly faster than the tools designed to reduce those risks increase in complexity. It seems that every day some new vulnerability appears in a product that just about everyone uses, including you. A single machine is hard to take care of when crackers spend the majority of their time looking for holes in your defenses—keeping a network safe is just about impossible. In fact, many network professionals say that security is their number one problem for the following reasons:

- The number of security vulnerabilities at both the OS and application levels is increasing.
- The number of machines managed by a typical network administrator have increased dramatically.
- More users are computing on the road, which means that network administrators need to manage a large distributed environment.
- Crackers are getting better at writing viruses and breaking into networks.
- The news media often provides conflicting reports about new security vulnerabilities, which means it takes more time to figure out which vulnerabilities a network administrator needs to concentrate on.
- There isn't a single method for managing vulnerabilities—a network administrator often relies on several tools with different interfaces and capabilities to get the job done.
- Managers who aren't computer savvy, but do read media reports about security problems, keep pressuring network administrators to fix more problems faster than before, even if no real threat to network security exists.

A home office network administrator may not need to worry about all of these problems, but many of them are important. For example, you won't have to worry about the manager getting upset about the schedule for implementing security fixes because normally you're self-employed (you're also the boss). However, the time problem is very real for anyone, especially someone who's self-employed and needs to spend time with company business rather than chase down computer security problems. On the other hand, all these list items do apply to the small business. A network administrator for even the smallest network will find the task of implementing security that's bulletproof frustrating to say the least.

Hackers and Crackers—*The media often uses terms in the wrong way and clouds issues by doing so. For example, you'll frequently see the term hacker used to define someone who has low-level computer knowledge and often uses it for malicious reasons. In other cases, you'll see the same term used for people who work for security agencies and probe a network for security vulnerabilities. The same term can't apply to both the good and bad guys. In fact, security professionals recognize two different terms and I'll use those terms throughout the book. A hacker is someone who has in-depth computer knowledge and uses it for the good of others (like a security professional will). Crackers are people who use their knowledge to maliciously attack computer systems.*

Part of the problem is that you can't look at your network the same way that a cracker does. A cracker looks at your network from the outside, doesn't know anything about your network to start with, has plenty of time to search for vulnerabilities in your security setup, and often views breaking in as some type of game. A cracker sees breaking your security as a way to have fun and there are cracker Web sites where crackers will boast about just how much damage they did to your system. One of the cracker's major motivations is feeling superior to anyone else who uses a computer—financial gain is often a secondary reason. In short, even getting into the mindset of a cracker would be difficult for a network administrator.

There are, however, tools at your disposal that will make it easier for you to detect security holes. Using these tools regularly will help you find new holes as they appear, such as a user password that any cracker would guess in a few seconds. In addition, there are tools that make your network more secure and other tools that help you detect problems when they occur, which leads me to this helpful way of looking at network security:

Networks are never completely safe from intrusion, so a smart network administrator is always on the look out for the security breach that will occur.

This chapter is going to show you how to detect, discourage, and monitor security problems on your network using the least time-intensive methods available. We'll look at the kinds of security threats that you need to be aware of and how you can protect yourself from them. In addition, we'll talk about ways to accomplish all of this at a relatively low cost.

No One Wants My Data, Do They?

As soon as you provide any form of outside communication for your computer, it becomes a target for break-in. Novice crackers aren't picky about the targets they choose—they just want the experience your network can offer. Just like anyone else, a cracker has to go to school to learn the tricks of the trade. That school is your network. In fact, the BlackICE monitoring software on my server (the only one connected to the Internet) often receives 9 or 10 hits per day and all I have at the moment is a dial-up connection. (We'll talk about products like BlackICE in the section, "Monitoring Your Network for Break-Ins," later in this chapter.) Imagine how high this number would be if I were online 24 hours per day like many companies are.

Once a cracker decides to break into your system, he or she will likely damage it in some way. The damage can be anything from inserting a virus on your server to erasing files to creating additional accounts so that other crackers can play on your system. In fact, according to the **Issues and Trends: 2000 CSI/FBI Computer Crime and Security Survey** (http://www.gocsi.com/prelea_000321.htm) by the Federal Bureau of Investigation (FBI) and the Computer Security Institute (CSI), the damage to your system can take many forms, all of which are devastating. Here are some statistics from the survey of 643 respondents that you need to know about:

- 120 percent increase in loss occurred last year (dollar value of damage).
- 90 percent reported a security breach in the last twelve months.
- 74 percent acknowledged financial loss due to computer break-ins.
- 70 percent reported serious attacks, all of which included data damage in some form. (This doesn't include common forms of security threats like computer viruses.)
- 59 percent reported a higher number of Internet attacks than previous years.

As you can see, the question of whether someone wants your data isn't the question you should ask at all. A few crackers may be after your data, but for the most part, the only interest they have in your network is creating some type of damage. So, when you're securing your network, you need to ask the questions like, "Where can a cracker cause the most damage?" rather than limit your questions to those about protecting your data. Looking at your system from a cracker's perspective makes a big difference because it allows you to see how many ways a cracker can make your life miserable. (Mind you, I'm in no way implying that you should become paranoid.)

There is a plus side to this revelation. By taking the cracker's view of your network, you're undertaking the first and most important step in making your network secure. When you stop thinking like a responsible businessperson and start looking at your network as a place to play dirty pranks on hard-working individuals, it becomes easier to see all of those holes. In fact, it was after learning about this perspective that I started securing application directories as well as data directories. I also started using the need-to-know approach in my network-security policies. If someone doesn't have a need to know about something, I don't tell that person.

A Look at the Other Side—*Sometimes it's hard to imagine what someone else will do, especially if you'd never do it yourself. That's why Hacking Exposed by Stuart McClure, Joel Scambray, and George Kurtz is such an important book. It allows you to learn more about the way crackers think. This book will also help you learn about standard holes in OS security (including Windows 95, Windows 98, Windows NT, Windows 2000, UNIX, and NetWare) that crackers employ to break into your network. In addition to OS-specific information, you'll learn how denial of server (DoS) attacks work and the best way to secure your firewall (or at least how crackers can see through your defenses). You can learn more about this book at Hacking Exposed (http://www.hackingexposed.com/).*

Passwords: the Cracker's Best Friend

Most people consider passwords a method of securing a network, and that's what they're supposed to do. The entry of a password is supposed to confirm that the person at the computer console is authorized to perform certain tasks. However, what should be a security aid can often turn into a security problem. Passwords often become a cracker's best friend because they give the network administrator a false sense of security and allow the cracker entry to a network.

In the following sections, we'll look at two important password issues. First, I'll talk about why passwords don't work on most networks today. Since passwords are the most economical method of determining a user's identity, finding ways to make them work is important. Second, I'll talk about some password alternatives that you need to consider. A word of warning—they're all new and all expensive. However, all of them work better than passwords and I'll tell you why.

Why Passwords Don't Work in Some Situations

I've spent quite a bit of time helping companies build their network and then maintain that network so that it provides a desired level of functionality. One of the concerns that I always address is network security, especially the use of passwords. It doesn't surprise me anymore when I see several user passwords posted on someone's monitor on a sticky note. There are several problems with this scenario. First, the user has written down the passwords, which is something no one should ever do. Second, the user has access to more than one password, which means that someone else in the company dropped the security ball as well. Finally, the user placed the passwords in plain view where anyone could see them (even if not looking for them). It's not unheard of for a professional cracker, who wants to break into a company for financial reasons, to pose as a janitor for the sole purpose of viewing those passwords.

You may assume that the users are the bad guys, in this case, and should be punished in some way for their action. Actually, the problem isn't all that simple. There are several reasons why the password could be written down and even more reasons why the user has access to more than one password, but never a good reason to keep passwords in a public place.

Let's address the problem of writing the password down first. Any organization with a network should have a written security policy that people working in that environment can refer to. It should be written clearly without any hint of legalese or geek speak. One of the policies that you should include within this document is a description of how to create a password and why the use of a password is important. This document should also tell the user that there's never a good reason to write a password down and spell out penalties for doing so. Finally, you should make it clear that it's never an imposition to ask the administrator for a new password when one is lost.

There's a reason I made this last point. At least a few companies have fined users for asking for new passwords too often because it inconveniences the network administrator and wastes time. Considering the relatively low cost of providing a new password and the high cost of a security breach, passing out new passwords should be the least of the network administrator's worries.

A good user password should be hard to guess and easy to remember. I look at the passwords provided by some organizations as a disaster waiting to happen. For example, a case-sensitive password like "XYZ123abcQnX" is really tough to guess, but invites the user to write it down, because no one can remember such a password. One of the hard-to-guess and easy-to-remember schemes I've been using for quite some time is two random words separated by a special character. For example, "Coyote?Glove" is a case-sensitive password that would be fairly tough to guess, yet relatively easy to remember. The user has no reason to write this password down. Users should avoid using single words, personal items, or dates as passwords. Someone with enough knowledge about the user will guess all of them with relative ease. In addition, passwords should be long enough to thwart password-guessing tools that crackers use—I normally suggest 10 characters. Using this type of easy-to-remember password makes a long password quite feasible.

Using Shifted Characters in Passwords—*Some OSs may have trouble using shifted characters like the caret (^) in passwords, so you may need to select special characters with care. In most cases, standard punctuation characters like the question mark (?) and exclamation point (!) work just fine, so you can usually use these characters in a password. Numbers will work as well, so you could use a password like Hello7Green without too many problems.*

Now let's talk about the second problem, multiple passwords used by a single user. In most cases, the other passwords on the note you find will belong to a superior or another employee with privileges the user doesn't have. One of three things is happening (in order of highest probability):

1. The offending users don't have sufficient privileges to complete their work. If this is the case, you should audit the users' accounts to ensure that all required privileges are available. Make sure you find out precisely which task requirements aren't answered by the current security constraints.
2. Other users feel they're too busy to help the user with special tasks. A manager, for example, may not want to manage user accounts and delegates that task to the offending user. Depending on the task, you might want to provide the user with additional access or ask other parties why they can't help. Explain that need-to-know security requires everyone to work together, which means that all users need to perform their assigned tasks. Also explain that the other parties are responsible for the way offending user uses their password.
3. The user is power hungry and wants more than the required access. Unfortunately, there isn't much you can do about this situation except deny such users access they don't require. It's important, however, to ensure that everyone knows there are penalties for misused passwords (including dismissal for cause). If the problem persists, you may need to ask management to take action.

Identification Alternatives to Logging In

A user name and password is normally the only form of access identification that a user needs to gain access to your server. In most cases, that's all you really need to ensure that the data on your system remains secure. However, even if the software that grants access to the system is totally bulletproof (an ever more difficult task as computers gain processing power), there are still problems with this approach besides the password written on a sheet of paper that I discussed in the previous section.

Even if all parties at a company do their best to protect security, and you have the best security available for your application, crackers often find ways around the security measures you have in place. Just the fact that your security relies on a password means that someone can guess what that password is given enough time and opportunity. In other words, using the name and password method of security is problematic at best. You can't rely on a password to provide total security for some types of extremely confidential data.

Some companies are combating these problems using alternatives to passwords—unique ways of identifying someone that don't rely on a password. One of the more common methods, at the moment, is the use of smart cards. A *smart card* is a credit card sized device with some built-in processing power. The user swipes the card in a special reader to gain access to the network. What happens is that the card provides a digital certificate that identifies the user in lieu of a password. One of the nice things about using a smart card is that you don't have to provide any identification like the numbers used by credit cards on the outside.

One company that's starting to make smart card readers a standard option is Hewlett-Packard (HP). Their Vectra Desktop PCs and Kayak PC workstations are now optimized to use either the Gemplus (a Veridicom product) or Schlumberger smart-card readers. In addition, the ProtectTools corporate security strategy offered by HP extends from the client to the firewall, which will allow a company to give outside partners secure access to company data. The HP TopTools Management software will allow managers to view client computers that have smart-card readers. In essence, there's already an infrastructure and products in place to allow a company to implement full security using smart cards. Here's where you can find out about all these companies:

Hewlett-Packard
http://www.hp.com/

Veridicom, Inc.
http://www.veridicom.com/

Schlumberger
http://www.1.slb.com/smartcards/

A smart card eliminates the problem of compromised passwords—at least without assistance. Without a password lying around, it would take a concerted effort by an inside party to break network security. Such an effort would be easier to trace than a break-in by an outside source. However, a smart card can still be lost and used by someone who knows what the card is used for and to whom it belongs. (There's nothing to stop the user from placing some form of identification on the card, even if the issuing company doesn't.) In addition, the issuing company has to bear the cost of issuing and maintaining the cards, which could be an expensive proposition.

There's a relatively new alternative to both passwords and smart cards. Biometrics is a statistical method of scanning users' unique characteristics to ensure that they are who they say they are. Some of the scanned elements include voiceprints, irises, fingerprints, hands, and facial features. The two most popular elements are irises and fingerprints, because they're the two that most people are familiar with. The advantages of using biometrics are obvious. Not only can't users lose their identifying information (at least not very easily), but with proper scanning techniques, the identifying information can't be compromised either.

At the time of this writing, there are two main problems with using biometrics: quality and price. Some managers don't want to use biometrics because of the time it takes to create quality scans that ensure absolute accuracy. The quality issue is being resolved as computer hardware gets faster. In addition, the price for a single scanner can range from $100 for something simple to thousands of dollars for complex solutions. Considering the number of access points a typical company has, the price of using biometrics for all but the most stringent security requirements could be prohibitive. Obviously, you have to weigh the cost of the data you're trying to protect against the cost of protecting it. Fortunately, the tide is turning for biometrics as more companies start to pursue this solution. Today you'll find biometrics in use in a wide range of government and high-security institutions; tomorrow you could easily find them even at smaller companies. Many industry experts say that forward-thinking financial organizations have already begun using biometrics as a means of identification. By late 2001, many corporations will view fingerprint identification as the access method of choice for remote communication. Iris identification may begin to overtake fingerprint identification as early as 2002 as the primary means of identification used by some corporations. Of course, it's going to be a long time before your ATM will read your eyes before allowing cash withdrawals. You'll eventually use a biometric device for the security of your home as this technology becomes more popular.

A few companies deal with biometrics today. One of the most popular systems, the IriScan System 2200, can scan the iris of an individual using a camera instead of direct contact. The system prompts users through the process of getting their iris scanned for the first time. In addition, this scanner works with someone who wears glasses (older systems required you to remove your glasses for scanning). The codes for the scanned individuals are stored in a Microsoft Access database.

If your company prefers to use fingerprints instead of other biometric techniques to enforce security, you might want to look at the fingerprint reader chip solutions provided by Veridicom, Inc., which is working with Intel to incorporate interfaces for biometrics into the Common Data Security Architecture (CDSA). CDSA is a comprehensive set of security services that will make secure transactions easier. It has a four-layer architecture: application, layered services and middleware, Common Security Services Manager (CSSM) infrastructure, and security service provider modules. CDSA is currently on The Open Group fast track to becoming a standard.

IriScan and Veridicom aren't the only companies getting into biometrics. Compaq computer has introduced a sub-$100 fingerprint reader that it developed with Identicator Technology. This fingerprint reader works for all but the most demanding small-business needs. (You may need something better to work with the government.) Here's a list of some of the biometric companies you'll want to know about:

Compaq
http://www.compaq.com/newsroom/pr/1998/pr070798b.html

IriScan, Inc
http://www.iriscan.com/

Common Data Security Architecture
http://www.opengroup.org/security/cdsa/

Saflink Corporation
http://www.saflink.com/

Visionics Corporation
http://www.faceit.com/

Keyware Technologies
http://www.keyware.be/

Vision Systems, Inc.
http://www.whovision.com/

Plugging Security Holes

One of the most time consuming, yet necessary tasks that you can perform on your network is plugging all of the security holes that pop up. It's a never-ending task. Any change in network configuration, staff turnover, software or hardware modification, or new discoveries of existing security holes by the cracker community will make your job harder. Security is one of those tasks where you can't be a bystander and expect to accomplish anything.

The important message to get from this section is that you need to spend time learning your OS and the applications it supports if you want to plug security holes before a cracker can use them. One of the cracker's biggest advantages over the network administrator is that the cracker normally spends a lot of time looking for these common security problems. Most security issues receive some type of press attention—retaining a notebook of these reports is one way to keep the current problems with your OS and applications in mind.

Knowing what problems you're likely to see is one way to ensure you get as many security holes plugged as possible. The following sections will help you understand some of the problems you'll run into when working with popular OSs and applications. There's a special section for Windows 3.x and Windows 9x users because this OS has specific problems that many people ignore or are completely unaware of. In addition to discussing the security issues that you'll run into, the section entitled, "An Overview of Security Standards," will talk about the standards on which security is based. Knowing the standards can save you a lot of time when it comes time to implement security for your network.

The Windows 3.x, Windows 9x, and Windows ME Security Dilemma

Some people are under the impression that the login dialog box you see when you first start Windows 3.x, Windows 9x, or Windows ME represents some level of security. The next time you log onto either of these OSs, press Escape instead of entering a password. You'll find that you can easily access the workstation and gain full access to all the features it provides. (Fortunately, you can't access the network using this technique.) Setting up a security policy for a Windows 3.x, Windows 9x, or Windows ME machine is a waste of time, because most users realize that it's not going to stop them from doing what they'd like to do with the machine. In short, these versions of Windows aren't very secure, and it's unlikely that you'll make them secure because of the design that Microsoft used.

Windows 3.x has appalling support for Microsoft's security application programming interface (API). An API is a set of programmer routines that allow the programmer to ask the OS to do something without using a lot of code. The Windows security API allows a programmer to determine what level of security a user has and whether the administrator wants to give the user access to certain OS features. Unfortunately, while Windows NT has a full set of security API features and Windows 2000 provides even more, Windows 3.x, Windows 9x, and Windows ME ignore many of these requests and send the requesting application a default answer. The application won't stop working because the security features aren't included; but your network isn't secure either because of the omissions.

Fortunately, many of these security problems affect the local machine and not network access. Windows 9x and Windows ME are better than Windows 3.x was, because they at least allow some level of verification by the server. While all three versions of Windows are relatively inexpensive to set up and operate, none of the versions are secure. I'm not here to tell you that Windows 98 is a terrible operating system that you should consider burning rather than using. A lot of people use Windows 98 and never have a security problem. The point of this section is that you need to know that Windows 3.x, Windows 9x, and Windows ME aren't the secure operating systems that you think they are—there are big holes in security that you could drive a semi through and those holes aren't going to go away. If cost is the big factor for your network, these OSs will probably work fine. However, if you require the utmost in security, the Windows NT or Windows 2000 (or a non-Windows OS) are better choices.

Understanding Security Holes

Security holes come in sizes both large and small. Finding them is imperative if you want to maintain any level of security on your network. You need to ensure that every piece of every application on your network provides the required level of security or there will be holes in the security measures for your network. One of the most common sources of security problems in corporations today is the user who doesn't understand the business rules regarding security. Adding security to both the application and associated components helps you overcome some types of user-knowledge problems, or at least alert the users that they're doing something outside of company guidelines.

Of course, few companies are islands anymore. You don't have just your network to worry about; you also have the Internet to worry about as well. Even if you don't open your Web site to the public, there are going to be ways for people outside your company to break in and cause havoc on your network. The Internet opens all kinds of potential cracker opportunities. It doesn't help that there are holes in the current API specifications for Internet security and in the implementation of those specifications by various applications. In some cases, these security holes aren't in the API itself, but in some of the creative solutions people used in the past to make the Internet work. In essence, problem solving in the past created security back doors in the present.

No matter what the source of the security hole is, you can be sure that some cracker is just waiting to find it on your system. Exploiting well-known security holes is one of the major tools of the cracker trade. It's not just accounts that you need to either disable or monitor (like the guest account found on many OSs); it's the way that applications are designed, directories are set up, and users interact with the system. Even Java, which uses the sandbox approach for security, has had holes in it. For example, crackers were able to use these holes to convince the Java Virtual Machine (JVM) that it needed to erase a file on a user's machine. Someone could use this hole to create a virus that would erase files while a user visits Web sites. While some of the security holes are small and difficult to gain access to, the fact remains that there's a hole in your security that a cracker can use to damage your network.

What Is the Sandbox Approach?—*Imagine your network as the entire world. It's open to anyone who has the right security, but it's also a dangerous place. Applications with an attitude can do a great deal of damage. Java adheres to the principle that it should stay in its own sandbox (area of the network) instead of going outside like most applications. This approach has several advantages for the user. For one thing, it should make Java less of a security problem, because it normally isn't aware of which machine it's operating on or what the capabilities of that machine are. All that Java is worried about is its own little world. While this concept is great in theory, there are holes in the current implementation, so sometimes Java does get outside the sandbox.*

Microsoft has been the object of much trade-press scorn in the recent past and that scorn shows no sign of letting up. Of course, a good amount of this attention is because Microsoft is one of the biggest players out there and, as a result, receives more than its fair share of attention. Crackers have found holes in everything from Internet Explorer to Microsoft Office. In a lot of cases, you can get around these security holes by setting up your applications a certain way. For example, you can tell Internet Explorer not to run scripts—a constant source of problems with Microsoft's products. In other cases, you need to install the latest patch for the OS or application from Microsoft. Unfortunately, these patches are often difficult to find and can create problems of their own.

Many security holes are found in the services that servers run. A service is a special piece of application code designed to perform a task in the background. For example, there's a service that checks the user's password. Another service monitors the uninterruptible power supply (UPS) for problems; while yet another service is linked to the database management system (DBMS). Each service has a specific use that makes it unique on the server. The server can't perform the tasks you want it to without these services, so stopping a service that has a security hole in it might not be an option. Now, consider how many services are running on your workstation and associated server. Even if every one of those services has just one security hole, the potential for a breach of security is immense.

One of the biggest reasons Linux advocates like that particular OS is that open source allows a lot of developers to look at the source code. All of these people peering into the heart of the operating system can find flaws that might otherwise go unnoticed. While there have been very few problems discovered with Linux, it doesn't receive the attention that products like Windows do. It remains to be seen whether the open-source model used by Linux really does result in more secure OS environments.

The Flow of Security

Setting security isn't a mystical experience. Most OS implementations today use the same methodology for determining the security settings of a directory (folder in Windows terminology) or file. Setting a security policy on a directory also affects all the files within that directory. Likewise, any directories below the current directory are affected by the security policy of the parent. Security is said to flow down from the parent to the children; whatever security you set for the parent is the security the children will have.

Of course, you can always change the security policy for a specific file or directory manually. Changing the security for a single file will change only that file. On the other hand, changing the security for a directory will mean that any new rights will flow down to the directories below it.

So, if the flow of security is the same for most OSs, how are they different? There are four major ways in which security differs between operating systems from a network administrator's perspective:

- Default security
- Granularity
- Security standards
- Auditing

The default security that a network provides can dictate how secure the network operation ends up being. Some network administrators never change any security settings they don't have to change. OS vendors have gotten smarter about this problem in the last few years, because they've made the default security for an OS more stringent. For example, Windows NT comes with the guest account enabled while Windows 2000 comes with the guest account disabled. A simple change like this plugs a security hole that network administrators often miss.

Security granularity is an important OS feature. It determines the rights that the OS will allow you to set for a file. Figure 8.1 shows that the granularity of Windows 2000 is fairly generic. It allows you to modify, read, read and execute, or write to the file. This is still better than Windows NT, which only allows you to set the read, change, and full control attributes for most files. Windows 2000

Figure 8.1: Windows 2000 offers a moderate level of access granularity.

also includes the Allow inheritable permissions from parent to propagate to this object check box. Any Windows 2000 object will inherit the parent's rights when you first create it. However, removing the check mark from this box severs that connection and allows you to set the security for the object separately. This can include denying rights that the parent grants.

Contrast the granularity of Windows 2000 to the NetWare dialog box shown in Figure 8.2. In this case, you get a set of eight rights that you can change including read, write, erase, create, modify, file scan, access control, and supervisor. This difference in granularity would allow you to truly hide a file under NetWare, yet allow the user to write to it. Under Windows 2000, there are always ways to see a file if you want to. In addition, you can restrict the user to only writing to a file under NetWare; under Windows 2000, writing usually means reading as well.

The thoroughness with which an OS vendor follows security standards will affect your ability to purchase third-party products to manage the OS. I'll discuss these standards more in the next section. Auditing features are one way to monitor your system for security breaches. They also allow you to charge other departments or companies for resources used on your network. We'll look at this particular security element in the section, "Using the Windows 2000 Auditing Features," later in this chapter.

An Overview of Security Standards

Security standards are an important part of your company's safety net. The section, "Understanding Security Holes," earlier in this chapter alerted you to the fact that there are holes in your security net that come from a variety of sources, including the OS and off-the-shelf

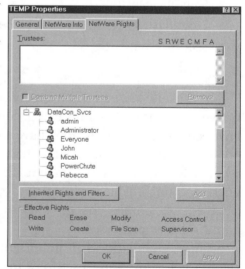

Figure 8.2: NetWare offers a fairly high level of access granularity.

applications that you rely on to conduct business. All of those problems are real, but you don't have to face them alone. Standards groups are working even as you read this to come up with methods for protecting data. All you need to do is learn the methods that these groups come up with for managing security on your network.

The advantages of using standards-based security are twofold. First, you won't have to reinvent the wheel and create everything from scratch. Second, your security methods will mesh with those used by other OSs, reducing the user learning curve and making it possible for you to use tools developed for other network administrators.

You need to think about two levels of security standards. The first includes the internal security that an OS provides. This is your first line of defense against local security threats that exist on your local area network (LAN) or wide area network (WAN). The second includes security for external communications like the Internet. In some cases, like Kerberos, a security standard can work in both environments. It's not essential that you know every security standard by heart; but you should know security standards exist and that they fulfill certain purposes for your network. Looking for these standards as part of products that you buy will ensure your network has the best possible chance of remaining secure and can interact with other networks. Here's an overview of these security standards:

Distributed Authentication Security Service (DASS) IETF RFC1507— DASS is an IETF work in progress. It defines an experimental method for providing authentication services on the Internet. The goal of authentication, in this case, is to verify who sent a message or request. Current password schemes have a number of problems that DASS tries to solve. For example, there's no way to verify that the sender of a password isn't impersonating someone else. DASS provides authentication services in a distributed environment. Distributed environments present special challenges, because users don't log onto just one machine—they could conceivably log onto every machine on the network.

DSI (Digital Signatures Initiative)—This is a standard originated by W3C to overcome some limitations of channel-level security. For example, channel-level security can't deal with documents and application semantics. A channel also doesn't use the Internet's bandwidth very efficiently, because all the processing takes place on the Internet rather than at the client or server. DSI defines a mathematical method for transferring signatures—essentially a unique representation of a specific individual or company. DSI also provides a new method for labeling security properties (PICS2) and a new format for assertions (PEP). This standard is also built on the PKCS7 and X509.v3 standards.

Internet Protocol Security Protocol (IPSec)—IETF has created the IP Security Protocol working group to look at the problems of IP security, such as the inability to encrypt data at the protocol level. It's currently working on a wide range of specifications that will ultimately result in more secure IP transactions.

JEPI (Joint Electronic Payment Initiative)—A standard originated by W3C, JEPI provides a method for creating electronic commerce. Transactions will use some form of electronic cash or credit cards. Data transfers from the client to the server will use encryption, digital signatures, and authentication (key exchange) to ensure a secure exchange. This is an emerging standard—some items, such as transport-level security (also called privacy), are currently making their way through the IETF.

PCT (Private Communication Technology)—The IETF is working with Microsoft on this particular protocol. Like SSL, PCT is designed to provide a secure method of communication between a client and server at the low protocol level. It can work with any high-level protocol such as HTTP, FTP, or Telnet.

Privacy Enhanced Mail Part I (PEM1) Message Encryption and Authentication Procedures IETF RFC1421—This is an approved IETF specification for ensuring that your private mail remains private. Essentially, it outlines a procedure for encrypting mail in such a way that the user's mail is protected, but the process of decrypting it is invisible. This includes the use of keys and other forms of certificate management. Some of the specification is based on the CCITT X.400 specification—especially in the areas of Mail Handling Service (MHS) and Mail Transfer System (MTS).

Privacy Enhanced Mail Part II (PEM2) Certificate-Based Key Management IETF RFC1422—This is an approved IETF specification for managing security keys. It provides both an infrastructure and management architecture based on a public-key certification technique. IETF RFC1422 is an enhancement of the CCITT X.509 specification. It goes beyond the CCITT specification by providing procedures and conventions for a key-management infrastructure for use with PEM.

Privacy Enhanced Mail Part III (PEM3) Algorithms, Modes, and Identifiers IETF RFC1423—This is an approved IETF specification that defines cryptographic algorithms, usage modes, and identifiers specifically for PEM use. The specification covers four main areas of encryption-related information: message encryption algorithms, message integrity check algorithms, symmetric-key management algorithms, and asymmetric-key management algorithms (including both symmetric encryption and asymmetric signature algorithms).

Privacy Enhanced Mail Part IV (PEM4) Key Certification and Related Services IETF RFC1424—This is an approved IETF specification that defines the method for certifying keys. It also provides a listing of cryptographic-related services that an Internet site would need to provide to the end user.

Secure/Multipurpose Internet Mail Extensions (S/MIME)—This is a specification being promoted by a consortium of vendors, including Microsoft, Banyan, VeriSign, ConnectSoft, QUALCOMM, Frontier Technologies, Network Computing Devices, FTP Software, Wollongong, SecureWare, and Lotus. It was originally developed by RSA Data Security, Inc., as a method for different developers to create message transfer agents (MTAs) that used compatible encryption technology. Essentially, this means that if someone sends you a message using a Lotus product, you can read it with your Banyan product. S/MIME is based on the popular Internet MIME standard (RFC1521).

Secure/Wide Area Network (S/WAN)—This is an initiative supported by RSA Data Security, Inc. The IETF has a committee working on it as well. RSA intends to incorporate the IETF's IPSec standard into S/WAN. The main goal of S/WAN is to allow companies to mix and match the best firewall and TCP/IP stack products to build Internet-based virtual private networks (VPNs). Current solutions usually lock the user into a single source for both products.

SHTTP (Secure Hypertext Transfer Protocol)—This is the current encrypted data-transfer technology used by Open Marketplace Server, which is similar in functionality to SSL. The big difference is that this method only works with HTTP. The Web Transaction Security, or WTS, group of the IETF was recently formed for looking at potential specifications like this one.

SSL (Secure Sockets Layer)—This is a W3C standard originally proposed by Netscape for transferring encrypted information from the client to the server at the protocol layer. Sockets allow low-level encryption of transactions in higher-level protocols such as HTTP, NNTP, and FTP. The standard also specifies methods for server and client authentication (although client site authentication is optional).

The Kerberos Network Authentication Service (V5) IETF RFC1510—This is an approved IETF specification that defines a third-party authentication protocol. The Kerberos model is based in part on Needham and Schroeder's trusted third-party authentication protocol and on modifications suggested by Denning and Sacco. As with many Internet authentication protocols,

Kerberos works as a trusted third-party authentication service. It uses conventional cryptography that relies on a combination of shared public key and private key. Kerberos emphasizes client authentication with optional server authentication.

Universal Resource Identifiers (URI) in WWW IETF RFC2396 (and others like RFC1630)—URI is an IETF work in progress. Currently, resource names and addresses are provided in clear text. A URL (uniform resource locator) is actually a form of URI containing an address that maps to a specific location on the Internet. URI would provide a means of encoding the names and addresses of Internet objects. In essence, to visit a private site, you'd need to know the encoded name instead of the clear-text name.

As you can see, there are many standards to keep track of. These standards change on a regular basis; but fortunately all of the changes appear on the Internet once they're approved by the organizations that sponsor them. Here's a list of URLs for the standards I just talked about:

Computer and Network Security Resources
http://www.andrew.cmu.edu/user/chuang/security.html

Distributed Authentication Security Service (DASS) IETF RFC1507
http://www.wu-wien.ac.at:8082/rfc/rfc1507.hyx/$$root

DSI (Digital Signatures Initiative)
http://www.w3.org/DSig/

Internet Protocol Security Protocol (IPSec)
http://www.ietf.cnri.reston.va.us/html.charters/ipsec-charter.html

JEPI (Joint Electronic Payment Initiative)
http://www.w3.org/ECommerce/Overview-JEPI.html

Naming and Addressing: URIs, URLs, ...
http://www.w3.org/Addressing/

Netscape Security Center
http://home.netscape.com/security/

OSISEC (Open System Interconnection Security Package) Documentation
http://www.cs.ucl.ac.uk/research/ice-tel/osisec/documentation/

PCT (Private Communication Technology)
http://activex.adsp.or.jp/Japanese/Specs/pct.htm

RSA Security S/MIME Central
http://www.rsasecurity.com/standards/smime/

RSA Security What is S/WAN
http://www.rsasecurity.com/rsalabs/faq/5-1-3.html

Secure/Multipurpose Internet Mail Extensions (S/MIME)
http://www.oac.uci.edu/indiv/ehood/MIME/

The Kerberos Network Authentication Service (V5) IETF RFC1510
http://info.internet.isi.edu/in-notes/rfc/files/rfc1510.txt

Web Transaction Security
http://www.ietf.org/html.charters/wts-charter.html

Security standards tend to change on a fairly regular basis. Part of the reason is crackers force network administrators and other professionals to continually update the standards used to protect their networks. Here are some links that will help you keep up to date on current security developments:

A Concise Selection of RFCs
http://afs.wu-wien.ac.at/usr/edvz/gonter/rfc-list.html

Cryptography Related Stuff
http://www.si.hhs.nl/~henks/comp/crypt.html

IETF—Current Internet Drafts
ftp://ftp.isi.edu/internet-drafts/1id-abstracts.txt

IETF—RFC Search
http://www.ietf.org/rfc.html

IETF—Working Group Charters
http://www.ietf.cnri.reston.va.us/html.charters/

RSA Security, Inc.
http://www.rsasecurity.com/

W3C Security Resources
http://www.w3.org/Security/

It's a surprising fact that vendor standards are probably the fastest growing area of the Internet right now. Businesses need these standards to ensure interoperability with the myriad of vendor products—a fact that's forcing the vendors to compromise in some areas for the sake of compatibility. You'll also notice that the majority of standards listed in this section of the chapter aren't from Microsoft or some other company—they come from one of two groups: the IETF (Internet Engineering Task Force) or a group known as W3C (World Wide Web Consortium). IETF has been around for a long time. It was one of the first groups to work with the Internet. Be prepared to read a lot about the W3C group as you delve into Internet security issues (and to a lesser extent other standards areas such as HTML tags). It's the group responsible for newer Internet standards of every kind.

Knowing Which Security Holes You Can't Patch

In some situations, your best efforts at securing your network won't be enough. For example, if an OS vendor leaves a security hole in a required OS component, there isn't much you can do about the security hole until the vendor issues a patch. There might be OS features that you can remove to make the problem harder to take advantage of; but the problem will still remain. OS vendors are normally good about providing feedback on security problems when they find them and issuing patches in a relatively short time.

In some cases, you can avoid security problems if you know about them in advance. For example, browsers and e-mail readers have both appeared in the news a lot lately because crackers have found more than a few security holes in them. If you find out about the security problem before you install the software, you can retain the current version or go with another vendor's product. However, once you install the software, you're often stuck with the problem unless you want to remove the program from your hard drive. In many cases, removing the program means not being able to read the data that it produced; so removing a security risk may not be an option.

Almost every hardware-related problem falls into the "can't self patch" category because hardware patches normally mean adding new chips to the device. For example, a router may contain faulty firmware (special software on a chip) that causes it to allow packets through to your network without filtering. In the past, a hardware failure of this type meant a trip back to the factory because few hardware vendors trusted users to replace chips within the unit. Because hardware vendors test their products extensively, however, it's unlikely that you'll run into a security breach that's associated with a device. In addition, the use of flash ROM technology means that many hardware patches can be applied by users in the field, rather than by a technician at the company.

Monitoring Your Network for Break-Ins

Always assume that someone will find a way to break into your network. It's the false sense of security that many network administrators develop that gets them into trouble. A security breach occurs and they never realize it has taken place because they aren't looking for it. The only time some network administrators figure out that there are problems with security on their network is when a scandal happens. Constant vigilance is an essential part of any security plan.

One of the first places you should look for trouble with your network is in the event log. The OS you choose will determine whether there is one or many of these logs and which utility you use to view existing the logs. Figure 8.3 shows an example of the Event Viewer for Windows 2000. In this case, there are three logs to look at: application, system, and security. The security log shows a single event consisting of a success audit.

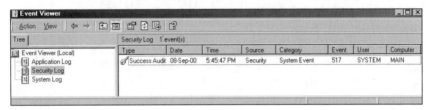

Figure 8.3: The Windows 2000 Event Viewer allows you to see incidents that have occurred on your system.

Security events don't always appear where you expect them. For example, many of the application security problems that have occurred on systems that I worked on ended up in the application log rather than the security log. The reason is simple: the application log is the place where Windows puts application events. Even though it might seem reasonable to place these security events in the security log, they almost always appear in the application log.

However, don't get the idea you can just look in one or two event logs. System login failures won't appear in the application or the security log because they're system events. If a user or an application is having problems logging into the system, you'll find an entry in the system log.

The point is that you need to monitor all of the server logs for important security information. It doesn't matter which application, service, or system routine generated the log; the important element is the data within the log. In many cases, there won't be a message saying that a security breach has occurred; but you'll be able to tell that something is wrong because the normal pattern of entries will change or an application that normally works fine will generate error messages. Monitoring often means spending hours in detective work only to find that a change in pattern really wasn't a breach after all.

Monitoring also means looking at your system configuration. You won't want to memorize every user on the system; but you should audit the user list from time to time. Crackers will often give themselves a fake account. Only by performing an audit will you find users who don't belong to your company. Even if they are legitimate users of the past, you should remove accounts that are no longer needed because they represent security holes in your network.

Another form of monitoring is resource usage. You'll see in the section, "Performing an Audit," later in this chapter that you can tell the operating system to show you unusual resource usage patterns. Of course, it's ridiculous to monitor every resource on the network—it would take all of your time to do so. However, by noticing that a user is creating a lot of new directories, you can at least narrow the number of resources to monitor down to that particular user.

Using the Windows 2000 Auditing Features

Like many OSs, Windows 2000 provides auditing features that you can use to verify the use of resources on your network. Verifying this information also allows you to check for security breaches. For example, if you have an audit log entry that shows Joe Smith used some space on the hard drive at midnight, yet you know that Joe Smith was away on a trip at the time, you've just found a breach in your security.

Crackers will often assume the identity of an employee to avoid suspicion. They'll call into the network at times when the employee is gone to avoid multiple login alerts the network administrator might otherwise receive. Stealing another user's identity does protect the cracker to a certain extent. Your only real defense is auditing the system and looking for odd behavior from an otherwise model employee.

The following sections of the chapter will help you understand the benefits of using auditing as both a resource management tool and a security aid. I'll talk about the issues that auditing is designed to solve and how you can keep your networking running well with a little behind-the-scenes monitoring. I'm looking at Windows 2000 in these sections, but many OSs provide auditing capability that's similar in functionality and purpose.

Understanding the Moving Target

Computer security is a moving target and one in which the environment changes constantly. Every time you hire a new employee, you're also taking on a new set of unknown security risks. Even if the new employee condescends to read the security bulletins your company provides, he or she may not understand those policies fully or may inadvertently circumvent them because of ingrained bad habits from another job. In addition, employees sometimes engage in illegal activities. Many computer break-ins occur from the inside rather than the outside. There isn't any way to know when you hire new employees whether they're friends or foes. Only time will tell you whether someone can be trusted with your data and often it's too late to get rid of a security problem by the time you find out one exists.

Employees aren't the only source of new security problems on a network. Any change in hardware configuration can cause security breaches. Hardware that isn't configured correctly can open your network to outside intrusions. Normally it pays to audit your system after a major hardware upgrade to ensure everything is configured properly. Fortunately, once you configure your hardware, it normally remains stable and you don't have to worry about it.

Software is another story. Any change to your software can create security holes. The problem is that you won't know about the security holes in many cases for weeks after the software is installed. Microsoft and other companies constantly release security updates to their software for this very reason. Of course, every new update can create yet other security problems.

The purpose of this section isn't to give you bad dreams at night—far from it. I want you to be aware of all of the sources of new security holes on your network. Constant auditing helps you discover these new holes and plug them before anyone else gets a chance to use them. In short:

Network security is a moving target that requires constant vigilance on the part of the network administrator.

Since network security is a moving target, you need to take measures to keep the target within sight. Here are some techniques you can use to keep closer watch on the security of your network and at least be aware of potential security threats:

- Always log every change to the network from updates in hardware to the installation or upgrade of software. Logging network events will allow you to pinpoint the causes of security breaches when you find them.
- Never allow users to install software from home, new company sponsored software, or software patches. The only way to be sure you know what the security risks for your network are is if you're also aware of changes to the network.
- Always read the README file that comes with a new product or an update. In many cases, vendors are aware of security problems with their software and will tell you about them if you look in the correct spot. Security holes aren't a major marketing point, so vendors tend to hide this information.
- Track security bulletins from vendors of any products that you use. In many cases, a security hole isn't easily fixed; so the vendor will tell you about settings changes that will make the software safe. Keeping a list of security bulletins with this type of information will allow you to reestablish a safe system after an upgrade.

- Keep user rights to a minimum. This may sound cruel; but the best way to keep a secret is not to tell anyone. If your company has secrets that only a few people should know (and what company doesn't), you need to restrict access to that information to only those who need it. No one else should even know that information exists.

Performing an Audit

Most OSs will allow you to perform some type of audit. For example, when you work with NetWare, you can monitor various types of resource usage, including processor time and hard drive space. This is actually a minimal level of monitoring compared to some OSs.

Windows 2000 will allow you to audit any object on the system; although it's not always easy to figure out how to do so, you can generally audit anything you like. File auditing is the easiest to set up. All you need to do is right-click a file within Windows Explorer and choose Properties from the shortcut menu. Select the Security tab of the Properties dialog box and click Advanced. You'll see an Access Control Settings dialog box that contains an Auditing tab. Click the Auditing tab, and then click Add. You'll see a Select Objects dialog box. Choose an object to audit, and then click OK. Figure 8.4 shows some of the ways that you can audit a file.

Notice that the list shown in Figure 8.4 is task oriented. Windows 2000 will allow you to audit the success or failure of each task. For example, you may want to monitor every failed attempt to write data to the file. This would allow you to see when an unauthorized person is trying to get into the file to see what it contains. Crackers are known to snoop files on the system they want to exploit. Normally, they're looking for security information; but some crackers are also looking for your company data or anything else they think they can sell.

Unfortunately, the audit coverage that Windows 2000 provides is incomplete. For example, you can't audit access to a DOS formatted drive, even if that drive is located on the same machine. Windows 2000 will only allow you to audit NTFS (Windows NT File System) drives, which makes the auditing

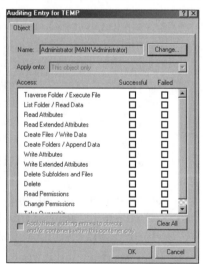

Figure 8.4: Windows 2000 allows you to perform a wide variety of auditing tasks on any object, including files.

feature of limited use in some environments. Contrast this with both Linux and NetWare, both of which allow you to audit any local drive.

Auditing Dangers and Limitations

Security audits are a useful tool in ensuring your network will remain secure from crackers, or that you'll be able to detect intrusions when they do occur. Performing security audits regularly will definitely improve the integrity of your network. However, security audits have some major flaws that you need to consider:

- They look from the inside out, which means they're not looking at the network from the same perspective that a cracker is looking from.
- They can be expensive to implement and time consuming to perform.
- The results can be difficult to understand, which limits the amount of information derived.
- They offer little in the way of risk assessment, so you really don't know how vulnerable your network is.
- Security audits use easily outdated techniques that fail to look for new security holes as they become evident.

Let's put a little reality into this picture; few crackers are going to consider a small network or a home office as a prize worth boasting about. Certainly, a small network isn't going to be a target for professional crackers who have the expertise to break into just about any network. If you make things difficult, a novice cracker (the kind most likely to attempt a break-in) will probably move on to the next network in search of an easier target. However, you also need to consider how much the loss of data will affect your company—it's important to cover all of the bases if you can. Here's the easiest way to look at this issue:

Take all of the reasonable precautions you can to protect your network; but don't become so paranoid about security that it causes your business to become less competitive.

There are a few ways to get around the auditing problems I listed previously. The easiest way is to hire a hacker (security professional) to check your network for the same vulnerabilities as a cracker would. A hacker would look from the outside in, just like a cracker would, and won't want to know anything about your network at the outset. Of course, you don't want to invite just anyone to break into your network. Make sure the hackers you hire have insurance, can prove that they have done this type of work before, and offer a client list that you can check with for credentials. In addition, the System Administration,

Networking, and Security (SANS) Institute certifies hackers by using the Global Incident Analysis Center (GIAC) training program. There are several levels of certification available, each of which raises the requirements the hacker must pass to qualify. You can find out more about these programs at **GIAC Training and Certification Program** at http://www.sans.org/giactc.htm.

Another method to get around the problem is to use a subscription service like **Sunbelt Software QualysGuard** (http://www.sunbelt-software.com/product.cfm?id=545). This approach costs a lot less than hiring a consultant, so you can get your network scanned more often. The subscription service uses special software that relies on artificial intelligence to duplicate the techniques of a cracker. Using subscription software means that you'll get updates as new security holes are discovered and the software can look from the outside in, just like a cracker would. This method does have limitations—computers can't duplicate the thought process of a human; they can only check what they're programmed to check. As a result, this method is probably less thorough than hiring a hacker would be, but still a lot better than anything you can do internally.

CHAPTER NINE

Network Administration Made Simple

For many people, networks stop with the topics that I covered through Chapter 8, *Network Security Essentials*. Designing and installing hardware and software and configuring the network is a process that ends with the first employee submitting a document for storage on a file server. No matter how well designed your network is, it will require administration if you want to keep it running smoothly. Here are some reasons why:

- Employees leave.
- Hardware is updated.
- Software is replaced with something newer.
- The network setup changes to meet business or personal needs.

In short, no matter what you do, you'll need to make changes to your network setup. The process of keeping the network's configuration current with business, personal, and environmental needs is called administration. It's a continuing process that most people dread because they perceive it as difficult or too time consuming. Yet, network administration doesn't have to be either difficult or too time consuming.

Home Networks Need Care Too!—*Don't get the idea that home networks are immune to change. Yes, they change more slowly than an office network, but change still occurs. For example, you may decide to give children more rights to network resources as they grow older or you might add more machines as required to handle business needs. Internet needs also tend to change a network's management requirements.*

The problem for most small networks is that the tools you get to manage them are designed for corporate networks. It's like using a sledgehammer to pound a tack into place. Sure, these tools will work, but you'll end up hitting your thumb more often than you'd like to admit and there isn't any way to guarantee your network will be any better for the effort. That's why this chapter is so important. I'll talk about ways to use the tools provided with most servers on a small network like the one found in a small office or the home. This chapter will also examine some policies that work great on a large network, but are doomed to failure within the small-town atmosphere of a small network.

Maintaining a good work environment is the topic of the first section of this chapter. A large network requires lots of monitoring, because people feel they can get by with more by getting lost in the crowd. This isn't true with a small network. People working on the network already know their work is easy to monitor and there isn't any way to hide in the crowd. As a result, an overzealous network administrator can be a hindrance. Too much monitoring reduces productivity and places artificial barriers in the way of progress.

I've talked about client/server and peer-to-peer networks throughout the book. A client/server network operating system (NOS) like Novell's NetWare provides a lot of management tools, because it's designed for use with large networks. On the other hand, peer-to-peer networks usually include just a few management tools, because they're normally used with workgroups. We'll see in the second section of the chapter that the lack of tools for a peer-to-peer network isn't a problem in most cases. In some situations, you'll want to buy third-party tools to fill in the gaps, but for the most part, a peer-to-peer network provides the right mix of tools for a home or small-office network.

Windows 2000 comes with some new management tools that may have some users confused. The third section of the chapter talks about the new Microsoft Management Console (MMC) snap-ins and how you can use them to manage your network. More important, it talks about how you can configure this tool, which is designed for large network use, for a small network. By creating a special configuration, you can reduce the complexity of using this tool, reducing the time required to perform administration. In other words, you can set up MMC to include the tools that a small network administrator would be interested in and ignore the other possibilities.

Every network administrator needs to know how to work with computers and users—that's the main point of network administration. The fourth section of the chapter helps you work with users and computers more efficiently. Network administration for a small network shouldn't be an all-day task—it's something you should be able to do in a relatively short time.

The last two sections of the chapter deal with maintenance tasks. You need to maintain your computer network just like you do a car or other complex device. While most people wouldn't consider running their car for a year without changing the oil, a lot of people run their computer system for years without any maintenance at all and then wonder why it constantly fails to perform as expected. The section, "Maintenance Tasks You Can't Ignore," talks about local maintenance tasks that you should perform on a regular basis; while the section, "Working With Remote Machines," talks about special maintenance considerations for remote networks.

No One Likes Big Brother

A lot of network administration texts on the market talk about the need for constant network monitoring. In fact, a lot of third-party vendors make the tools required for constant network monitoring available for every NOS and network configuration on the market today. For the most part, these tools and associated advice are designed to help the network administrator of a large network. A small office or home network doesn't require such intense monitoring and it's actually detrimental to perform such monitoring for the following reasons:

- Intense network management requires a lot of network administrator time.
- Too much network management reduces employee efficiency.
- The trust relationship between the network manager and employees is different on a small network than on a large network.

Administrator time is the issue that hits most small companies the hardest. In many cases, a small company will rely on a consultant to perform network administration tasks, and the cost of hiring a consultant is high. Even if you use an internal network administrator, every moment spent monitoring the network is time that could be spent doing some other type of work. In some cases, the people responsible for network administration become so sidetracked that they don't get any other kind of work done. If your company has a 10-node or less network, an hour or two per week should be more than enough administration time unless one of the following events occur:

- Employee hiring or departure
- New equipment purchase or old equipment retirement
- Software installation or update
- Security breach
- Change in company policy

An overzealous network administrator can make the situation worse by interfering with the work of other employees. For example, a network administrator should maintain tight security on the network, but not deny employees access to resources they need. Likewise, the timing of maintenance is important. Performing database maintenance (like compressing the files or indexing records) when other employees require access to the database file usually means that the other employees spend their time waiting rather than working. Scanning the server's hard drive for errors or performing other forms of hardware maintenance is another task that should wait for times when other employees have no need of the server (like on a day your business is closed). In other words, there's a tightrope the network administrator must walk to provide enough security and administration, yet keep the network running quickly and safely.

Network administrators for a large network may not see users often enough to know their names, much less their usage habits. In the case of an extremely large corporation, the network administrator may never see most of the employees they manage. This means there's no trust relationship between the network administrator and the employees. On the other hand, a network administrator for a small company will likely know the employees by name and will probably spend time during off-hours with at least some of them. A trust relationship develops, which allows the network administrator to judge certain requirements without monitoring. The small-town atmosphere of a small company or home office is something that companies like Microsoft don't take into account when developing their products.

As you can see, network administration for the home or small-office network is completely different than network administration in a large company when it comes to human issues. Too much monitoring is going to be detrimental, because the employees will resent monitoring at a personal level. In addition, excessive monitoring typically produces a lot of friction and even hatred—something to be avoided in a small-company environment. The small-company network administrator has to take a different tack—one that accounts for the personal needs of the employees.

Letting Users Figure Out Tasks—*There's a lot to be said for letting users figure out some of the tasks they need to perform on their own, even if it takes them more time to do so. Anyone who learns to associate certain types of functionality with specific tasks will be able to make the switch from one version of the same product to another with relative ease. In addition, self-taught users are also less expensive to support and often provide valuable input to the network administrator. Of course, there's a point where frustration takes over and the user isn't learning anything—it's important to help a user before frustration leads to bad habits, broken equipment, or both.*

I've run into two types of network administrator who work well in the small-office environment. The first acts like the small-town sheriff—friend to everyone, but vigilant when required (think of Sheriff Taylor of the "Andy Griffith Show"). The second is more like a librarian who encourages creative thought, but keeps the library quiet so others can work. Network administrators who have worked on large networks usually won't transition well to a small-network environment, because they're used to having too much control over individual users.

Of course, no matter how large or small your network is, a network administrator will have to perform certain monitoring tasks. For example, every network requires monitoring for security breaches. People using small networks abuse system resources just as easily as those on large networks, so resource monitoring is a must. Equipment wears out on large and small networks alike; software still requires updates. Proactive monitoring of these nonhuman elements keep any network running better and the people using it will complain less about slow downs and other network-specific problems. However, you can accomplish this type of monitoring without making it look like Big Brother is peering over the shoulder of every user on the network. You can sum up network monitoring for a home or small-office network as follows:

Monitor your network for hardware, software, and security faults, not as part of a power trip that will destroy the network you're trying to build.

Security breaches require special monitoring, even if you run a small network. There are more than a few sources of security breaches, and operating systems (OSs) don't provide a complete set of tools to check for them all. (Make sure you read Chapter 8 to gain a full appreciation of network security threats.) Here are some places you'll want to check for network-security monitoring tools (all tools support Windows unless otherwise noted):

Big Brother System and Network Monitor (Windows NT, Mac OS, NetWare, UNIX, and Linux)
http://maclawran.ca/bb-dnld/

Computer Incident Advisory Capability–Unix Network Monitoring Tools
http://ciac.llnl.gov/ciac/ToolsUnixNetMon.html

NetSaint Network Monitor (Linux and UNIX)
http://www.netsaint.org/

Network and Network Monitoring Software
http://www.alw.nih.gov/Security/prog-network.html

Network ICE
http://www.networkice.com/

Shields Up!
http://grc.com/su-firewalls.htm

Peer-to-Peer Means Little Administration

There's a relationship between network complexity and the time required to manage it. As the network complexity increases, so does the time you spend managing it. Peer-to-peer networks represent the least complex network that you can install. As a result, they also place the smallest burden on the network administrator—at least if you set the network up correctly. Of course, even the least complex network can quickly become a management nightmare if you don't sustain some level of organization and perform at least a little maintenance each week.

Let's talk about the organization issue first. A peer-to-peer network can be something as small as a two-node setup for gamers. In this case, there isn't much to organize. Everyone will have approximately the same rights to network resources, and there won't be much difference in equipment. However, once you get beyond this small, two-node network, you need to consider some organizational issues, including the following:

- Equipment configuration
- Peripheral device location and connection points
- Employee security
- Resource access rights

More than a few times, a company has asked me for help with a system, but no one at the company knows what equipment is installed or how that equipment is configured. In some cases, someone might know the vendor name, but that's not enough information to perform any sort of evaluation—you need to know specifically which equipment is in use. Normally, I end up performing a survey of the equipment and ordering any lost product manuals before going any further. Any sort of repair progresses at a snail-like pace until the manuals arrive and I've determined just what it is that I'm working with.

Maintaining equipment-configuration records is important. These records should list the configuration of each machine, at a minimum. For example, if a workstation has a display adapter, you should include the vendor name, the model number, the amount of memory, and any other configuration details. If the display adapter has any special options installed, you should record them in your configuration records. Of course, you'll want to maintain similar records for any other peripherals on the inside of the workstation (including the motherboard and hard drive configuration). Most installed peripherals come with separate manuals, so that you can see the information without opening the machine first. It's still a good idea to open a new machine and perform an inventory to ensure you do have all of the required manuals. Keeping good records means that anyone who helps you will have the information required when diagnosing problems like bad device drivers.

Hold Onto Those Manuals—*Nothing's more frustrating than to get to a job site and learn that the client has lost every manual for every machine on the premises. Getting copies of manuals verges on impossible a year after a machine is released. There are two ways to take care of the manual problem. Either store the manuals in a central location and use your configuration records to choose the correct manuals during servicing, or store the manuals with the machine and hope the user doesn't take them home.*

The original design for a network may require you to place a printer in a central location within a building. A year after you begin using the network, the printer location may prove less than ideal. This is especially prone to happen on a peer-to-peer network where the lack of a central server makes peripheral-device placement an error-prone task. One of the administration tasks for a small network is moving equipment around as needed. You want to ensure that the equipment is easily accessible by those who use it most, yet isn't causing environmental hazards, like too much noise. In addition, as user roles change, you may find that moving a peripheral improves system performance. This is especially true of performance-robbing peripherals like printers.

I previously talked about security as part of the "No One Likes Big Brother" section of this chapter. It's important to realize that security is actually a bigger issue in some ways on a peer-to-peer network because you have less flexibility in maintaining a secure environment. For example, most peer-to-peer networks don't offer security settings at the file level; you may find that you have to reconfigure systems to place shared files in a central directory or even dedicate a drive for that purpose. In addition to the paucity of security settings, user security is normally a pass–fail arrangement. Either users can work with the file in every way possible, or they can't work with it at all.

Small companies tend to have limited resources. In most cases, you'll want to provide complete access to resources like printers, because your company may have only one or two printers to serve everyone's needs. On a peer-to-peer network, you may find that you have no choice about sharing certain types of resources. Printers may be available to anyone who asks, whether you want them to have access or not. This is a situation when you may need to count on peer pressure to maintain some level of resource management. A peer-to-peer network may require a hands-off approach when tools to manage a particular resource don't exist or aren't capable of doing the job.

The second major area of peer-to-peer network administration is equipment maintenance in the form of diagnostics and repair. Maintenance on a peer-to-peer network can be tricky. Unless you maintain very good records, it may not be obvious that a particular workstation also shares its hard drive with everyone on the network. Removing such a workstation from service would be a mistake, because users would be unable to access their data. In most peer-to-peer network setups, it's a good idea to perform maintenance after hours, rather than at a time when someone might need the services of the workstation in question.

An Overview of Microsoft Management Console Snap-Ins

Microsoft Management Console (MMC) is an application that you'll find installed with Windows 2000 and, in some cases, Windows NT as well. (Windows NT doesn't come with MMC installed—you need to install the Windows NT Option Pack, or Service Pack 4 or above to get it. You can start MMC by selecting Start|Run, typing MMC in the Open field of the Run dialog box, and then clicking OK. You'll see an empty MMC dialog box like the one shown in Figure 9.1.

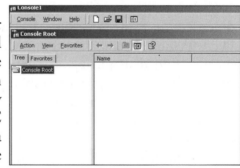

MMC is what's known as a container application—one that's specially designed to hold special objects. In this case, the special objects are MMC snap-ins. An MMC snap-in is a tool. The easiest way to view the relationship between MMC and the MMC snap-in is to think about a ratchet and a socket. MMCs are ratchets—you only need one of them for your toolkit. The MMC snap-in is the socket—you need one socket for each size bolt that you want to work with. Likewise,

Figure 9.1: MMC is a container application that allows you to perform various kinds of maintenance tasks with Windows 2000.

you'll need one MMC snap-in for each kind of task that you want to perform.

You can create your own special toolbox by combining MMC with one or more MMC snap-ins. In fact, I'll tell you how to do this in the "Creating Your Own MMC Consoles" section later in this chapter. The combination of MMC and a set of MMC snap-ins is called a console. Microsoft provides several preconfigured consoles in the Administrative Tools folder as shown in Figure 9.2. Selecting one of these options will display a copy of MMC with one or more MMC snap-ins loaded for you. Unfortunately, many of these preconfigured consoles are designed for large-network use or are too generic to provide full functionality by themselves. You can save MMC console settings and use them later, which makes it possible to create custom consoles. In fact, when you try to save console settings, MMC will normally suggest placing them in the Administrative Tools folder so that you can find the MMC console later.

Terminal Services Client ▸
Active Directory Domains and Trusts
Active Directory Sites and Services
Active Directory Users and Computers
Certification Authority
Cluster Administrator
Component Services
Computer Management
Connection Manager Administration Kit
Data Sources (ODBC)
DHCP
Distributed File System
DNS
Event Viewer
Internet Authentication Service
Internet Services Manager
Local Security Policy
Performance
QoS Admission Control
Remote Storage
Routing and Remote Access
Services
Telephony
Telnet Server Administration
Terminal Services Licensing
Terminal Services Manager
WINS

Figure 9.2: Windows 2000 comes with several preconfigured consoles that are targeted toward enterprise users.

Microsoft isn't the only company that develops MMC snap-ins. You can get MMC snap-ins from just about any company that creates applications for Windows NT or Windows 2000. Like a socket, the MMC snap-in is designed in such a way that it will always fit the ratchet (the MMC application). So, a developer can create a tool for you without knowing much about your system just by creating an MMC snap-in.

There are many ways to classify the tools that network administrators commonly use on a network. In days gone by, these tools would have been created as individual applications that the network administrator would have learned one at a time. Each tool would have had a different user interface and there wasn't any guarantee that the tool would work on your system. Using container applications like MMC means that the tools can now use a common interface; so they're easier for the network administrator to find and learn to use. Using MMC snap-ins also has advantages for the developer. For example, it takes a lot less time to develop and debug an MMC snap-in, because the user interface has already been created. All the developer needs to do is decide what special needs the MMC snap-in has.

Now that you have a better idea of what MMC snap-ins are, let's look at them in more detail. The first section that follows talks about the various uses for MMC snap-ins. It's important to know when an MMC snap-in will work well, and when it won't. Just as you wouldn't use a hammer to drive a screw, you shouldn't use an MMC snap-in for tasks that it's not good at performing. Some vendors will probably try to use MMC for these tasks because it's a new technology and they have gadgetitus. The next section tells you how to create your own MMC consoles. This is especially important, because you'll want to set up your tools to access the network quickly. In addition, having all of your tools in one place ensures you don't waste time looking at information you don't require to fix a given problem.

Uses for MMC Snap-Ins

MMC snap-ins are limited to one specific use—developers can create MMC snap-ins that fulfill a variety of needs. Of course, it's helpful to know what types of tools you can expect to see on the market in the near future. An obvious method of classifying a tool is to determine what you'll use it for in a general way. For example, do you want a tool to monitor the network and alert you to possible problems, or do you need a proactive tool that performs maintenance on a regular basis so that there won't be any need for monitoring in the first place? The following list talks about some of the ways to define tool type by general usage:

Monitor—This is the type of software network administrators use on a daily basis. It helps them track the status of the network. For example, monitoring software can tell a network administrator how much memory the server has left or the status of the hard drives. Network administrators normally want to monitor the network from the workstation at their desk. MMC allows this kind of flexibility without any special programming. You won't get this kind of support using desktop applications unless the developer adds special codes to do it. Even if the developer adds the specialized code, you'll likely find that the code is network specific rather than the general interface provided by MMC. Figure 9.3 shows a typical monitor MMC snap-in in the form of the System Monitor. Notice that there are actually two MMC snap-ins shown in this figure—the second is the Performance Logs and Alerts snap-in.

Analysis—At times, simply knowing the network's statistics doesn't really do everything you need it to do. Analysis software takes raw input from monitoring software, studies it, and then returns the result. For example, an analysis tool might try to predict hardware failures based on certain network trends such as the number of errors found while doing normal hard disk maintenance. Analysis software is another category of administrative tools that work well with MMC, because the network administrator will want to track this information from the local workstation.

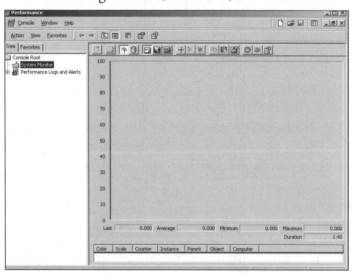

Figure 9.3: Performance Monitor is an example of a typical monitor MMC snap-in.

Security—You'll see MMC snap-ins used for a variety of security needs. For example, the Local Security Settings console (Security Settings MMC snap-in) allows you to change the local security policies. Figure 9.4 shows what this MMC snap-in looks like. Likewise, the Certification Authority console allows you to manage security certificates for your company.

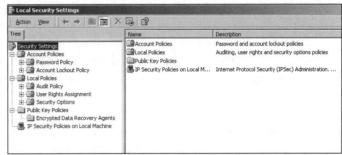

Figure 9.4: The Local Security Settings Console allows you to change the security settings for the local machine.

Event—These tools don't always provide some type of pro-active feature; they may be reactive instead. A hard drive failure is something that you can prepare for and even anticipate; but it's not something that you can predict with absolute accuracy. Some developers create desktop applications that periodically poll the servers for failure conditions. This is one place where MMC isn't the best choice, because you have to manually start MMC to use it. The best way to monitor failure conditions is to install a service application and then allow that service to send e-mail to the network administrator and create an event log entry when a failure occurs. Figure 9.5 shows the Event Log snap-in for a Windows 2000 Professional machine. Servers typically have more logs, and applications can create specialized logs if necessary. If you do get an MMC snap-in for event monitoring, make sure you ask the vendor about any limitations. For example, you need to know whether the snap-in has to be active to gather event information.

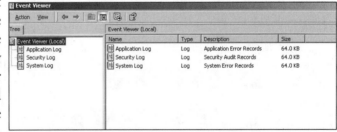

Figure 9.5: The Event Viewer MMC snap-in allows you to see events that have already taken place on the machine.

Automated maintenance—Some types of maintenance that you need to perform daily don't require any form of network administrator input. For example, tape backup software has been automated for quite some time. The network administrator only needs to set up the parameters once, and then the software can automatically perform this maintenance from that point on. Any time you can automate a maintenance task, it increases network-administrator efficiency and reduces the chance of error. Automated maintenance is one type of administrative software that requires two levels of application support. An MMC snap-in allows the network administrator to configure and monitor the background task; while a service actually performs the task in the background. It's usually not safe to assume that you can answer every administrative software need using a single application.

Setting Alerts Can Help Track Events—*The network administrator can use the Alerts portion of the Performance Logs and Alerts snap-in to send messages to the network administrator when certain events occur. An alert can also make an entry in the event log, start a performance data log, and run an application in an effort to recover from the problem. Using several MMC snap-ins together allows you to overcome the limitations of a single tool in many cases, which means that you need fewer third-party tools to manage your network.*

Manual maintenance—Testing software was probably one of the first network administrator tools created. It's important to test the network and verify that it actually works as intended—that there isn't some hidden flaw waiting to cause data corruption or other problems. Some of these testing tasks require constant monitoring, input, or even analysis on the part of the network administrator. These kinds of tasks are perfect candidates for manual maintenance utilities. Figure 9.6 shows the Disk Defragmenter snap-in. The simple act of defragmenting your hard drive as needed can greatly improve system performance. We'll talk more about testing soft-ware in the "Maintenance Tasks You Can't Ignore" section that appears later in the chapter.

Figure 9.6: The Disk Defragmenter snap-in can improve system performance by reducing fragmentation on a hard drive.

Configuration—Software today is more flexible than ever before, which means that there are more configuration options. Sometimes OS vendors hide some of the more powerful configuration options, because they fear that the user will use them incorrectly. Since you can assign individual security restrictions to your MMC snap-ins, they make perfect configuration utilities. You can hide dangerous utilities from prying eyes by setting the correct security and making it a manual addition to a console rather than a default console setting stored in the Administrative Tools folder. Of course, the configuration tools that everyone knows about appear in the System Tools MMC snap-in. It contains MMC snap-ins like the Device Manager shown in Figure 9.7, which allows you to manage system hardware.

Installation—Administrators constantly perform installations of all kinds—everything from word processors to new OSs. As a result, this is one area in which even a small amount of automation can produce a large increase in administrator productivity. However, while you might be able to configure an automated installation set-up using an MMC snap-in, normally you'll want to use the Windows 2000 Installer to perform the actual installation process.

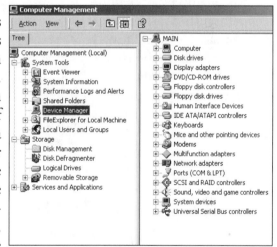

Figure 9.7: The Device Manager is accessible through an MMC snap-in; it allows you to add, update, and remove devices.

User assistance—All of the large software companies have come to the same conclusion about user support: It's less expensive to write software to do the job than it is to hire support personnel. Witness all of the automated methods these vendors employ to direct your attention to some other source of help. Telephone lines usually have menuing systems that offer everything from fax-back support to recorded message help. Online sites provide complex search systems that allow users to find information themselves, rather than depend on human support. User assistance software requires constant configuration, monitoring, and updates. You can use MMC snap-ins to perform all these required tasks.

Informational—A lot of times, help-desk personnel need to know information about the user's machine. Getting the information out of the user, however, can try anyone's patience. The main problem is the information is spread out into places the user normally doesn't look. Informational MMC snap-ins would allow the user to see all of the required information in one place. For that matter, the administrators or help-desk personnel could look at the information from their MMC console without even asking the user for input. One example of an informational MMC snap-in is the contents of the System Summary folder of the System Information MMC snap-in shown in Figure 9.8.

Tracking—Records are the mainstays of many administrators. Unfortunately, few administrators have the time to keep records that are both complete and up to date. Automating the task of tracking various maintenance and error events on a server makes it easier for an administrator to locate problems based on the history of the

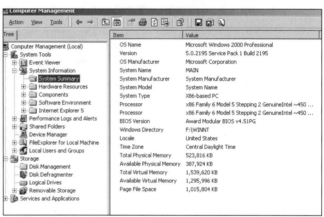

Figure 9.8: The System Summary folder contains one of the rare examples of an information-only display for Windows 2000.

system. Of course, all default Windows 2000 monitoring is accessed using an MMC snap-in. You'll find this MMC snap-in in the Performance console using the Performance Logs and Alerts MMC snap-in shown in Figure 9.9.

As you can see, there are a lot of different uses for MMC snap-ins. The difficulty is figuring out how the various MMC snap-ins work together and then grouping them in a way that fits your work style. Obviously, if you find that you're using a particular MMC snap-in a lot, you should place it with your general tools to ensure you can

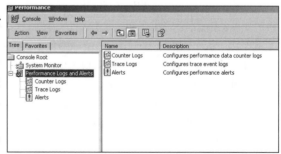

Figure 9.9: MMC is a container application that allows you to perform various kinds of maintenance tasks with Windows 2000.

find it quickly when needed. Its also helps if you create task-related consoles. I normally use the following three consoles on smaller networks; but there isn't any right or wrong way to set up a console for your own use.

- Performance and security
- Maintenance
- Computer and user

Creating Your Own MMC Consoles

It's relatively easy to create MMC consoles of your own, and if you don't like a particular console, you can simply erase it from your hard drive and start again. I normally create MMC consoles based on the types of tasks that I'm performing. Keeping all of the MMC snap-ins related to a specific task in one place means I can open a single console and not have to worry about looking anywhere else for tools. However, there aren't any rules that say you need to create a console in a particular way—you can create any number of consoles that you want, and they can be configured in any number of ways. The following steps show you how to create a simple MMC console:

1. Start MMC. You'll see the empty MMC window shown in Figure 9.1.
2. Select Console|Add/Remove Snap-in. You'll see an Add/Remove Snap-in dialog box.
3. Click Add. You'll see an Add Standalone Snap-in dialog box like the one shown in Figure 9.10. Notice that some of these MMC snap-ins are created by other companies.
4. Select one or more MMC snap-ins from the list by highlighting the entry and clicking Add. For the purposes of this example, I'll select the Disk Defragmenter. MMC may display a dialog box asking you which machine

Figure 9.10: The Add Standalone Snap-in dialog box contains a list of all the MMC snap-ins installed on your machine.

you want to configure the MMC snap-in to use. We'll cover remote machine monitoring in the "Working With Remote Machines" section that follows.
5. Click Close to close the Add Standalone Snap-in dialog box. You should see the list of MMC snap-ins that you selected in the Add/Remove Snap-in

Figure 9.11: The Add Standalone Snap-in dialog box contains a list of all the MMC snap-ins installed on your machine.

dialog box shown in Figure 9.11. Notice that you can learn more about an MMC snap-in by clicking About or remove it from the list of MMC snap-ins by clicking Remove. In many cases, the vendor will include contact information for the MMC snap-in as part of the About dialog box.

6. Click OK. You'll see the MMC snap-ins you selected displayed in the left pane of the MMC console. Selecting one of the MMC snap-ins will display a detailed view of the information that MMC snap-in monitors in the right pane of the MMC console. At this point, you can manipulate the display so that the information is presented in the best way for use.

7. Select Console|Options. You'll see the Options dialog box shown in Figure 9.12. This dialog box allows you to choose which level of control the user of the MMC console will have over the environment. The most powerful selection is Author mode. You can limit the number of panes users see and their ability to add new MMC snap-ins. In other words, you can set the MMC console up to provide safe access to specific machine information without giving the user access to more information than needed. You also use this dialog box to assign a name to the MMC console and give it a unique icon, if desired. There are a lot of icons to choose from in system files like Shell32.DLL, which you can access by clicking the Change Icon button shown in Figure 9.12.

8. Click OK to close the Options dialog box.

9. Click Save. You'll see a Save As dialog box. Notice that this dialog box automatically asks to save the MMC console in the Administrative Tools folder. Saving the MMC console here will allow it to appear automatically in the Administrative Tools folder on the Start menu.

10. Type a name for the MMC console, and then click OK.

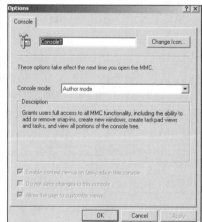

Figure 9.12: The Options dialog box allows you to customize an MMC console before you save it.

Keeping Track of Your Tools—*In some cases, I set up a custom folder below the Administrative Tools folder to keep the custom MMC consoles that I've created separate from those provided by Windows.*

As you can see, creating custom MMC consoles is relatively easy. Of course, creating useful MMC consoles will take time, because you'll need to learn how the various MMC snap-ins work together. The important concept to remember is:

Always create MMC consoles that contain a selection of MMC snap-ins that you normally use together to make administering the network more efficient.

Working with Users and Computers

The two elements that you'll work with the most on a network are users and computers. Even low-end networks usually include several ways to manage both users and computers to allow a company to work at top efficiency. The main limiting factor from an administrative perspective is how much flexibility the NOS offers. Whether the limitations are pertinent to your company depends on your company's size and how strictly you need to maintain security. A home office with two people using a peer-to-peer network may not experience the same problems that a small company with ten users and the same peer-to-peer configuration would. The number of users and the complexity of the company make a difference when it comes to user and computer configuration requirements.

One of the most straightforward and easily configured user setups is found with NetWare. Figure 9.13 shows a typical user configuration dialog box. The important consideration here is that you get a lot of flexibility with NetWare, yet there aren't any confusing alternative configurations like you'll find with other OSs such as Windows. You'll always configure user settings with this dialog box, no matter how many users you get or how the network is configured in

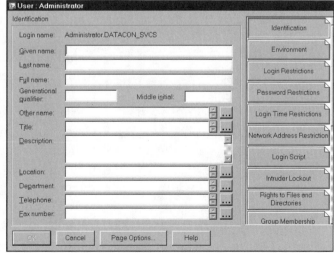

Figure 9.13: NetWare offers a straightforward, yet flexible method to configure user and computer settings.

other ways. The same principle holds true with computers. You'll find that they're configured precisely the same way every time you add a computer to the network.

Windows 2000 uses two different configuration methodologies, depending on how you have your network configured. In fact, you'll find that you have to use two different MMC snap-ins, depending on which type of configuration you want to perform. When creating a domain setup, you'll normally have Active Directory installed, which means using the Active Directory-specific tools. Likewise, when using a workgroup setup, you'll need to use the Local Users and Groups MMC snap-in. The reason for the dual-setup modes is that Active Directory provides centralized storage of user and computer information; whereas a workgroup setup relies on local storage. You'll want to avoid using a workgroup setup once a network grows beyond 20 users, because replicating the settings across multiple machines manually can use up a great deal of network administrator time. The information Windows 2000 collects when set up for Active Directory is equivalent to the information gathered by NetWare. On the other hand, Windows 2000 gathers hardly any information at all when in workgroup mode, as shown in Figure 9.14.

Windows 9x presents yet another challenge. There are several different ways to configure this OS depending on which features you want to use. Windows 9x defaults to a share-level access control scheme when initially set up for networking. Many people don't realize that you can also choose a more secure user-level access-control scheme by manually selecting the option from the Access Control tab of Network Neighborhood. If you decide to use share-level access control, you'll also need to provide the name of domain controller on the network. Windows 9x will ask the server for a list of names every time someone requests access to a resource, making the resource much more secure in the process.

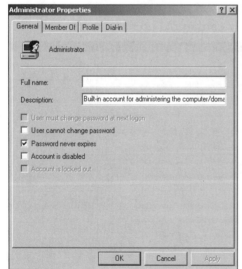

Figure 9.14: Local workgroup storage for Windows 2000 means that you lose a lot of flexibility and storage capacity that this OS is supposed to offer.

You can also choose to provide a separate desktop for each user under Windows 9x—another feature that is turned off by default. Open the User Profiles tab of the Passwords applet in the Control Panel and you'll see a Password

Properties dialog box. While there's no way to absolutely ensure a user has to use a specific desktop under Windows 9x, assigning a specific desktop and linking it to network access ensures the desktop will be used when it most counts—working with sensitive company data.

Ultimately, the security in Windows 9x is extremely flawed, because you can bypass it with relative ease by pressing Esc at the main login dialog. While doing this prevents access to the network, the user still has access to the local machine. So, while there are certain protections under Window 9x, the user and computer settings are better used to help users get the most from the working environment than as a means to secure network data.

Maintenance Tasks You Can't Ignore

The administration task that every network administrator hates the most is maintenance. Computer maintenance is something every network administrator should take seriously, but few do. The following list discusses the three reasons that most network administrators don't perform regular maintenance on their machines:

Time—Most network administrators rush through their day putting out fires. Trying to convince them to spend a few additional hours after work completing maintenance tasks is nearly impossible. Even network administrators need to sleep, unlike authors.

Resources—Even small companies want their servers up and running 24 hours a day, 7 days a week. Trying to convince management that it would be a good idea to take a server offline for maintenance is difficult, to say the least.

Difficulty—Most maintenance packages are viewed as being difficult to use and even harder to interpret. They don't offer remote capability for the most part, which means the network administrator has to run from machine to machine to get the work done.

The problem with this reasoning is that it trades a shortsighted goal for a long-term payoff. A properly maintained network will always outperform one that languishes for lack of maintenance. In addition, proper maintenance assures that the network will run when you need it most—during peak usage hours. Yes, it will cost the network administrator some time to run diagnostics, but the network administrator will save a lot more time not having to run around putting out fires.

Management team members are usually worried about server down time, because they view it as a system failure rather than a preventative maintenance effort. In most cases, once management sees that proper maintenance results in fewer network emergencies, getting a reserve server ordered isn't a big deal. You can achieve the 24/7 up-time goal required by many companies today by cycling servers out of the loop. Conducting maintenance on the server that's out of the loop allows the network to remain online while keeping it in peak condition. A reserve server also makes good sense because it allows a company to recover quickly when a server goes down unexpectedly during peak usage hours.

Maintenance software can be difficult to use; there isn't any doubt about it. Few packages allow any type of remote activity. Those that do are often inefficient or not effective at finding the sources of potential problems. However, a network administrator can set a system up to allow for batch processing of diagnostics. Placing a floppy in a machine and rebooting shouldn't be too much of a problem. This is one of those areas where a little planning up front can allow you to complete an unpleasant task with a minimum of effort.

So, what types of maintenance are essential? It depends on your computer system to a certain extent. However, these are the tasks that you should always perform:

Cleaning—Every machine on your network should be cleaned. Accumulated dust can cause shorts in the system and will cause components to heat up more. Dust also gets into moving parts and causes bearings (like those found in hard drives) to fail. A clean system will have fewer failures and will be able to withstand those losses of air conditioning with fewer problems. Don't forget to use CD-ROM and other disk cleaners when necessary. Cleaning mice and monitor screens will improve their longevity as well.

Backup—If your data is important to you, back it up. Make sure you create a tape of updated data every day. Creating a complete backup of the whole system once a week is also a good idea. Backup software can be completely automated, so there are very few excuses for not creating a good backup of your system.

Diagnostics—Testing your system for flaws is a must. Some components tend to warn you of imminent failure far enough in advance that you can take proactive measures rather than react to the problem. This is especially true of components with moving parts. Frequently, devices like hard drives will provide a warning in the form of bit failures that good diagnostic software can detect. Make sure you perform any diagnostics that come with a particular device. For example, most display adapters provide special diagnostics that test all of their internal features, not just the common ones supported by off-the-shelf diagnostic software.

Defragmenting—Most OSs do a poor job of keeping data organized on the hard drive. Whenever data becomes disorganized, the hard drive has to work harder to find it and get it to the user. It doesn't take too many delays in data retrieval to become a noticeable problem.

Scanning—It pays to scan your system for problems. I normally begin every day with a scan of the hard drive for viruses, followed by a scan for data errors. Scanning your system for problems takes only a few seconds, but gives you a sense of security throughout the day.

You'll find that most OSs are lacking in diagnostic software. This is especially true of Windows. Here is a list of some of the diagnostic packages you may want to consider for your network:

#1-PC Diagnostics Company TuffTEST
http://www.tufftest.com/

BCM Diagnostics
http://www.bcmcom.com/utilities/wdiag102/

Micro 2000, Inc. Universal Diagnostic Toolkit
http://www.micro2000.com/

PC Doctor
http://www.ws.com/

PC Tools Diagnostics
http://www.pc-tools.com/

TouchStone Software CheckIt
http://www.checkit.com/

Ultra-X Diagnostic Tool Kits
http://www.uxd.com/

When Systems Won't Boot—*The interesting part of some of the available diagnostics is that they either come with their own OS (TuffTEST) or are hardware based (PC Tools Diagnostics), so they work with any system. In fact, when working with the hardware-based products, you can often test a machine from a remote location, even if the machine isn't booted. (Of course, this can be expensive, because you need one diagnostic card per machine.)*

Working with Remote Machines

Any time you have a network installed, you will have to deal with remote machines. Even if that machine is right across the hall, the fact that it's not sitting right in front of you makes it a remote machine—at least from a certain perspective. As PC networks have gotten larger, the need for some way of accessing these remote machines for administrative purposes has increased. Imagine forcing a network administrator to run across town every time a machine in a satellite office breaks down.

Small offices can also benefit from remote access capability. Keeping a network administrator at his or her desk means higher efficiency. Instead of running from room to room in a mad panic every time a user stubs a toe, the network administrator can calmly view the information required to fix a problem and then make a trip to the user's machine if necessary. In many cases, a problem can be solved by making a small change in the user's configuration right from the network administrator's desk.

Windows 2000 excels in providing easy-to-use, remote machine capability. There are several ways to access this capability. For example, when you set up a new MMC console, you can choose either the local machine or a remote machine for certain MMC snap-ins. You can also set the console up to allow changes to the target machine from the command line.

If your network is small enough, you can create a special console that allows you to view more than one machine at the same time. Figure 9.15 shows an example of such a console. Notice that all three MMC snap-ins are the same—only the target machine is different. This is a technique that works great with small networks, but quickly loses its appeal once the network grows beyond five or six computers.

Some MMC snap-ins also allow you to select another computer from the root node. For example, the Computer Management snap-in shown in Figure 9.15 allows you to change computers. Right-click Computer Management, and select Connect to another computer from the shortcut menu. You'll see a Select Computer dialog box that allows you to select another computer on the network. By creating a MMC console with two copies of the Computer Management snap-in, you could compare any two computers on the network. This would allow you to make upgrade decisions with greater ease and could reduce trouble-shooting time significantly in many cases.

Whether you're working with local or remote machines, the ability to manage system resources is crucial for any network. Maintaining the machines on the network is no longer a matter of checking an individual machine—you need to check how each machine is affecting the network as a whole. In the long term, having a good set of network administration tools is essential if you want to keep a network up and running all of the time.

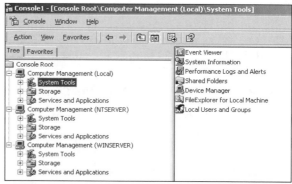

Figure 9.15: You can create custom consoles that allow you to view certain statistics for every machine on the network at the same time.

CHAPTER TEN

Remote Communications

It's only been in the last few years that people have gotten connected to their homes and business from every location imaginable. Cell phones and other technologies promise to make it possible to talk with people no matter where they are. I see commercials and television poking fun at this new connectivity by placing people in truly awkward situations, only to have their cell phone ring. The reality is that cell phones and other portable communication have an important role to play in today's mobile society. They allow you to talk with loved ones when you need to, rather than wait until everyone is in one location. Likewise, people work best with computers when they communicate with the office when they need to, rather than when they're physically at the office.

Computers have gone through the mobile communication revolution as well, but it's been a slower and longer road. Remote communications used to consist of connecting a home computer to the office through a local connection to perform tasks like checking e-mail or working on documents stored on the network from home. Someone thought it would be a good idea to make computers mobile, so they invented the luggable—a computer that was portable in name only. Luggable computers allowed users to communicate from a motel room, but not anywhere else, because of their size and weight. The main reason that people wanted a luggable computer is to remain in contact with the office while on the road and to work on reports as needed, instead of writing them when they got home. These 40-pound behemoths gave way to lighter laptops, which have now become the computer to get for those who spend any time at all on the road. Laptops are great, because they extend remote access to the conference room where people can take notes or hold conferences with the home office. Laptops allow people to communicate with the home office from any location that has a telephone line and electricity. While laptops are nice, they're still not portable enough—size and weight still confine them to certain environments. Computers are getting ever smaller as we progress from laptops, to notebooks, and finally palmtops.

Using cell phone technology will allow an employee to call the home office from almost anywhere in the world. All that the road warrior will really need once voice technology is perfected is a palmtop with voice interface and a small screen for displaying data that can't be translated into words with ease.

All of these new technologies mean one thing. If you're setting up a network today, you need to consider remote communication as part of the design. It's not a matter of *if* you'll need the capability, but *when* you'll need it. Whether the communication takes place from home or on the road, most businesses require some type of remote communication to remain competitive today. If you haven't guessed it already, we'll be looking at a variety of remote communication technologies in this chapter. (We'll talk about Internet specific strategies in Chapter 11, *Communicating Over the Internet*.)

The overall goal of this chapter is to show you how remote computing can become a natural extension of your existing network. Some people have the idea that remote communications have to be difficult to use, limited in functionality, or expensive. Remote communications don't have to fall into any of these categories. A properly configured remote communication setup can operate trouble free—at least most of the time. Of course, you can't control problems like the availability of a telephone line and the quality of the line that you do get.

Since this book focuses on the home and small-office network, the "Getting to the Office From Other Places" section of this chapter talks about communicating with the office from home and other places. Part of the problem of creating good remote communications is getting the right software package. The "Software Packages You Should Know About" section of the chapter examines some of the packages currently available on the market and helps you understand the pros and cons of each package type. Collaboration between professionals represents another use of remote communications and one that's on the rise. We'll not only look at the various collaboration packages available on the market today, but the kinds of problems that you might have using them in the "Using Conferencing Tools" section of the chapter. This section of the chapter also looks at conferencing. A conference allows one or more speakers to communicate with a group of people over an intranet or the Internet.

Getting to the Office from Other Places

For many home office and small business network users, time spent away from the office represents opportunities lost. However, staying in the office all day isn't an option for at least some of these users. Consider a business that depends on retail sales at craft or other shows across the country. The owner of the business may be on the road four or five months out of the year. One or two employees may staff the home office and fulfill orders; but the owner still has to remain in contact with the home office to make decisions. Without remote communication, the owner could lose touch with the business and miss opportunities. A mobile world doesn't wait around for someone to get home after a business trip; business owners often need to make a decision immediately after hearing about an opportunity.

Even if you're not on the road four months out of the year, remote communication is still an important facet of your network to consider. Data transfer between home and office is the most important type of remote communication for many small businesses, because a small business owner often needs access to company records from home. For example, a business owner may not want to go back to the office after dinner to get some nighttime work completed—it's easier to call into the office from home. In addition, small business owners can't afford to lose entire days of work by being sick; a home connection to the company network allows the owner or employee to get work done without making everyone else in the office ill. Even trade shows represent an unwelcome interruption in workflow if you don't have remote communication with the office. Many professionals need to attend trade shows associated with their craft, yet the time spent in training means a loss of communication with the office.

Communications are important to the health of every company, but not every company has the same needs. You may have heard that the Internet is the best solution for all of your communication needs, but that isn't entirely true. While large companies use methods that allow continuous communications to keep disparate parts of the organization in contact, small companies seldom need continuous remote communications. One of the most common solutions to the problem of remote connectivity is to use a virtual private network (VPN), which means using the Internet to extend a local network directly. We'll talk about VPNs in Chapter 11, *Communicating Over the Internet*, but for the most part, they answer a specific need and assume you have a local Internet connection at your disposal. What happens if all you have is a telephone line? In addition, VPNs are quite expensive to setup and maintain; cost becomes a concern if the VPN isn't paying for itself. It's still possible to create a perfectly usable low-cost dial-up connection to your network. The dial-up setup won't operate at the same speed as a network connection; but it still allows you to complete work assignments while on the road and stay in contact.

The following sections help you understand what you need to create a remote connection using just a telephone and some special software. Of course, the first question you should ask is whether your business needs require the investment for a remote communication setup, however small. Remote communications normally provide a limited set of features at reduced speed, so they're not the best alternative in some cases. Even if you do create a remote connection, you'll want to optimize it to keep costs down, which is the topic of the next section. We'll also talk about the importance of security for this connection. Even though a dial-up connection to your network is lower risk than an Internet connection in some respects, dial-up connections are often the access point of choice for professionals.

Do You Need a Remote Connection?

The question of whether you need a remote connection might seem simple at first. After all, you need to exchange data with the home office, so a remote connection is the best option. A remote connection seems like a low-tech approach to a problem with communication, but it can just as easily turn into yet another problem if not managed properly.

Many small businesses look at the initial cost of a computer solution without fully considering the long-term cost. The advantage of a remote connection is that it requires only a telephone line, two computers, and a bit of software. Newer versions of some operating systems include the required dial-up software. Telephones are relatively easy to find and reliable as well, so creating a remote connection to your network shouldn't be a problem. Except for the cost of an additional computer, there's a good chance that your remote connection will cost little or nothing. In fact, if you were planning to use a laptop while on the road anyway, the cost of a remote connection is effectively free. This also holds true if you already have a home computer in place and want to connect to your office.

The problem with a remote connection is that the telephone call can become a continuous drain on your checking account. A connection from your home to your office isn't a problem, because telephone companies typically charge a flat rate for a local call. Using a remote connection, in this case, makes good sense, because it provides enough bandwidth for most business needs. (For a discussion on bandwidth, see the "How Fast is Fast Enough?" section of Chapter 5, *Cabling and Other Masses of Wire*.)

When you're on the road, however, things change because you have to pay long distance charges. If you plan to spend a lot of time communicating with the home office, those long distance charges can really mount up. You'd need to provide something of significant value to the company during that time to compensate for the cost of making the call. So a remote connection is best used for small data transfers like downloading the latest price list or reading your e-mail when you need it on the road.

So, the first consideration is the cost of the phone call and any extra equipment contrasted to the value of the information exchange to the company. If you regularly use a remote connection to enter orders into the company database for processing, a remote connection is a highly cost-effective addition to your company's network. The bottom line is that remote communication must pay for itself or there isn't any reason to use it.

Calling Cards: the Cheap Alternative—*The size of your long distance bill can depend on how wisely you purchase telephone minutes. Some motels add a surcharge to long distance calls to pay for improvements in telephone facilities for travelers. Make sure you check for this surcharge before making a reservation. However, even without the surcharge, calling long distance from a motel can be an expensive proposition and calling collect isn't an option. A third alternative, calling cards, are one way to keep costs under control. Not only do calling cards offer competitive rates, they're also convenient to use while on the road. In addition, allocating each employee a specific number of minutes of long distance communication time is a good way to keep remote communications within budget.*

Another factor is convenience. Most motels in larger cities offer modem connections within the rooms and recognize that business people will need these connections to communicate with their home office. Unfortunately, there isn't any guarantee that you'll always be in a large city; you might spend most of your time traveling between small towns. Even if a remote connection would pay for itself in terms of new sales, you need some guarantee that the telephone line will be available. Fortunately, the cell phone makes it possible to create a connection even if a permanent telephone line isn't available, but you need to factor in higher costs for the call. (We'll talk more about this solution in the "Optimizing Remote Connection Components" section that follows.) An alternative to using a cell phone for wireless connectivity on the road is to use a wireless modem service like **Metricom Ricochet** http://www.ricochet.net/. Unfortunately, this alternative is limited to specific service areas and you couldn't use it to travel across country.

The final consideration is frequency of use. A remote connection is fine for connecting from your home to your business if you use it for an hour or two each night, or on the occasional sick day. If your company requires remote connectivity on a continuous basis or more than a few people need this feature, it pays to look at alternatives like VPN. A remote connection of the kind that we'll discuss in this chapter will provide a 56 Kbps connection at best. It's far more likely that you'll end up with a connection in the 40 to 50 Kbps range, which is fine for small files, but not good for working with large files on the server.

Optimizing Remote Connection Components

A quick definition of remote connectivity is two computers that you connect using a telephone line. Using this definition, the list of components required to create a connection is relatively small. Some people assume that few components automatically means high reliability and ease of use. However, there are some performance and reliability issues to consider for these components. The most important performance-related issue is communication speed. The highest bandwidth you can hope to achieve given current technology is 56 Kbps, so it's important to get the best connection you can between the client and host machines. Here are some ways to ensure you can get the maximum speed from your setup:

Check modem features—Modem vendors often provide special features designed to make the modem run faster. For example, the vendor may provide a nonstandard way of compressing data that allows the modem to transmit more data on the relatively limited bandwidth provided by a telephone line. Unfortunately, modem features and their implementation vary by vendor, so you can't always access them. Getting all the modems for your remote communication needs from the same vendor ensures you can access these special features.

Verify the modem setup—Having access to a special modem feature doesn't mean your system will use the feature. In many situations, operating systems like Windows and the Mac OS will initially set a modem up for a default set of features. This allows the modem to communicate with the broadest range of modems possible, but means the modem can't perform up to its full potential. Of course, you'll want to know how to set the modem to use the default features so that you can communicate with machines other than the remote server.

Avoid telephone line noise—Telephone lines are susceptible to noise, because they rely on unshielded cable. Even if you get a high connection speed between client and server, line noise will greatly reduce throughput. In many cases, you can reduce line noise by checking the connections within the telephone line's junction box (the little box you plug the telephone line into). Loose connections will always produce noise, as will excess lengths of stripped wire. In some situations rerunning the telephone line along a different route to avoid noise sources will reduce line noise as well.

Check the connection speed—A momentary spike in line noise or other environmental factor can affect the connection speed of the modem. Checking connection speed before you begin work is one way to ensure you'll have the maximum bandwidth available. It's less expensive to disconnect and make a new connection than to suffer through a remote computing session using a 14.4 Kbps connection. This factor is important enough that most operating systems make it easy to check. For example, Windows will display the connection speed if you momentarily place the mouse cursor over the connection icon on the taskbar.

Perform modem diagnostics—Most modems provide diagnostics that are built right into the hardware. However, accessing these diagnostics can be a painful experience if you don't have software to automate the task. Some operating systems, like the Windows support found on the Diagnostics tab of the Modem Properties dialog box, provide rudimentary software diagnostic support that accesses the diagnostics buried in the modem hardware. In other cases, you'll need to perform the diagnostics using an application provided by the vendor. Make sure you run modem diagnostics on a regular basis. A modem can appear to work fine and still experience some type of failure. The loss of features like hardware data compression will affect your remote communication session speed.

Understand remote-communication program features—Remote-connection programs vary greatly in their ability to provide good connections. For example, some remote-connection programs allow you to take control of the server so that you can operate it by remote control. This feature allows you to replace lengthy data transfers with short commands in many cases. All you need to do is transfer the result of a session to the client machine. In addition, some remote-connection applications provide software compression. The important consideration is to balance product cost with communication cost. A high-end remote-communication program is necessary when you perform most of your remote communication using a long-distance connection. On the other hand, using the remote-communication program that comes with the operating system is a good choice when you normally work with a local telephone connection.

Reliability is another issue that you need to consider when defining a remote connectivity strategy. You can't always guarantee that you'll have a telephone line to use for a remote connection. If you're staying in a smaller or older motel while on the road, the rooms may not be equipped to handle computer connections. However, if you have a cell phone available, you can normally make the connection using a special adapter kit. Here are some companies that make the special adapter kits for computer modem to cell phone connections:

AirBridge Products: Mitsubishi MobileAccess 120 Phone and PC Connection Kit
http://www.bam.com/wireless/mitsubishi.htm

Connect Cell Phones to the Mac
http://www.sentman.com/mac_pcs.html

Connect Globally Mobile to Cell Phone Adapter Cables
http://www.connectglobally.com/note_cell/modem_to_cell.asp

Xircom Xcessories Family Page
http://www.xircom.com/cda/page/1,1298,0-0-1_1-319,00.html

Once you have a good connection in place, you'll find that optimizing a remote-communication session comes down to making the right choices with the communication software. If your company plans to provide remote-communication software to employees on the road, make sure you have a training session to teach employees how to use the product efficiently.

I remember watching an insurance agent come to my home and fiddle with his remote-communication software for the better part of fifteen minutes before getting a simple data transfer completed. The agent complained that the company had spent a grand total of thirty minutes teaching employees how to use both the product and the remote-communication software. If the company had taken time to train the insurance agent, it would have saved on their long distance bill. More important, the long wait times were annoying—I had to wonder how much business the company lost, because the agents ended up looking inept. Here's a simple rule to remember:

You'll more than make up for any money you spend in remote-communication training with savings in long distance bills and lost business.

If you're a one-person company, make sure you spend time with the remote-communication product at your office by using a second line to actually call the host machine. There won't be anyone at the home office to help you out with the remote connection while you're on the road, so checking the reliability of the connection is important. In addition, working with the product before you go on a trip will help you make adjustments in your usage plans. You may find that some applications work so slowly that it's best to wait until you return home to use them. In other cases, you may need to perform some local configuration before you go on the road to ensure the data you need is available immediately. For example, you may need a report from your database manager each morning. Scheduling the report to run automatically will save time and allow you to obtain the report with a simple download rather than wait for the computer to generate it first.

Everyone can benefit from remote communication planning. Creating checklists of common tasks is a good idea. They allow you to perform tasks quickly without having to think about each step. Since many remote-communication tasks are repetitive, you can refine these checklists over time to get tasks done faster and keep your long-distance bill small. Using checklists also ensures that you perform the tasks the same way every time, making remote communication more consistent and predictable so that you can estimate costs with greater accuracy. Finally, checklists guarantee that you complete all data-transfer tasks with one call. Multiple calls waste both time and money.

Doubling the Effect of Remote Communication—*Everyone assumes that remote communication is a one-way street. An employee calls into the home office network, performs some tasks, uploads or downloads files, and is on the road again to another client. However, it's possible to reverse the connection and make remote communication a benefit to the home office as well. A remote connection of this type has several uses, but the most helpful is for support personnel. Using a remote connection will allow support personnel to examine a user's hard drive for problems that would be difficult to troubleshoot using voice communication. A file that's corrupted, erased, or overwritten doesn't have to be a catastrophe; the support person can simply upload a new file. This option would also allow the support person to look for error logs and other important diagnostic information.*

Remote-Connection Security

Some people may wonder about the necessity for remote-connection security. They consider a dial-in connection secure, because the telephone number to the host connection is hard to guess and most crackers have turned their attention to the Internet. It's true that novice crackers are more likely to attack you through an Internet connection, but veteran crackers use any connection they can find. In addition, many companies disregard the threat posed by ex-employees, to their embarrassment later. I talked about other fatal security assumptions in Chapter 8, *Network Security Essentials*.

Any time you make an external connection to your network, security is an issue. In fact, before the emergence of the Internet, dial-in connections were the only option that most companies had available. The methods required to break into a company network are therefore older and better established than the newer Internet break-in methods. In short, ignoring remote-connection security is akin to leaving the front door to your house unlocked before going on a long vacation. You can be certain that crackers won't miss an opportunity like an unsecured dial-in connection if they're serious about breaking into your network.

Security for a remote connection doesn't have to involve costly software or hardware. It's possible to use rudimentary security measures with any remote-connection package even if it costs little or nothing. While a third-party security package provides many features you can't get with a standard OS setup, such as auditing and event logging, simple security measures often fill in the chinks in the security armor of your network. As a result, you'll want to use these simple methods even if you do install an expensive security setup later:

Don't publish the number—A number of small businesses that I've worked with use their fax line as a remote connection line. The business publishes the fax number in the telephone book so customers can send in orders or other information. Of course, crackers know this and often try the fax number to see whether they can gain access to your company. Keeping the telephone number of your remote connection unlisted means the cracker has to find the number first. It doesn't stop the cracker for long; but any delay is helpful, because delays make it more probable that a cracker will give up on your network and move on to something easier.

Set a password—If you're working with a reasonably secure OS like Windows 2000, the OS will likely set the password option by default. On the other hand, third-party software and less secure OSs like Windows 98 will leave the host connection unsecured. It's essential to use an easy-to-remember, yet hard-to-guess password if you only have one password for the connection. Using individual passwords for each user is the next best option. The best option is selecting a password for each remote-connection user that differs from that user's normal login password.

Limit access—Some remote-connection packages allow you to limit the drives that the remote access software can use. In many cases, the limitation is the local drive; but in other cases, you can also choose a mapped drive like the data drive of your server. If the remote-connection software doesn't provide a feature that limits access, make sure that you log any users off the host workstation before you allow an outside connection to take place. Mapped drives give users almost unlimited access to the system and are a major security hole.

Limit open time—Most secure operating systems allow you to limit the login time for any object on the network, including users. Crackers will often study a network for days trying to discern the login patterns of the users. They'll use an existing user's account to gain access to the network during a time when the user is no longer active. In other words, the cracker wants to keep a low profile so the network administrator doesn't see abnormal occurrences on the network. Placing a login time restriction will deny a cracker this route of access, or at least severely diminish the time the cracker has to make use of such a connection.

Disconnect the line—Crackers like to access networks during weekends and holidays, because network activity is low. The chances of the network administrator catching the cracker are smaller as well. A cracker can't access your network if the telephone line is disconnected. If no one from the company plans to use the connection during a weekend or holiday, unplugging the line won't hurt business and will keep your network safe.

Maintain logs—Almost every OS out there allows you to log remote-access connections. If you can't stop the cracker immediately, it's important to detect the presence of the cracker on your network. Logging calls is important, because the log will cue you in on cracker activity. Once you detect some type of activity, you can take measures to keep the cracker outside the network. Of course, you'll have to read the logs on a regular basis for this option to work.

Use host callback—Some remote-communication packages provide a feature called host callback. When using this feature, a user calls into the remote access host and provides identification. The remote host hangs up, and then calls the number provided in the user's record for remote access. If the user's computer answers, the user has access to the remote host. Otherwise, the remote host assumes that a cracker was trying to gain access to the network and notifies the network administrator. This feature is extremely hard for crackers to circumvent, because they can't gain access to the network easily unless they call from the user's home.

Some of the least expensive (or free) remote-communication packages come without much in the way of security. Your company may decide the cost of buying a high-end package that offers good security is too high and that a third-party security package is too difficult to install or use. Another way of taking care of the security problem is to place the host machine outside the normal network connection using a firewall. Many firewall programs allow for this type of connection. Using a firewall means that there's a physical barrier between the host connection and the rest of your network. The same firewall package can also protect your network from outside access from the Internet—allowing a single piece of software to perform double duty. We'll talk more about firewalls in the "Firewalls, a Wall of Protection for Internet Users" section of Chapter 11, *Communicating Over the Internet.*

No matter which security methods you decide to use, vigilance is still the prime factor in ridding yourself of security threats. Only by watching for the trail that crackers leave behind can be you confident that your network is secure.

Every security expert will tell you that security measures delay break-ins and make them more apparent, but only the network administrator can detect and remedy the break-ins when they occur.

Software Packages You Should Know About

Remote-access software is an important addition to a network in light of today's mobile computer user. Fortunately, Microsoft has made the decision of which software to use easy for Windows users. Most versions of Microsoft Windows have a remote connection host program called Dial-Up Server as part of the package. If your version doesn't, you can get it as a separate add-on contained in the Microsoft Windows Plus Pack or as part of the Windows Resource Kit. Wherever you get the host program, the cost is quite low. This program provides you with basic hosting capability, which is more than sufficient for home-to-office connections.

There are a few problems with the remote-access software provided by Microsoft. While it does offer encrypted password protection, there's only one password for everyone who logs into the workstation. This means that everyone gets the same rights, making it impossible to tailor remote access to an individual user's needs. In addition, there isn't any auditing capability, which means there are no logs you can check for cracker activity. So, while this free add-on is good enough for some purposes, it won't do the job for long if your company's remote access needs increase. This isn't a good solution for long-distance connectivity either if more than one person will need access to the network.

Because of the limitations in Dial-Up Server, you may want to get a different remote communication package. The software you use for remote communications should be easy to use and flexible enough to handle line problems—yet the software also needs to answer the needs of your particular business. Here are some of the remote communication alternatives on the market today:

Artisoft (CoSession)
http://www.artisoft.com/

Compaq (Carbon Copy)
http://www5.compaq.com/services/carboncopy/

Danware (NetOp)
http://www.danware.dk/eng/

Funk (Proxy)
http://www.funk.com/

Hilgraeve (KopyKat and HyperAccess)
http://www.hilgraeve.com/products/

Laplink
http://www.laplink.com/

Netopia (Timbuktu)
http://www.netopia.com/software/products/tb2/

Shiva (Access)
http://www.shiva.com/remote/

Symantec (pcAnywhere)
http://www.symantec.com/pca/

Not all of these products are Windows specific. For example, Hilgraeve KopyKat is an OS/2 product. Its HyperAccess product comes in both Windows and DOS versions. Netopia offers both Windows and Macintosh versions of its Timbuktu product. Shiva offers Windows and UNIX support for remote access servers, but only Windows support for viewers. In addition, many of these products sport great language support. For example, Danware NetOp comes in several languages, including Danish and English.

All of these packages share one common feature: they all allow you to connect with a remote-access host from your workstation. Most of the packages allow you to take control of at least one host machine and perform any task with it that you could if you were sitting in front of the console. Some of these packages, like Laplink and pcAnywhere, boast incredible levels of security, making it unlikely that anyone will listen in on your remote session, much less break into your server using the remote-connectivity software. All of these programs offer security features that exceed those offered by Dial-Up Server.

In addition to standard features that you'd expect, many of the packages have special features that make them better at performing a specific task. NetOp sports a special add-on designed to make it easier to use in a PC classroom environment. Products like Proxy and pcAnywhere focus on connectivity over any media and the ability to control more than one machine at a time from a single workstation. HyperAccess is the product to use if automation is a major concern. You can control HyperAccess using Visual Basic, VBScript, Visual Basic for Applications, C++, or Java. Laplink is one of the few packages that includes cables for local copying of files in addition to remote access capability— you have your choice of parallel, serial, or USB connections.

Using Conferencing Tools

One of the bigger initial changes that the Internet brought to business was a new way to communicate. No longer did an employee need to call the office—a business could meet just about any communication need through e-mail. Unfortunately, e-mail isn't enough in some situations. At times, you need more. Help-desk personnel find e-mail an exceedingly slow and cumbersome way to deal with employee needs on the road. It's much easier to fix a problem if you can see the computer's display and hard drive. Likewise, brainstorming slows to a trickle when e-mail is in the loop. A group can't build the synergy required for a free exchange of ideas when communication requires days rather than seconds. In short, e-mail is nice, but it's not good enough for complete communication.

Conferencing software allows people to interact using several methods. Depending on the conferencing software that you use, network nodes can exchange audio, video, text, and files using a single connection. The combination of instant voice and visual feedback is the element that other forms of computer communication lack. You can react to those around you, even if they're not physically present when using conferencing software. The addition of text as a media and the ability to exchange files makes conferencing software provide features on par with a face-to-face meeting in many cases.

The following sections of the chapter talk about how you can use conferencing software in general, followed by ways you can optimize your use of conferencing software. They also talk about Microsoft's NetMeeting, which is a free program you get with newer versions of Windows or can download from Microsoft's Web site.

Conferencing Tools in General

You might be wondering why we're talking about conferencing software in a chapter on remote communications. For most people, conferencing software is an application used on the Internet to collaborate with others. Fortunately, most conferencing software is a lot more versatile than that—you can use it for other needs as listed here:

- Engage in impromptu meetings using a remote connection to discuss immediate needs like making a customer sale.
- Hold meetings over an intranet in a company setting. This allows everyone to participate equally when a lot of hands-on discussion takes place.
- Training groups of users to perform new tasks. A training specialist could hold company-wide training where anyone could join in.

- Brainstorming new ideas. Rather than wait until you can get everyone together for a formal meeting, you could discuss an idea with a few colleagues while the idea is fresh in your mind.

- Obtaining hands-on help from help-desk personnel using a remote connection. A network administrator normally can't answer questions effectively when a user is on the road. Using NetMeeting could allow the network administrator to show users how to perform a task even if they're at a remote location.

Using conferencing software allows you to expand the horizons of your business. You're no longer a small business conducting transactions locally; you can become a major player in creating new connections with other companies. The ability to interact with employees on the road is an important one for several reasons. The most important of these reasons is that the employee no longer feels alone—there's someone to talk with and interact with a phone call away. The psychological effect of such communication can greatly enhance business transactions and make the employee more successful.

One of the challenges with small businesses is that everyone wears more than one hat. An employee on the road may have valuable contributions to make to the home office. A sales trip becomes inconvenient, because the employee is no longer available to perform other office functions. Now an employee can participate in critical meetings and collaborate with others while on the road. The inconvenience of travel is less.

Of course, conferencing software can reduce the need for travel in the first place. A conference with business partners over an Internet or remote connection can make travel an unnecessary expense. Not only do you save money on travel, but also the information is handled in a timely manner and more people can participate.

Optimizing the Use of Conferencing Tools

There's a dichotomy between making your workstation efficient and allowing it to perform a variety of tasks. In the "Windows Features You Can Live Without" section of Chapter 6, *Configuring Windows for Network Use*, I talked about applications that you probably wouldn't want to install right away. NetMeeting was one of them. Remote access to your computer isn't going to be the first task that you want to complete. Rather, it's something that you'll spend time working on and will eventually add as a feature if necessary. The point is that the workstation you use for remote access won't be a new machine; it's going to be an established machine.

Part of the optimization process for installing conferencing tools is going to include cleaning up the target workstation. You'll want to remove accumulated software and files that the workstation no longer needs. Installation of a new application is a perfect time to clean things up, especially if the application is as resource hungry as a conferencing tool.

You'll also want to consider the conferencing features that the company needs. For example, video is an interesting addition to conferencing software; but it uses up a lot of workstation and network resources. Unless you actually need video to communicate ideas, using the resources to transfer images from one part of the network to another may not be cost efficient. Of course, there's the additional cost of placing a camera at each workstation to consider—adding video can quickly transform an extension of your network that's essentially free into a high-cost undertaking.

Most conferencing tools include features that allow you to monitor the network for an incoming conference request. The act of monitoring the network will use up resources on the local workstation. While it's reasonable for a large company that uses conferencing tools to enable monitoring because there's a lack of communication between employees, small companies don't need this feature. Scheduling conference times will work better and reduce the resource needs of the conferencing software dramatically.

Limit the number of conferencing machines. Installing conferencing software on one or two machines may be sufficient. Every machine that has the conferencing software installed represents another load on the network. Add enough loads to the network and the low-cost installation you began with won't be able to handle the processing load. Eventually, you'll have to upgrade the network to support what amounts to specialty application. It's important to keep the purpose of conferencing applications in mind when you set your network up to use them.

Working with Microsoft NetMeeting

NetMeeting is the conferencing software that comes free with Windows, making it the perfect product to try when deciding whether conferencing software will meet your company's needs if your network runs Windows. Like most software in this category, NetMeeting is still a product that's under development. A few features don't work as well as they could. For example, taking over an application on another user's machine can still produce unanticipated results. You may find that some meetings still require personal face-to-face contact due to these limitations. Yet, NetMeeting is an outstanding tool in some situations. For example, if you have a meeting in which everyone will need to provide some form of input, NetMeeting may actually be a better solution than a face-to-face meeting. Consider the possibilities for a moment. No one will feel inhibited, because of the public nature of the meeting, and you'll find that people participate better when they can actually see what's going on.

NetMeeting is relatively easy to install if you didn't install it as part of the initial Windows installation process. All you need to do is check the NetMeeting option in the Communications folder of the Add/Remove Programs applet in the Control Panel. Just follow the prompts to complete the installation. You'll need to have your Windows disk handy to complete the installation in most cases. What we'll look at in the rest of this chapter are some basic usage techniques that you can use to reduce the NetMeeting learning curve. The following sections will show you how to set NetMeeting up for use and talk about the features this product provides.

Getting Set Up

The first time you use NetMeeting, you need to provide some information about yourself. NetMeeting sends this information to other users when you join a meeting in progress. It also lets other users know what part of the country you're in, and so forth. The following procedure takes you through the process of setting up NetMeeting for the first time. I based this procedure on the latest version of NetMeeting to ship with Windows ME and Windows 2000. You may notice some variances from your version of NetMeeting. Microsoft has made many changes to NetMeeting as it's matured, so you may want to get the latest version of the product at **Internet Explorer Downloads** at http://www.microsoft.com/ Windows/ie/download/ before you begin the setup process.

1. Start NetMeeting. You'll see an initial NetMeeting dialog box, which isn't the window you'll normally see when using the product.
2. Click Next. You'll see a dialog box in which you supply the information needed to converse with other people. At a minimum, you have to provide your first name, last name, and e-mail address. I suggest filling out all the entries so that you don't have to do it during long-distance meetings in the future.

Other Uses for the Comments Field*—You could use the Comments field of this dialog box for a variety of purposes. Two of the more important items that you could include are your position within the company and the department for which you work. Coming up with a standard, company-wide approach to using this field makes it even more useful.*

---

3. Click Next. NetMeeting asks whether you want to log on to a directory server automatically (which implies Internet use) and which directory

server you want to use. The directory server helps you find other people to talk with. However, unless you plan to use NetMeeting exclusively on the Internet, it's a good idea to clear the directory server option. Otherwise, when you use NetMeeting without an Internet connection, you'll notice significant delays in completing tasks as NetMeeting looks for an Internet connection. NetMeeting also asks whether you want to list your name in the directory service of your choice. You'll want to clear this option if you plan to collaborate with people outside the company on a regular basis. Otherwise, check this option to maintain your privacy.

4. Choose whether you want to automatically log on to a directory server and then choose a directory server from the drop-down list box, if necessary. Decide whether you want to publish your name and e-mail address within the directory.

5. Click Next. NetMeeting asks you to select modem speed. (You can also choose a LAN or ISDN connection if those options are available to you.) The speed of your modem affects the amount of data it can transfer. Even though the audio-compression algorithms NetMeeting uses to transmit voice over the Internet have improved, the speed of your modem still affects the quality of the sound that you hear. (It also affects the quality of the sound you send to the other party and the speed of the connection as a whole.) As you can see, the lowest speed modem you can use with NetMeeting is 14.4 Kbps.

6. Choose a modem speed; then click Next. NetMeeting will ask which video capture device to use if you have one or more video capture devices installed on your machine. In many cases, you'll have more than one video capture board from which to choose. It always pays to check each entry on the list. Select the entry for the highest speed adapter or the one that provides a separate processor. You want to keep the load on the main processor for your workstation as low as possible, and video capture can quickly gobble up any extra processing cycles the processor might have available.

7. Choose a video capture device; then click next. NetMeeting will display a dialog containing two check boxes. The first check box allows you to place a shortcut to NetMeeting on your Desktop. The second check box allows you to place an icon on your Quick Launch toolbar (on the Windows taskbar).

8. Choose zero or more icon options; then click Next twice. You'll see a dialog box that allows you to tune your speaker volume. This dialog box may also allow you to tune your microphone volume. Depending on the hardware setup of your computer and manner in which you installed Windows, you may see one or two dialog boxes at this point. If you don't see both the

speaker and microphone volume settings on the same dialog box, you'll need to click Next to adjust the microphone volume.

9. Make sure that you have a microphone attached to the microphone input of your soundboard (this last section of the procedure is optional—you don't have to use a microphone with NetMeeting). Click the Start Recording button so that NetMeeting can get a sample of your speaking voice and set the volume properly. Keep speaking until the Audio Tuning Wizard tells you to stop. (You see an indicator move as NetMeeting gathers the sound sample.) If you haven't recorded any sound, the Audio Tuning Wizard displays an error message. Otherwise, the counter counts down to 0.

10. Click Next after you finish recording a sound sample. (If you see an error message, fix any problems and try to record the voice sample again.)

11. Click Finish to complete the audio-tuning process. At this point, you see a standard Connect To dialog box if you choose to use a directory server. Connect to your ISP. The Setup program takes care of a few additional setup requirements and then displays the main NetMeeting dialog box.

Using NetMeeting with the Company Intranet

I don't see the Internet as the first place you'll use NetMeeting. The first place I expect to see this tool used is on an intranet or LAN. If you're using a dial-up connection for the Internet, the speed at which we communicate online right now is just a little too slow to get the high-quality connection that people expect. Even a remote connection performs better than an Internet connection, because a remote connection experiences less latency than an Internet connection. *Latency* is a lag in transmitting data from node to node on the Internet. Any latency uses up some of the bandwidth you'd normally have for communication needs. Since bandwidth is already at a premium for a dial-up connection, losing some bandwidth to latency is going to make most NetMeeting features too slow to use. Having said all this, you should keep in mind that no matter where you use NetMeeting, the usage details are the same.

Let's begin by creating a simple conversation. Several people in the same company need to discuss a project, but no meeting rooms are available or one of the people is on the road. Each person has a copy of NetMeeting running, so calling someone over the company LAN isn't a problem. All you need to do is click the Call button (telephone icon) and then enter the name of the machine you want to call. You also should choose Network in the Call Using drop-down list box. When you receive a call, you see a dialog box asking whether you want to accept or ignore the call. If you're attempting to communicate with someone on the road using a remote connection, make sure you set the time for the meeting well in advance. Ensure the person can actually call in before you start adding people to the NetMeeting connection.

The person receiving your call will need to decide whether to accept it. If the person accepts the call, NetMeeting displays a list people involved in the meeting. The initial connection relies on audio communication; but you can choose to use any of the other communication options as well. For example, the Chat button will display a dialog box that you can use to enter text. What happens when someone talks? You see some sound waves coming out of the speaker icon. (Look at the speaker icon onscreen, and you'll see an animation of sound waves coming out.) When working with someone on the road, test the audio connection first. If you can't get the audio connection to work, ask everyone to use text communication instead.

Using Video with NetMeeting—*If you're one of the lucky few with the capability to send video of yourself using a video capture board in your computer, it might be tempting to turn this feature on while using NetMeeting. Video has a highly detrimental effect on network bandwidth, so use this feature sparingly for local communications and high-speed Internet connections. Don't use video if you're working with a dial-up connection, even a remote connection without any latency. A dial-up connection won't have the bandwidth required to transfer video.*

Unless you just happen to be a gadget nut, seeing sound waves coming out of a speaker isn't that exciting. You can definitely get better sound quality from a telephone connection as well. The point is that you can communicate using voice and other methods at the same time using a single connection. Let me introduce you to the buttons on the toolbar (this list includes buttons from all versions of NetMeeting, in case you're using an older product):

Call or Place Call—Click this button to call someone else. You'll see a dialog box that asks who you want to call and which connection to use to find them. The Automatic option in the Using field will tell NetMeeting to search every available connection for the party you want to talk with.

Hang Up or End Call—Use this option to stop your participation in the current meeting.

Find Someone in a Directory—This button is only available when using the version of NetMeeting that ships with Windows 98 SE, Windows ME, or Windows 2000 (which is version 3.0). It allows you to find someone you've recently called using a history directory. You can also look names up in your address book or the Microsoft Internet Directory.

Switch—This button allows you to start using audio and video with another person. NetMeeting allows you to use audio and video with only one person at a time. Switching allows you to give another person a chance to speak. You won't find this button on NetMeeting 3.0 or above.

Share or Share Program—This feature allows two people to work together with an application. That doesn't necessarily mean that both people actually get to use the application at the same time. This is a useful feature for training or demonstration purposes. A training expert can show how to perform a task and then ask a trainee to demonstrate the technique. Because everyone has his or her own machine, each person gets a maximum participation benefit.

Collaborate—This button works with the Share Application option. It allows two people to work together on a project. Both parties have total control over the application (although only one of them actually gets to edit the document at a time). Clicking the Collaborate button a second time allows you to work alone. This button isn't included with NetMeeting 3.0, because the newer version handles collaboration using buttons associated with the application.

Chat—Sometimes you can't hold a decent voice conversation, transfer files, use the Whiteboard, and share an application all at the same time. Even a LAN doesn't provide this kind of bandwidth. The alternative is to cut out one or more activities. At this point, the Chat button comes into play. It opens a Chat dialog box, which you can use to type text to other people. Sure, it's not as handy as talking, but it does work in a pinch.

Using Chat to Your Advantage—*One way that the Chat feature actually works better than voice communication is when you're creating minutes for a meeting. If you use the Chat feature, the meeting notes are already typed. Just select File\Save to save everything said at the meeting to disk. I can guarantee that these minutes will be more accurate and in-depth than meeting notes that rely on voice communication.*

Whiteboard—Every meeting needs some place for people to draw their ideas. That's why the Whiteboard is included with NetMeeting. Clicking this button will display a Whiteboard that looks similar to the Paintbrush application that comes as part of Windows. You get a full set of drawing tools, including the normal circle and square drawing tools. Just so you don't get the Whiteboard confused with a regular drawing program, it also includes things such as a highlighter. One of the nicer features is the remote pointer. It looks like a great big pointing hand. You can use it to point to things on the Whiteboard in a way that everyone can see.

Transfer Files—This is a new button for NetMeeting 3.0 that displays a File Transfer dialog box. This dialog box allows you to transfer files from your machine to another machine participating in a NetMeeting call. A salesperson on the road could use this button to upload written requests from the customer or download new prices to use during a negotiation. You can also use this dialog box to view the files that you've received from other people.

Start Video/Stop Video—This button determines whether you're sending video images to other parties in the NetMeeting call. This button is only available with NetMeeting 3.0. Use it with care in a LAN conference call and not at all with a dial-up connection.

Picture-in-a-Picture—The large display area contains the video that you're receiving from someone else. Clicking this button allows you to also see the video that you're sending in a small picture in the corner of the display. This is a new feature for NetMeeting 3.0.

Adjust Audio Volume—This new NetMeeting 3.0 feature displays volume controls for both speakers and microphone. It also contains check boxes that allow you to mute either the speaker or microphone. This is a handy feature if you want to hold a private conversation before talking with another person over a dial-up connection.

Sharing Applications with NetMeeting

Let's look at sharing an application. This feature is one of the more important uses for the current version of NetMeeting, because you can use it in so many ways. We've already talked about two uses: a help desk and for training. You can also use this feature for collaboration; it allows two people to work on a document together. Sharing an application will also make remote sales easier and offer people an opportunity to try products before they buy them. Developers could use this feature to show form layouts and demonstrate application functionality.

How do you share an application? Begin by opening the application. You may also want to open any files that you intend to use, because the application could get a bit sluggish after you establish the NetMeeting setup. After the application is open, click the Share Program button in NetMeeting, and select one of the running applications from the list that NetMeeting presents in the Sharing dialog box. Click Share. The Unshare and Unshare All buttons are enabled once you share the application, allowing you to stop sharing the application at any time.

At this point, you're sharing the application with someone else in the work-alone mode. The way you can tell this from your machine is to look for a check mark next to the application in the Sharing dialog box. The other party is able to tell, because his or her cursor will change to a circle with a slash through it when he or she moves it over the application. The application has the initiating user's name at the top. This way, you can tell who "owns" the application.

Click the Allow Control button in the Sharing dialog box, and everyone involved in the meeting can change the contents of the application. There are also two check boxes associated with the Allow Control button. The first, Automatically Accept Requests for Control, means that you won't have to grant each request for control individually—control is granted automatically. The second, Do not Disturb with Requests for Control Right Now, temporarily disables other people's ability to take control of the application. However, the other users will also get a message saying that you're busy working with the application at the moment. Remote users take control of the application by using the Control|Request Control command in the <Username> Programs window. Only one person can take control of the application at one time. Everyone else has a pointer to click to take control. The pointer also contains the initials of the person who has control, so you don't have to monitor the NetMeeting window.

CHAPTER ELEVEN

Communicating Over the Internet

The Internet has opened many new possibilities for anyone with a connection. Most people are aware of Web sites, newsgroups, and e-mail; but that's only the beginning. The Internet is a fully functional network, just like the network in your office; it's just bigger. It's the fact that the Internet is a really large network that allows you to use it for other types of communication needs. For example, just like your office network, you can use the Internet to share files with other people. However, unlike your office network, the people don't have to be in the same building or even the same country.

The uncommon uses of the Internet as a communication device are the most interesting. Many telephone companies are complaining about the potential loss in long-distance revenues as companies begin to use the Internet as a long distance voice communication media. Read the "Working with Microsoft NetMeeting" section of Chapter 10, *Remote Communications*, if you'd like to know more about this particular use of the Internet. While the quality of the voice communication isn't the same over the Internet, the price is definitely right.

In this chapter, we're going to look at various methods of communicating over the Internet. This is actually a follow up of the remote-communication strategies found in Chapter 10. We'll begin by looking at the Internet connection and how it has changed the way people communicate. Like any other technology, the Internet offers pluses and minuses as a communication media.

Sharing data comes next. We'll look at Internet Explorer Web Folders first. This technology allows for off-line viewing of Internet content, a handy feature for users on the road. We'll also talk about various methods for sharing files over the Internet. In many situations, an employee needs to access a file left behind at work or transmit data to someone in file form. Obviously, there are ways to do this if the need is known about in advance, but what happens when you're in a motel in another city and need the file at midnight when there isn't anyone at work? We'll talk about this question and more.

The telephone is a central part of any business venture today. Imagine trying to run your business without a telephone. How would people send in orders? How would you request services from others? The Internet can double as another kind of telephone. Two of the more promising technologies are instant messaging and voice conferencing. We'll look at both types of communication and talk about how you can integrate them into your business in an effort to save money and make communication easier.

Virtual Private Networks (VPNs) are the most complete way to extend your network so that it's difficult to tell where your network ends and the Internet begins. Unfortunately, setting up and implementing a VPN can be expensive—too expensive for many small companies. We'll look at what you can expect from VPNs in this chapter. In addition, we'll talk about an alternative to using VPNs for your extended networking needs. This inexpensive VPN alternative wouldn't work for a large company, but it will work fine for most home and small-office networks.

The final section of the chapter introduces you to firewalls. Essentially, a firewall is a piece of hardware or software that keeps crackers out and yet allows you to use the Internet with relative ease. There are a lot of firewall products on the market, most of which are priced for the corporate environment. However, we'll look at a few products that are perfect for the small office. Firewalls are an essential part of your defense against crackers on the Internet today, so be sure to include one as part of your network design.

How the Internet Is Changing Communication

The Internet has quickened the pace of communication around the world today. A business deal that used to require a month to negotiate might take less than a week today, because of the speed at which communication takes place. *Internet time* has come to mean an event that occurs in a moment—blink and you might miss it. Internet time is reflected in everything from the maniacal pace of technological development to the increasing speed of information transfers. Internet time also affects your business, because your competitors are more numerous and farther reaching, so you have to react quickly to new opportunities.

Accomplishing tasks faster can be good for business. Making more business deals per hour or sales per minute will make the bottom line look good. However, as the failure of many dot-com businesses shows, speed isn't everything. The Internet is proving that higher speed requires better management—a commodity that has always been hard to come by. A small miscommunication by management is likely to lead to devastating results for a company as a whole.

Communication is at the center of this chapter. In the following sections, we'll talk about how a small business can maintain good communications in today's fast-paced economy. Even if you're not going to sell products in China, it pays to keep a world view in mind as you formulate your business plan. While China may not be on your agenda, a businessperson in China may have your customers in sight. The point is that you may sell shoes in a small town in Wisconsin and may not desire to sell beyond the community you serve today, but that won't prevent people in England from selling their shoes to your customers.

The World View of the Internet

There are many facets to communication on the Internet. Language is an important issue if you plan to sell products overseas. For that matter, it may be an important issue even if you sell your product locally. Consider the place where I buy sausage. A man and his children run the place and they make some of the best sausage I've ever tasted. To serve their customers, each person in the family speaks two or three languages. As a whole, the family knows eight or nine different languages fluently enough to make a sale. Part of the reason this business is so incredibly successful (people line up outside the door on Saturday) is that this business communicates well with the customer. Here's another way to look at this philosophy:

Communication is the key to the success of any business.

What's the point of my language reference? Like my corner sausage shop, the outside world exposes your business to many communication possibilities every day. You may not have a need to speak another language, but the need to communicate well using electronic media is a requirement if you're planning to use your network to its full potential. When your business does make an appearance on the Internet, the need to communicate will become even greater. The ability to handle requests by people who speak other languages becomes important. The way you communicate ideas to people who visit your Web site could change your business in ways that you never thought possible.

Getting Help with Communications—*Humans communicate directly, both visually and audibly. Your body movements and tone augment the words you say so that someone who's talking with you directly fully comprehends what you want to say. Unfortunately, when you're talking with electronic media, there isn't any way to provide body language or tone with your message. As a result, some meaning is lost and the other person may misunderstand you. Human communication is such a big issue that many people are studying its effect on the Internet, like the Human Communication Research Centre http://www.hcrc.ed.ac.uk/Site/. Another great place to look for information on electronic communication skills is Computer-Mediated Communication (CMC) Information Sources http://www.december.com/cmc/info/.*

One large area of communication change is in the way companies deliver information. At one time, a company had to deliver everything on paper. Today, paper can be a slow and archaic way to deliver information that you need immediately. Even if companies aren't selling their product online, many of them are using the Internet to deliver information. In fact, the number of sources for a particular piece of information has become so large that it is impossible to sift through all of the data you don't need. Information overload is a term that came into use slightly before the Internet appeared on the scene; but the Internet has made things worse. According to some recent studies, many professionals will double their online time in the next year or so. The main reason for this increase in online time is the increase of e-mail that professionals will receive and an increase in online research. The Internet has significantly changed how we send and receive information.

All of this leads back into the purpose of this chapter. As a small business, you may feel that you can't use the Internet for your business needs. Selling on the Internet might be out of the question, because you can't guarantee prompt delivery or enough products to satisfy requests. Providing information might be useless if you're a baker. Research might be something you'd need to do, but not frequently. However, even if you can't exploit the Internet for any of these other uses, there's bound to be some way that the increased communication capability of the Internet can help your business succeed. You may find that all you need the Internet for is to communicate with employees on the road. Even a small communication requirement, like keeping in touch with an employee, means that you'll need to learn new rules—ways to communicate in the absence of body language and tone. You may even find that you need to learn an entirely new human language to get the job done.

Managing the World View as a Small Business

Let's look at ways that you can use the Internet for communication purposes. After all, if the Internet is going to come knocking at your door anyway, you may as well make the best use of it that you can. You may even find that electronic communication makes life easier and your business more productive—that's why the vast majority of the people on the Internet today keep signing on. The best way to begin using the Internet is to view it as an opportunity rather than a business requirement. In fact, you can summarize the Internet phenomenon like this:

The Internet is your portal to opportunity, a potential door to success.

One of the ways that a small business can use the Internet is to keep in touch with other professionals. Many professions have special newsgroups or Web sites. You may find a less expensive source for parts or new ideas on how to make products faster. You wouldn't normally communicate with these other professionals without the Internet—this is a new place for you to look for information, help, and even moral support.

The mechanics of the Internet also make it a good place for a small business to look for productivity enhancements. For example, employees on the road can use e-mail to keep in touch with the company and you can use e-mail to send out important information like new price lists. A type of two-way communication can take place that you didn't have access to in the past. Yes, you could transmit much of this information over the telephone, but it would be neither convenient nor fast to do so.

You can also use the Internet as a type of long-distance telephone service. The voice quality isn't as good as using a standard telephone and there may be odd delays in communication, but at least it won't cost much to reach an employee in another country. We already visited this issue in the "Working with Microsoft NetMeeting" section of Chapter 10, *Remote Communications*. This particular use of the Internet is becoming more prevalent as businesses begin to realize just how much of a financial benefit that using the Internet for telephone service can be. We'll discuss this use in more detail in the "Reducing Your Phone Bill With Voice Conferencing" section that follows.

The Internet can also allow you new possibilities for written communication. For example, you could create your own newsletter to tell other people about changes in your business. One clothing retailer uses a newsletter to update people on sales and new products. It's cheaper than sending out fliers and allows the clothes store to do more with the information. For example, the clothes store could never afford to use color on fliers, but color is a free addition to newsletters. Using a newsletter is also advantageous, in this case, because the store doesn't want to set up a Web site that could attract sales it's ill-prepared to handle.

Finally, you can look at the Internet as a vastly expanded version of your office network. It allows you to transfer files and perform other tasks in real time that you could only do with your local network in the past. Obviously, you won't get 100 Mbps speeds from the Internet unless you pay for a connection of the right type; but connection speeds are improving as new technology becomes available. Small-business users can treat the Internet as a slow addition to their office network.

Pros and Cons of Internet Connection Types

Gaining access to the Internet means having a connection. Home users are used to dial-up network connections. Cable modems are also gaining popularity. Eventually, you'll also see more digital subscriber lines (DSL) used in the home.

Businesses are using all of these solutions, in addition to higher speed alternatives. There are, in fact, a vast number of ways to create a physical connection to the Internet.

Before you can create a connection to the Internet, you need to consider how the individual users on a network will access the Internet. Large companies always provide a proxy server that makes the connection to the Internet for everyone. In many cases, this is the only practical way for a large company to handle Internet access. Providing a separate modem and outside telephone line for everyone to use for Internet access would be too expensive. In addition, there are security concerns to consider—providing a firewall for each user would be a difficult task. However, using a central connection might not be the best choice for a small business for many reasons. The alternative to a centralized connection, of course, is to provide separate connections for each user. We'll discuss the differences between individual and centralized connections in the first section that follows.

The second issue you need to consider is the kind of connection that you get and the amount of bandwidth it provides for your business needs. Companies with two or three people can probably use individual dial-up connections in most cases. However, if you're constantly downloading large graphics files, a dial-up connection may not provide enough bandwidth. As the amount of available bandwidth increases, so does the cost of the connection. There's a balancing act companies play; they need enough bandwidth to get work done on time, yet keep costs low.

Individual versus Centralized Connections

The choice between an individual and centralized connection may seem obvious at first. Many people view the centralized connection as more efficient, because vendors who service large businesses believe that it's the most efficient connection. If you're a large business with hundreds of Internet connections to service, a centralized connection is the only answer. A large business already has the required infrastructure in place to handle centralized communication, so using individual connections is ludicrous.

A small business won't have hundreds of connections to service. If you're in a home office, you may have one or two connections to service. Storefronts may have three or four connections, while small offices could have up to twenty connections to service. You need to answer questions like, "At what point does it make economic sense to use a centralized connection?" and "When do I need to use a centralized connection as an employee convenience, rather than for economic reasons?"

When answering either of these questions, the first issue you need to consider is whether you have a server in place. A centralized connection requires a server (or a machine to act as a server). If you don't have one now, you'll need to purchase a server to implement a centralized connection. So, how does the cost of two modems compare to the cost of a new server? The answer seems obvious. The two modems are less expensive, so the individual connection is the right choice when the number of machines is low. Unfortunately, things aren't always as clear-cut as they seem.

An office may be set up as a peer-to-peer network. If you're working with Microsoft Windows, you have access to Internet Connection Sharing (ICS); so, theoretically you could use a single connection even if you don't have a machine set aside specifically as a server. Light Internet usage won't bog down the machine—the workstation's user may not even know that you've connected to the Internet if you turn the modem's speaker off. On the other hand, heavy Internet usage will bog down the machine, making it a lot less useful for the person who needs it. So, the choice of an individual versus centralized connection when in a peer-to-peer network would seem to hinge around the amount of usage the Internet connection will receive and the load each user places on their machine.

Internet connections also vary by bandwidth. We'll talk about how bandwidth affects this whole picture in the "How Much Bandwidth Do You Need?" section that follows. For now, what you need to know is that the bandwidth of the Internet connection affects the speed at which you can transfer data. As data-transfer speed increases, so does the load on the host machine. A high-speed Internet connection may require a separate machine simply because the connection bandwidth requires it. In addition, since high-speed Internet connections are extremely expensive, getting two for a small office would be unreasonable.

It's time to make a little sense of the individual versus centralized connection. This is the set of criteria I use to determine whether a business warrants an individual or centralized connection in order of priority from highest to lowest:

1. Does the business have a server that isn't already heavily loaded? If so, a centralized connection makes good business sense.
2. Will the users of the Internet connection need to transfer large data files, making a high-speed Internet connection economically feasible? If so, the high cost of the high-speed Internet connection will eventually make the cost of a server more palatable. This makes a centralized connection the best choice.

3. Are there fewer than ten users who will use the Internet intermittently? If so, individual connections are the best choice, because a centralized server will never pay for itself. You can save money by using the same telephone line for voice and Internet. Of course, this means that the user won't be able to use the Internet and talk on the telephone at the same time.

4. Are there fewer than ten users on a peer-to-peer network who will use the Internet moderately? If so, try using a centralized connection on the least loaded workstation. If this doesn't help, using individual connections with separate telephone lines for voice and Internet will probably be the best choice. Only if you plan to add employees or expect Internet usage to increase should you buy a separate server and create a centralized connection using it. Get a high-speed Internet connection to go with your new server.

5. Are there fewer than three users who make light to moderate use of the Internet? If so, use individual connections to a shared telephone line to reduce costs. Users will need to ask before they dial, but the cost reduction should be worth the effort. If sharing a single telephone line becomes a problem, try using individual phone lines or a shared dial-up connection on a workstation.

As you can see, it's not always easy to figure out which connection type will provide the best access speed while keeping costs down. You can summarize the problem as follows:

Determining which type of Internet connection to get depends on how much you'll access the Internet, the number of users you need to support, and the amount the connections will cost.

How Much Bandwidth Do You Need?

Part of the Internet connection issue is determining how much bandwidth you need. A company that performs a lot of research on the Internet will need a moderate speed connection; someone who downloads large video files all the time will require a high-speed connection. E-mail users may only require a dial-up connection unless they receive large files on a daily basis. You could surmise that the question of bandwidth depends on the type of access you perform—the amount of data you download. This theory follows along with the discussion in the "Deciding How Much Bandwidth to Get" section of Chapter 5, *Cabling and Other Masses of Wire.*

However, you can't stop at determining the type of access you need for the Internet connection. You also need to consider how many users will require the connection and how often they'll need it. Always use the actual number of access hours, rather than the number of users for your Internet bandwidth requirement calculations. An administrative assistant may get on the Internet twice a day to pick up e-mail and that's it. Certainly this doesn't constitute full-time use and you shouldn't allocate enough bandwidth to accommodate full-time use. On the other hand, someone looking for new sales leads may spend a considerable amount of time on the Internet downloading Web pages. This doesn't represent a heavy load, so you shouldn't treat it as such, but you do need to allocate enough bandwidth to allow this person to continue working unhindered.

Another consideration is the kind of Web sites you'll visit. The speed of your connection depends on four factors:

- The speed of your connection to the ISP
- The speed of the ISP's connection to the Internet
- The size of the load (amount of activity) on the Internet
- The speed of the target server and its connection to the Internet

Providing bandwidth that the Web sites you visit can never use will cost you money that you won't recover through use of the Internet connection to build sales. You can only receive data as fast as the server for the Web sites you visit can provide it. So, you need to consider the effects the Web sites you visit will have on your Internet connection when figuring out how much bandwidth you need. If you visit sites that are consistently bogged down in traffic and the site owner shows no interest in upgrading the site, providing a high-speed connection to that site doesn't make sense. On the other hand, well-maintained sites use the bandwidth and allow you to get your work done much faster— making the extra bandwidth well worth the cost.

Testing Your Connection Speed—*Learning how much speed you're getting out of an Internet connection is difficult. First, there's the speed that the connection device is capable of providing. For example, most modern modems are capable of transferring data at 56 Kbps. Of course, you won't actually see that transmission speed, because there are losses between your computer and the Internet Service Provider (ISP). If you're using Windows or another OS that monitors connection speed, you'll probably see a connection in the range of 49 Kbps for a modem. Of course, that's the speed between you and your ISP. A connection speed of 49 Kbps may not reflect what you're actually getting—your 49 Kbps connection speed to the ISP may result in a 43 Kbps Internet connection speed. That's where Bandwidth Speed Test Results at* http://www.computingcentral.com/topics/bandwidth/ *comes into play. A quick check of this Web site will tell you the actual speed you're getting from your Internet connection (which can vary from one call to the next). This Web site also has some great information on all of the factors that affect connection speed.*

The final consideration for Internet bandwidth is the value of the data received to your business as a whole. Unlike bandwidth planning for your local area network (LAN), planning for the Internet requires some type of immediate payoff, because you'll pay a monthly charge for the connection. In other words, you can't make a large investment today and pay it off during a number of years—the charges will continue to accumulate the entire time you have the connection in place.

It pays to know about the types of connections available. Some connections are less expensive than others are, so it pays to shop for the lowest cost alternative to your Internet communication needs. In addition, some connections are more readily available in some areas than others. For example, I have ready access to DSL in my area but no access to cable modems yet. So, if I want a high-speed connection, I need to pay the additional cost of getting a DSL line and appropriate modem. Fortunately, the Internet provides a vast array of resources to help you make your connection decisions. Here are a few of those resources:

Methods of Accessing the Internet
http://www.nlc-bnc.ca/pubs/netnotes/notes2.htm

Understanding Your Internet Connection
http://www.elementkjournals.com/int/9405/int0001c.htm

Wow Nebraska Connection Methods
http://uswest.univnorthco.edu/wowjr/wowne/resources/connect.htm

Working with Internet Explorer Web Folders

Deciding how to use the Internet to provide access to a network isn't always easy, because there are more than a few solutions, all of which look like they'll work at the outset. Some companies choose to provide access to company resources to employees on the road through a Web site. Working with a Web site, however, has definite disadvantages. For example, it's hard to upload files when you're working from a Web site designed to provide data viewing and downloading.

Internet Explorer comes with Web Folders, a new way to interact with a Web site. It allows you to work with the contents of a Web site just as you would work with folders and files on your own hard drive. In short, you get a view of the Web site as a group of files. Of course, this feature only works on Web sites to which you have the right level of access. For example, you couldn't use Web Folders to view Microsoft's Web site.

Let's take a better look at how this works. Use the File|Open command of Internet Explorer to display the Open dialog box shown in Figure 11.1. Notice that there's an Open as Web Folder check box in the dialog box.

Open
Type the Internet address of a document or folder, and Internet Explorer will open it for you.
Open:
Open as Web Folder
OK
Cancel
Browse...

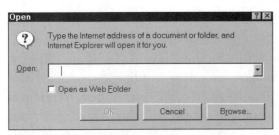

Figure 11.1: The Open dialog box in Internet Explore contains an Open as Web Folder check box that allows you to view Web sites in a new way.

Type in a Web site location and check Open as Web Folder. Click OK. After a few moments, the Internet Explorer display will change. Depending on how you set your browser, you'll see a window similar to the one shown in Figure 11.2. This window shows the Details view. You'll also have access to all of the other views supported by Internet Explorer.

The interesting thing about the display in Figure 11.2 is that you can interact with it just as you would any display on your hard drive. This means you can copy, paste, move, delete, and create new files within the Web Folders display. Of course, the network administrator has to provide the proper rights for working with the files.

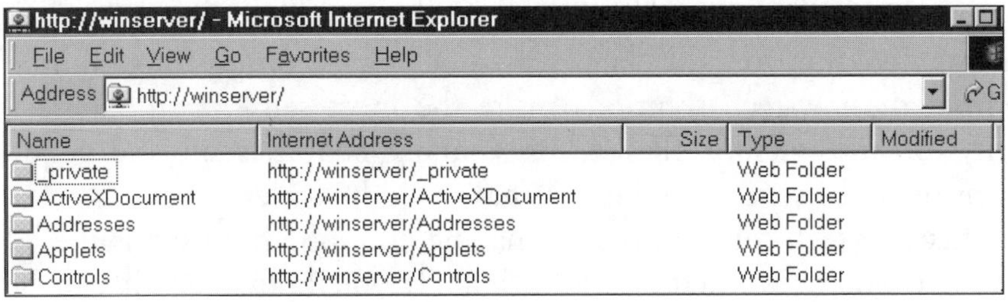

http://winserver/ - Microsoft Internet Explorer
File Edit View Go Favorites Help
Address http://winserver/
Name
Internet Address
Size
Type
Modified
_private
http://winserver/_private
Web Folder
ActiveXDocument
http://winserver/ActiveXDocument
Web Folder
Addresses
http://winserver/Addresses
Web Folder
Applets
http://winserver/Applets
Web Folder
Controls
http://winserver/Controls
Web Folder

Figure 11.2: Internet Explorer displays Web Folders much like the displays you'll see in Windows Explorer.

You won't need to provide any special Web servers or software to make this feature work. All that's required is that you install the Web Folders feature with Internet Explorer versions 5.0 and above. I've even tested this feature with the Personal Web Server provided with Windows 98 and it works fine. This means you can potentially use Web Folders as an alternative method for accessing your desktop machine while on the road. I'll show you the technique in the "An Inexpensive VPN Alternative" section later in this chapter.

Microsoft doesn't force you to use Web Folders from only Internet Explorer. Once you install this feature, you'll find a Web Folders in Windows Explorer too. Any Web sites you open in Internet Explorer using the Web Folders option will appear here, allowing you to access them quickly the next time you need them. You can also create new Web folders using the Add Web Folder icon in the Web Folders folder.

Sharing Files over the Internet

Data sharing is an important part of the Internet experience today. One way that people share data is through Web site displays and downloads. Many different types of information are shared this way, including application updates and shareware. Of course, all of this information is for public distribution. While you may want clients to obtain a copy of the latest software patch for your application, you wouldn't want them to get a copy of secret company documents, like the specifications for your latest application idea. This represents private data that you may want to share with a few individuals, but that's it.

In the previous section, "Working With Internet Explorer Web Folders," we saw just one way to share files over the Internet. By setting rights to the data on your Web server, you can maintain control over what individuals see. Make the Web site private, and you'll keep the data safe from prying eyes. That's the point of using Web Folders, making data easy to share over an Internet connection without too many problems.

Not everyone has a Web site for sharing data. Some people have to share data using the decidedly low-tech solution of the e-mail message. In a world of businesses looking for the latest method of accomplishing simple tasks, sometimes the low-tech solutions make the most sense. I still share the vast majority of my private files using e-mail. People send me requests for information and I send it to them. What could be easier?

Another low-tech solution that I imagine everyone has used is the FTP site. However, if you've worked much with FTP, you know that it can be a real nuisance. The native capabilities provided with OSs like Windows are appalling. It feels like you're back in the Stone Age trying to work with files using text commands. Internet Explorer makes this a little easier, but not much. Besides, it doesn't automate the task of going to the FTP site and logging in. You can, however, make the task of getting onto FTP sites easier using add-on products.

Two of the solutions you should try when working with FTP sites are **FTP Explorer** http://www.ftpx.com/ and **WS_FTP Pro** http://www.ipswitch.com/Products/WS_FTP/. These product provides a method for storing all of your favorite FTP site parameters and provides a Windows Explorer display. You can set alternate ports, choose to log in anonymously, provide a name and password, and choose firewall support. Working with FTP is one of the easier ways to share files over an Internet connection, because it doesn't require any special training.

Another method for sharing files is to provide them directly as part of an electronic conference. For example, NetMeeting provides this feature as part of the package. It's possible to send a file to an individual or an entire group as the meeting progresses. You can read more about NetMeeting in the "Working with Microsoft NetMeeting" section of Chapter 10.

Online Storage Technologies

One of the methods that people are using to share data is online storage technologies like **Xdrive** (http://www.xdrive.com/). This new technology has a lot of potential, but I can't really recommend it for anything other than read-only, non-confidential data storage at the moment. Here are a few good reasons you should consider using something other than online storage technologies:

- There is no guarantee your data will remain safe from crackers. Even supposedly secure sites like Microsoft's Web site get hit by cracker intrusions.
- You'll experience usage problems like the inability to organize your data in folders and capitalize filenames as you see fit.
- None of these sites take any responsibility at all for your data. If the data gets lost, you don't have any recourse for recovering it. (Make sure you read the terms of service carefully for other liability exclusions.)

Having said that, there are certainly advantages to these types of systems and thousands of people are using them and like them. If you do decide to use an online storage system, be sure to make backup copies of your data on a regular basis. For a list of these companies visit http://dir.yahoo.com/Business_and_Economy/ Shopping_and_Services/Communication_and_Information_Management/Internet_and _World_Wide_Web/Personal_Information_Management/File_Hosting/.

Reducing Your Phone Bill with Voice Conferencing

Voice conferencing is one of the more popular alternate uses for the Internet. You'll find it in many general and special-purpose applications today. Normally, you use a microphone to talk into the computer. The voice data gets digitized and sent over an Internet or intranet connection to another party, who hears it on his or her speaker. We talked about this feature a little with regard to NetMeeting in Chapter 10, *Remote Communications*. However, NetMeeting is just the tip of the iceberg. You'll find that many vendors supply voice conferencing products, including the following:

3Cube PhoneCube
http://www.3cube.com/

Genesys Conferencing
http://www.genesysna.com/

DaveCentral Conferencing Software
http://www.davecentral.com/conf.html

ICUII Internet Video Community
http://www.icuii.com/

Firetalk Communications Firetalk
http://www.firetalk.com/

ICQ Voice, Video, Data Conferencing
http://www.icq.com/icqchat/VoiceVideo DataC/

This list represents just a few of the many Web sites selling voice-conferencing products or services. Note that some of these sites include both voice and video conferencing. We may not have reached video conferencing with standard telephones yet, but it's right over the horizon. Unfortunately, you still can't use these products to replace your telephone. However, employees can use voice conferencing to replace calls to the home office and you can use it with other people who have the capability of using voice conferencing. In addition, most of voice-conferencing packages offer a full set of telephone features like voice mail, Caller ID, call screening, and conference calls. They also offer some features you could only get on the Internet, such as the ability to chat with someone else as you surf the Internet. Chatting while you surf may not seem like a business-oriented activity, but you can use this feature to check out competitor Web sites and plan sales strategies. In some ways, voice-conferencing technologies make the old telephone experience appear a little dated.

The TeamSound Web site is interesting, because it's specifically set up to meet the needs of gamers. Business users aren't the only ones using voice conferencing. In the future, you may find that almost all of your telephone conversations take place over the Internet as telephone companies begin to make the move to digital. The goal is to eventually allow all voice and data to use the same transmission lines—larger telephone companies have already begun buying equipment to make this dream a reality.

You owe it to yourself to spend time at **DaveCentral**. Even if you decide to use one of the other third-party products on the list, you'll find a wealth of ideas on this Web site. For example, some products allow people to participate in conferences using 3D virtual worlds (see http://www.davecentral.com/ conf3d.html). While the usefulness of such software may be limited at present, it could become something that you'll want to work with in the future. Imagine being on the road and able to meet with co-workers for lunch at the same time. This technology represents a very useful business tool for the future. Although such technologies aren't ready for prime time yet, they do present interesting possibilities.

Need Help Getting Started?—Several consulting groups on the Internet help companies get started using technologies like voice conferencing. For example, The Meta Network at http://www.tmn.com/ provides access to consultants who keep a company workgin together, even when employees spend most of their time on the road. However, it's important to remember that consulting services can get quite expensive. Make sure you check out the thrid-party products in thie sectio nfirst. Getting voice conferencing started ins't hard, but it can take time.

If you'd really like to make the voice-conferencing experience seem like making a telephone call, some companies offer telephone hardware to accommodate you. For example, **Polycom** at http://www.polycom.com/ makes voice-conferencing telephones that almost look like works of art. This company also makes monitor-mounted video recorders to allow video conferencing as well.

VPN Pros and Cons

You may have heard the term virtual private network (VPN) floating around. Of course, the first question is what is a VPN? The second question is how can it help your business become more productive?

The first question is easy to answer. A VPN is a way to use the Internet to extend your network directly. You access the company network using the same methods you would use when you're home. It's similar to using remote connectivity, but instead of using a telephone wire, you're using the Internet as a data-transfer medium. The VPN service wraps data sent to and from your network in a secure envelope so that no one can see it. The data-wrapping technology is referred to as *tunneling*—the VPN service creates a secure data-transfer tunnel between the user's machine and the server.

The second question is a lot harder to answer, because VPN is a relatively new and untried technology. A lot of people say that a VPN is the right choice for extending most networks on the Internet, because it provides secure, direct access to network resources. Other people say the technology is too new, too costly, and presents too many security problems to use effectively without risk to your business. Both groups can't be right, but separating fact from fiction can be difficult given the dearth of studies and other scientifically based information available on the topic.

The VPN is a useful tool mired in a sea of misinformation and emotionally charged saber rattling by the supporters of each side of the issue. From a usage standpoint, a company has a lot to gain by using a VPN for remote communication if the company can secure a local ISP connection at both ends of the connection. Paying long-distance charges to allow someone access to the company network is an expensive proposition. However, as we'll find out as the section progresses, there are hidden costs you should consider.

Another reason that some people consider VPNs a good alternative to dial-up networks is ease of use. Dial-up solutions usually require the user to follow special connection procedures. A VPN sever can implement a seamless connection using the Internet connection already configured on the user's machine.

Because of the way a VPN creates the connection between the client and server, it's an extremely useful tool in some circumstances. It can change the entire landscape of your business by making it appear that all those sales people on the road are actually at home and contributing to the company as normal. The VPN is so useful that the software to implement it comes as a standard add-on for many versions of Windows and other OS vendors are sure to follow suit eventually.

One of the major problems with VPNs is that they rely on various network technologies to accomplish their work. A user's workstation may follow one set of rules; the Internet may follow another set of rules, and the server may follow yet another set of rules. Depending on how you route VPN, it may need to work with several layers of *protocols*—sets of rules for working with data transmissions—on each machine that it visits. As a result, many experts view VPNs with suspicion. A VPN is only as good as the standards used to secure it and those standards are many. VPN setup suffers from the diversity of standards (and lack thereof) that seems to hinder the Internet at every turn. There's an overview of the standards problems at **Mick Bauer, Network Analyst and Musician**, http://www.visi.com/~mick/.

Some people feel that VPNs are too expensive to implement for all but the largest businesses, because there are many hidden costs that they only discover as they attempt to implement the technology. Here's a list of the common sources of hidden costs you need to know about:

- **Separate server**—Most security experts say that you should maintain a separate server for VPN use that isolates incoming requests from the rest of the network. Otherwise, you take the chance that a security breach will devastate your entire network, since a VPN is designed to provide seamless access to network resources.

- **Firewall**—Every machine involved with a VPN will need a firewall to keep crackers at bay. The cost of buying a firewall for every server and workstation can quickly mount.

- **Complex administration**—A VPN isn't something you set up once. Some industry experts maintain that VPNs require almost constant maintenance, because of a lack of standards.

- **Security issues**—Along with a firewall, you'll need to consider other security issues. For example, a network administrator can monitor the local network for security incursions; but how about the remote user's machine? A cracker could break into the user's machine and add a virus to it. When the user makes contact with the home network, the virus can travel onto the network undetected in some situations, because of the trust relationship established between client and server.

- **Technical support**—No matter how easy a technology is to implement, users will have questions that you need to answer. VPN technology is often sold as a no-brainer solution requiring minimal technical support. Because this technology is new, you'll find that users have plenty of problems with it. In fact, you may find that a VPN requires more technical support than a dial-up solution does.

Total cost of ownership—It's important to consider the total cost of ownership for any solution you implement on your network. So far in this section, we've discussed lots of software, a new server, and many additional work hours for both technical support staff and the network administrator. The cost of owning a VPN is relatively high, and it's a recurring cost that you'll pay for each month.

Performance—There's evidence that a dial-up solution provides better performance that a VPN does. The reason is easy to understand when you think about it. The VPN can't compress an encrypted data stream or it'll lose the chance of decrypting it later. If a VPN doesn't compress the data before encrypting it, the data goes across the VPN at full size. Even if the VPN does compress the data, encrypting it will increase the size of the data slightly. Finally, VPN compression algorithms aren't as efficient as those used by a modem, because the VPN compression is software-based.

As you can see, VPNs have a lot of offer, but they also cost a lot. Yes, a VPN can offer users on the road seamless access to network resources and reduce training costs that you'd normally incur using other technologies. However, for most small businesses, a dial-up network connection is still going to cost a lot less than a VPN. In fact, you'll find a comparison of these costs at **Remote access: VPN vs. dial-up** at http://www.idg.net/crd_vpn_7658.html.

An Inexpensive VPN Alternative

There's an alternative to creating a VPN. This is one of those two-tin-cans-and-a-string ideas; while the physics are simple, it won't work for everyone. This alternative relies on the unique IP address assigned by the ISP when you connect to the Internet. For many home-office and small-business users, this technique provides everything needed for file transfer while on the road. Even if this technique won't meet your needs, it's free, so trying it costs you nothing.

Each time you connect to the Internet, your ISP assigns you an IP number. This number uniquely identifies you on the Internet for the entire session. For dial-up connections, the number changes for every session. So when you hang up, you no longer have access to that IP number; but it doesn't matter, because you don't need it anymore. The important thing to remember is that you always get a unique IP address and that it's always unique for the entire Internet. No one else has that number. You might be wondering, "If the Internet IP address changes with each new connection, how can my employee use it?" I'll answer that question later, but first you need to know how to find the IP address.

If you've installed a Web server program on your workstation, the Web server features are available to anyone who might want to use them online when they call into the Internet, including employees on the road. All the employees would need to know is your IP address, so that they could type it in at their browser's address field. The employee would type http:\\<IP Address> instead of the more familiar http:\myplace.com, because your machine isn't a registered server. To translate a human readable name to an address, the Web site has to register that address with an authority. Of course, this isn't a prerequisite for accessing a site; it just makes things easier.

So, the first step is finding your IP address. If you're using Windows, the procedure is relatively easy, but varies with the version of Windows you use.

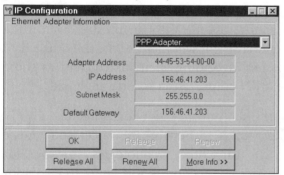

Windows 9x users have the easiest time finding their IP address. Use Start|Run to display the Run dialog box; then type WinIPCfg in the Open field. Click OK. You'll see a dialog box similar to the one shown in Figure 11.3. Select the PPP Adapter as shown in the figure. The IP address that someone would need to reach your Web server is listed in the IP Address field.

Figure 11.3: Windows 9x makes it easy to find the IP address assigned by the ISP to your workstation.

If you're using Windows 2000, you follow a different procedure to find your IP address. Right-click My Network Places and select Properties. You'll see a Network and Dial-up Connections dialog box. Right-click the connection you're using to connect to the Internet and select Status, and then select Details. You'll see a Status dialog box like the one shown in Figure 11.4. Notice the Client IP Address field at the bottom of the display. This is the address someone would use to access your server.

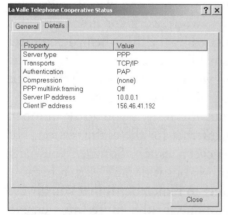

Once the employee has access to your Web site, you can use Web Folders or an FTP site to exchange information. Using this alternative makes use of a commonly known property of the Internet and allows you to communicate freely. Of course,

Figure 11.4: Windows 2000 requires you to use a different procedure to find the IP address.

there are some negatives to consider. The first is that any data you send over the Internet will be open for inspection. This isn't as big a problem as you might think. Unless someone is specifically looking for the data that you're sending, it will probably go by unnoticed. You can also secure the information before you send it. Programs like WinZIP allow you to compress the data and secure it with a password, effectively duplicating the encryption feature provided by VPNs.

The biggest problem is letting the employee know which IP address you're using that day, since the IP address changes each time you connect to the Internet. The easiest way to take care of this problem is to send the IP address in an e-mail. Sending the IP address in an encrypted message will protect the location of your site.

The final word of caution is security. If it's this easy for you to use a Web application installed on your workstation, imagine how easy it would be for a cracker to find using scanning software. Always secure your Web site—protect it with a password and ensure that you secure every folder that someone can access from the Web site as well. Shut down the Web server when you don't need to use it—someone can't break in if you keep the door closed. Use a firewall as well. We'll discuss firewalls in the next section, "Firewalls, a Wall of Protection for Internet Users."

Firewalls: Walls of Protection for Internet Users

Firewalls provide protection for your network from intruders by monitoring the data stream between the Internet and your server. First, a firewall prevents access to any data ports except the ones that you say users can access. Consider a data port as a door—lock the door and no one can come in. An open door still requires a knock. If people on the other side of the door have the right credentials, the firewall will let them into your network.

Most firewalls also check for problems in the data stream. For example, if the vendor designs the firewall to look for viruses, it will stop any file if it recognizes a virus signature in the file. The firewall examines every byte for potential corruption before allowing it to pass. In effect, the firewall is the network's guardian, filtering any input the network receives to ensure the network remains safe.

Firewalls come in two forms. Hardware firewalls provide everything you need in a separate box. These products are designed for high-end users with a lot to protect and normally aren't a good deal for a small company from a cost perspective. Software firewalls run on the Web server or a separate machine set aside for the purpose. Some of these packages are expensive as well; others are low-cost products that a home office or small company can afford. There are many firewall packages on the market, but this list concentrates on those that sell for a reasonable price and offer good protection:

Digital Robotics Internet Firewall 2000
http://digitalrobotics.com/IFW2000.htm

DoorStop Personal Firewall
http://www2.opendoor.com/doorstop/

eSafe Desktop
http://www.ealaddin.com/esafe/

McAfee.com Personal Firewall
http://www.mcafee.com/

Network ICE BlackICE
http://www.networkice.com/

Norton Personal Firewall
http://www.symantec.com/homecomputing/

Shields UP!
http://grc.com/su-firewalls.htm

If you didn't find a product you liked in this list, there are a lot more available online. In addition, you can check Web sites like **SECURE-ME.COM** at http://secure-me.com/directory/ to find more products for your network. This site provides a wealth of security links on every security topic imaginable—everything from crackers to the latest in biometrics technology. (We discussed biometrics in Chapter 8, *Network Security Essentials*.)

CHAPTER TWELVE

Networks That Pay for Themselves

While it's difficult to design a network and harder to build a network that functions precisely as you envisioned it would, creating a network that pays for itself may be the most challenging feat of all. Throughout the book, we've looked at the many costs associated with building and maintaining a network. By the time you get a network up and running, tallying the cost could bring tears to your eyes and emphasize the extreme price you paid for some conveniences while skimping on necessities. Even large companies have this problem. You may have heard the term *total cost of ownership* (TCO) used in some computer magazines—that's the daily cost of using an individual workstation on the network. For many companies, a network is a necessary expense rather than the profit center it should be.

The problem of TCO is so significant that the sole purpose of entire consulting firms is to help companies bring TCO in line with company needs. One such example is **Manuel W. Lloyd Consulting** at http://www.mwlconsulting.com/, a company intent on helping you make all of the pieces work together to reduce TCO. Even larger consulting companies, like **Unisys** at http://www.unisys.com/srvcs/networks/tco.asp, have made TCO a major part of their business. Networking professionals have researched, categorized, and analyzed TCO to the point of abstraction, yet many companies still find themselves with a bottomless pit of profit-grabbing network needs. To get some idea of the significant amount of research put into this problem, check out the **Network Industry Surveys** at http://www.ins.com/knowledge/surveys/.

The main purpose of this chapter is to show you how to change your network from a necessary expense into a profit center. No, you won't see your coffers fill with cash the instant you add a new workstation to the network; but the way you manage your system will make it cost less than the profit you eventually make as a direct result of having a network. For a home-office or small-business network, the change is important. Large companies can absorb additional cost centers to make money in other ways. Most small businesses don't have that option. Every cost is an important one. Here is another way to put this:

Manage your network or the network will force you into an abyss of endless costs.

We'll look at a three-step process to profitability in the first three sections of this chapter. In the first section, we'll look at how networks can save you money. If you can't get your network to make money, saving money is the next best thing. In the second section, we'll talk about how you can compute the actual cost of installing and running your network. Most businesses don't know how much their network costs and can't do any financial planning for it as a result. The third section of the chapter will show you how to take the information found in the first two sections and use it to turn your network into a paying proposition. While these ideas won't work for everyone, they represent a good place to start.

The fourth section of the chapter will talk about getting enough software and hardware for your network. Some companies starve their network in an attempt to save money. What they end up doing is costing their company more money, because the network can't operate efficiently. A network that doesn't work well won't make any money. Instead, you'll end up spending all of your time supporting disgruntled users and fixing overextended machines.

Of course, you can go to the opposite extreme, too. Spending too much money on your network is a sure way to eat up any profits that you might have otherwise derived from it. We've talked about the need to match the hardware and software on a network to the needs of your company. That's not a one-time decision—it's an ongoing process as your company evolves and technology becomes more advanced. The network that works well for you today may not work well tomorrow when your company is twice the size it is now.

Networks Can Save Money

Everyone likes a good deal—something that will save money, make life easier, reduce the time to perform a task, or best of all, do all three. Computer systems are no exception. Many businesses look for a quantifiable way to prove a network is saving them money. Often this goal proves to be elusive, because the company looks in the wrong places or doesn't research the matter completely. Looking for a monetary bottom line that's easy to prove using company accounting information will usually fail. Here are some of the places you should look for cost savings when working with a network:

- Faster order fulfillment, resulting in better cash flow
- Better inventory control, resulting in fewer duplicate purchases and lost inventory items
- Higher employee productivity, resulting in faster task accomplishment and reduced need to hire new employees
- Online marketing and sales, which broadens your market
- Reduced customer support costs through the use of online help desks by employees and customers alike
- Employee work-at-home benefit—a sick employee can put in a partial day, in many cases, rather than take the whole day off
- New business opportunities that you couldn't take advantage of without a computer network
- Better communication with employees on the road, resulting in a higher percentage of completed sales

In the book, I've covered many other ways in which networks save money, especially near the end of Chapter 1, *Do You Need a Network?* The vast majority of these money-saving ideas won't have a direct affect on the entries in your accounting program, but they will affect your bottom line. Of course, some cost savings will be difficult, if not impossible to prove. For example, it would be difficult to prove the effects of a network on the ability of employees to communicate ideas, yet this ability saves money. The intangible savings of a network are often more important than the tangible savings, but it's the tangible savings that interest most people.

You need to emphasize two elements: determining how to configure your network to your point of view and your goals. We'll discuss point of view a lot as the chapter progresses. It's essential to determine which costs you need to monitor given your business needs. For example, a home office won't need to worry about major renovations as part of wiring a business nearly as much as a small business will. A small business won't need to worry about the availability of power as much as a home office will—at least, not in most cases. Both groups will need to worry about the cost of hardware and software, but a small business may need to add services to the list.

Point of view also determines how you calculate intangible benefits. For example, an intangible benefit of adding some network features is improved employee attitude. You can't measure an attitude directly, but you can measure attitude indirectly through improved performance, reliability, and work attendance. How you measure improved attitude depends on the needs of your business.

A business also needs networking goals. For example, if you're providing a service, it might be more important to measure the computer network's ability to reduce personnel costs. On the other hand, if you're selling a product, it might be more important to measure the increased number of sales and average sale value. The networking goal has to fit your company's goals before any numbers you derive will provide value.

Once you understand your company's point of view and goals, you can use them to help your network save money. For example, if your company concentrates on making sales, providing better resources to sales people makes sense. A database that shows how customers spent money in the past, what approach worked best, and even personal information so that a sales person can build a rapport quickly are all good investments if you want to make sales. A bad investment in the same situation would include buying high-end graphics hardware. The sales person will never use this hardware, so you've incurred a cost without any benefit. This happens all the time. A buyer for a company will purchase a stock unit designed for gaming rather than ask for a modified version of the same stock unit with a more realistic feature set. Many vendors replace high-end components with generic ones for free at the time you order your system and you get the system for a lot less money, because the generic component costs less.

Saving money also means looking at your network realistically and cutting through sales hype from vendors. Microsoft may tell you that Windows 2000 is going to wake you in the morning with a fresh cup of coffee and brush your teeth on the way to work. That's not going to happen. Some real hype is just as silly when viewed from the perspective of a small company. For example, if you upgrade to Windows 2000 from Windows NT, you'll likely need new hardware, user training, updated software, and reconfiguration time. You need to ask whether all of these expenses will really help an administrative assistant type faster. The answer is probably no and you can save money by not making the upgrade.

Counting the Cost of Your Network

How much does your network cost you? The answer often proves elusive to the best analysts. Of course, they're normally working with large companies with hundreds of machines and many servers. As the size of a network increases, the difficulty in calculating the cost increases, because the complexity of the network increases. For a small network, however, it's relatively easy to count the cost if you dissect the problem into smaller pieces, analyze each piece, and put the results back together.

As part of your preparation for counting the cost of your network, it pays to spend a little time figuring out what your goal is. Do you plan to put a dollar figure on precisely what the network has cost? Is it important to include intangible benefits? Will you use the numbers internally or as part of an effort to clue a new consultant in on problems your company is experiencing with network costs? These questions are important, because they affect how you count the cost of your network.

The kind of business that you're in also determines how you count the cost of your network. I found it interesting that there are special Web sites that help educational institutions count the cost of networking. Look at **Taking TCO to the Classroom** at http://www.cosn.org/tco/ and you'll find some interesting information that could apply to any business, not just schools. For example, unlike most TCO plans on the market, this plan takes the cost of retrofitting the building into account. Schools need to consider the cost of removing asbestos and lead from the building as part of any networking effort, because installing cables necessarily exposes these once hidden contaminants. In addition, schools have to consider the cost of adhering to the American with Disabilities Act, a cost that large businesses often hide in other cost accounting areas. This report is enlightening for a small business, because they end up counting many of the same costs for their TCO. Unlike a large business, these costs add up for a small business and you need to consider them as part of your cost analysis.

You can see that the art of calculating TCO is imprecise and requires you to employ goal seeking as part of the calculation process. To say there's one TCO for a network is incorrect; the cost and benefits are clearly a matter of perception. It's more accurate to say there's a TCO that best reflects your company's needs and business orientation. There are, however, some sites on the Internet you should look at for guidance:

Anzer Business Systems
http://www.anzer.com/tco.htm

GartnerGroup's Products and Services
http://www.gartner.com/public/static/home/ourservices/use/tco/home.html

Inter-Corporate Total Cost of Ownership
http://www.inter-corporate.com/products/network/tco/

Total Cost of Ownership
http://www.zdnet.co.uk/pcmag/labs/1998/06/corp_pc/8.html

Taming TCO
http://www.seatmanagement.com/content/article_taming_tco.htm

One mistake that many companies make when calculating TCO is not using a consistent TCO model. Any change in the TCO model affects the results of the calculation and your perception of the results of that model. It pays to document the method used to calculate TCO and use that same model every year. If you change the model to account for a new business need or orientation, you can't use previous TCO results for direct comparison. In essence, every change in the TCO model means starting over, collecting historical data for comparison purposes. It's also important to create a TCO report, a document that provides specifics about your TCO calculations to avoid losing the documentation for your TCO calculations.

Now that you have a good idea of where we're going with cost counting in this chapter, let's talk about some specifics. The following sections look at the areas most businesses consider most important in their TCO calculations. Knowing how much your system is costing you is extremely important if you want that system to provide some type of return. Here are the topics that we'll talk about:

- Hardware
- Software
- Personnel
- Administration
- Maintenance
- Replacement
- Building

***Corporate Costs versus the Small Business**—Almost every piece of TCO literature you'll read considers the corporation, not the small business. You'll hear staggering figures on the annual cost of maintaining a single workstation in the corporate environment. Unless you're doing something completely wrong, the costs for a small business should be about half- to three-quarters of those for a corporation in a given year, because you have fewer high-cost personnel working for your organization. If a business owner fixes a PC, that's unpaid time; but it doesn't cost as much as hiring a high-priced network administrator like a corporation would. The only area where corporations have a decided advantage is in the initial purchase. By buying in bulk, a corporation can often reduce the purchase price of products substantially. A small business also pays more for professional services, so it pays to hire a consultant only when you actually need one to solve a difficult problem.*

Hardware

The hardware costs placed in your TCO report depend on how you manage the network. The one cost that you'll always include is the initial purchase price of computers, peripherals, and associated equipment. Some businesses place new equipment in the hardware category and place updates in the maintenance or replacement categories to show that an expenditure saved the cost of buying new equipment. How you account for hardware update and repair isn't important. What's important is that you account for the purchase and do so consistently.

Some companies account for new computer desks and other computer-specific furniture as hardware purchases. Other companies view computer desks as standard office equipment they would have purchased anyway. Still other companies count the difference in cost between computer desks and standard desks of the same type. As you can see, there are hidden costs that some companies count and others don't, which is part of the reason for such a wide disparity in TCO figures from different consulting firms.

Furniture Modification Rather Than Replacement—*A lot of small companies have older furniture that has been part of the business for a long time or purchased used to meet a specific need. In many cases, it's less expensive to modify this furniture for computer use than it is to replace it with new furniture. There are kits that allow you to convert the top drawer of most executive desks into a keyboard drawer. It's relatively easy to drill holes in the top of the desk and add plastic inserts for cables and other computing needs. (Many woodworking catalogs contain the required inserts at low prices.)*

A final hardware category is fixtures. For example, if you need an additional receptacle for the computer, the network administrator will add it in as part of the purchase price of that computer. Again, not everyone agrees about the merit of this addition to the TCO report; but it's important to at least think about the cost of various fixtures.

Software

Most TCO reports account for two types of software: individual and shared. Individual applications, like a word processor, require one license for each machine; no one shares. The TCO for a workstation is the cost of that application. Shared applications, like database management systems (DBMSs), are used by more than one person. The TCO for a workstation is that workstation's portion of the entire cost of the DBMS.

Accounting for single-use applications is relatively easy. All you need to do is add the cost to the TCO for the workstation. However, shared-application accounting can become complex. Dividing the cost of the DBMS or other shared application evenly between all workstations won't account for differing usage patterns. One user may require access to the application more often than others do. While this is an important issue for large businesses where departmental accounting takes place, it's less of a concern for small companies.

One software issue you do need to consider is the cost of unauthorized software brought in from the outside of the business, such as the employee's home. If this software fails, a support call is generated and your company will end up paying for the cost of fixing the failed system. This represents one of the biggest reasons that large corporations want to begin using PC alternatives, like the network computer (NC) or the Network PC (NetPC). For more information about these alternatives see the section entitled, "Using Network Computers and Network PCs," later in this chapter. The damage done by unauthorized applications is significant; it costs companies a lot to fix and reduces worker productivity. Even if you have a policy in place regarding the use of outside applications, you should plan to add troubleshooting for this type of problem to your TCO report.

Personnel

People can represent the highest cost of your network. Training people to perform a task can cost more than the system they'll use. Support costs continue to skyrocket as computer systems become more complex. Supposedly simple systems cost more to learn today than they ever have in the past. The use of the Internet increases these costs. Despite the benefits of Internet use, it increases the complexity of systems. New methodologies like Microsoft's .NET architecture may further increase the learning curve, resulting in yet another round of training costs if your company decides to implement this technology. All these costs are fairly straightforward and easy to account for in a TCO report.

Workers also make support requests like the ability to connect to the company network from remote locations. You should consider these additions carefully, because once you set a policy, it's hard to undo. Additions, like remote access, incur costs like additional administrative time, new equipment, user training, and software updates or modifications. Of course, remote access normally pays for itself in a relatively short time; but other additions aren't as certain to pay dividends. Even with the extra cost of additions, you can usually predict the extended costs accurately and add them to the TCO report for the affected workstations.

What may not be easy to account for are items like peer support, which is one user helping another user complete a task. Large businesses discourage peer help, in many cases, because peers can provide incorrect answers or make assumptions that go against company policy. In addition, large businesses have support staff on the payroll, making it easy to access professional help as needed. Small businesses rely heavily on peer support, because a small business seldom has support staff on the payroll; help comes in the form of an expensive outside consultant. On the other hand, a small business is unlikely to have complex management requirements so the probability of getting good peer support is much higher as well.

The problem still remains that accounting for items such as peer support is difficult, if not impossible. You should account for the time, because the employee wasn't performing an assigned task at the time that peer support took place. If a problem takes several hours to correct, the business loses several hours that an employee could have worked on new sales. One alternative to this problem is to ask employees to account for their peer-support time.

Administration

Home offices seldom incur administration costs unless you want to provide cost accounting for your own time or you decide to hire an outside consultant. On the other hand, corporations always have at least one highly paid network administrator. This is an area where home offices have an edge when it comes to TCO. It's also one of the reasons that home systems always have a lower TCO compared to corporations. Corporations require the professional services of network administrators, because there's so much work to do; a home office would never generate a workload requiring a full-time network administrator.

Small businesses are far more likely to incur administration costs. If you have 20 or more users on a network, it usually pays to have someone assigned as a part-time network administrator. However, a small-business network won't incur the high network-administration costs that a corporate network will. In many cases, you can call in an outside consultant for a few hours each month to perform any difficult maintenance. Someone in the company can wear the network administrator's hat when the consultant isn't available.

Network-administration costs can cover everything from installing new machinery to configuring software. In some cases, the network administrator is responsible for writing macros and other simple applications. A network administrator may be responsible for testing new off-the-shelf applications and recommending their use within the company. In short, a network administrator is responsible for keeping the network running smoothly.

Most corporations also have some training staff. A small company may rely on the network administrator to perform simple training tasks. An outside consultant normally handles any difficult training tasks. In some cases, you can also rely on training tapes or schools to train users on the latest equipment. No matter how you train users to work with new equipment, you need to account for the cost somewhere in the TCO report.

Maintenance

All computer systems require maintenance. This includes cleaning, updates, repair, and some types of replacement (see the "Hardware" section for details).

Normally, the network administrator is responsible for these tasks, but a consultant could perform maintenance in some situations. The point is that performing this maintenance is less expensive than repairing a faulty computer. Just keeping a computer clean can extend its life and reduce the number of service calls it requires.

Some computer maintenance requires consumable products. For example, dusting the inside of the computer requires the use of compressed air. Monitors require cleaning, as do floppy drives and CD-ROM drives. All the consumables used for these tasks should appear on your TCO report.

Replacement

Eventually, every computer system will require replacement or at least the replacement of parts. Many companies account for replacements separately, so there's no confusion between new equipment purchases and upgrades. Most analysts predict a computer system you buy today will require replacement in three to five years. A home office or small business can generally increase that number by moving a computer from job to job. For example, a computer may begin life as a high-powered graphics workstation, move to the administrative assistant's slot, go to the file-server position, and end up as the kid's computer. In some cases, a home-office computer can last seven years with careful management.

One way to keep this TCO category low is to get some type of return on investment. For example, you could sell old systems to employees at low prices to recoup part of their purchase price. Another popular alternative is to give the computer to charity for a tax write-off. Be warned that many charities are setting limits on what they'll accept as a baseline computer. If your machine is too old, the charity may not accept it. This is the time to decide whether it contains any salvageable parts you can use for spares before you scrap the remainder, or whether to sell it to your neighbor, the experimenter. A common use for out-of-date systems is home control systems where a PC controls lights and provides some level of automation when the owner isn't home.

Another way to extend the replacement cycle is to update the computer in steps. Many people view this as a constant exercise in repair, which it would be for a large business. A small business can get by with this strategy, because it has fewer computers to maintain. You can replace motherboards one year, display adapters the next, hard drives the next, and so on. Yes, you'll eventually end up with a new system, but at a more manageable pace. The interim updates prevent the computer from getting completely out of date and allow the user to remain more productive than if you allow the computer to continue to lapse out of date.

Building

It's important to place the building-specific TCO recommendations you read in online sources in perspective. Most corporations are located in buildings designed for large company use. This makes a difference in the way the buildings are constructed. The architect is more likely to design the building with modifications in mind. In addition, most corporate buildings are relatively new, which means there's a good chance the architect wired them for computer use. Buildings used by small businesses are more likely to use hard-to-modify construction and extremely unlikely to provide pre-wired computer closets. This difference in building design affects the way you compute TCO. Using the same TCO figures that large companies do will result in a lower estimate of building costs than you'll actually experience.

You need to consider how the construction of the building you use for your computer system affects the choices you make. For example, if the building has older walls and a decorative metal ceiling, you may find that opening the walls to run cabling is out of the question, as is using a radio frequency network. (The decorative metal ceilings that are prevalent features of Victorian era buildings interfere with radio-frequency networks, making them a poor choice in such a situation.) However, running the cables in a conduit is a good choice, because the poured plaster walls in older buildings provide good support. Of course, conduits cost quite a bit, so you need to add that cost into the TCO for your network.

Older buildings may harbor unexpected problems. For example, you may find asbestos or lead pipes that the state or local government will insist that you replace as part of any renovation efforts. If the renovation is for computer-specific reasons, you may need to include them as part of the TCO for the network. There's a lot of discussion about whether the inclusion of necessary building repairs in TCO are justified since a business would need to perform the work at sometime in the future. Naturally, since the costs of such repairs are high, they tend to exaggerate TCO.

One building-specific concern shared by all computer users is ergonomic considerations such as area lighting. A building may have inadequate lighting or the lighting may be in the wrong place. For example, placing lighting in the wrong area could increase computer screen glare or make screen flickering more prominent. Unless you want workers going home every day with severe headaches, you need to take care of these ergonomic problems and add the cost to the TCO for the network.

Learning How Your Network Makes Money

In the "Replacement" and "Building" sections of this chapter, we talked about how you can save money with your network and how to determine TCO. For some companies, knowing that their network has a low ownership cost would be enough. However, a small business needs to know that the network is materially contributing to its business. If the network is producing more income than it costs, the network has become a profit center for the organization. The problem is separating the money your business would have made without computers from the additional money that computers provide.

I partially quantified this problem in the "Networks Can Save Money" section of the chapter. When you know how a network is saving money, you also have some idea where the line between computer profit begins and other business profit ends. Some businesses, like computer consulting, wouldn't exist without computers. As long as the business is making a profit, the computers are, too. Unfortunately, most people aren't working in computer-centric businesses. Some people are even working in businesses that would do fine without a computer (imagine that).

What if your business is Pat's Fine Furniture? How do you determine whether the network you installed three years ago has helped the business become more profitable or is an anchor weighing your business down? You already know from the first section of the chapter, "Networks Can Save Money," whether the network has made employees more profitable or brought in business that you might not otherwise have. All you need to do now is assign a dollar amount to those conclusions based on what you know about your business.

Let's look at an example. Three years ago, before the computer network was installed, Pat was able to produce five new chairs a day. At that time, Pat was using all paper documentation and sometimes it took a while to find just what he needed in the warehouse. Today Pat is producing six new chairs a day. In other words, either Pat is working faster due to better training, or the computer is contributing to Pat's newfound efficiency. You decide to split the difference and give the computer a half a chair per day. Chairs have a profit margin of $100, so the computer is worth about $50 in this area. You've just quantified the contribution the computer is making to the business.

Of course, you still don't know whether the computer is a profit center or a business loss. The TCO for the computer is $3,000 per year. Pat works with the computer 250 days per year, so the TCO per day is $12. Since the profit on the chair is $50, the actual profit after computer costs is $38 or $9,500 per year. You now know that Pat's computer is a profit center. Of course, you'd need to perform the same calculation for all of the other computers in your business.

You'll find that some computers cost money to operate no matter what you do. For example, it's hard to derive a profit from the administrative assistant's work; but this is a necessary business function and you have to have it. As long as the bottom line shows a profit, the network as a whole is making money.

This example points out some real-world principles about calculating whether the computer is a valuable asset to your business. If the network isn't providing a positive contribution to the business, you may find that lowering the TCO will help or using the computer in more ways will allow it to earn more. The point is that you actually know something that most businesses don't—the real value of your computer system. This information provides you with a basis for optimizing network operations. You at least have some idea of what to do next.

This example also points out the reason that large corporations hire expensive consultants to perform this work. At Pat's Fine Furniture, you have five computers to worry about and can probably figure out everything in an afternoon. Imagine having several hundred computers to work with and job descriptions that run the gamut from administrative assistant to CEO. As a business grows in complexity and the size of its network increases, the ability of anyone to understand the contribution the computer network makes to the business diminishes.

Reducing Costs and Maintaining Quality

Keeping costs under control is an important element in any network strategy. Knowing the TCO for your system is important; knowing how to reduce the TCO makes it easier to create a profit center out of your network. However, reducing costs isn't a complete solution. When the quality of a network decreases, the ability to use the network to perform useful work decreases as well. So, you can only truly reduce costs when you maintain quality. The following strategies decrease costs without decreasing quality:

- Comparing current costs with historical costs to look for trends
- Using new technologies that cost less, yet produce the same results
- Reducing costs using group buying power

We'll look at these topics in the remaining sections of this chapter. However, it's also important that you look for specific ways to reduce costs and increase quality in your company. While the following sections provide good starting points for any company, you may be able to find unique ways to reduce costs and keep quality high in your company's particular situation.

The Advantage of Comparison

Many companies have no idea of how their computing picture is changing. They fail to keep track of resources and how people use those resources within the company. In addition, there isn't any effort to track the effect of decisions. For example, did the purchase of larger hard drives really make the company more efficient, or did they simply allow users to accumulate even larger mounds of useless data? Without some type of statistical information to use as a basis for comparison, you'll find it difficult to answer questions about resource usage.

Creating a TCO model and tracking TCO statistics every year provides one measure of the success of certain decisions. If you see a gradual rise in productivity over three years even though costs remain the same, it probably indicates that network policies are doing their part to maintain company health. Likewise, a rise in certain TCO costs, like hardware maintenance, may indicate a need to spend more time working with those resources.

Making single comparisons is a dangerous practice; you should always couple statistics to gain a fuller understanding of how your company is progressing. Saying that equipment costs are lower means nothing if you can't show that user productivity has remained the same or increased. Lower equipment costs may signal a loss in quality, which the user statistics would reflect.

It's important to look at performance as part of the comparison process. We'll talk about performance issues in Chapter 13, *Performance Issues*. Cost measurement doesn't mean much if the performance of your network is affected. As machines age, their performance goes down, which means that their price increases even if all other factors remain the same. In fact, older machines require more maintenance. At some point, the machine will require either update or replacement to keep users productive. Unfortunately, you won't know where this point is in the life cycle of the machine unless you monitor all of the factors that affect usefulness.

Using Network Computers and Network PCs

Some larger companies are experimenting with network computers (NCs) and network PCs (NetPCs). An NC is a computer with no local storage devices. It does contain local memory and a processor. NCs are designed to run Java applications stored on a server. As a result, they always require a connection to the server to operate. A NetPC has a hard drive, but no CD-ROM or floppy drive. The local hard drive is only large enough to store user data and to improve performance by storing temporary data locally. Again, this type of PC needs a connection to a server to work. You can find out more at the **Network PC System Design Guidelines** Web site at http://www.microsoft.com/HWDEV/netpc.htm.

The initial cost of either system is under $1,000, in most cases, making it a cost-effective purchase. Both of these systems reduce TCO for an individual workstation by managing the user's computing environment. The reasoning is that if users can't change any element of their environment and only use applications stored on the server, there will be fewer support calls and the user will waste less time. In addition, both setups rely on a sealed case to prevent tinkering and theft. A lack of expansion slots means that every NC or NetPC has a specific hardware setup, which reduces repair and maintenance time. A network administrator can monitor the vitals of each workstation from a remote location and is unlikely to need direct machine access to troubleshoot most problems. Whether this kind of setup actually works is a subject of much debate. Many large companies aren't buying into the hype and some that did have reported mixed results.

A home-office user should never consider using NCs or NetPCs as part of a network setup, because there isn't any way to upgrade their capabilities. While it's expensive for a large company to troubleshoot and repair vast quantities of PCs, a home-office user actually benefits from the flexibility that PCs offer. I normally upgrade my systems as needed rather than get entirely new boxes. Only when there's a major technology change does a new box become essential. By carefully purchasing needed hardware upgrades, I've managed to significantly cut my annual hardware purchases without reduced productivity. For the home-office user, an NC or NetPC means buying a server as well. Considering that most home offices are peer-to-peer network setups, the addition of a central server will actually add to the cost of the network, not save money.

A few small businesses might benefit from using an NC or NetPC. Of course, the only time you should consider using either system is if you already need a central server for your business. If a peer-to-peer network will do the job, it makes little sense to complicate your network by using these alternative technologies. However, even if you already have a server, you need to consider the costs carefully. Using an NC or NetPC allows you to better control ongoing costs at the user end; but you need to consider whether those savings are eaten up by costs at the server end. Since both an NC and NetPC rely on the server for application and configuration support, you might need to buy a larger server to support user needs. In addition, if the network administrator isn't familiar with these new technologies, you spend time and money on training.

You also need to consider a hidden cost of these technologies. In the "No One Likes Big Brother" section of Chapter 9, *Network Administration Made Simple*, we discussed the problems with too much administration. For some users, an NC or NetPC will feel much worse than any amount of administration. Every aspect of their work environment is strictly controlled—from the wallpaper on their desktop to the arrangement of applications on the Start menu. Some users are likely to experience loss of productivity and even depression in such an environment. A user's work environment is important. Although an NC or NetPC will save money in hardware, support, and maintenance costs, if you don't gain some level of user productivity, the effort is for nothing. While NCs and NetPCs are worthy of consideration for a small business, it pays to have all of the facts before you make a decision.

Forming a Cooperative

Corporations have a decided advantage when buying new equipment, because they can buy it in bulk. Companies, like Compaq, are interested in making big sales—the sale of an individual unit is insignificant to them. Unfortunately, many small businesses can only afford a single new machine at a time; buying in bulk isn't an option.

Fortunately, you can leverage your buying power with others in the same position by forming a cooperative. Create a cooperative from all of the businesses that use computers in your area or with businesses that have a similar interest. You'd be amazed at the savings that buying 5 units instead of 1 garners—25 units garners even bigger savings.

Farmers and other individuals have used cooperatives for years to keep their costs low and raise the price received for goods. The quality of the products you receive won't change, just the price you pay for them. While using a cooperative isn't for everyone, you should consider joining or forming one if the price of computer hardware, software, and services is a concern.

CHAPTER THIRTEEN

Performance Issues

Many networks are fully functional, yet they still require additional work. The problem is that networks can do everything you ask them to, but not perform these tasks quickly. Slow networks are a universal problem. Every computer system from the mainframe to PC has problems with slow execution and wait times that would try the patience of a saint. Most people recognize the problem, yet many network users have to live with slow execution speeds as part of their daily computing experience.

Part of the problem is that performance is always the second concern of the network administrator; it comes right after making the network function. Obviously, if the network isn't able to do anything at all, performance tuning is a moot point. Unfortunately, some network administrators are always in reactive mode and never get past first base to tune the performance of their network. This chapter assumes that you've taken the proactive approach to network management that we've talked about in all of the previous chapters and now have time to speed up your network.

Performance is more than monitoring the speed of your network or making it miraculously work faster. Getting your network to perform better requires observation and an understanding of what makes your network tick. Speed problems can disguise themselves in a number of ways and you'll never know what the problem is for certain until it goes away. It's time to put on your detective's cap; this chapter is about performance problems, both subtle and obvious.

Some people don't understand how performance problems occur. For example, I often monitor Internet newsgroups and the first performance culprit on everyone's lips is the display adapter. Sometimes the problem really is the display adapter and when the person receiving advice reports success, the newsgroup members nod their heads and repeat the mantra that the display adapter is always the culprit. Proponents of the one-device fix usually meet a failure report with accusations of using the wrong device to fix the problem. I just read along and scratch my head.

A performance problem is the result of a bottleneck. The bottleneck could occur at the display adapter; but it could also be the result of a memory shortage or a problem with the hard drive. Network interface cards (NICs) and hardware failures also share part of the blame for performance problems. In fact, I once chased down a subtle performance problem to the terminator on the end of a network cable. The first section of the chapter discusses the types of performance bottlenecks you're most likely to run into. Just as with any detective, you need to know where the performance bottlenecks in your system are likely to hide.

In the second section of the chapter, we'll talk about the Performance Monitor. This is the tool that Microsoft provides as part of Windows. However, some third-party vendors extend Performance Monitor, so they can use it to check the performance of their applications, too. A lot of people find Performance Monitor complex and difficult to use, because it provides so many counters—methods of measuring system performance. This section will help you understand Performance Monitor better and how it can verify that you have specific bottlenecks on your system. A good detective knows the tools of the trade.

The final four sections of the chapter are the epilogue of the detective story—the part where the criminal is unmasked. These four sections show you time-tested methods for eliminating performance problems once you understand where they are and why they exist. In many cases, you'll find that a simple performance problem is actually the source of other troubles on your network. The easiest example to understand is a faulty or poorly tuned NIC. Not only does the NIC affect the performance of the local machine, but it affects the performance of all the other machines around it since signals to these other machines are likely pass through the faulty NIC during their travels.

Understanding Performance Bottlenecks

Some people make the subject of performance a lot more complicated than it needs to be; others don't give it enough thought. It's easy to get lost in the reams of highly scientific data about performance issues out there that make the labyrinths of ancient Greece seem like child's play. On the other hand, a performance problem doesn't go away; it just gets worse.

Let's begin with a simple definition of a performance bottleneck. Imagine you're at a subway or railway terminal, or even an amusement park, where turnstiles regulate the flow of traffic through the gate. What would happen if everyone got tired of waiting at the same time and decided to rush the turnstile? A few would make it through immediately; the rest would be crushed and eventually make it through, but much more slowly than if they had waited. The mental picture you're seeing right now, while comical, is also what's going on inside your computer when a performance problem occurs. All of those electrons try to get through the gate at the same time and end up slowing things down considerably. Because of the cause-and-effect relationship between system components, a performance bottleneck is likely to slow more than just one application; it can slow them all.

From a user's perspective, performance bottlenecks always occur in the operating system (OS), applications, or hardware. A user rarely blames the processor and may not even know the processor exists. Many users refer to the entire PC box as the "brain" and leave their understanding of the computer at that basic level. Some users blame the network administrator for performance problems. The point is that a user's perspective is based on the visible aspects of the computer: What does the monitor display? How fast does the system accept input? How fast does it produce output? In fact, you'll find out later in the chapter that tuning does occur at these three levels, plus a fourth level, the user. To find the performance culprit, however, you need to look somewhere else.

For now, we need to talk about the real sources of performance bottlenecks. They don't occur in the visible elements of the system, but in the background areas where the computer is performing work. Here's a list of the four culprits normally responsible for performance bottlenecks in a system:

- Processor
- Memory
- Disk
- Network

We'll talk about other problem areas as well, but you'll find that these other problem areas affect a main system bottleneck directory or that you can't tune this particular area. For example, the system bus can become a performance bottleneck, but you can't tune it or replace it, so we'll talk about the effect of the bus, but won't consider it in the four tuning sections at the end of the chapter. Likewise, problems with the display adapter manifest themselves as processor problems in most cases. We'll talk about those rare instances when you do have to replace the display adapter with a higher speed alternative, but we'll also talk about ways that you can tune the system to make the display adapter more efficient. A machine set up for business purposes rarely requires a display-adapter update.

The following sections explore these four sources of bottlenecks. Once you understand why these four areas are the problem, you'll understand why the user could never see them by simply viewing the computer or attempting to use it. That's the problem with the culprits in most detective stories—they work in the background unnoticed until the detective shines a light on them and exposes the problems they create.

Processor Bottlenecks

The concept of a processor bottleneck isn't difficult to understand. You can view the processor as equal parts traffic cop, decision-maker, and accountant. The easiest way of looking at this performance bottleneck is to say that the rest of the machine is waiting on the processor to perform its work or that the processor is overwhelmed with requests. In other words, other subsystems, like the disk drive, are idle while they wait for the processor to perform some given tasks. Most professionals view processor bottlenecks as something that affects the entire system, because application and OS alike need the processor to perform just about every task. Because the processor is a central part of activity for the entire machine, peaks in processing load occur. However, it's when the processing load peaks and remains at that point that you have a problem.

You might think that processor bottlenecks are the worst thing that could happen to your machine—that you need to do everything to stop them. In part, this view is true. Processor bottlenecks do tend to cause network administrators the greatest amount of grief from angry users who want to perform some task as simple as a login or database query. However, saying that a processor bottleneck completely stops the machine from operating really isn't accurate, because it neglects to look at quite a few factors that influence processor bottlenecks. For example, some disk-drive controllers can perform direct memory access (DMA) transfers in the background. In a DMA transfer, data moves directly from memory to the hard drive without any processor assistance. Depending on your machine setup, some level of system activity occurs despite a processor bottleneck.

Let's take this discussion out of the realm of the abstract into the user's perspective. Some applications require more processor time than others do. A spreadsheet application always uses a lot of processing cycles, because it performs many calculations without requiring disk access (the whole spreadsheet normally resides in memory). Most people use spreadsheets to perform complex analyses, which is another processor intensive task. The fact that people normally use spreadsheets for graphing, as well, only increases the potential for this application to use all of the available processing cycles. When users complain that their system has slowed to a crawl and you see that they're using processor-intensive applications, like spreadsheets or graphics applications, you have your first clue as to the source of the problem.

Memory Bottlenecks

Memory bottlenecks are one of the easiest to discover and the hardest to diagnose problems you'll run into. They're easy to discover, because the OS normally starts complaining that it's low on memory; the size of the *page file* grows dramatically, or the hard drive light stays lit most of the time. (The page file is an actual file on the hard drive that contains pages of RAM; many versions of Windows use PAGEFILE.SYS or WIN386.SWP as the page file filename.) While the performance drop in a system with processor, disk, or network bottlenecks is slow, a memory bottleneck appears quickly so the user notices the performance drop almost immediately. If a memory problem becomes severe enough, the system may crash or it could exhibit weird behavior. Applications that normally work fine begin to crash; you may see some corruption on the display, or the system may refuse to perform some tasks. A memory problem is more likely to produce hard-to-miss results than any other form of performance bottleneck.

Memory comes in assorted sizes and shapes. There are more types of memory out there than most people care to think about. All of these forms of memory have different operating characteristics. Some types of memory are faster than others are, some provide nearly permanent storage, while other types lose their contents as soon as the user removes power. You need to know about the memory found in your machines. Reading the manuals for your display adapter and motherboard (the places you'll find configurable memory) is important. It's also important to understand the meaning behind the memory acronyms you're likely to run into, such as dynamic random access memory (DRAM), synchronous DRAM (SDRAM), double data rate (DDR) SDRAM, synchronous link DRAM (SLDRAM), and Direct Rambus DRAM (RDRAM). When working with display adapters, you may also run into video random access memory (VRAM), while processors often require static random access memory (SRAM). These Web sites can also help you understand the memory in your machine:

Enhanced Memory Systems
http://www.edram.com/

Fujitsu Microelectronics
http://www.fujitsumicro.com/

Hitachi Semiconductor America
http://semiconductor.hitachi.com/

Hyundai Electronics America
http://www.hea.com/hean2/semi/home.htm

Intel
http://www.intel.com

Rambus, Inc.
http://www.rambus.com/

SLDRAM Consortium
http://www.sldram.com/

Synchronous DRAM: The DRAM of the Future
http://www.chips.ibm.com/products/memory/sdramart/sdramart.html

Texas Instruments Memory Reference
http://www.ti.com/sc/docs/products/memory/

Some applications use more memory than others do. For example, a spreadsheet application can use a lot of memory, because the application normally reads all of the data required to populate a spreadsheet into memory. Word processors and DBMS can be memory efficient; they page data into memory as the user needs it. However, both of these applications are feature rich and all of the widgets that people install require memory. It's important to remember that memory usage is cumulative. You don't get a discount for running five or more applications. Each application requires memory and depletes the stock of memory you have on hand. So even if you're running small applications, you can run out of memory.

Disk Bottlenecks

Have you ever watched the drive light on your machine flicker on, and then stay on for what seemed like hours? Perhaps you could hear the OS grind the drive to dust as it requested data from the hard drive repeatedly. Eventually, if the drive system doesn't get a rest, the drive will fail—it's a mechanical device after all and can only withstand so much abuse. However, long before the drive fails due to abuse, the users of your network will begin to complain about slow processing times and ever longer waits for database applications. You might even see the machine freeze, because it runs out of the one resource it must have to operate—disk space.

These are all symptoms of a disk bottleneck—an extreme disk bottleneck in most cases. Even small disk bottlenecks can cause devastating consequences on a network machine. You might see anything from strange glitches, to unexplained data loss, to the more benign slow application response. Fortunately, most modern applications test for adequate disk space before they write to the hard drive, because lack of drive space has been a problem in the past. It's rare to see an application fail due to lack of hard disk space.

The most common disk bottleneck scenario is that the system begins to slow over a period of months. The loss of speed is so gradual that no one really notices, at least until the day the problem becomes so severe that the system forces someone to notice by displaying an error message. A disk bottleneck is a somewhat predictable, yet extremely slow event. This is the slow-kill bottleneck of networks and standalone systems alike.

You'll see two types of application when it comes to the disk drive. Database applications write many small records into one or more files on a server. The use of small records means that the hard drive must perform many seeks. Disk bottlenecks often occur because the drive search hardware is overwhelmed. Word processing applications tend to make large data requests. The long read time of contiguous data makes the hard drive search hardware work more efficiently, but can also block requests from other users. The disk bottleneck is just as real no matter which type of access problem occurs.

Network Bottlenecks

The whole purpose of a network is to allow users to share both data and peripheral devices, which makes a network a way to improve efficiency. However, like most things in life, the benefits of using a network don't come free. Sharing a resource means not getting exclusive access to it. A single machine on the network can slow the entire network down. If a user abuses network resources, there's a good chance that everyone on the network will notice. A partially failed NIC or a poorly designed DBMS application can generate excess packets, which slows the network down. You may find as your company grows that the original network infrastructure can't handle the load and that you need to perform an upgrade. Everything and everyone on the network affects network performance and can become a network bottleneck.

Network bottlenecks tend to have a variety of causes and effects. However, network bottlenecks also tend to exhibit patterns across multiple machines. For example, if one person is complaining of a slow hard drive, but no one else is, the cause is likely a local problem on that machine. On the other hand, if everyone is complaining about disk access, it's time to look at the application type. If you find the applications in question require network access, there's a good chance you'll need to look at the server. Groups of users can see network bottlenecks as well. A damaged cable tends to affect the users on the client side of the damage. Users on the server side of the damage won't see a performance drop.

Using Performance Monitor

Finding the performance bottlenecks on your system depends on observation and analysis of performance data. You need some way to measure current system performance against some benchmark that shows whether system performance is slower than anticipated or that the activity level of a specific part of the system is higher than expected. Most new versions of Windows ship with some type of performance-monitoring tool. The name of the tool varies by version, but the operation is similar. We'll use the Windows 2000 Performance console, which includes System Monitor and the Performance Logs and Alerts Microsoft Management Console (MMC) snap-ins. We talked about MMC snap-ins in the "An Overview of Microsoft Management Console Snap-Ins" section of Chapter 9, *Network Administration Made Simple*.

System Monitor relies on counters to check system performance. A counter is a mini-application that monitors the system for a certain event. For example, you may want to know how many times the system sends a packet on the network. The counter counts each time the event occurs during a given time frame and then sends that number to System Monitor. The counter may also manipulate the raw count data in some way. For example, when you want to see the percentage of processing power used for OS specific tasks, the counter has to track user application usage as well and calculates the percentage based on all the counter data. Depending on how you set up System Monitor, data may appear in chart or tabular form.

The following sections look at four important System Monitor tasks. We'll begin by looking at the views you can create with System Monitor. Certain views work better for specific types of monitoring tasks. Next, we'll take a quick tour through the standard performance objects, each of which contains one or more counters, provided with System Monitor. Not every version of Windows includes every performance object, and the performance objects contain differing numbers of counters. In addition, third-party applications may add special performance objects to your system. Once you know what the performance objects are, we'll look at adding counters to the System Monitor display in the third section. Finally, we'll talk about how you can automate the monitoring process using logs.

Understanding the Views

When you start System Monitor for the first time, you get a blank screen. Before you can do anything, you need to select some events to monitor. I decided to monitor CPU usage statistics for the machine I was testing (the percentage of time spent performing user-related tasks in this case). Figure 13.1 shows one way to display this information.

Let's look at the System Monitor toolbar. The first two buttons from the left are New Counter Set and Clear Display. You use New Counter Set to remove all of the counters for the current display. It allows you to create the blank screen

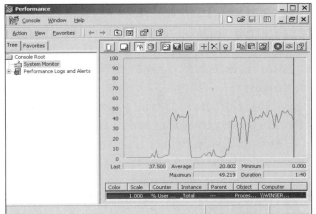

Figure 13.1: System Monitor provides several views of data, such as the Chart view shown here.

you'll see when you first start System Monitor. Clear Display removes the current data without removing the counters. This allows you to start a chart over again so that old data isn't cluttering the screen.

The next five buttons on the System Monitor toolbar change the way you track information: View Current Activity, View Log File Data, View Chart, View Histogram, and View Report. The first two view options determine whether you view current system activity or the contents of a log that you've created. We'll talk about logging data in the "Creating and Using Logs" section later in this chapter. Some types of system configuration changes require the log-file approach, because you'll need to see how the change affects system performance over an entire day or even longer. You may also want to track performance when certain events occur. A log file can make it easier to track event-generated monitoring requirements.

The View Chart, View Histogram, and View Report System Monitor toolbar buttons affect the actual presentation of information on screen. You'll use the View Chart display shown in Figure 13.1 to monitor system performance over

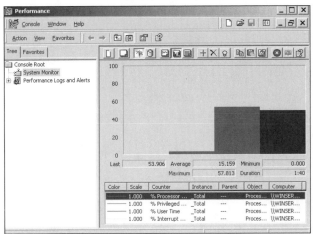

Figure 13.2: The Histogram view allows you to make quick performance data comparisons between like statistics.

a long interval. This view also helps you to see the interaction between various statistics over time. However, the problem with this view is that the current value is hard to read. The historical information tends to clutter the display and makes quick reading impossible.

The View Histogram option, shown in Figure 13.2, provides the best method for performing instantaneous comparisons of system data. You can use this view to make quick comparisons of two statistics when you're adjusting a configuration option that makes a relatively large change in system performance. The instantaneous display is also easier than the Chart view to read. Historical data doesn't get in the way and cause incorrect readings. Obviously, this view isn't any good for long-term data display.

The third button, View Report, is extremely useful when you need to compare large quantities of related data or save the information to an application that normally requires text input, such as a spreadsheet. Figure 13.3 shows an example of this view. Note that you can change the presentation of the data; this figure shows the default view that you'll normally see when you first select this view. Notice that System Monitor organizes the data by machine, then by performance object, then by counter, and finally by instance. This view is helpful, because it shows how Windows organizes the performance data and provides some clues about the manner in which performance statistics are collected.

Let's talk about counter organization for a few moments. The four levels you need to consider appear in the following list:

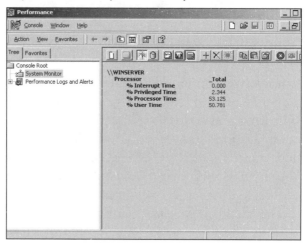

Figure 13.3: The Report view is useful for comparing large numbers of counters or saving statistics as text for import into other applications.

Machine—Every machine has a separate set of counters. You can compare counters across machines. This allows you to determine whether one machine is heavily loaded while another remains idle. Comparing statistics also allows you to check the performance of a known good machine against one that's experiencing performance problems.

Performance object—Windows groups performance into functional areas. Each area appears within a single DLL. Loading the DLL creates a performance object that contains multiple counters associated with the functional area in question. For example, the Processor performance object contains counters that monitor the amount of time the processor spends in activities like servicing OS and user needs.

Counter—Each counter measures a specific statistic. For example, when working with the Memory performance object, there are separate counters that measure memory reads and memory writes.

Instance—A system requires one instance of each counter for every device you want to monitor. For example, if a machine has two processors, an instance allows you to monitor the processors separately or together. There are 0 (processor 1 only), 1 (processor 2 only), and _Total (both processors) instances in this case.

Some people worry about the effect of the counters on system performance indicators. It's a valid concern, because loading System Monitor and counters uses system resources. Each performance object you load is contained in a separate DLL, so that you can select more than one counter within an object and not add to the memory load of the system. However, every counter and instance you choose adds to the machine's processing load; adding too many counters affects performance measurements like processor time.

Performance Monitor uses a default-monitoring period of one second, which is great if you're troubleshooting a bad NIC or want instant feedback on a configuration change. However, this might be too fast in certain situations. For example, if you're performing long-term monitoring, you might want to set the monitoring period to a high value. Click the Properties button within any of the views to change this setting. Figure 13.4 shows the dialog box that changes the interval for the Chart presentation.

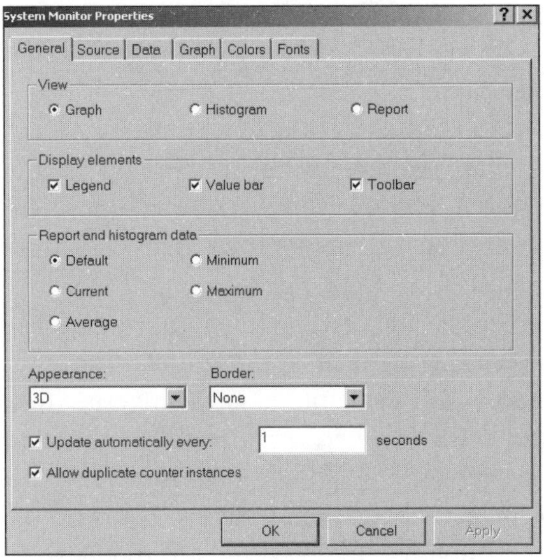

You can also use this dialog box to embellish the default Performance Monitor views. For example, you can add both a horizontal and a vertical grid to either the Chart or the Histogram view. There are also options for changing the chart colors, font, and other display features. The Source tab allows you to choose between current system data or logged data. This tab also allows you to select a source of logged data.

Figure 13.4: Use the System Monitor Properties dialog to change the various view options for Performance Monitor.

Understanding the Performance Objects

Windows 2000 ships with a vast number of performance objects. You can monitor just about every aspect of your machine using them. The problem is that there are too many performance objects for the average person and even some corporate network administrators have trouble figuring them all out. Most home offices and small businesses can do a great job performance tuning their systems using a subset of these performance objects. The following list contains the performance objects you'll use more often and a summary of why you'd use them:

Cache—This performance object allows you to check how efficiently the file system cache is working. The cache retains parts of the hard disk in memory to improve system performance. A large Data Map Hits % counter value indicates the file system cache is working efficiently. A low number in this counter indicates that you need to increase the size of the file cache to allow better performance. In most cases, this means adding memory to the machine in question.

Gateway Service for NetWare—You'll find several performance objects that have the same names as services you installed for your network. The counters within these performance objects tell you how well the services are operating. For example, the Gateway Service for NetWare performance object includes a Server Reconnects counter. A high number for this counter indicates the server is disconnecting from the workstation too often and indicates there's a problem with the NIC, network cabling, or other network-specific hardware in many cases.

IP—Besides monitoring network services, System Monitor can check on the performance of protocols. Again, high numbers in error counters usually indicate some type of network problem. However, in this case, the problem is more likely memory or configuration oriented rather than hardware oriented.

Job Object—A job object is a task that you've scheduled to run in the background. This performance object doesn't track applications running in the foreground or OS-specific tasks. You schedule a job using the Task Scheduler. Sometimes background tasks can become a problem, because they rob the system of essential resources. Checking the counters for this performance object allows you to detect when scheduling problems occur.

Memory—This performance object provides an overview of the current memory status for the workstation. Monitoring counters like Page Faults/sec can tell you when you need to add memory to a system. A high number indicates that the system is using disk cache too often. Reducing the number of tasks that you run concurrently will also help in this situation.

Network Interface—We've already looked at two types of network performance indicators: protocol and service. This performance object monitors network performance as a whole and is the one that's most useful for tuning purposes. For example, the Current Bandwidth counter tells you the bandwidth available to each adapter or interface supported by the machine. Knowing how much bandwidth you have available allows you to make decisions about how much bandwidth to allocate for tasks like Website access.

Objects—This is a somewhat nebulous performance object for many people, because they don't understand what it represents. You can use this performance object to measure the number and types of objects the OS creates. Every object requires system resources and processing time, yet this is the only way you can effectively measure that load on the system. An application that creates many objects places heavier instantaneous loads on the system. However, this application may operate more smoothly by using processing cycles that the user would normally waste. Knowing what type of application you're working with and why it's creating the objects is helpful in determining when you need to tune application performance to create fewer objects.

Paging File—Windows normally wants to set the paging (swap) file size for you automatically. However, the automatic routines normally set the size of the file too big, and could select the slowest hard drive on the system. Hand tuning this feature requires careful monitoring of the counters in the Paging File performance object to ensure you make the file big enough, but don't waste space by making it too large.

Physical Disk—This is the partner to the Cache performance object discussed earlier. You can use the counters in this performance object to monitor actual disk accesses. The goal is to get the % Idle Time counter as high as possible. A high value here means the hard drive is working as little as possible to answer user requests for data.

Process—This performance object works with the Objects performance object described earlier. Every application running on the server has an entry here. You can use the counters within this object to measure individual application performance. This performance object also helps you figure out whether an application uses more disk or processor resources. A high % Processor Time value indicates the application spends a lot of time using the processor; while high IO values indicate the application spends a lot of time using the disk. A high IO Data Operations/sec value tells you that an application uses small data writes like a DBMS. You can also see how many objects the application creates and how it uses resources like memory.

Processor—Use this performance object to get an overall picture of processor performance for the system. You can use this performance object to check the system for processor problems. If you see that the various percent values stay high, there's likely a processor bottleneck on the system and you need to investigate further.

Server—If the machine in question is a server, it's important to know how well it's doing its job. This particular performance object contains a lot of error counters that you should monitor for problems. For example, if you see a high Errors Logon value and no one has complained about server access, you may be seeing cracker activity.

System—This performance object allows you to monitor system specific operations. For example, the Context Switches/sec counter tells you how well the system is moving from one task to another. A high value could indicate that the system is overloaded and isn't able to devote much time to each task. It could also indicate that one application is using too many threads and wasting system resources. You'll normally use this performance object on a server to measure server efficiency and productivity.

Thread—It's easy to get lost with this particular performance object, but you need to know how to use it when working with problem applications. This performance object contains counters that allow you to monitor every aspect of the individual threads within an application. Normally, this information is completely useless to network administrators, because they have no idea of what those threads are doing. However, when working with the application developer, you can help locate problem threads—those that waste resources—and get them fixed.

Note that there are other performance objects available and you may need them on special occasions. For example, the Active Server Pages performance object allows you to monitor the performance of Internet Information Server (IIS). If your business uses IIS for its Web server, this statistic could become important if users complain that the Web site seems slow. Counters under the Active Server Pages performance object, like Errors During Script Runtime, tell you when IIS is running into problems processing user requests. An update to IIS could affect its ability to use old scripts and this counter would be your cue that you need to check the script code.

Adding and Removing Counters

Before you can use System Monitor, you need to know how to add and remove counters on the display. Right next to the view buttons that we talked about in the "Understanding the Views" section earlier are three buttons that affect the counters used to display information for Performance Monitor. These three buttons enable you to change and highlight the items that Performance Monitor displays.

Use the Add button to add new items to the list. Figure 13.5 shows a typical Add Counters dialog box. You select an object to monitor, such as the processor, the specific counter you want to use, and an instance of the selected counter. In

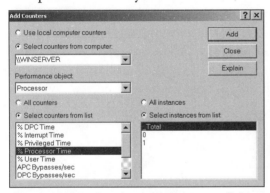

the case of a processor, you may only have one *instance*, but disk drives usually provide several instances. (The term instance denotes a single object—a single processor or a simple copy of an application.) Notice that there are special radio buttons for adding all counters for a specific object, or all instances of a specific counter, to the display. You can also monitor statistics from more than one computer by selecting another in the Select Counters from Computer field.

Figure 13.5: Use the Add Counters dialog box to add new counters to your Performance Monitor display.

Use the Delete button to remove an item from the monitoring list. Remember that the more items you display onscreen, the less screen area each item receives. This, in turn, limits the accuracy of the readings you take. Make sure that you monitor only the essentials. For that matter, you might want to break the items into groups and monitor a group at a time.

Finally, the Highlight button allows you to highlight a specific item found in the monitoring list. This particular feature is only available in Chart view, where highlighting a line helps you see it better. The highlighted line defaults to an extra wide white line that you can see with relative ease when compared to the other lines on a chart.

Creating and Using Logs

You can create log files of counters that you plan to monitor over a long period of time. The first thing you need to do is create the log before you can view the results. The following steps show you how to create a new log:

1. Open the Performance Logs and Alerts\Counter Logs folder.
2. Right-click in the right pane, and select New Log Settings from the shortcut menu. You'll see a New Log Settings dialog.
3. Type a name for the new log setting (the example uses Temp). You'll see a <log settings name> dialog box. The General tab contains the log file name, a list of counters recorded in the log, and the interval used to make log entries. When you create a new log, the list of counters is blank. The one requirement for every log is selecting one or more counters to track.
4. Click Add. You'll see a Select Counters dialog box that looks similar to the Add Counters dialog in Figure 13.5.
5. Select one or more counters to track. Highlight the counter and instance information that you want and click Add. The example uses all instances of the % Processor Time counter found in the Processor object. Click Close in the Add Counters dialog box when you've finished adding counters. At this point, your counters are ready to go, but you haven't decided when to record the log.
6. Click the Schedule tab and you'll see a dialog like the one shown in Figure 13.6. Notice that you can start the log at a specific time or manually start it using a shortcut menu command. Likewise, stopping the log can be automatic or manual. There are special considerations when stopping the log. For example, you can stop the current log at the end of a specific time interval and automatically begin a new one. The log will always default to starting the log immediately and requiring you to manually stop it.

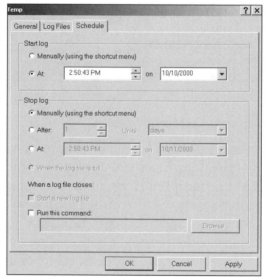

Figure 13.6: The Schedule tab allows you to determine when the log starts and stops.

7. Choose the starting and ending time for your log, and then click OK. The example uses the default settings. The log settings are now ready to use.

Depending on how you've set up your log, Windows may start recording it automatically. You can also right-click the log entry in the Counter Logs folder and choose Start from the shortcut menu. Stopping the log recording process is just as easy. Just select Stop from the shortcut menu when you right-click the log settings icon. Log file icons are red when stopped and green when started, making it easy to see what Windows is currently logging for you.

So, what do you need to do once you've created a log? Open System Monitor and click View Data Log File on the toolbar, select a filename in the Select Log File dialog; then click Open. Performance Monitor opens the log file and shows you any of the counters that you select using the Add Counter dialog. Note that when you open the Add Counters dialog box, instead of seeing all of the available counters, you'll see only those that are recorded in the log.

Now that you can see the recorded counters, let's look at another important feature of Performance Monitor. If you're recording data for days or even weeks, you won't want to look at all the data in one big lump. Wouldn't it be nice if you could look at just a small piece of it? Performance Monitor enables you to do just that. Right-click the chart and choose Properties from the shortcut menu. Click the Source tab and you'll see a dialog box similar to the one shown in Figure 13.7.

Notice the Total Range bar at the bottom of the dialog box. On the upper-left side is the starting time for the log; the upper right side shows the stopping time. On the lower-left side is the starting view time; the bottom right side shows the stopping view time. You can move the two thumbs on this bar to change the starting and stopping view time, which, in turn, affects the display you see in the chart.

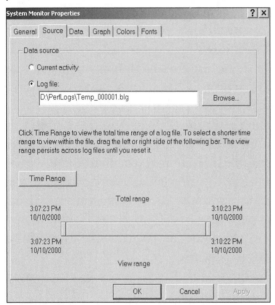

Figure 13.7: The Source tab of the System Monitor Properties dialog allows you to select log file options.

OS Tweaks that Really Work

Getting the OS tuned correctly affects every other aspect of the system. A simple OS tweak can make a vast different in the performance you see, because the OS affects every application you run. The OS also affects network performance, because the OS provides all of the services, protocols, and clients the network needs to operate. In short, if the OS isn't tuned, it may not pay to tune anything else. Here are some simple tweaks to try first:

Look at the Performance tab or dialog box—Most versions of Windows have a Performance tab on the System Properties dialog box or a button you click from within the System Properties dialog box to access the Performance dialog box. In both cases, you need to ensure that these performance settings are correct for your machine. Windows often uses less than optimal settings for your machine. For example, it may not use full disk acceleration or you may find that it chose to favor background instead of foreground tasks.

Shutdown unneeded services—Windows comes with a wealth of services and many third-party vendors install even more. In most cases, the services are set to start automatically if the vendor thinks you need them. Checking the services installed and started on your machine using the Services MMC snap-in is important. Shut down any services you don't need and set them to start manually rather than automatically.

Schedule tasks whenever possible—Windows includes a Task Scheduler that you can use to start tasks that require no user interaction at night or times when the user won't need the machine. This allows you to perform maintenance when the user won't notice the performance drop.

Use virtual memory efficiently—Use the Paging File performance object to determine the paging file size you need. Set virtual memory to use a drive other than your normal drive if possible. Defragment the hard drive so that there aren't any fragmented areas. Finally, set virtual memory to use the freshly defragmented drive. Set the minimum and maximum virtual memory size the same, so that the page file doesn't grow and shrink. Doing so reduces processor cycles used to maintain the page file to a minimum and reduces fragmentation within the page file.

Defragment the hard drive—Fragmented hard drives greatly reduce system performance, not only for virtual memory use, but also for file access reasons. Defragmenting the drive puts all pieces of a file in order, making the drive hardware run more efficiently. We discussed disk defragmentation in Chapter 9, *Network Administration Made Simple*.

Disk caching optimization—The OS uses some of the RAM on a machine to store commonly used data from the hard drive. Since RAM is much faster than the hard drive is, caching the data in RAM makes the hard drive appear much faster. The only way the system will experience a performance boost from caching is to use physical memory. Increasing physical memory also increases the size of the disk cache and system performance.

Software Tweaks that Really Work

The software portion of the system-tuning process is relatively straightforward and easy to understand. In most cases, you don't have access to the source code for the applications you use, so there isn't any way to make the code more efficient. However, there are still ways to make the software more efficient. Here are some methods to try:

Manage application feature sets—Install only the application features you need. If you don't install a feature, it won't sit on your hard drive using up hard disk space and potentially killing performance.

Use only the features you need during a session—Every time you access a new application feature, the OS reads that feature into memory. Unfortunately, the OS takes its time removing the feature once installed. By accessing only the features you need, you can keep memory free for other tasks.

Configure for background processing—Most applications allow you to perform some level of background processing configuration. For example, you can choose to print in the background or in the foreground. Printing in the foreground uses less memory and ensures that the printout is available as soon as the Print dialog box goes away. Printing in the background allows you to resume work immediately, but may slow down both printing and the other work that you then perform.

Using small applications when possible—A small version of a full-fledged application can reduce system load and provide more memory for other applications. For example, you could use a text editor in place of a word processor when taking notes.

Check for memory leaks—Some applications have memory leaks. This means that every time you close the application, some memory isn't deallocated. As the day wears on, your system will experience a memory drain if you open and close this application. Keeping such an application open the whole day (or at least as long as you need it) will keep the memory leak under control. In many cases vendors become aware of memory leaks after releasing the product—make sure you install patches and service releases that may fix these problems.

Disable automatic updates—When you ask an application to do something for you automatically, you're assigning resources and processing time to the application that you won't get back. In some cases, the loss of performance is worthwhile. For example, using automatic save with a word processor solves more problems than it creates. On the other hand, you may want to check your e-mail manually, rather than ask the application to check your e-mail automatically every half-hour.

Hardware Tweaks That Really Work

Hardware upgrades or complete replacements are the basis of many bottleneck solutions today. The idea is a simple one. Make the data pipe bigger and faster so that it can handle all of the data that today's applications generate. In addition, better hardware can perform some tasks automatically or reduce the load on the server. However, there's a lot more to ensuring your hardware is prepared for optimum performance than simply plugging in new hardware. The following tips provide you with some ideas on how to enhance hardware performance:

Ensure it works—Hardware doesn't necessarily fail completely; it can partially fail. These partial failures can cause havoc with system performance. In some cases, the performance drop is noticeable, such as when a NIC begins transmitting packets at random. In other cases, the performance drop is noticeable, but not the cause. For example, a damaged network cable could induce noise into the system that forces workstations to resend packets.

Use vendor supplied drivers—In most cases, using vendor-supplied drivers will provide a performance boost for your system. Drivers supplied with the OS are outdated or generic in many cases. The vendor drivers you download from a Web site are performance tuned and less buggy.

Widen the pipe—Anytime you can create a larger data path you'll also increase system performance. In many cases, a motherboard has more than one option for peripheral devices. For example, you may have a choice between using a PCI or an AGP bus display adapter; the AGP bus is wider and allows better performance in many cases.

Buy quality components—Some companies consider price the only criterion on which to base a buying decision. In some cases, vendors price their hardware higher, because it provides more features and better performance. Careful shopping means looking at what you're getting for the price. Sometimes you need to spend more to get a performance gain and help users get work done more efficiently.

Users: A Hidden Performance Issue

Users represent the most frustrating part of tuning your system. In some cases, users defy any attempt at making the system more efficient. Adding a new procedure means testing the procedure with a subset of users, optimizing the procedure, and training users to perform the task using the new method. This leads to the confusion syndrome. Some users end up using the old method, some users one of the failed methods, and still others the optimized method that you created.

Before you decide that you never want to train a user to do anything new, remember that new procedures are important. You designed the network to make users more efficient; the user has the greatest impact on network performance. Users who aren't completely sure how to use the network waste precious network bandwidth trying to figure out the best way to get their work done. In addition, poorly trained users won't know that the network can perform certain tasks for them automatically, which means they'll waste time doing things in some convoluted manual fashion. So, the first user-oriented network bottleneck solution is to ensure that everyone is actually trained to use the network.

This brings up another problem—resource usage. No matter what you do, some users will insist on abusing network resources. With this in mind, part of your user-oriented system bottleneck solution should be to check network security. Ensure that users can only reach the applications they need to use. In some cases, you may need to perform the additional work required to secure high-bandwidth applications, like NetMeeting, until the user needs them to perform work. However, a good network usage policy (and requisite enforcement) should keep this kind of micro-management to a minimum.

At some point, you'll have the users fully trained to use the network. They'll be aware of all of the security and application usage policies for the company. Even with these two goals met, you may still find that network performance lags. That's where certain types of monitoring come into play. You don't want to become "Big Brother," because that will kill user productivity and could cause your company to lose valuable employees. What you do want to look for are application-usage problems, especially with custom applications. In some cases, you may find that a change in the design of the application interface nets improved network performance; in others, you may find that more user training on specific procedures is mandated. Whichever route you go, it's important to understand what kind of problem the user is facing before you assume that a network-performance–inhibiting usage habit is all the user's fault.

The one thing you never want to do is force users to perform tasks a specific way if another way works equally well. A relative of mine related an incident where a company trainer was convinced the only way to use a database application was with a mouse. The trainer wouldn't even consider telling employees how to work with the keyboard except for data-entry purposes.

Unfortunately, everyone was using the database application for high-speed data entry, and removing their hands from the keyboard didn't make sense. After a lot of complaining to management, the company replaced the trainer with someone who would teach the keyboard method in addition to using the mouse. User performance increased dramatically and everyone is happier. As you can see, there are many ways to improve system performance. You need to consider everything from the hardware, to the software, and even the users of the system.

CHAPTER FOURTEEN

First Aid for the Network

It's easy to view a network as a conglomeration of wiring, some software, and a lot of hardware. The truth is that networks also include the people who work on them. In addition, environment and the level of care provided affect the health of a network. It's not surprising when you consider the complexity of a network that they get sick. Yes, I know I'm giving human qualities to what amounts to a machine, but until you gain this perspective, you'll find that troubleshooting a network is hard at best and impossible in many situations.

This chapter will help you give your network first aid when it becomes ill. In the first section, we'll dispel the notion that only computer gurus can fix network problems. The fact is that networks aren't all that mystical and many of the problems you'll encounter with them are easy to fix. There isn't a good reason to pay a consultant hundreds of dollars to fix a faulty cable—you should save these expenditures for those times when a consultant's services are really needed.

Once you decide to fix your own network, it's time to learn how to diagnose network problems. The second section of the chapter will help you locate many of the simple problems that a network can experience. We'll talk about hardware, software, and even human problems in this part of the chapter. Getting a good diagnosis is extremely important if you don't want to waste a lot of time trying solutions that have little or no chance of working.

The next three sections of the chapter show you how to repair the most common network problems. Hardware has become incredibly reliable over the years and software is becoming more reliable as computer technology improves. In many situations, there's nothing wrong with either the hardware or the software; simple configuration errors can create more problems than you might think. Software problems do occur, however, and you have to know how to deal with them. Even software errors can often be traced to something as simple as having the wrong version of a DLL installed. Cables are another problem area. They get damaged relatively quickly because they're small, flexible, and exposed to abuse. We'll look at other hardware issues as well, but you'll find many of your network problems have something to do with cables or associated hardware like connectors. Finally, Windows is known for experiencing odd problems when changes in the OS affect the way drivers work. In many cases, a driver that used to work fine will stop working after a Windows component is updated. As a result, you'll want to check for new drivers for your hardware on a regular basis. This last repair section will provide you with tips for working with drivers.

The sixth section of the chapter tells you what to do when network problems become too complex for simple troubleshooting techniques. You'll probably need to call a consultant at this point, but there are ways to protect yourself from paying too much for a network repair. For example, you may know that the problem exists with the computer's software, because you've completely tested the hardware. This little piece of information can help reduce the time the consultant requires to locate a problem. Providing a consultant with complete and documented information about your network and the current problem can drastically reduce the cost of a service call.

Paramedics Need Not Apply

You don't have to be a computer guru to figure out the ills of your network. Consultants often make their connection with the network seem mystical—it's not. Good network troubleshooting includes patient observation of the problem and analysis of the information you see. In fact, here's my number one rule of troubleshooting networks (or computer problems of any kind):

> *Getting angry with the computer just wears you out—the computer isn't impressed at all.*

The following sections will look at some of the common problems you'll find: hardware, software, and user. Locating problems in these areas doesn't have to be hard. These sections will provide you with tips on where you need to look for problems and why you won't look in some places.

Understanding Hardware Problems

Most people immediately assume any problem with their computer is going to be hard to find and both difficult and expensive to fix. Some problems are obvious. If you can't use your mouse, either the mouse is broken or the port the mouse is connected to no longer works. In either case, the problem is easy to fix and not expensive. If you can use a screwdriver, you can fix this problem.

You may have noticed that I didn't even mention software. Unless you just installed a new mouse driver or performed a major upgrade of the OS, it won't be the software. The software has remained stable, so it doesn't pay to look at it as a suspect. This is an area where analysis comes into play. Look for what changed or what can break when searching for a problem.

It's true that other problems are subtler than a broken mouse. For example, intermittent losses of connectivity with the network could be a little more difficult to find. However, the simple act of examining the network cable often fixes this problem. I've fixed more broken cables than I care to think about—most of which were routed incorrectly in the first place. In many cases, finding a subtle problem is more a matter of knowing where to look than having a detailed knowledge of how networks are put together. Fortunately, a lot of the "where to look" information has been recorded for you at these Web sites:

A Complete Illustrated Guide to PC Hardware
http://www.karbosguide.com/

BIOS Error Beeps/Messages/Codes
http://sysopt.earthweb.com/biosbmc.html

BVR Tech Repair
http://millbury.k12.ma.us/~hs/techrepair/

Internet FAQ Archives – LANs
http://www.faqs.org/faqs/LANs/

Micro House Technical Library
http://www.supportsource.com/mtltrial/whatis.htm

PCMechanic
http://pcmech.pair.com/

Peter den Haan's Storage Page
http://thef-nym.sci.kun.nl/~pieterh/storage.html

Tom's Hardware Guide
http://www.tomshardware.com/

Troubleshooters.com
http://www.troubleshooters.com/troubleshooters.htm

Wim's BIOS Page
http://www.ping.be/bios/

Some of these documents are a little complex, but they're all useful resources. Even if you can't act on the information they provide directly, knowing where to find the information can help you validate the input you get from consultants. In addition, as you spend more time with your network, your proficiency will grow. Technology that seems foreign and difficult to learn today will be within your grasp tomorrow.

The hardware portion of the network is relatively logical and problems make sense when you locate them. Crimp a cable, and network communication will suddenly cease for at least part of the network. Lose a display adapter and a user will claim the machine can't be turned on. If you could somehow talk to the network and ask it what it feels, diagnosis of the problem would be instantaneous. Unfortunately, the network isn't talking, so you'll need to rely on tools to solve your problems. Once you master the tools, however, you'll find that hardware problems become almost too easy to fix.

Overcoming Parts Problems—*Not all of us can afford the latest equipment; some of the equipment in use today is well past its prime. The problem is that many stores stop stocking parts for older equipment about a year after the equipment is released; making repairs difficult to say the least. You can find a lot of these older parts at ThePartsFinder (http://www.thepartsfinder.com/). In many situations, repairing an old, dependable piece of equipment with enough oomph to do the job is a lot less expensive than buying new equipment with capabilities you don't need.*

Understanding Software Problems

Software problems are another story. There may not be a single source of problems in software as there is for hardware. Unlike hardware, software doesn't break. It can act erratically, but it's not used up or broken in the normal use of the term. This makes it hard to determine whether a piece of software is no longer working like it should—there are no good or bad indicator lights to go by. In addition to the lack of positive indicators, every piece of software on your system is linked with one or more other pieces. These interactions are often the source of a software failure. So, it's often a problem to figure out which piece of software to replace. Several pieces are involved with the problem and replacing just one piece will fix the problem, but determining which one to replace can be hard.

Fortunately, there are techniques you can use to minimize the number of hard software decisions you have to make. For example, it's common practice to replace old drivers in an effort to repair a software problem that occurs after an OS update. DLLs can become corrupt or conflict with newer DLLs on the system. Replacing an old version of a DLL with a new one is usually a good idea. (There are exceptions that we'll talk about in the "Exorcising Software Demons" section later in this chapter.) Consultants rely on years of experience of looking at the same problem over and over again to determine what to check first. However, this is information you can learn through experience and by reading books like this one. There are also some important Web sites you should check out when it comes to diagnosing software problems:

Apple Services and Support
http://www.apple.com/support/

AppleCare Tech Info Library
http://til.info.apple.com/techinfo.nsf/

Bud's Troubleshooter
http://www.geocities.com/~budallen/

Computing.net
http://computing.net/

HelpTalk Forums
http://www.helptalk.com/supportlist.htm

InfiniSource (Windows-Help.net)
http://www.windows-help.net/

Macland.net
http://www.macland.net/help/

Microsoft Support Knowledge Base
http://search.support.microsoft.com/kb/

The Internet Access Company Support
http://corp.tiac.net/support/software/

Troubleshoot Your Computer at Wayne's Computer World
http://www.wayneswebworld.com/wcw/troubleshooting.html

Some of these URLs, like the Microsoft Support Knowledge Base, are OS specific. Others, like The Internet Access Company Support, are useful no matter which OS you have. In fact, The Internet Access Company provides support for Windows, Mac OS, UNIX, and OS/2. Of course, each Web site provides information on a specific topic; you may find that the answer you need lies on another Web site. Besides these general Web sites, make sure you check the Web sites for your software vendors as well. These sites normally contain a wealth of information, some of which is probably buried where you least expect it. Newsgroups are also a good resource. Many of the larger vendors, like Microsoft, have extensive newsgroup selections that answer just about any software diagnostic need.

Software problems are normally a matter of following a specific set of repair steps rather than using clairvoyance to detect the problem based on the current position of the moon and stars. Still, the interaction between software components is complex. Software-related problems are one area where you may find the help of a consultant most useful. Some subtle problems may require a combination of changes in configuration and updates to fix. Consultants often have the real-world experience needed to locate and fix these complex problems without spending a lot of time doing so.

Understanding User Issues

Human issue problems are the most difficult to fix, because you have the least control over them. Users who always turns their machine off without shutting Windows down first will probably continue to do so unless you can find some method of convincing them to do otherwise. (Electroshock does wonders from what I hear.) Users who try to get software to perform tasks that it was never designed to do are common and no amount of persuasion on your part is likely to change behavior.

Training can help reduce user problems, as can written company policies with remedies spelled out for offenders. Often the subtle approach works best. Again, consultants don't have a corner on the human-interaction market. In fact, this is one area where you might be better qualified than a consultant to fix a problem with your network, because you know the human players involved. The principle of observing the problem and patiently finding a solution usually works best.

Discovering the Source of a Network Problem

The most complex problem that many network administrators deal with is the network. The combination of machines, cabling, and software are too complex for most people to grasp without help. Network problems usually occur in the following situation:

- After you initially put the network together
- After a major upgrade or other disturbance like a company move
- After maintenance
- When a new user begins working alone after training
- Randomly as the result of component failure

Normally, you can reduce the scope of the problem by observing network behavior and determining what has changed in the last week or so. Looking at behavior allows you to eliminate hardware from your list of culprits. For example, if some people can work with the server and others can't, the server isn't the problem. Determining what events took place in the last week tells you what to avoid searching. If nothing has changed, you can usually ignore problems like server configuration and many software problems. Notice I didn't say you could ignore workstation configuration—users are notorious for making simple changes that produce unpredictable results.

When working with network problems, the divide-and-conquer approach works best. Try to localize the problem to a single machine, hub, cable, or peripheral if possible. When working with a hub, see if the indicator lights show that a particular line is dead when you plug a workstation into it. Try unplugging workstations one at a time to rule out a single workstation failure. When working with a bus configuration, try unplugging part of the network. (Remember to terminate the active segment.)

Get the Full Scoop on Hardware Problems—*Many network administrators start out with limited hardware knowledge. In fact, it's likely that most network administrators know more about software to start with and learn hardware as an afterthought. If you fall into this category, you don't have to feel intimidated by computer hardware. Many hardware maintenance courses teach the basics of computer hardware design. One option is PC Architecture (*http://www.can.ibm.com/ services/learning/course/V5100CA.html*).*

Once you've eliminated the hardware, look for software problems. Software problems do occur, but not independently of other factors. Remember that software doesn't break or get old. In most cases, software fails as the direct result of some action. Users may change their network configuration, or you might install a new application that causes a network problem. Application and DLL corruption can occur in some instances due to the action of the OS; but this is rare. Asking users about changes and looking into your own maintenance logs is the right place to start looking for software problems. The item that changed is the culprit in most situations.

There are also human problems to consider. Human aren't predicable and any attempt to analyze them will only result in much head scratching with little problem resolution to show for the effort. As a network administrator, you need to get used to the weird and unforeseen when dealing with the human factor on your network. In fact, I know of network administrators who have scrapbooks of their favorite human crisis experiences, which is a little odd when you think about it.

Here's one of my favorite real-world experiences. I kept getting calls from one company with intermittent network problems. Many searches of the software, cabling, and hardware turned up nothing. I eventually discovered a user who unplugged a computer from the network every day to avoid being bothered by e-mail. Once the user completed a task, the computer would get plugged back into the network, e-mail would get checked, and then the computer would get unplugged again. The user always plugged the computer in before leaving work, which is why I didn't spot the problem at first. (I tried to do my work after everyone went home.) No, these kinds of problems don't happen every day, and they're always unexpected when they do; but, as a network administrator, you have to be prepared for any eventuality when it comes to finding human-related problems.

Configuration Fixes that Help or Hinder

System configuration is an accident waiting to happen. For example, in an effort to increase system speed, you decide to turn off a service that you no longer need. It doesn't take long for problem reports to come pouring in; users no longer have access to a much-needed application on the server. The idea of configuring the system for higher speed was a good one; but it failed to produce the intended results. Many configuration changes fall into this category. You need to try them, because they could produce a good result; but you're never sure until you actually do try them.

Solving Speed Problems for Games—*Many older software products, especially games, can't run on today's modern computers. The reason is simple: the computer is just too fast. These older products have timing loops that can't keep up with the speed provided by a modern system. The solution to this problem is obvious. If the application can't keep up with the computer, you need to slow the computer to the application's level. Many shareware products do just that—temporarily slow your system so that you can use these older applications. One of the best places to look for slow-down utilities is The NEW PC Slow Down Page* http://home.att.net/~pc_slowdown/.

Not every system configuration task is as experimental as finding ways to get more speed. In some cases, a configuration is a necessary task that you must perform to get the system to work at all. For example, many servers install a new service like dynamic host configuration protocol (DHCP) support. Before this new service can do any work, you need to configure it by providing a list of addresses the DHCP service can rent to clients on the network. So, while you could reverse a change that might produce an increase in system throughput, you must make DHCP configuration work.

An error that most network administrators make is to try to configure more than one system element at a time. Most network administrators try to work on blocks of items to keep up with the constant load of network-related tasks. System configuration is one of the few tasks that a network administrator should perform one at a time. Not only does this allow the network administrator to reverse the change more easily; but it also allows better analysis of the effect of the change.

One type of system configuration change you should avoid is the "gee-whiz" modification. In many cases, these configuration changes aren't necessary and only increase the chance of problems later. For example, it might be nice to add music to the user's login experience every morning; but it's not a necessary change. In fact, a change like this could really backfire on you, because not every user machine includes a soundboard to play the music. Obviously, this is a simple example; but many configuration changes are equally unnecessary. Whenever you decide to make a configuration change, ask yourself first whether the change is really necessary or if it falls into the gee-whiz category.

Exorcising Software Demons

Most software demons fall into the OS interface arena. Something about the interaction between application, OS, and perhaps hardware isn't right. Since access to hardware is controlled by drivers in modern OSs, you can limit your search (except in rare cases) to a problem between the OS and the application. Of course, the difficulty is narrowing the cause of the interface disagreement still further; is the culprit the application or the OS? One way to narrow the problem is to try the application on another machine. If the application works there, you're seeing either a configuration or an OS problem. On the other hand, if the application won't work on any test machine, it goes back to the store for a full refund.

After you check for a configuration problem, it's time to look at the OS. Normally, it pays to check for DLL or other low-level system problems first. No matter how well behaved any application is, there's always a chance that a common DLL used by one application will conflict with another version of the same DLL used by another application.

Every time Microsoft provides upgrades for the DLLs used in Windows, that's one more version of the DLL that vendors have to think about supporting. The problem is that developers often program around behaviors or bugs they see in the common Windows DLLs. In other words, the application is dependent on a certain DLL behavior (something that Microsoft doesn't recommend). When Microsoft corrects bugs in the DLL or enhances the DLL in some way, the application breaks.

Here's where a conflict comes into play. An older application needs the old version of the DLL to function properly. Yet, a new application might need Microsoft's latest version of the DLL to operate, because it relies on the fixed or enhanced behavior that Microsoft has provided. Since both DLLs can't appear in the Windows system folder at the same time, you get a conflict situation that some network administrators call DLL hell.

Microsoft is aware of the problems of DLL hell, and is taking steps to fix the problem. In some cases, this means coming up with unique solutions, because network administrators require the functionality of both DLL versions to make the network run as anticipated. The best solution, however, is to upgrade the applications to use the same DLL version whenever possible, or at least test the utility with the latest DLL version to see whether it'll work.

One solution is to make registry changes and run an application called DUPS.EXE. DUPS is short for DLL Universal Problem Solver. The DUPS tool is a set of utilities that allows you to monitor the version numbers of DLLs stored on multiple Windows machines, making it possible to look for incompatibilities across your entire network. You can find an article, "**An End to DLL Hell**" by Rick Anderson at http://msdn.microsoft.com/library/techart/DLLdanger1.htm that details the problem of DLL hell. The DUPS tool and accompanying documentation appears at **SAMPLE: Using DUPS.exe to Resolve DLL Compatibility Problems** http://support.microsoft.com/support/kb/articles/q247/9/57.asp.

Updating Drivers and Windows

As Windows evolves, the drivers you use with Windows must change as well. In many cases, this means obtaining new drivers and loading them on the machine. Most mainstream vendors are good about providing a Web site location in their documentation where you can download new drivers. In some cases, you may have to call the vendor's technical support to obtain new drivers. Of course, not every vendor provides update information and you may find that you can't locate a new driver when you need it most. When you run into problems finding a driver you need, you'll want to check out the following Web sites:

Driverzone.com
http://www.driverzone.com/

FTP Search
http://ftpsearch.lycos.com/

Microsoft.com Download Center
http://www.microsoft.com/downloads/

Paperbits Support Center for Windows NT
http://www.paperbits.com/

Updates.com
http://updates.zdnet.com/updates/drivers.htm

WinDrivers.com
http://www.windrivers.com/

WinFiles.com
http://www.windows95.com/

Most of these Web sites have one thing in common; they allow you to look for files. In some cases, they allow you to perform a general search; in other cases, the search is limited to pieces of hardware. You can use these search engines to find new drivers for your hardware. Don't be too surprised if users rather than vendors support some of the download sites. If the vendor won't support a product, quite often the users of that product band together in an attempt to provide peer support.

What to Do When All of This Great Advice Fails

There's no doubt about it, some of the problems that you'll run into require professional help to fix. Compatibility problems are the worst; trying to get two applications to work together at one time verges on the impossible. Some hardware problems defy identification without the proper tools. Network cabling can look great, but still contain flaws. In short, you may not be able to fix every problem you run across. While these unfixable problems represent perhaps as much as five percent of all of the system errors you'll ever need to fix, they can also be the most bothersome and time consuming.

Before you get a consultant, try peer help. Talk to other people you know and spend some time on newsgroups. Perform searches on the Internet for magazine articles that may help. Few problems in computing are so rare that no one has heard about them. However, finding just the right information can be difficult, and you have to consider several factors before you search too long. When a workstation is disabled, there are three costs involved: the cost of your time to search, an employee's time to wait, and business loss of lost resource time. In addition to cost, there's the frustration factor; eventually most people get too frustrated to see a solution even if it pokes them in the eye.

Consultants cost a lot to hire—at least good consultants do. Before you make a telephone call, gather all of the information the consultant will require. This saves time and money. The consultant needs complete documentation for the system; organizing the documentation by machine will help. You should include maintenance logs for your system and a complete written description of what you did to try to fix the problem. Make sure that all software is available and that you've performed maintenance on the system (especially a backup that you've verified). Blow the dust out of your machines so that the consultant can actually see to work.

When the consultant arrives, make sure he or she fully understands the situation and knows the location of all the materials you gathered. If you find the consultant is ignoring all of this input, get a new consultant. Some consultants are only interested in making a buck, not fixing your system anytime soon. They'd love to make a career out of fixing your system. Get a consultant who has a list of happy clients (call to verify they're happy) and who will listen to what you have to say. Even if this second type of consultant charges a higher hourly rate, you'll find that you spend less money, because a responsible consultant will fix the problem faster.

CHAPTER FIFTEEN

Planning for the Future

We've talked about every other networking topic so far except the future. Most people do some type of planning for the future—both personal and business. Like everything else, networks require some form of future planning. Otherwise, you'll end up with a network that's not supported and will eventually fail to deliver the features and performance you need to conduct business.

When you plan for the future of your business, you take many factors into account. For example, you probably set money aside for necessary building repairs, equipment upgrades, advertising, and the like. Each of these individual requirements adds to the business as a whole and allows you to plan for the future in a proactive, rather than a reactive, manner. A computer network also requires future planning at several levels; each level contributes toward the health of the network as a whole.

This chapter looks at many planning issues that businesses fail to consider. The first topic is planned obsolescence. Computers become less useful as they get older. Some of the newer software packages won't run on them, maintenance costs increase, and minor problems start to creep in that a user has to consider as part of the daily use of the machine. If you don't plan for the retirement of your old computer equipment as part of an upgrade strategy, you may find yourself with an attic's worth of old hardware sitting around without a home.

Small businesses don't typically need to buy computer equipment in bulk. Large purchases occur even less often with a home office network. However, there are still times when it pays to plan for the future by getting what you need in bulk at a lower cost. For example, your company may have a growth plan in place. If you know for sure that the company will be adding five new employees in three months and you can save by purchasing NICs in bulk, the risk of doing so is justified. Eventually, the new staff will arrive and you'll save the company money.

Most companies keep detailed records of their business. These records provide the information required for statistical analysis. For example, sales records might indicate that additional advertising in a specific area of the world would help with sales during a given timeframe. Likewise, records of network maintenance actions, client and application load, tuning, and other statistics help you plan for your network's future. Of course, you don't want to get so mired in paperwork that you never get anything else done. The third section of the chapter looks at a reasonable level of record keeping that can help you plan for future needs based on network performance today.

The final section of the chapter talks about breaking the upgrade hardware cycle that many companies fall prey to because of a simple marketing strategy that feeds on the desire to be part of the "in" crowd. It seems like Intel introduces a new processor each month. When Intel fails to introduce a new processor, someone else is always ready to take their place. The point is that you could upgrade your hardware continuously and never catch up to current technology. Of course, the ads say you'll get left behind if you don't have the latest 100 GHz processor running on a machine with 4 TB of RAM. Software vendors tend to support the insanity that began with the hardware vendors. They would lead you to believe that the old word processor with 100 features you didn't use is going to require replacement by the new, super word processor with 101 features you still won't use. Let's face it, if you write one letter a year, even the oldest word processing package will fulfill your needs. The only time you actually need new software is if it contains a feature that will make your business more productive.

Keeping Your Attic out of the Office

We talked about computer replacement as part of total cost of ownership planning in the "Replacement" section of Chapter 12, *Networks That Pay for Themselves*. In that chapter, we focused on the computer system. Planning for the replacement of computer system equipment isn't limited to individual workstations; every element of your network requires some type of replacement plan. This includes the cabling, furniture, manuals, software, and peripherals. If you want the maximum throughput from your network, each element needs periodic replacement.

The problem for many companies is that they don't inventory their systems. When you buy a computer, peripheral, hub, or other hardware, record the date of purchase, along with the dates of purchase for individual parts within the computer. Making individual entries allows you to update them as you replace failed components. It also pays to document dates cable segments are installed and replaced. The copper within a cable gets old and brittle after a while. Cables require replacement if you want to continue getting the maximum signal strength. Even office equipment requires replacement. An old chair may still support your weight; but if the padding is worn out, you'll get backaches from sitting all day. If you don't want to replace the chair, at least have it recovered. The point is that you need to record purchase information for your network and plan for the day when you'll need to retire a piece of equipment.

So, how long can you expect parts of your network to last? Most experts agree that a computer system last from three to five years. It won't wear out in that time; but the components inside the case will become so outdated that modern software won't run on it. Of course, that brings up the issue of whether you need the latest software; in some cases, you don't, which means you can also get more use out of the associated hardware.

But there's still a concern about old computers. Connectors and other high-stress components begin to loosen, so you spend more time fixing problems with systems by reseating cards and performing other tasks you wouldn't need to perform with a new system. If you continue to use the same software year after year, it still pays to monitor computer performance and replace it as the system shows signs of additional maintenance time or large performance losses.

A network is a complete picture—everything from the computer systems to the cable to the furniture you sit on. To obtain maximum user productivity, you must consider ergonomic as well as other concerns. Ergonomics is the study of human-to-machine interface; a better work environment makes the computer easier to use and allows someone to work longer without fatigue. Therefore, it pays to look at the entire picture from a future needs perspective. You need to answer this question, "When will my company's furniture wear enough that it affects user productivity?" Furniture longevity is a matter of use. According to some government statistics, most furniture lasts 20 years. It's probably true that a filing cabinet or a desk lasts that long. However, most people don't have that experience with ergonomically essential equipment like chairs. Generally I replace or reupholster my chair every five years.

Cabling lasts a relatively long time. You can normally expect seven or eight years from a piece of networking cable if no one stresses or mistreats it. Some people use their cables even longer; but they'll begin to notice losses in performance and increased maintenance. The cable is probably good (with reduced capacity due to aging); but connectors wear and cutting the cable to replace the connectors after seven or eight years of use doesn't produce good results. It's easier to replace the cable and get the additional speed a new cable and connectors provides.

Hubs and other sealed equipment have a longer life expectancy than some computer equipment. Generally, I wait for these devices to fail or become outdated before I replace them. In some cases, the sealed device won't wear out;

but some component of it will require replacement. For example, a UPS generally won't fail unless it's hit by lightning. However, the battery inside the UPS will eventually require replacement. It's a good idea to plan for battery replacement every three years. The UPS tells you when the battery isn't able to handle a load anymore—generally as part of a diagnostic test.

Lightning and Power Lines—*Lightning doesn't have to strike your house directly to cause problems. It can strike anywhere on the power line and feed back into your house. This means that you may see damage to your computer even if the lightning strike is a few blocks away. Considering the number of times lightning hits power lines, because they provide a convenient discharge path, it doesn't take long to see several strikes at your power line.*

This brings up the topic of surge suppressor and UPS life. Some people assume that as long as these devices can provide power to your computers, they're just fine. That's a mistaken notion that could cost you the life of your workstation during the next lightning storm. Some components within a surge suppressor are only good for three or four lightning hits. UPS vendors usually provide longer lasting components, but they eventually fail due to exposure to the high voltage of a lightning strike as well. Surge suppressors almost never provide any form of monitoring circuitry that tells you when it's no longer doing the job. In low lightning areas—places where few storms occur—it's a good idea to replace your surge suppressor every four years even if it still provides good connectivity. In high lightning areas, it pays to replace the surge suppressor every year. The price of a surge suppressor is less than the cost of a new computer; so this is cheap insurance. Fortunately, a UPS normally provides monitoring circuitry that tells you when the device is no long providing surge protection. However, you'll want to check with the UPS vendor to be certain and adjust your replacement strategy to match.

Some peripherals have amazing life spans (at least for computer equipment). For example, I use one dot matrix printer on my network to print multipart invoices. It's 12 years old and shows no sign of giving up. However, this device isn't my first printing choice. A much newer laser printer is the first choice for black and white printouts, while an inkjet serves as the output device of choice for color. Some people may think that keeping the dot matrix printer around is a waste of time. However, I have lots of forms and plenty of ribbons for the printer so there isn't any reason to get rid of it.

When Buying a Dozen Network Cards Does Make Sense

Many small businesses buy computer equipment on an as-needed basis when they could buy the equipment in bulk to save money. In the "Forming a

Cooperative" section of Chapter 12, *Networks That Pay for Themselves*, we talked about the advantage of combining purchases with other businesses. A cooperative can save a great deal of money, because the buying power of many small businesses compares well to one large business. However, you won't always be able to use this approach, especially if your network has unique requirements. That's where buying in bulk comes into play.

You may notice that some devices on your network fail more often than others do and the devices don't change. For example, network cards appear to fail more often than some types of cards, because they take more abuse. Part of the problem is that network administrators check them more often when network failures occur. Serial and parallel port boards are another category of board that fails somewhat often. In some cases, the cables attached to all of these boards cause problems, because users get stuck in them, they get moved around by cleaning personnel, and the cable acts as a conduit for all kinds of outside energy. Whatever the cause of failure, they fail more often than some types of boards in the computer. Since the device doesn't change often, you can buy in bulk and save money. In many cases, stores promote this idea by offering the boards at special rates in bulk to retail customers.

Of course, there are also situations when buying in bulk is a mistake. For example, buying display adapters in bulk isn't a good idea. Display adapters do fail, but not as often as other board types. The fact that vendors heavily shield cabling for a display adapter and the cable includes a ferrite bead to reduce radio frequency interference reduces the chances of induction of harmful voltages from outside sources. The technology for display adapters also changes on a continual basis, which means that any board you buy today will be out of date tomorrow. Of course, you may want to maintain one spare display adapter as an emergency repair item.

Some boards fall into a gray area when it comes to buying in bulk. For example, IDE host adapters haven't changed much recently and it's unlikely they'll change anytime soon. However, motherboard vendors usually build these boards into the motherboard today and the lack of outside contamination makes them reliable. In short, you don't need a separate IDE host adapter to begin with on a new computer system, but may need one if the IDE host adapter fails later. Given the low failure rates of the boards, you may find it hard to justify a bulk purchase of five or more boards.

In some cases, you need to depend on records to determine the need to purchase some boards in bulk. We'll talk about this issue in the next section of the chapter.

The point of this section is that you can use your knowledge of the network to save money and decrease repair times. Having spare parts available in the right quantity is essential if you want to have the part on hand when a failure occurs. Buying spare parts in quantity reduces network-operating costs and keeps the total cost of ownership in line. It's this type of future planning that can keep you from operating in a reactive mode all of the time; planning makes it easier to take a proactive stance to your computing needs.

Keeping Records Today to Plan for Tomorrow

We've talked in various places in the book about the need to keep records. However, we haven't talked about the various records a network needs for full documentation. The following list is an overview of the network records that I maintain:

- **Hardware purchase**—Make sure you include any new equipment purchase. I include the equipment name, manufacturer, serial number, date of purchase, date of installation, and cost.
- **Software purchase**—Be sure you include every new piece of software. I include the application name, manufacturer, serial number(s), date of purchase, cost, and quantity. I also include a notes section to record special software features and associated packages. For example, I included a note about the Windows 95 Plus Pack in my Windows 95 entry.
- **Equipment purchase**—Any equipment that isn't hardware or software goes into this log. I include the equipment description, manufacturer, date of purchase, date of installation, serial number, cost, quantity, and location.
- **Workstation or server maintenance action**—Each machine has a maintenance log. However, I keep all of the logs in one database so that I can search for past problems for any machine. The log includes machine name, date of action, a category, a note area for a description, and an area for a drawing. I don't make the entry long; but I do include everything I think I might need in the future. If I think a drawing will help show the problem, I'll sketch something quickly and paste it in the database.
- **Planned updates**—This is my five-year plan for the network. I try to keep an eye on equipment that will require replacement soon based on purchase date. This log includes the date of purchase, date of repair, and equipment description.
- **Performance log**—I don't track the performance of everything on my network, but I do track specific performance figures for each machine. These figures include disk access, processor load, and network bandwidth

usage. Just these three sets of figures provide me with a picture of general network health.

As you can see, most of these records are common sense. You need to know when you buy hardware, software, and other equipment for warrantee purposes anyway, so these records won't place an additional burden on your company. In the long run, the maintenance action log will actually save you time, because it represents a store of knowledge that you can refer to as needed to help repairing new problems. A few minutes spent recording problem and solution information today may save you hours of work tomorrow. The planned updates log is a little harder to justify if you have a home office. Normally, a network administrator wants this log when talking with management about future expenses. It does make a good log for planning purposes no matter how big or small your company is. My performance log reflects the needs of a home office. If you work for a larger organization, you may want to record other performance information. Just remember that every hour you spend in paperwork is an hour you won't have for other purposes.

Of course, I stopped maintaining paper records long ago. I keep these records in an Access database on my machine. That's one of the reasons I listed the information I record for each log; you can use this information for creating your own database. Likewise, you may find it easier to maintain electronic records to keep clutter to a minimum and make the records easier to search. For example, you may remember fixing a problem in the past, yet not remember when you did it. Searching through paper records could be time consuming, electronic record searches are almost instantaneous.

Stopping the Vicious Hardware and Software Upgrade Cycle

Have you noticed that hardware vendors come out with a new and more exciting device every six months to a year? Software vendors tend to support these upgrades by adding features to their applications that rely on the new hardware. As a result, some users feel like they're in a dangerous upward spiral. Constant software and hardware upgrades threaten to kill budgets and reduce network administrators to tears. Not only do you upgrade software and hardware, but there are training concerns to consider and new procedures to write. In short, you can spend all of your time performing nothing but upgrades.

Vendors power this upgrade using one tactic—the fear most users have of being left behind. If you look at the ads for all of these new products, the vendor portrays those who don't perform the upgrade as being the last to get a contract or achieve some other goal. The fact is that you may not get left behind. You may find that leaving the network as is actually allows you to move ahead of other companies, because you can focus on doing something other than upgrades.

So, how do you make the decision to plan for an upgrade sometime in the future? We've talked about many criteria throughout the book, but let me summarize them here:

- The performance of your network has decreased and tuning doesn't help.
- The equipment is nearing the end of its life expectancy.
- Your company wants to grow into a new area and the old equipment can't handle the load.
- Your company hires additional personnel.
- An equipment failure leaves you without any other choice.

Because you decided to plan your network, purchase hardware and software with care, and configure everything correctly, you don't need to worry about chasing every new fad in the computer industry. While you don't want to become complacent about the capabilities of your network, you also know that your network does everything you need. Breaking the vicious hardware and software upgrade cycle requires nothing more than knowledge and the ability to say no.

GLOSSARY

This glossary defines the terms and acronyms used throughout the book. These definitions are specific to the book. In other words, when you look through this glossary, you're seeing the words defined in the context in which they're used. This might or might not always coincide with current industry usage since the computer industry changes the meaning of words so often. Finally, the definitions here use a conversational tone in most cases. This means they might sacrifice a bit of puritanical accuracy for the sake of understanding.

While this Glossary is a comprehensive view of the words and acronyms in the book, you'll run into situations when you need to know more. What happens if you can't find the acronym you need in the computer dictionary you just bought? It may mean that you won't fully understand the installation instructions for a new computer or a piece of software. More importantly, you won't understand a concept you need to know to run your business. Fortunately, there are a lot of sites on the Internet that you can go to for help:

Acronym Finder
http://www.acronymfinder.com/

Microsoft Encarta
http://encarta.msn.com/

University of Texas Acronyms and Abbreviations
http://www-hep.uta.edu/~variable/e_comm/pages/r_dic-en.htm

Webopedia
http://webopedia.internet.com/

yourDictionary.com (formerly A Web of Online Dictionaries)
http://www.yourdictionary.com/

Web sites normally provide acronyms or glossary entries—not both. An acronym site only provides the definition for the acronym that you want to learn about; it doesn't provide an explanation of what the acronym means with regard to everyday computer use. The two extremes in this list are Acronym Finder (acronyms only) and Webopedia (full-fledged glossary entries).

Acronym Finder isn't updated as often as the University of Texas site is, but it does have the advantage of providing an extremely large list of acronyms from which to choose. At the time of this writing, the Acronym Finder sported 164,000 acronyms. Most of the Web sites for computer terms are free. In some cases, like Microsoft's Encarta, you have to pay for the support provided; but it's still worth the effort to seek these locations to ensure that you understand the terms used in the jargon filled world of computing. The University of Texas site is updated fairly often and provides only acronyms (another page at the same site includes a glossary). Webopedia has become one of my favorite places to visit, because it provides encyclopedic coverage of many computer terms and includes links to other Web sites. I like the fact that if I don't find a word I need, I can submit it to the Webopedia staff for addition to their dictionary, making Webopedia a community-supported dictionary of the highest quality. One of the interesting features of the yourDictionary.com Web site is that it provides access to more than one dictionary and in more than one language.

Active Directory—A method of storing machine, server, and user configuration within Windows 2000 that supports full data replication so that every domain controller has a copy of the data. This is essentially a special purpose database that contains information formatted according to a specific schema. Active Directory is designed to make Windows 2000 more reliable and secure, while reducing the work required by both the developer and network administrator for application support and distribution. The user benefits as well since Active Directory fully supports roving users and maintains a full record of user information, which reduces the effects of local workstation down time.

API—*See* Application Programming Interface.

Application Programming Interface (API)—A method of defining a standard set of function calls and other interface elements. It usually defines the interface between a high-level language and the lower level elements used by a device driver or operating system. The ultimate goal is to provide some type of service to an application that requires access to the operating system or device feature set.

ASP—*See* Association of Shareware Professionals.

Association of Shareware Professionals (ASP)—A group formed to assist with shareware needs. For example, members gain assistance with marketing and distribution. ASP also provides a forum for members to discuss shareware issues and promotes professionalism among members. The association also terms shareware as user-supported software.

Asynchronous Transfer Mode (ATM)—A data transfer method that relies on packets (cells) of a fixed size. The cell size used with ATM is smaller than used with older technologies, which enhances network efficiency by reducing the number of padding characters required to create complete cells. An ATM network typically transfers data at 25 to 622 Mbps.

ATM—*See* Asynchronous Transfer Mode.

Bandwidth Throttling—A method of reducing the amount of bandwidth required by a device during transmission.

Bandwidth—A measure of the amount of data a device can transfer in a given time.

BBS—*See* Bulletin Board System.

Basic Input/Output System (BIOS)—A set of low-level computer interface functions stored in a chip on a computer's motherboard. The BIOS performs basic tasks like booting the computer during startup and performing the power-on startup tests (POST).

Bindery Emulation—A method used to make NetWare Directory Services (NDS), used by NetWare versions 4.x and later, to appear as a NetWare 3.x bindery to older clients.

Bindery—The set of files used to store network-specific configuration information on a network. These files contain user data, security information, and other network configuration data. You can't start the file server without this information. Corruption of any of these files might prevent the network from starting properly as well.

Biometrics—A statistical method of scanning an individual's unique characteristics, normally body parts, to ensure that they're who they say they are. Some of the scanned elements include voiceprints, irises, fingerprints, hands, and facial features. The two most popular elements are irises and fingerprints, because they're the two that most people are familiar with. Not only can't the user lose their identifying information (at least not easily), but also with proper scanning techniques the identifying information can't be compromised either.

BIOS—*See* Basic Input/Output System.

Bottleneck—The perceptible slowing of a system due to excess resource requirements by an application or user. A bottleneck may also appear when there's a disparity in the performance potential between two system components. Network professionals normally classify bottlenecks by type. For example, an application that uses disk resources excessively or hardware that's incapable of keeping up with other machine elements, like the processor, could cause a disk bottleneck.

Buffer—The area in memory where program variables or other data are stored. For example, applications normally read more than one page from a word-processed document to improve performance. The applications store pages in addition to the one currently viewed by the user in the buffer until needed.

Bulletin Board System (BBS)—A form of electronic message center that relies on a dial-up connection. BBSs normally provide services for special interest groups, software vendors, or hardware vendors. The BBS server allows reading and uploading of messages, as well as downloading of software and text.

Business Logic—The rules a business uses to perform various tasks. Business logic normally refers to business math and the application of that math to accounting needs. For example, business logic dictates how a business calculates shipping and handling costs for an order.

CAD—*See* Computer-Aided Drafting.

CD-ROM—*See* Compact Disk Read-Only Memory.

CDSA—*See* Common Data Security Architecture.

Certified NetWare Engineer (CNE)—The Certified NetWare Engineer is an intermediate-level Novell networking certification. Many people who obtain the CNE certification are consultants, system integrators, or employees of companies that need a person with a high skill level to maintain the network.

CGM—*See* Computer Graphics Metafile.

Client/Server—A method of networking that relies on a file server as a central repository for data. The file server acts as the server for a workstation (client).

Client—The recipient of data, services, or resources from a file or other server. This term can refer to a workstation or an application. The server can be another PC or an application.

Cluster—A group of servers that are joined together to service the needs of a large group of clients. A router normally controls access to the cluster. Networks use clusters for a wide range of activities, including load balancing.

CNE—*See* Certified NetWare Engineer.

Common Data Security Architecture (CDSA)—A comprehensive set of security services that makes secure transactions easier. It has a four-layer architecture: application, layered services and middleware, Common Security Services Manager (CSSM) infrastructure, and security service provider modules. CDSA is on The Open Group fast track to becoming a standard.

Common Security Services Manager (CSSM)—The interface used to provide access to cryptographic service modules and certificate libraries by applications when working with Common Data Security Architecture.

Compact Disk Read-Only Memory (CD-ROM)—A device used to store up to 650 MB of permanent data. You can't write to a CD-ROM like you can to a hard or floppy disk. The disks look like audio CDs, but require a special drive to interface it with a computer.

Computer Graphics Metafile (CGM)—A standard method of storing graphic images in vector format. Like all vector graphic formats, CGM allows infinite scaling and provides better resolution characteristics than bitmapped graphics. This is a favorite format of many application programs, like spreadsheets, because the files are easily transported between operating system platforms like the PC and the Macintosh.

Computer-Aided Drafting (CAD)—A special type of graphics program used for creating, printing, storing, and editing architectural, electrical, mechanical or other forms of engineering drawings. CAD programs normally provide precise measuring capabilities and libraries of predefined objects, such as sinks, desks, resistors, and gears. Some people refer to CAD as *computer-aided design* as an interchangeable term.

Connectivity—A measure of the interactions between clients and servers. In many cases, connectivity begins with the local machine and the interactions between applications and components. Local area networks (LANs) introduce another level of connectivity with machine-to-machine communications. Finally, wide area networks (WANs), metro area networks (MANs), intranets, and the Internet all introduce further levels of connectivity concerns.

Counter—An application designed to measure performance on a Windows system. The counter is part of a performance object. It's normally stored with other counters associated with the same performance object within a dynamic link library (DLL) on the host machine. A counter may allow monitoring of one or more instances of the same type of device or other object as individual performance statistics.

Cracker—Crackers use their skills for misdeeds on computer systems where they have little or no authorized access. A cracker normally possesses specialty software that allows easier access to the target network. In most cases, crackers require extensive amounts of time to break the security for a system before they can enter it. See also Hacker.

CSSM—*See* Common Security Services Manager.

DASS—*See* Distributed Authentication Security Service.

Data Store—The accumulated information resources for a single business or business entity.

Database Management System (DBMS)—A method for storing and retrieving data based on tables, forms, queries, reports, fields, and other data elements. Each field represents a specific piece of data, such as an employee's last name. Records are made up of one or more fields. Each record is one complete entry in a table. A table contains one type of data, such as the names and addresses of all the employees in a company. It's composed of records (rows) and fields (columns), just like the tables you see in books. A database may contain one or more related tables. It may include a list of employees in one table, for example, and the pay records for each of those employees in a second table.

DBMS—*See* Database Management System.

DDR SDRAM—*See* Double Data Rate Synchronous Dynamic Access Memory.

Defragmenting—The process of organizing files on a storage media so that the file system can access each sector of the file sequentially. Most operating systems call the application responsible for performing the optimization a disk defragmenter.

Device Driver—A special program used to extend the functionality of an operating system. Device drivers normally contain specific code used to control a hardware or software device. Hardware devices include tape drives and high-resolution monitors, and software devices include RAM disks and expanded memory managers.

DHCP—*See* Dynamic Host Configuration Protocol.

Dial-Up Networking (DUN)—The ability of a workstation to connect to a remote server using a modem or other long distance connection. DUN connects a client to a private server that's running the DUN server, or the user can employ it to access public networks like the Internet. From the Windows client perspective, the connection created looks just like any other network connection; the main difference is that the DUN connection is slower than a local connection.

Digital Signatures Initiative (DSI)—A standard originated by the W3C (World Wide Web Consortium) to overcome some limitations of channel-level security. For example, channel-level security can't deal with documents and application semantics. A channel also doesn't use the Internet's bandwidth efficiently, because all the processing takes place on the Internet rather than the client or server. This standard defines a mathematical method for transferring signatures—essentially a unique representation of a specific individual or company. DSI also provides a new method for labeling security properties. (W3C also built this standard on the PKCS #7 and X509.v3 standards.)

Digital Subscriber Line (DSL)—A term used to refer to any of a number of technologies that allow higher communication rates over standard telephone lines than standard modems normally allow. DSL is normally used between a remote location such as a home or office and the switching station or ISP. It isn't used between switching stations. Types of DSL include asynchronous DSL (ADSL), symmetric DSL (SDSL), and high bit-rate DSL (HDSL). The technologies vary by their ability to pack data onto the copper line, distance from the switching station, and other characteristics. ADSL allows communication from 1.5 Mbps to 9 Mbps downstream (to the remote connection) and 16 Kbps to 640 Kbps upstream (from the remote connection). SDSL allows communication up to 3 Mbps in both directions. HDSL allows communication up to 1.544 Mbps in both directions.

Digital Video Disk (DVD)—A high-capacity, optical storage media with capacities of 4.7 GB to 17 GB and data transfer rates of 600 KBps to 1.3 GBps. A DVD can hold the contents of an entire movie or approximately 7.4 CD-ROMs. DVDs come in formats that allow read-only or read-write access. All DVD drives include a second laser assembly used to read existing CD-ROMs.

Digital Video Disk Random Access Memory (DVD-RAM)—A form of DVD drive that allows both reading and writing of data. DVD-RAM functions in a manner similar to a CD-RW drive. The DVD Consortium sponsors this drive.

Direct Memory Access (DMA)—A method-addressing technique in which the processor doesn't perform the actual data transfer. The transfer occurs as a direct connection between memory and the requesting device. This method of memory access is faster than any other technique.

Disk Defragmenter—An application used to reorder the data on a long-term storage device such as a hard or floppy disk drive so that it appears in sequential order by file, reducing the time required by an application to access and read the data. Sequential order allows you to read an entire file without moving the disk head at all, in some cases, and only a little in others. This reduction in access time normally improves overall system throughput and therefore enhances system efficiency.

Disk Operating System (DOS)—The underlying software used by many PCs to provide basic system services and to allow the user to run application software. The operating system performs many low-level tasks through the basic input/output system (BIOS). The revision number determines the specifics of the services that DOS offers; check your user manual for details.

Distributed Authentication Security Service (DASS)—Defines an experimental method for providing authentication services on the Internet. The goal of authentication, in this case, is to verify who sent a message or request. Current password schemes have a number of problems that DASS tries to solve. For example, there's no way to verify that the sender of a password isn't impersonating someone else. DASS provides authentication services in a distributed environment. Distributed environments present special challenges, because users don't log on to just one machine; they could conceivably log on to any machine on the network.

DLL—*See* Dynamic Link Library.

DMA—*See* Direct Memory Access.

DNS—*See* Domain Name System.

Domain Name System (DNS)—An Internet technology that allows a user to refer to a host computer by name rather than using its unique Internet Protocol (IP) address.

Domain—An area of control in a network. Members of a domain can share resources controlled by one or more member servers. One or two servers normally control the security of the network; these servers are normally called domain controllers.

DOS—*See* Disk Operating System.

Double Data Rate Synchronous Dynamic Access Memory (DDR SDRAM)—This is a memory technology that's built upon the data storage techniques used by SDRAM. The only difference is that this type of RAM transfers data on both the up and the down clock. In essence, it transfers data at twice the speed, because it transfers data twice per clock cycle.

DSI—*See* Digital Signatures Initiative.

DSL—*See* Digital Subscriber Line.

DUN—*See* Dial-Up Networking.

DVD—*See* Digital Video Disk.

DVD-RAM—*See* Digital Video Disk Random Access Memory.

Dynamic Host Configuration Protocol (DHCP)—A method for automatically determining the Internet Protocol (IP) address on a Transmission Control Protocol/Internet Protocol (TCP/IP) connection. A server provides this address to the client as part of the setup communications. Using DHCP means that a server can use fewer addresses to communicate with clients and that clients don't need to provide a hard-coded address to the server. You must configure your server to provide these services.

Dynamic Link Library (DLL)—A specific form of application code loaded into memory by request. It's not executable by itself. A DLL contains one or more discrete routines that an application may use to provide specific features. For example, a DLL could provide a common set of file dialog boxes (like the Open dialog box used in Windows) to access information on the hard drive. More than one application can use the functions provided by a DLL, reducing overall memory requirements when more than one application is running.

EMF—*See* Enhanced Metafile.

Encapsulated PostScript (EPS)—A graphics file format used by the PostScript language. PostScript is a page description language that uses text to define the elements of a drawing. Like all vector graphic formats, PostScript allows infinite scaling and provides better resolution characteristics than bitmapped graphics provide. Use of PostScript requires an interpreter on every machine where the language is used.

Encryption—The act of making data unreadable unless the reader provides a password or other key value. Encryption makes data safe for transport in unsecured environments like the Internet.

Enhanced Metafile (EMF)—Used as an alternative data-storage format by some graphics applications. This is a vector graphic format, so it provides a certain level of device independence and other features that a vector graphic normally provides.

EPS—*See* Encapsulated PostScript.

Failover Support—A method of enhancing server reliability by allowing one server to take over the load of a second failed server. In most cases, the client is completely unaware of the server failure; the transfer of load occurs seamlessly. Both servers must provide the same services and use the same centralized data store.

FCC—Federal Communications Commission.

File Transfer Protocol (FTP)—One of several common data-transfer protocols for the Internet. This particular protocol specializes in data transfer in the form of a file download. The site presents the user with a list of available files in a directory-list format. An FTP site may choose DOS or UNIX formatting for the file listing, although the DOS format is extremely rare. Unlike HTTP sites, an FTP site provides a definite information hierarchy using directories and subdirectories, much like the file-directory structure used on most workstation hard drives.

Firewall—A system designed to prevent unauthorized access to or from a network. Firewalls are normally associated with Web sites connected to the Internet. A network administrator can create a firewall using either hardware or software.

FTP—*See* File Transfer Protocol.

GIF—*See* Graphics Interchange Format.

Graphical User Interface (GUI)—A system of icons and graphic images that replace the character mode system used by many machines. The GUI can ride on top of another operating system (like DOS and UNIX) or reside as part of the operating system itself (like OS/2 and Windows). Advantages of a GUI are ease of use and high-resolution graphics. Disadvantages consist of higher workstation hardware requirements and lower performance over a similar system using a character mode interface.

Graphics Interchange Format (GIF)—One of two standard file formats used to transfer graphics over the Internet. (JPEG is the other.) There are several different standards for this file format; the latest of which is the GIF89a standard you'll find used on most Internet sites. A secondary form of the GIF is the animated GIF. It allows the developer to store several images within one file. Between each file are one or more control blocks that determine block boundaries, the display location of the next image in relation to the display area, and other display features. A browser or other specially designed application displays the graphic images one at a time in the order in which they appear within the file to create animation effects.

GUI—*See* Graphical User Interface.

Hacker—An individual who works with computers at a low level, especially in the area of security. A hacker normally possesses specialty software that allows easier access to the target application or network. The two types of hackers include those that break into systems for ethical purposes and those that do it to damage the system in some way. The proper term for the second group is *crackers*. Hackers often work for firms that specialize in finding holes in a company's security. However, hackers work in a wide range of computer arenas. For example, a person who writes low-level code (like that found in a device driver) after reverse engineering an existing driver is technically a hacker.

Host—A form of server normally associated with communications. A terminal makes data or other requests of the host application through a remote connection. The terminal normally makes a connection using a modem and telephone line; but this isn't a requirement. For example, most people use the term host to refer to the servers on a TCP/IP network, most notably the Internet.

HTML—*See* Hypertext Markup Language.

Hub—A device used to connect two or more nodes on a network. A hub normally provides other features such as automatic detection of connection loss.

Hypertext Markup Language (HTML)—HTML is one method of displaying text, graphics, and sound on the Internet. HTML provides an ASCII-formatted page of information read by a special application called a browser. Depending on a browser's capabilities, some keywords are translated into graphics elements, sounds, or text with special characteristics, such as color, font, or other attributes. Most browsers discard any keywords they don't understand, allowing browsers of various capabilities to explore the same page without problem. There's a loss of capability if a browser doesn't support a specific keyword.

ICS—*See* Internet Connection Sharing.

Industry Standard Architecture (ISA)—The original bus used for expansion cards by IBM in the PC. The bus appeared in 8-bit and 16-bit formats. Several attempts to extend the bus to 32 bits met with limited success. Most modern machines use buses other than ISA.

IEEE—*See* Institute of Electrical and Electronics Engineers.

IETF—*See* Internet Engineering Task Force.

Infrared Data Association (IrDA)—The standards association responsible for creating infrared data port standards. These ports are normally used to create a connection between a laptop and a device or network. Devices include printers, PCs, modems, and mice.

Institute of Electrical and Electronics Engineers (IEEE)—A standards group for the electronics and computer industries. This group developed the 802 standard, which defines protocols for local area networks (LANs).

Internet Connection Sharing (ICS)—A special type of server that allows more than one workstation on a peer-to-peer network to share a single Internet connection. ICS requires that one workstation act as the server and have a connection to the Internet through dial-up or other means. All other workstations act as clients and access the Internet through the connection provided by the server.

Internet Engineering Task Force (IETF)—The standards group tasked with finding solutions to pressing technology problems on the Internet. This group approves standards created inside and outside the organization. If approved, the technologies would become an Internet-wide standard performing data transfer and other specific kinds of tasks.

Internet Packet Exchange (IPX)—A Novell-specific peer-to-peer communication protocol based on the Internet protocol (IP) portion of TCP/IP.

Internet Protocol (IP)—The information exchange portion of the TCP/IP protocol used by the Internet. IP is an actual data transfer protocol that defines how the sender places information into packets and transmits from one place to another. Transmission Control Protocol (TCP) is the protocol that defines how the actual data transfer takes place. One of the problems with IP, which standards groups are addressing right now, is that it doesn't encrypt the data packets; anyone can read a packet traveling on the Internet. Future versions of IP will address this need by using some form of encryption technology. In the meantime, some companies have coupled TCP with other technologies to provide encryption technology for the short term.

IP—*See* Internet Protocol.

IPX—*See* Internet Packet Exchange.

IrDA—*See* Infrared Data Association.

ISA—*See* Industry Standard Architecture.

Job Object—A Windows computing task scheduled to run in the background automatically at a specific time or as the result of an event. Normally, a user schedules a job using the Windows Task Scheduler.

Joint Photographic Experts Group File Format (JPEG)—One of two graphics file formats used on the Internet. (GIF is the other.) This is a vector-file format normally used to render high-resolution images or pictures.

JPEG—*See* Joint Photographic Experts Group File Format.

Kerberos—This is Microsoft's primary replacement for the Windows NT LAN Manager (NTLM) security currently used to ensure that your data remains safe when using Windows. Kerberos Version 5 is a relatively new industry-standard security protocol that offers superior security support through the use of a private-key architecture. This protocol supports mutual authentication of both client and server, reduces server load when establishing a connection, and allows the client to delegate authentication to the server through the use of proxy mechanisms.

LAN—*See* Local Area Network.

Latency—The amount of time spent waiting for a response. For example, the time a client waits for a server to fulfill a request or the time the CPU waits for data to arrive from a disk drive. Latency reduces overall system performance by adding wait cycles.

LDAP—*See* Lightweight Directory Access Protocol.

Lightweight Directory Access Protocol (LDAP)—A set of protocols used to access directories that's based on a simplified version of the X.500 standard. Unlike X.500, LDAP provides support for TCP/IP, a requirement for Internet communication. LDAP makes it possible for a client to request directory information like e-mail addresses and public keys from any server. In addition, since LDAP is an open protocol, applications need not worry about the type of server used to host the directory.

Local Area Network (LAN)—Two or more devices connected using a combination of hardware and software. The devices, normally computers and peripheral equipment such as printers, are called nodes. A network interface card (NIC) provides the hardware communication between nodes through an appropriate medium (cable or microwave transmission). There are two common types of LANs (also called networks). Peer-to-peer networks allow each node to connect to any other node on the network with shareable resources. This is a distributed method of sharing files and peripheral devices. A client-server network uses one or more servers to share resources. This is a centralized method of sharing files and peripheral devices. A server provides resources to clients (usually workstations). The most common server is the file server, which provides file-sharing resources. Other server types include print servers and communication servers.

MAN—*See* Metro Area Network.

Memory Leak—A condition where an application doesn't release all of the memory it allocated during execution prior to termination. The memory becomes unavailable to other applications, since the operating system doesn't know the status of the memory. A memory leak can lead to reduced system performance or an increase in system crashes.

Metro Area Network (MAN)—A special form of wide area network (WAN) where all of the connections are within the same metropolitan area.

Microsoft Management Console (MMC)—A special application that acts as an object container for Windows management objects like Component Services and Computer Management. The management objects are actually special components that provide interfaces that allow the user to access them within MMC to maintain and control the operation of Windows. A developer can create special versions of these objects for application management or other tasks. Using a single application, like MMC, helps maintain the same user interface across all management applications.

MMC—*See* Microsoft Management Console.

MSDN—Microsoft Developer Network.

NC—*See* Network Computer.

NDPS—*See* Novell Distributed Print Services.

NDS—*See* Novell Directory Service.

NetPC—*See* Network PC.

NetWare Storage System (NSS)—A partition formatting method used to support large volumes under NetWare without the usual performance problems that traditional NetWare partitions suffer. NSS doesn't support data migration, data duplexing, disk mirroring, disk striping, file compression, transaction tracking, File Transfer Protocol (FTP), VREPAIR, Network File System (NFS), or file name locks. In addition, NSS uses more resources than a traditional NetWare volume does.

Network Cabling—The physical media used to transfer data across a network. Designers use a variety of copper and fiber optic cable configurations with networks. Each cable type has different characteristics and capabilities.

Network Computer (NC)—A low-cost computer with no local storage devices. It does contain local memory and a processor. Vendors design NCs to run Java applications stored on a server. As a result, NCs always need a connection to the server to operate.

Network Interface Card (NIC)—The device responsible for allowing a workstation to communicate with the file server and other workstations. An NIC provides the physical means for creating the connection. The card plugs into an expansion slot in the computer. A cable that attaches to the back of the card completes the communication path.

Network Operating System (NOS)—The operating system that runs on the file server or other centralized file or print sharing device. This operating system normally provides multi-user access capability and user accounting software in addition to other network specific utilities.

Network PC (NetPC)—A low cost computing solution that has a hard drive, but no CD-ROM or floppy drive. The local hard drive is only large enough to store user data and to improve performance by storing temporary data locally. This type of PC has to have a connection to a server to work.

NFS—Network File System.

NIC—*See* Network Interface Card.

NICI—*See* Novell International Cryptographic Infrastructure.

Node—A single element in a network. In most cases, the term node refers to a single workstation connected to the network. It can also refer to a bridge, router, or file server. It doesn't refer to cabling, or other passive or active elements that don't directly interface with the network at the logical level.

NOS—*See* Network Operating System.

Novell Directory Service (NDS)—An object-oriented approach to managing network resources. (Novell originally called this technology NetWare Directory Services, but subsequently renamed it.) It includes a set of graphical utilities that allow the network administrator to view the entire network at once, even if it includes more than one server or more than one location. NDS includes a variety of object types including servers, printers, users, and files. NDS not only allows the administrator to manage the resource, but it provides security as well. NDS gives each object a unique set of properties that the administrator can change as needed.

Novell Distributed Print Services (NDPS)—A method of managing printers on a large NetWare installation. NDPS includes a series of client and server additions that make it easier to allocate a large number of printers between multiple clients and ease printer congestion.

Novell International Cryptographic Infrastructure (NICI)—The set of NetWare modules used to encrypt keys and documents. Novell designed NICI to provide the highest level of encryption allowed by local governments.

NSS—*See* NetWare Storage System.

Packet—A packet is an individual data grouping. Packets define the envelope for transferring data on electronic media. Many networking protocols have unique names for packets. For example, the Internet Protocol (IP) uses the term *datagram.*

Paging File—A method used to simulate memory within an operating system to allow applications to allocate more than the available physical memory. The paging file is an actual file on the hard drive that contains pages of RAM; many versions of Windows use PAGEFILE.SYS or WIN386.SWP as the paging file filename.

PC Card—*See* Personal Computer Memory Card International Association.

PCI—*See* Peripheral Component Interconnect.

PCMCIA—*See* Personal Computer Memory Card International Association.

PCT—*See* Private Communication Technology.

Peer-to-Peer Network—A group of connected computers where every computer can act as a server and a client. Selected computers normally provide services to others; but unlike a client/server network, the network administrator can distribute the processing load over several machines. In addition, all nodes of a peer-to-peer network also act as workstations.

PEM—*See* Privacy Enhanced Mail.

Peripheral Component Interconnect (PCI)—A type of computer system bus that has relatively high access speeds and a minimum of 32-bit access to the system's memory and processor. Older forms of the bus provided a 33 MHz bus speed. A newer form of the PCI bus allows 64-bit data access and a 66 MHz or higher bus speed; although the older 32-bit data path is normally supported for compatibility purposes.

Personal Computer Memory Card International Association (PCMCIA)— A standards group responsible for the credit-card–sized devices originally used in laptop PCs. A PCMCIA card could contain devices such as a modem or network card. Some of the more esoteric uses for this card include solid-state hard drives and added system memory. Some people refer to a PCMCIA card as a PC Card. The typical bus speed of PCMCIA is 8.33 MHz.

PKI—*See* Public Key Infrastructure.

Point-to-Point Tunneling Protocol (PPTP)—A technology jointly created by Microsoft, US Robotics, and other members for the PPTP forum used to create virtual private networks (VPNs). A VPN is a private network of computers that uses the Internet to connect some nodes. PPTP incorporates various forms of security to ensure the data transmitted across the Internet (essentially an open network) remains secure. A VPN would allow a user to dial into the corporate network from home.

PPTP—*See* Point-to-Point Tunneling Protocol.

Print Queue—The network version of a print spooler. It spools all print jobs for a particular printer to a network drive or the drive of a print server. In most cases, the print queue doesn't affect local workstation performance. The print queue uses file or print server CPU cycles to perform its work.

Print Server—A computer set aside to provide print services to clients. The network or user can exploit the computer for other purposes. Print servers reduce the load on other network computers by spooling print jobs locally.

Privacy Enhanced Mail (PEM)—A multi-part specification that defines how to maintain the privacy of e-mail. It includes sections on e-mail encryption, security key management, cryptography, and security key certification. The cryptography portion of the specification includes algorithms, usage modes, and identifiers specifically for PEM use.

Private Communication Technology (PCT)—An Internet security standard that enables a client and server to engage in private communication with little chance of being overheard. This level of security depends on digital signatures and encryption methodologies to do its work.

Protocol—A protocol is a set of rules that defines a specific behavior. For example, protocols define how networks transfer data. Think of a protocol as an ambassador who negotiates activities between two countries. Without the ambassador, communication is difficult, if not impossible.

Public Key Infrastructure (PKI)—A protocol that allows two sites to exchange data in an encrypted format without any prior arrangement. The default method for initiating the exchange is to create a secure sockets layer (SSL) connection. The main difference between this technology and others on the market is that it relies on a public key system of certificates to ensure secure data transfer. The latest specification for SSL is SSL3, which the IETF is calling transport layer security (TLS) protocol. A newer addition to the mix is Private Communication Technology (PCT). PCT still uses public-key encryption. One of the benefits of PKI is that there's no online authentication server required since well-known certification authorities (like VeriSign) issue the certificate when the sender uses the technology publicly.

Queue—Commonly, a programming construct used to hold data while it awaits processing. A queue uses a FIFO (first in, first out) storage technique. The first data element in is also the first data element processed. Think of a queue as a line at the bank or grocery store and you'll have the right idea. There are also hardware queues, which emulate the processing capability of their software counterparts.

Radio Frequency Interference (RFI)—A problem that occurs when a radio frequency emission source, such as a computer, produces a radio frequency transmission that's the same as another radio frequency emission source, such as a radio station. The resulting interference from the computer can partially or fully block the radio station signal, resulting in a loss in radio functionality. On the other hand, outside signals can interfere with computer communications.

Raster Graphic—A file format that contains one entry for each pixel in a bitmap. All entries are precisely the same size. Standard pixel sizes include 1, 4, 8, and 24 bits. Contrast this with vector graphics that depend on math equations to define an image rather than storing its representation as a bitmap.

Registry—A freeform database used to hold settings, configuration, and other information for Windows. The registry is a hierarchy or tree consisting of keys and associated values. The operating system searches the registry tree for keys that it requires and then requests values for those keys to perform tasks like configure an application. The registry is organized into hives. Each hive contains settings for a particular operating system element such as user information and hardware configuration. Users share common hives, such as those used for hardware, but have separate hives for their information as long as Windows is configured to provide separate desktops for each user.

Registry Key—This is a registry heading—a method of organizing registry data. It provides the structure required to hold configuration values and other information required by both Windows and the applications it runs.

Registry Value—An individual record within the Windows registry database. Each value provides some type of configuration information. There are three types of registry values: string, DWORD, and binary. Of the three, the only human-readable form is string.

Resolution—The number of horizontal and vertical pixels produced by a display. The display resolution affects the readability of text and the clarity of graphics. Resolution also refers to these same qualities in other output devices, such as printers.

RFI—*See* Radio Frequency Interference.

S/WAN—*See* Secure Wide Area Network.

SAN—*See* Storage Area Network.

Scalability—A definition of an object's ability to sustain increases in load. For example, companies often rate networking systems by their ability to scale from one to many users. Software scalability determines the ability of the software to run on more than one machine when needed without making it appear that more than one machine is in use.

SDRAM—*See* Synchronous Dynamic Random Access Memory.

Secure Hypertext Transfer Protocol (SHTTP)—A technology designed to encrypt messages sent using the Internet. This technology is similar in purpose to Security Sockets Layer (SSL). However, SSL secures the connection between two computers; SHTTP secures the individual messages. It's possible to use both technologies together to provide enhanced security.

Secure Socket Layer (SSL)—A digital-signature technology used for exchanging information between a client and a server. An SSL-compliant server requests a digital certificate from the client machine. The client can likewise request a digital certificate from the server. Companies or individuals obtain these digital certificates from a third-party vendor, such as VeriSign, who can vouch for the identity of both parties.

Secure Wide Area Network (S/WAN)—This is an initiative supported by RSA Data Security, Inc. The IETF has a committee working on it. RSA intends to incorporate the IETF's IPSec standard into S/WAN. The main goal of S/WAN is to allow companies to mix and match the best firewall and TCP/IP stack products to build Internet-based virtual private networks (VPNs). Current solutions usually lock the user into a single source for both products.

Server—A server is an application or workstation that provides services, resources, or data to a client application or workstation.

SHTTP—*See* Secure Hypertext Transfer Protocol.

Smart Card—A type of user identification used in place of passwords. The use of a smart card makes it much harder for a third party to break into a computer system using stolen identification.

Snap-ins—Component technologies allow one application to serve as a container for multiple subapplications. A snap-in refers to a component that's designed to reside within another application. The snap-in performs one specific task out of all of the tasks that the application as a whole can perform. The Microsoft Management Console (MMC) is an example of a host application. Network administrators perform all Windows 2000 management tasks using snap-ins designed to work with MMC.

Sneaker Network—A type of "network" where users pass data from one person to the next on a floppy disk, rather than electronic means.

SOHO—Small Office/Home Office.

SQL—*See* Structured Query Language.

SSL—*See* Secure Socket Layer.

Storage Area Network (SAN)—One of several methods used for network-specific storage because it offers several distinct advantages over the normal methods of storing data locally within the server. A SAN is a special form of local area network (LAN). A SAN is a high-speed subnetwork that consists exclusively of storage devices. The goal is to take the hard drive out of the individual server, create a new entity out of the existing peripheral device, and make it accessible to multiple servers on the same network. The concept of a SAN has been around in mainframe systems for quite some time. The original mainframe version relies on a bus technology known as Enterprise System Connection (ESCON). ESCON allows the mainframe to connect to many peripheral devices dynamically, including drive arrays and clusters. In fact, the DEC VMS network environment is based on a combination of SANs and clustered servers.

Structured Query Language (SQL)—Most DBMSs use this language to exchange information. Some also use it as their native language. SQL provides a method for requesting information from the DBMS. It defines which table or tables to use, what information to get from the table, and how to sort the information. A typical request includes the name of the database, table, and columns needed for display or editing purposes. SQL can filter a request and limit the number of rows using special features. Developers also use SQL to manipulate database information by adding, deleting, modifying, or searching records. Today it's a favorite language for most PC DBMS as well. There are many versions of SQL.

SWAT—Samba Web Administration Tool.

Synchronous Dynamic Random Access Memory (SDRAM)—A type of memory that improves on the access speed of standard DRAM using specialized access methods. It assumes that applications seldom need to access a single bit of data. SDRAM is designed to deliver a minimum of 4 bits or 8 bits of data at a time. The secret to the speed of this DRAM is that the RAM itself provides the address of the next bit of data to retrieve. In other words, the RAM delivers data in bursts. The processor programs a burst length and burst type into the SDRAM and then allows the RAM itself to deliver the requested data as quickly as possible. In most cases, the new memory architecture allows a burst mode operation of 100 MHz.

Tagged Image File Format (TIFF)—A bitmapped (raster) graphics file format used on the PC and Macintosh. The TIFF file format offers a broad range of color formats, including black and white, gray scale, and color. One of the advantages of using TIFF is that it provides a variety of compression methods and offers smaller storage form factor. Files on the PC often use a .TIF extension.

TCO—*See* Total Cost of Ownership.

TCP/IP—*See* Transmission Control Protocol/Internet Protocol.

Thread—One executable unit within an application. Running an application creates a main thread. One of the things the main thread does is display a window with a menu. The main thread can also create other threads. Background printing may appear as a thread, for example. Only 32-bit and 64-bit applications support threads.

TIFF—*See* Tagged Image File Format.

Total Cost of Ownership (TCO)—A measure of the investment required to keep a device or group of devices operational. TCO normally measures the cost of an individual workstation on a network, but companies can use the information for other purposes.

Transmission Control Protocol/Internet Protocol (TCP/IP)—A standard communication-line protocol developed by the United States Department of Defense. The protocol defines how two devices talk to each other. Think of the protocol as a type of language used by the two devices. TCP/IP is the only protocol used on the Internet and a common protocol for local area networks (LANs).

UNC—*See* Universal Naming Convention.

Uniform Resource Identifier (URI)—A generic term for all names and addresses that reference objects on the Internet. A URL is a specific type of URI. *See* Uniform Resource Locator (URL).

Uniform Resource Locator (URL)—A text representation of a specific location on the Internet. Web-based URLs normally include the protocol (http://), the target server type (World Wide Web or www), the domain or server name (mycompany), and a domain type (.com for commercial). It can also include a hierarchical location within that Web site. The URL usually specifies a particular file on the Web server, although there are some situations when a Web server will use a default filename. For example, asking the browser to find http://www.mycompany.com, would probably display the DEFAULT.HTM file at that location.

Uninterruptable Power Source (UPS)—A UPS, usually a combination of an inverter and a battery, provides power to one or more electrical devices during a power outage. A UPS normally contains power-sensing circuitry and surge-suppression modules. Some UPSs provide standby power and a direct connection between the power source and the protected equipment. Other UPSs use the power source to charge the battery constantly. The protected equipment always derives its power from the inverter, effectively isolating the equipment from the power source.

Universal Naming Convention (UNC)—A method for identifying network resources without using specific locations. In most cases, a user employs this convention with drives and printers; but the user can also apply it to other types of resources. A UNC normally uses a device name in place of an identifier. For example, a user might refer to a disk drive on a remote machine as "\\AUX\DRIVE-C." The advantage of using UNC is that the resource name won't change, even if the user's drive mappings do.

Universal Serial Bus (USB)—A form of serial bus that allows multiple external devices to share a single port. This technique reduces the number of interrupts and port addresses required to service the needs of devices such as mice and modems.

UPS—*See* Uninterruptable Power Source.

URI—*See* Uniform Resource Identifier.

URL—*See* Uniform Resource Locator.

USB—*See* Universal Serial Bus.

Vector Graphic—A vector graphic is a method of defining graphics based on mathematical equations. The application using the vector graphic must create a bitmap using the data points found within the vector graphic file. Contrast this with raster graphic files, which contain one entry for each pixel in the bitmap.

Virtual Private Network (VPN)—A special setup that newer versions of Windows provide for allowing someone on the road to use the server at work. The connection is virtual, because the user can make or break the connection as needed. The reason that this connection has to be private is to deny access to either the client machine or remote server by outside parties. A user gains initial access to the server through an ISP using Dial-Up Networking. After initiating access to the Internet, the user employs Dial-Up Networking to make a second connection to the server using Point-to-Point Tunneling Protocol (PPTP). The setup is extremely secure because it actually uses two levels of data encryption: digital signing of packets and encrypted passwords.

VPN—*See* Virtual Private Network.

WAN—*See* Wide Area Network.

WBEM—*See* Web-Based Enterprise Management.

Web-Based Enterprise Management (WBEM)—A Microsoft initiative for managing computers and other devices using Web-based tools rather than traditional desktop applications.

Wide Area Network (WAN)—An extension of the local area network (LAN), a WAN connects two or more LANs together using a variety of methods. A WAN usually encompasses multiple physical sites, such as a buildings. Most WANs rely on microwave communications, fiber optic connections, or leased telephone lines to provide the internetwork connections required to keep all nodes in the network talking with each other.

Windows MetaFile (WMF)—A special format of the enhanced metafile (EMF) file format, a WMF is used as an alternative storage format by some graphics applications. It's also used by a broad range of application programming languages. This is a vector-graphic format, so it provides a certain level of device independence and other features that a vector graphic normally provides.

Windows Scripting Host (WSH)—The Windows capability to write and execute scripts at the system level. WSH allows a user to reduce the number of repetitive tasks required to get applications to work together. A user can use a script, for example, that scans the hard drive for errors, backs it up, and then optimizes it—all without any work on the user's part except for the initial script execution. The user may have to perform additional work if the script encounters an error, but nothing more than the user would normally do. Scripts can employ one of two default languages, JavaScript or VBScript. The user can also create scripts via languages like REXX and Perl when working with a third-party add-in product.

WMF—*See* Windows MetaFile.

WSH—*See* Windows Scripting Host.

X.500—A standard created by the International Organization for Standardization (ISO) and the International Telecommunication Union (ITU) that defines a hierarchical directory structure. Each entry in the directory is at a separate level with sublevels that further define the entry.

Fifty Tips for a Successful Network

This appendix offers 50 tips consolidated from this book.

1. Spend time deciding whether you really need a network. While a network is a highly practical tool for most small businesses, it turns into financial nightmare for others.

2. Design your network carefully. The more time you spend looking at various needs before you spend any money, the less money you'll waste on items you didn't need in the first place.

3. Be prepared to work at your network. No one is going to offer to perform the required work for free and consultants are extremely expensive. Relying on your own abilities is one way to reduce the total cost of the installation and ensure you can maintain the network once installed.

4. Always look at your needs before you decide on software. Use the software as a basis for other items like the operating system and hardware.

5. Don't bite off more networking that you can chew. A network you don't complete is money wasted. Even a small network will save money and you can always expand it later if necessary.

6. You don't need to have a vast knowledge of computers to repair system problems. Consultants fix many problems with careful observation and patience, not with technical expertise.

7. Networks require consistent care. Perform maintenance tasks as often as required to assure worry free operation.

8. Always look for the low-cost solutions to your networking problems. For example, alternative networking technologies provide flexible networking support for home offices and other small networks.

9. Use the right networking technology for the job. An infrared connection works great for line-of-sight applications, like transferring data from your laptop to your desktop machine, but won't work for other applications.

10. Avoid getting a central server unless you need one. Peer-to-peer networks operate efficiently and cost less to maintain than client/server networks do. However, once you do decide on a client/server configuration, ensure you spend enough to create a workable network.

11. Allocate bandwidth wisely. Don't allow users to waste bandwidth on collaboration or video applications unless the user needs these applications to perform useful work.

12. Make sure all users will have the bandwidth required to get their work done and that you keep some bandwidth in reserve for future needs.

13. Consider an uninterruptible power supply (UPS) as cheap insurance against lightning strikes and power outages. The data you save may be your own.

14. Look for the best deal when buying software. Sometimes last year's product contain all of the features you need and at bargain bin prices.

15. Computers don't understand or care that you're frustrated. Getting angry with a will only wears you out and thwarts any effort at repair.

16. The best password is easy to remember, yet hard to guess. Making passwords long and hard to remember only encourages users to write them down—something that crackers just love to see.

17. The best way to keep a secret is not to tell anyone. Maintain a tight lid on any data you want to protect. The only people that need to know that it exists are those who work with it.

18. Reduce the problems you'll experience with any installation by keeping the number of features to a minimum. Fewer features means less things can go wrong and you'll find that performance is better as well.

19. Never assume that the vendor knows which features you need. Always perform a custom software installation, so that you can control which features the installation program places on the machine and how it configures them.

20. Networks work best when you keep complexity to a minimum. Never use two protocols when one protocol will do the job. Likewise, avoid adding services that no one needs to do their work.

21. Knowing the right command-line switches will save you time and effort during an installation. The Microsoft Windows Setup program offers a variety of switches to control the installation process, as do other applications.

22. Never assume you know everything a program has to offer. Reading the manual will save money on support calls.

23. There's always a logical reason for a device failure. In many cases, device configuration errors prevent a device from working. In other cases, the device driver is corrupted, out-of-date, or missing. However, don't keep kicking a dead device in an attempt to make it work; know when to get an upgrade.

24. No one likes big brother. There are easier ways to maintain vigilance over network operations without peering over the user's shoulder. Sometimes all it takes is a friendly chat.

25. Applications require hardware. If you don't have the hardware required by the application, you can't expect the application to do anything worthwhile.

26. If only an idiot can break an application, don't hire idiots. Always treat network users with respect and you'll find that they'll surprise you.

27. Don't forget to count all of the costs of your network when estimating total cost of ownership. On the other hand, don't forget to add in all of the ways the network benefits you when estimating its value.

28. Finding the source of a performance problem involves detective work. Always look for the source of a problem, rather than throw money at the symptoms.

29. Don't expect an operating system to provide features it can't support. Expecting Windows to work on old hardware is going to disappoint you, as is using a mouse with Novell NetWare. Always use a product in a way that emphasizes virtues and minimizes negative traits.

30. Blasting holes in the walls of your house to run cabling is the hard way to install a network. Try other technologies like radio-frequency or home phoneline networks.

31. Remember that many devices automatically add entries to the NetWare NDS tree for you. Always look for the entry before you make a new one. Having two of the same device in the tree makes administration more difficult.

32. Always have a boot disk on hand when you work with the operating system. It's too late to create a boot disk after the operating system has crashed. Windows creates an emergency boot disk for you during installation; Novell NetWare provides one as part of the license disk. However, it still pays to create a custom boot disk for emergency use.

33. Required maintenance items for every network include cleaning the machines, backing up the data, and optimizing performance by doing tasks, like defragmenting the hard drive. Always perform these three tasks and you'll find that your machine run longer and with fewer worries.

34. Never allow users to bring software from home. Not only can they contain viruses you won't want your network to catch; but they also introduce configuration problems that can cause the network to fail.

35. Training isn't an option; users need to know how to use the network. However, training doesn't always mean going to school. There are books, training tapes, online courses, and other methods of gaining the required information.

36. Avoid stomping out creativity. If a user can accomplish a task successfully using an alternative set of steps, congratulate the user for his or her resourcefulness.

37. Perform a complete check of the system looking for failures. Sometimes it's the small things in life, like terminators, that cause the greatest problems.

38. Attempt to get more out of your network by reselling old hardware whenever possible. Giving the hardware to charity will net a tax break. Scrapping the hardware for spare parts is at least useful.

39. Vendors may tell you that the latest product feature is the greatest thing since sliced bread. In many cases, this is a true statement for a corporate network. Always view new features with your network in mind; reduce the effects of hype by learning as much as you can about the product before you install it.

40. Just because you're small doesn't mean you have to get stomped on by giants. Form alliances with other small businesses to get parts and services cheaper by making it look like you're a large business.

41. Crackers are hoping you're asleep when they attack. Maintain a watch on your network. Look for differences in user patterns, strange files, new accounts, and other bits of information that will give a cracker away.

42. Don't forget the paperwork. The notes you keep today will probably save you time tomorrow. Failures tend to repeat themselves with unerring regularity.

43. Performance problems involve users as well as hardware and software. Remember to tune the users when you tune the rest of the system.

44. Make life easier for yourself. Use templates, scripts, and other aids to automate work whenever possible. The few minutes you spend creating a script today will net many hours saved over the life of the network.

45. A hot server is an unhappy server. If you keep a server in a closet, make sure the closet stays cool enough to keep the server happy.

46. Keep your users comfortable. Learn about ergonomic concerns; then implement the things you learn throughout the company. A comfortable chair and good light go a long way toward reducing network problems.

47. Look for ways to save money without reducing the quality of your network. As quality decreases, so does network performance and user productivity.

48. Don't be afraid of getting peer help with a problem. Suggestions offered on a newsgroup are free and often contain the same advice for which a consultant requires payment.

49. Check for new patches and service releases for all of your hardware and software at least once a month. These updates will often solve problems that you've noticed, but haven't been able to fix.

50. Always answer user questions honestly even if the answer is, "I don't know." If you don't know an answer, try to research it as quickly as possible to ensure users continue coming to you for help.

INDEX

Other Titles in the Poor Richard's Series

NEW! *Poor Richard's Internet Recruiting*
Easy, Low-Cost Ways to Find Great Employees Online
Here's how to use the Internet to find employees fast—using industry sites, professional organizations, state and city job banks, search engines, mailing lists, and much more.

NEW! *Poor Richard's Creating eBooks*
How Authors, Publishers, and Corporations Can Get Into Digital Print
Why publish electronically? How should content be formatted and marketed, sold, and protected? These are just a few of the questions this book answers.

NEW! *Poor Richard's Internet Marketing and Promotions, 2nd Edition*
How to Promote Yourself, Your Business, Your Ideas Online
Hundreds of proven techniques for getting attention online.

Poor Richard's Building Online Communities
Create a Web Community for Your Business, Club, Association, or Family
Create a *loyal, active* audience with an online community.

Poor Richard's Web Site, 2nd Edition
Geek-Free, Commonsense Advice on Building a Low-Cost Web Site
How to build a Web site without spending lots of time or money and without having to learn a complicated programming language.

Poor Richard's E-mail Publishing
Newsletters, Bulletins, Discussion Groups & Other Powerful Communications Tools
All of the information and tools needed to start and maintain an e-mail newsletter.

For more information or to place an order
Visit: http://TopFloor.com/
Call: 1-877-693-4676
Or visit your local bookstore.

For lots of FREE information about setting up a Web site and promoting a Web site, visit http://PoorRichard.com/. You can also sign up for the FREE newsletter, *Poor Richard's Web Site News*. With more than 45,000 subscribers, this is one of the most respected newsletters on the subject.